lonely planet

P9-DHJ-674

FLORIDA & THE SOUTH'S
BEST TRIPS

28 AMAZING ROAD TRIPS

This edition written and researched by

**Adam Skolnick, Amy Balfour,
Adam Karlin, Mariella Krause**

SYMBOLS IN THIS BOOK

✓ Top Tips	📖 History & Culture	📷 Essential Photo
🅢 Link Your Trips	👪 Family	🏃 Walking Tour
💬 Tips from Locals	🍷 Food & Drink	🍴 Eating
↱ Trip Detour	🌳 Outdoors	🛏 Sleeping

🎜 Telephone Number	@ Internet Access	📖 English-Language Menu
🕓 Opening Hours	🤶 Wi-Fi Access	🙀 Family-Friendly
🅟 Parking	🥗 Vegetarian Selection	🐾 Pet-Friendly
🚭 Nonsmoking	🏊 Swimming Pool	
❄ Air-Conditioning		

MAP LEGEND

Routes

Trip Route
Trip Detour
Linked Trip
Walk Route
Tollway
Freeway
Primary
Secondary
Tertiary
Lane
Unsealed Road
Plaza/Mall
Steps
Tunnel
Pedestrian Overpass
Walk Track/Path

Boundaries

International
State/Province
Cliff

Population

- 🟢 Capital (National)
- ◎ Capital (State/Province)
- ● City/Large Town
- ● Town/Village

Transport

- ✈ Airport
- Cable Car/Funicular
- 🅟 Parking
- Train/Railway
- Tram
- Underground Train Station

Trips

- **1** Trip Numbers
- **9** Trip Stop
- 🧍 Walking tour
- ↱ Trip Detour

Highway Route Markers

- 97 US National Hwy
- 5 US Interstate Hwy
- 44 State Hwy

Hydrography

River/Creek
Intermittent River
Swamp/Mangrove
Canal
Water
Dry/Salt/Intermittent Lake
Glacier

Areas

Beach
Cemetery (Christian)
Cemetery (Other)
Park
Forest
Reservation
Urban Area
Sportsground

CONTENTS

Contents cont.

Classic Trips

Look out for the Classic Trips stamp on our favorite routes in this book.

Miami View of Miami Beach

WELCOME TO
FLORIDA &
THE SOUTH

Life is rich – make that indulgent – in the southern states. The food, music, culture, history: all of it is robust, spiced to the hilt, and alive.

The 28 road trips in this book will introduce you to that way-out crab shack, that sweltering juke joint and that lonely trail. We'll show you upscale kitchens and the romantic jazz club of your dreams, and we'll tell you the best (though not necessarily the quickest) way to get there.

From the mighty Mississippi River to the Florida Keys, from a Blues Highway to the Nashville honky-tonks, from the Smoky Mountains and the Appalachian Trail to the vibrant, thrumming cities of Atlanta and Miami, you'll find your rhythm in this extraordinarily diverse region. And if you only have time for one trip, then make it one of our nine Classic Trips, which take you to the very best of Florida & the South. Turn the page for more.

➜

FLORIDA &
THE SOUTH
Classic Trips

What is a Classic Trip?

All the trips in this book show you the best of Florida & the South, but we've chosen nine as our all-time favorites. These are our Classic Trips – the ones that lead you to the best of the iconic sights, the top activities and the unique Florida & the South experiences. Turn the page to see the map, and look out for the Classic Trip stamp throughout the book.

5 **Overseas Highway to Key West** Skim above aquamarine waters as you island-hop towards Cuba

11 **Savannah to the Golden Isles** Absorb genteel Savannah's wealth of antebellum architecture, such as the Owens-Thomas House

6 **Blue Ridge Parkway** Take in the peaks, waterfalls and wildlife of the beautiful Appalachians

ALTRENDO / GETTY IMAGES ©

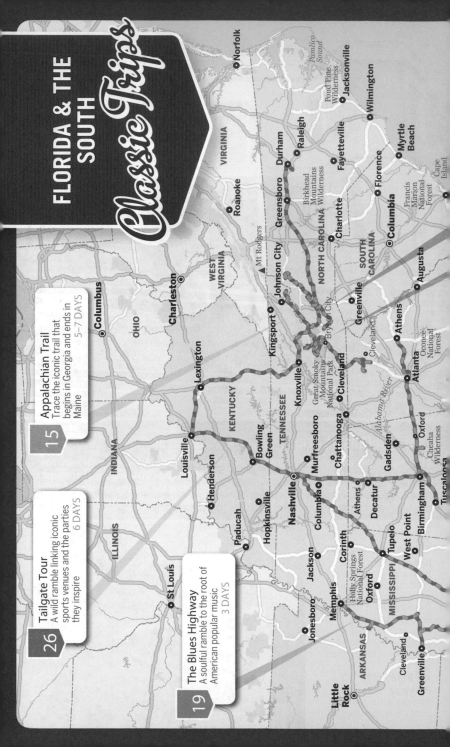

FLORIDA & THE SOUTH

Classic Trips

15 Appalachian Trail
Trace the iconic trail that begins in Georgia and ends in Maine   5–7 DAYS

26 Tailgate Tour
A wild ramble linking iconic sports venues and the parties they inspire   6 DAYS

19 The Blues Highway
A soulful ramble to the root of American popular music   3 DAYS

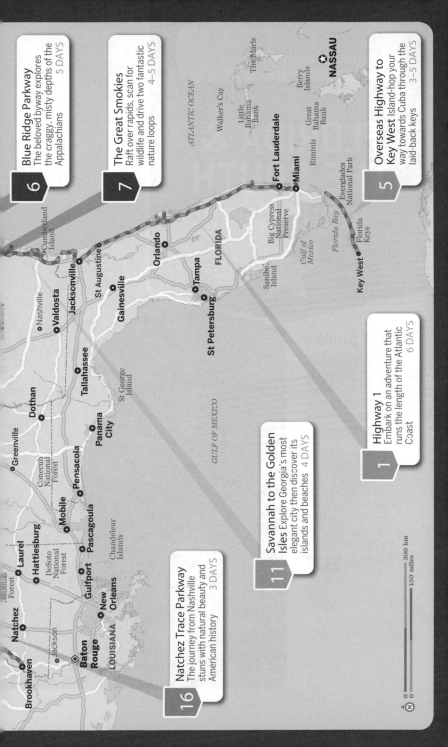

6
Blue Ridge Parkway
The beloved byway explores the craggy, misty depths of the Appalachians   5 DAYS

7
The Great Smokies
Raft over rapids, scan for wildlife and drive two fantastic nature loops   4–5 DAYS

5
Overseas Highway to Key West Island-hop your way towards Cuba through the laid-back keys   3–5 DAYS

1
Highway 1
Embark on an adventure that runs the length of the Atlantic Coast   6 DAYS

11
Savannah to the Golden Isles Explore Georgia's most elegant city then discover its islands and beaches   4 DAYS

16
Natchez Trace Parkway
The journey from Nashville stuns with natural beauty and American history   3 DAYS

FLORIDA & THE SOUTH
HIGHLIGHTS

Great Smoky Mountains

For one-of-a-kind thrills with cinematic backdrops, grab the wheel tight for **Trip 7: The Great Smokies**. Here, the Appalachian Trail climbs to mysterious, fog-wrapped peaks. Class III rapids crash through a narrow gorge. Black bears prowl like they own the place. And the tail of a dragon lures a few brave souls on a drive they'll never forget.

TRIPS

Great Smoky Mountains A mosaic of fall colors viewed from the Foothills Parkway

HIGHLIGHTS ★

Antebellum Architecture River Road mansion, Oak Alley Plantation

Antebellum Architecture

Most elaborate mansions that defined the Old South were torched in the war. Which is why the Georgian and Federalist architecture in Charleston (**Trip 10: Lowcountry & Southern Coast**), Gothic Revival in Savannah (**Trip 11: Savannah to the Golden Isles**) and the mansions of Natchez (**Trip 28: Big Muddy**) are so compelling.

TRIPS

Disney World

Maybe you'll immediately don some mouse ears and give yourself over entirely. Or, it could take a minute. Either way, it's hard not to fall under Disney's spell, especially if you're traveling with children on **Trip 4: Doing Disney & More**. The Magic Kingdom is the heart of this sprawling resort that includes four theme parks and a host of activities 'imagineered' for optimal glee.

TRIP 4

The French Quarter

Wrought-iron balconies, Creole cottages and Caribbean architecture: the French Quarter reveals itself on **Trip 17: Southern Gothic Literary Tour**. Ignore the adult adolescents on Bourbon St, and wander lanes named for French royalty (Chartres, Dauphine and Bienville) to see antique shops, art galleries, historic buildings, literary landmarks and possibly the oldest bar in the USA.

TRIPS

14

Mississippi River Steam-powered riverboat *Natchez*

BEST ROADS FOR DRIVING

Highway 1 Roll down Florida's east coast.
Trip 1

Tail of the Dragon Swerve breathtaking hairpin turns. **Trip** 7

Overseas Highway Island-hop in your car.
Trip 5

Natchez Trace Parkway Where history and natural beauty collide. **Trip** 16

Arkansas State Highway 23 A simply stunning mountain drive. **Trip** 22

Mississippi River

America's most important river – historically and economically – wends through the south uniting and defining it, blending cultures, sharing stories and mixing music. On **Trip 28: Big Muddy** you'll get an up-close view of this tempestuous beast. From Memphis to Natchez to New Orleans, you'll witness its natural beauty, grasp its immense power and consider its ecological fragility.

TRIPS 16 18 19 28

Beaches South Beach, Miami

Beaches

Nicknamed the Sunshine State, Florida could just as easily be called the Shoreline State. Thanks to its unique geography, you're never more than 60 miles from the beach. And those sandy stretches of coastline on **Trip 1: Highway 1** are as varied as they are plentiful, offering white-sand beaches bordered by emerald water, party towns where it's always spring break, peaceful barrier islands, and cosmopolitan city beaches.

TRIPS

BEST OUTDOORS

Great Smoky Mountains National Park Bald summits, lonely trails and waterfalls.
Trips 7 15

Natural Bridge State Park Home of the Red River Gorge, a rock-climbing mecca. **Trip** 24

Buffalo River Paddle a pristine, wild and scenic river. **Trip** 22

Everglades National Park Mangroves, manatees and alligators. **Trip** 2

Gulf Islands National Seashore White sands and emerald waters. **Trips** 3 21

17

Civil War Monuments Vicksburg National Military Park

Graceland Elvis Presley's grave in the gardens of Graceland

Civil War Monuments

Visit a battlefield and you'll learn they have a certain gravity. They are gifted with the power to silence even the busiest mind. Whether you're a history nut, a warrior or a pacifist, when you wrap your mind around the Battle of Shiloh on **Trip 27: Memphis to Nashville**, or Vicksburg on **Trip 28: Big Muddy**, there really is nothing left to say.

TRIPS 27 28

Graceland

Graceland is no mere tourist attraction. It's a pilgrimage site for Elvis likers and lovers, glimpsed on **Trip 23: Elvis Presley Memorial Highway**. We are talking about a mansion, bought by Elvis in 1956 for $100,000, done up in the king's signature no-holds-barred, bling-blang aesthetic. Here's a jungle room, there's a carpeted ceiling, over here is a racquetball court, and over there is a private jet called *Lisa Marie*.

TRIP 23

Appalachian Trail

Any time you have the opportunity to trek along the same trail in three states, you should take advantage of it. On **Trip 15: Appalachian Trail** you'll follow it through a stunning river gorge, wander up a series of bald mountains with layered Blue Ridge Mountain vistas, and rejoice in the silence and majesty only the wilderness can bring.

TRIP 15

Southern Barbecue

Whether it's dry rub or open-pit whole hog, classic pork shoulder or sauce-slathered ribs, you should be able to follow your nose to the nearest smoker wherever you find yourself in Georgia. On **Trip 13: Hogs & Heifers: a Georgia BBQ Odyssey**, you'll travel from the mountains to the cities in search of the holy grail of succulent and spicy Georgia BBQ.

TRIP

The Everglades

Take a walk on the wild side in the weird and wonderful Everglades. Encompassing more than 1.5 million acres, the unique ecosystem of this national park is home to hundreds of species of birds, fish, reptiles and mammals. On **Trip 2: The Everglades** you can kayak alongside graceful manatees, spot nesting ibis, herons and ahingas, or hike among enigmatic alligators lolling near the water's edge.

TRIP

(left) **The Everglades** Wildlife-spotting from an observation tower

(below) **Civil Rights Sites** Martin Luther King Jr National Historic Site

WENDELL METZEN / GETTY IMAGES ©

ZORANI / GETTY IMAGES ©

Civil Rights Sites

The roads in and around Atlanta, Montgomery, Selma, Birmingham and Memphis are graced by the memories of America's most fearless citizens, and stained with their blood. On **Trip 14: Civil Rights Tour** you'll visit the stages where the great drama unfolded, and where so many gave of themselves to change a nation for the better.

Trip

BEST LIVE MUSIC

Red's A real-deal Clarksdale juke joint.
Trips `18` `19` `28`

Station Inn A classic bluegrass honky-tonk. **Trips** `16` `27`

Chickie Wah Wah A wonderful jazz club in the Quarter. **Trip** `28`

Rum Boogie Beale St blues courtesy of a tight house band. **Trips** `19` `23` `27`

Bluebird Café Where singer-songwriters reign supreme. **Trips** `16` `27`

21

IF YOU LIKE...

Appalachian Trail Hiking America's iconic track (Trip

Music

We'll take you to the ragged, downbeat juke joints of Mississippi, then upriver to smoky Beale St nightclubs. You'll hear country stars of tomorrow wail in Nashville honky-tonks, and jazz men bring down the house in the Crescent City. Night music abounds.

19 The Blues Highway
Get to the roots of American popular music on this iconic romp through the Mississippi Delta.

27 Memphis to Nashville Think soul music museums, Beale St clubs, the Country Music Hall of Fame and hell-raising honky-tonks.

28 Big Muddy Listen to the soundtrack of the mighty Mississippi from Memphis to the Delta and down to New Orleans.

Beaches

Explore dollops of white sand off the Overseas Hwy, take Hwy 1 to South Beach in Florida, get windswept on the sensational Outer Banks of North Carolina, then discover the most incredible driftwood beach in Georgia.

5 Overseas Highway to Key West Roll along above azure waters and enjoy frequent layovers on powdery stretches of sand.

1 Highway 1 Hit all of Florida's east-coast hot spots and finish it off in South Beach.

8 North Carolina's Outer Banks Dunes and lighthouses hug the highway in the Outer Banks, a stretch of barrier islands sheltering North Carolina's mainland.

11 Savannah to the Golden Isles See vast estuaries, old-world architecture and miles-long stretches of pristine sand.

Adventure

The whole point of a road trip is to get out of the car and onto the trail, or into the river, to cultivate that raw blast of nature love. And we've offered ample opportunity to indulge your wild side.

2 The Everglades
Paddle through mangroves, spot manatees, nesting ibis and herons, and hike among enigmatic alligators guarding the water's edge.

7 The Great Smokies
Ramble through one of America's favorite national parks – hike, camp, mountain-bike and stargaze.

15 Appalachian Trail
Hike through a river gorge, beneath towering waterfalls, to the top of bald summits with a view.

22 Backroads Arkansas
Shove off into the wild Buffalo River then hike to a precipice and absorb the silence.

Smoky Mountains National Park A timber cabin near the village of Gatlinburg (Trip 7)

History

Tangled up in so much history, the South is knotted with tension and wise with soul. Far from avoiding its past, the South confronts it – is even proud of it, for better or for worse. From Native Americans to early explorers, from Civil War to civil rights, here lie stories.

14 Civil Rights Tour
An iconic journey through the battlegrounds of the American Civil Rights movement.

18 Historical Mississippi This state is heavy with history, deep with regret and as soulful as any state in the union.

16 Natchez Trace Parkway Explore the history of indigenous medicine men and early American explorers, plus Civil War battlefields and a town saved by southern hospitality.

Architecture

Modernists beware: this part of the country is better known for its old-world grace. Savannah, Charleston, Natchez and the French Quarter in New Orleans lure legions by maintaining and restoring their relics with aplomb and charm.

10 Lowcountry & Southern Coast Stroll past stunning Georgian- and Federalist-style homes in downtown Charleston.

11 Savannah to the Golden Isles One of the most beautiful cities in America, Savannah's abundance of period row houses surround shady old town squares.

28 Big Muddy Run the gamut from the antebellum homes and plantations of Natchez and the River Road to the, yes, Spanish accents of the French Quarter.

Southern Cuisine

You ain't here for the health food. If you like fried chicken and shrimp, crawfish boils, po'boys and barbecue, then you will be in your own high-calorie, deep-fried, open-pit wonderland. So you may as well add a bourbon chaser. Why wouldn't you?

10 Lowcountry & Southern Coast Savor shrimp and grits, Frogmore stew and other seafood dishes, which often have a West African spin.

13 Hogs & Heifers: a Georgia BBQ Odyssey Sample pulled and chopped pork, ribs and more as you roll from big-city to small-town Georgia.

20 Cajun Country Spicy jambalaya, rich gumbo and étoufée swimming in buttered-up deliciousness await hungry travelers in Cajun Country.

NEED TO KNOW

CELL PHONES

Mobile phone network coverage is solid, so your Google Maps app will work except in the Ozarks and Blue Ridge Mountains. Hands-free driving only, or you'll be cited and fined.

INTERNET ACCESS

Wi-fi is available in the vast majority of hotels and most cafes. Due to the proliferation of smart-phones, dedicated internet cafes are less necessary and less common, but midrange and top-end hotels always have at least one terminal available for guests.

FUEL

Gas stations are everywhere, except in national parks and some mountain areas. Expect to pay $3.50 to $4 per gallon.

RENTAL CARS

Budget (www.budget.com)

Hertz (www.hertz.com)

Enterprise (www.enterprise.com)

Dollar (www.dollar.com)

IMPORTANT NUMBERS

AAA (☏1-800-222-4357)

Emergencies (☏911)

Freeway Aid (☏511)

Climate

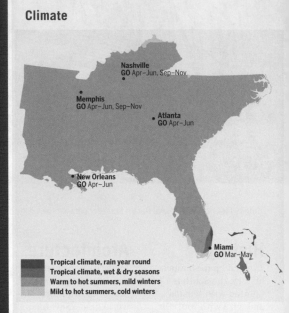

Nashville
GO Apr–Jun, Sep–Nov

Memphis
GO Apr–Jun, Sep–Nov

Atlanta
GO Apr–Jun

New Orleans
GO Apr–Jun

Miami
GO Mar–May

Tropical climate, rain year round
Tropical climate, wet & dry seasons
Warm to hot summers, mild winters
Mild to hot summers, cold winters

When to Go

High Season (Holidays, Mar–Aug)

» South Florida beaches peak with Spring Break.

» Spring and summer music festivals sprout in Tennessee, Mississippi and New Orleans.

» Rooms can be scarce and should be booked well ahead.

Shoulder Season (Feb & Sep)

» In South Florida, February has ideal dry weather, but no Spring Break craziness.

» It can stay cold (we're talking snow) in much of the southeast.

» Room prices drop from their peak by 20% to 30%.

Low Season (Oct–Jan)

» Beach towns are quiet until winter snowbirds arrive.

» Hotel prices can drop from their peak by 50%.

Daily Costs

Budget: Less than $100
» Dorm beds/camping: $15–$30

» Supermarket self-catering and cheap eats: meals $5–$10

Midrange: $150–$250
» Budget to midrange hotels: $80–$150

» Casual cafes with the occasional splurge: $35–$50

» Target theme park/beach shoulder seasons

» Nights out: $20–$30

Top End: Over $300
» High-season luxury hotel: $250–$400

» High-end dinner for two including wine: $100–$200

Eating

Roadside and big city diners Cheap and greasy.

Casual cafes and gastropubs More creative and flavorful.

Vegetarians Self-catering will be vital in more remote areas.

Eating price indicators represent the cost of a main dish:

$	less than $10
$$	$10–$20
$$$	more than $20

Sleeping

B&Bs Quaint and romantic; available in every coastal, historical and mountain town. Generally affordable.

Hotels From adequate roadside corporate numbers to rather boutique and inspiring sleeps.

Camping Popular option for road-trippers. The bare-bones

sites without plug-in options are the best for car campers.

Sleeping price indicators represent the cost of a double room with private bathroom:

$	less than $100
$$	$100–$200
$$$	more than $200

Arriving in Florida & the South

Miami International Airport
Taxis Outside baggage claim, taxis to South Beach run $32.

Shuttles SuperShuttle costs about $21 each way to SoBe.

Buses The Airport Flyer operated by Metrobus gets you to SoBe for $2.35. Take the MIA Mover to Miami Central Station.

Hartsfield-Jackson Atlanta International Airport
Rental Cars A courtesy monorail connects to a single rental car complex where all companies are located.

MARTA (Metropolitain Atlanta Rapid Transit Authority) Trains cost $2.50, leaving regularly, 6am to 11pm.

Shuttle It costs $16.50 to $20.50 to Downtown, Midtown and Buckhead.

Taxis Fares are $30 to $40 for Downtown and Buckhead.

Charlotte, North Carolina
Rental Cars Counters are on the Lower Baggage Claim level.

Bus Green Sprinter bus (Rte 5) goes to Charlotte Transportation Center in Uptown every 20 to 30 minutes.

Taxis Fares are $25 to city center; minimum $14 for drop-offs with-in 3 miles of airport.

Money
ATMs are widely available everywhere; credit cards are almost universally accepted.

Tipping
Restaurants 15% to 20% ; taxis 10% to 15%; bars $1 per drink; porters $2 per bag.

Opening Hours
Bars ⏰5pm to midnight Sunday to Thursday, to 2am or 3am Friday and Saturday.

Restaurants ⏰breakfast 7am to 11am, lunch midday to 3pm, dinner 5pm to 11pm.

Shops ⏰10am to 6pm Monday to Thursday, to 7pm Friday and Saturday, 11am to 5pm Sunday.

Useful Websites
Lonely Planet (www .lonelyplanet.com/florida) Pre-trip planning and peer advice.

Scout Mob (www.scoutmob .com) What's new in Atlanta.

Mississippi Blues Trail (www.msbluestrail.org) Maps, towns and markers, along with historical information about the stops on the trail.

Kentucky Bourbon Trail (www.kybourbontrail.com) The official website of all things bourbon in Kentucky.

For more, see Florida & the South Driving Guide (p332).

MIAMI

From the copious murals of artsy Wynwood to the vibrant Cuban community in Little Havana, Miami delivers exactly the cornucopia of experiences you would expect from a major metropolis. Just across the causeway, dazzling Miami Beach beckons with lush, sandy beaches, glamorous nightlife and streets lined with art-deco gems.

Getting Around

You can get around downtown Miami with the free Metro mover – equal parts bus, monorail and train – or rely on cabs. For the sprawling suburbs, your best bet is a car. Once you get to Miami Beach, though, ditch the car and walk or rollerblade like everybody else.

Parking

Metered street parking is available in T, but municipal parking garages are usually the easiest and cheapest option; look for giant blue 'P' signs. Downtown, street parking is scarce but not unheard of; most attractions offer garage parking.

Miami Art deco district, South Beach

Where to Eat

The best new spots for dining are in Wynwood, Midtown and the Design District; Coral Gables is also an established foodie hot spot. You can find inexpensive Cuban food all around town, but most notably around Calle Ocho in Little Havana.

Where to Stay

Miami Beach is chock-a-block with lodging options along Collins Ave and Ocean Dr, most of which occupy renovated deco properties. Downtown has high-end chains, the most sumptuous of which are located on Brickell Key.

Useful Websites

Visit Florida (www.visitflorida.com) Official state tourism website.

Florida State Parks (www.floridastateparks .org) Links to state parks.

Lonely Planet (www.lonelyplanet.com/florida) Planning and fellow-traveler advice.

Trips through Miami:

1

For more, check out our city and country guides. www.lonelyplanet.com

New Orleans Wrought iron balconies, French Quarter

NEW ORLEANS

New Orleans is American, but also identifiably elsewhere – Caribbean, African, French, Spanish and, occasionally, another galaxy. The faded beauty, prioritization of food, drink and music over deadlines, elegant architecture and gorgeous entropy, plus a population that includes artists, poets and eccentrics, all combine into one sultry breath of travel romance.

Getting Around

Outside of the French Quarter you need a car or bicycle to properly explore New Orleans in a timely manner. Streetcars ($1.25/3/9 per trip/one-day/three-day pass) are romantic but slow. Buses ($1.25) are faster, but require route map memorization. Taxis cost around $3.50 from flag drop plus $2 per mile.

Parking

Street parking is prevalent outside of the French Quarter and central business district. If you end up using a hotel lot or public garage, bank on at least $30 a day for the privilege.

Where to Eat

Some of the best restaurants in the city are in the Garden District and Uptown; many are located on or near Magazine St, the city's top shopping strip. The French Quarter has both good restaurants and tourist traps. Go to the Bywater for new stars in the New Orleans gastronomic sky.

Where to Stay

Lovely hotels with modern amenities ensconced in historical buildings pepper the French Quarter. Head to the Central Business District and Warehouse District for big box hotels, and the Garden District and Faubourg Marigny for cute B&Bs.

Useful Websites

New Orleans Online
(www.neworleansonline.com)
Database of all things New Orleans.

Best of New Orleans
(www.bestofneworleans.com)
City's best events calendar.

Trips through New Orleans: 17 28

Atlanta Downtown cityscape

ATLANTA

With a young population, a thrumming economy, a dab of Hollywood glitz, plenty of hipster panache and some damn fine places to eat, sip and sleep, Atlanta has never been more inviting. Although it can sprawl, there's solid mass transit and enough green to make it utterly liveable.

Getting Around

Atlanta is bigger than it looks, but the MARTA system (part subway, part bus line; single trip $2.50) has decent coverage, and once you're Midtown or downtown, you can walk. If you want to get to Decatur or the Eastside, though, it does make sense to drive.

Parking

Parking lots in Decatur are easy to find. Park on the street or at meters in Little Five Points and the Virginia Highlands, but in Midtown and downtown you'll need to find a lot or a garage ($15 to $20 per day).

Where to Eat

Westside Provisions looms bright like a gourmet lantern near Midtown, which has an abundance of great choices. Barbecue is best downtown, Decatur has some imaginative hipster kitchens, and the rough-edged Eastside has a lobster roll destined for the hall of fame.

Where to Stay

Boutique hotels sprinkle Midtown, making it the clear choice for centrality and variety; the corporate towers downtown aren't bad. Buckhead is rather isolated, but the rooms are plush. Virginia Highlands has a tried-and-true neighborhood feel.

Useful Websites

Atlanta (www.atlanta.net) Atlanta's Convention & Visitor's Bureau portal.

Atlanta Magazine (www.atlantamagazine.com) A glossy monthly, and an authority on the restaurant scene.

Scoutmob (www.scoutmob.com) A terrific resource on what's new and hot in the city.

Dixie Caviar (www.dixiecaviar.com) Recipes and restaurant recommendations from a young local foodie in the know.

Trips through Atlanta: 13 14

Florida

VACATIONERS HAVE FLOCKED TO FLORIDA SINCE THE LATE 1800S, when Henry Flagler built his famous railroad down the coast. The state's status as vacation paradise was cemented when Walt Disney snapped up a sizeable chunk of it in the 1960s to build his new theme park.

There's no denying the state's appeal, and its incessant sunshine and natural beauty make it particularly well suited to road-tripping. The narrow peninsula packs in the hedonistic pleasures, from white-sand beaches to fantasy-fueled amusement parks, with historical monuments, natural wonders and roadside attractions sprinkled liberally along the way.

Florida Keys Aerial view (Trip 5)
JUPITERIMAGES / GETTY IMAGES ©

Florida

Gulf of Mexico

0 ——— 200 km
0 ——— 100 miles

✓ DON'T MISS

Fort George Island

Peek into old Florida at this Cultural State Park, one of several historical stop-offs in Trip 1

Flamingo

It's a bit of a trek, but rowing in solitude among mangroves and manatees makes it totally worthwhile. Learn more in Trip 2

Mennello Museum

This tiny Orlando museum showcases the work of Earl Cunningham and other primitive and folk artists. Check it out in Trip 4

Indian Key

To see this abandoned island settlement in all its decaying glory, you have to work for it: it's only accessible by boat in Trip 5

African Queen

More than just a roadside relic, the famous steamboat chugs along while passengers re-create scenes from the movie in Trip 5

Miami Beach Ocean Dr at dusk (Trip 1)

33

Miami Beach Art deco treasures
as far as the eye can see

Highway 1

Glittering Miami provides a spectacular grand finale to this epic coastal road trip featuring miles and miles of beaches interspersed with fascinating historical sights.

TRIP HIGHLIGHTS

START 1 — **0 miles**

Jacksonville

4

Amelia Island
Where history, beaches and the old South meet

85 miles

St Augustine
The oldest permanent settlement in the US

07 miles

Canaveral National Seashore
Mile after mile of undeveloped beach

8

77 miles

Miami Beach
Dazzling art deco and beautiful beaches

Palm Beach

14 FINISH

6 DAYS
475 MILES / 764KM

GREAT FOR...

BEST TIME TO GO
November to April, when it's warm but not too hot.

ESSENTIAL PHOTO
Rows of colorful art-deco hotels along Ocean Ave at Miami Beach.

BEST FOR HISTORY
St Augustine, the oldest permanent settlement in the US.

35

1 Highway 1

Drive the length of Florida all the way down the coast and you'll get a sampling of everything we love about the Sunshine State. You'll find the oldest permanent settlement in the United States, family-friendly attractions, the Latin flavor of Miami and – oh, yeah – miles and miles of beaches traveling right along beside you, inviting you to stop as often as you want.

TRIP HIGHLIGHT

❶ Amelia Island

Start your drive just 13 miles south of the Georgia border in Amelia Island, a glorious barrier island with the moss-draped charm of the Deep South. Vacationers have been flocking here since the 1890s, when Henry Flagler's railroad converted the area into a playground for the rich. The legacy of that golden era remains visible today in Amelia's central town of **Fernandina Beach**, with 50 blocks of historic buildings, Victorian B&Bs, and restaurants housed in converted fishing cottages. The best introduction to the town is a half-hour horse-drawn carriage tour with the **Old Towne Carriage Co** (☎904-277-1555; www.ameliacarriagetours.com; half-hour adult/child $15/7).

✕ 🛏 p44

The Drive » Meander down Hwy 1A for about half an hour, passing both **Big and Little Talbot Island State Parks**. After you enter Fort George Island, take the right fork in the road to get to the Ribault Club.

❷ Fort George Island

History runs deep at **Fort George Island Cultural State Park** (12157 Heckscher Dr; ◷8am-sunset, visitor center 9am-5pm Wed-Sun). Enormous shell middens date the island's habitation by Native Americans to over 5000 years ago. In 1736 British General James Oglethorpe built a fort in the area, though it's long since vanished and its exact location is uncertain. In the 1920s flappers flocked to the ritzy **Ribault Club** (www.nps.gov/timu; ◷9am-5pm) for Gatsby-esque bashes with lawn bowling and yachting. Today it houses the island's visitor center, which can provide you with a CD tour of the area. Perhaps most fascinating – certainly most sobering – is **Kingsley Plantation**, (11676 Palmetto Ave; admission free; ◷9am-5pm), Florida's oldest plantation house built in 1798. Because of its

START
① **Amelia Island**
Fernandina Beach

② **Fort George Island**

③ **Jacksonville**

Green Cove Springs

④ **St Augustine**

⑤ **Fort Matanzas National Monument**

Palatka

⑥ **Daytona Beach**
⑦ **Ponce Inlet**

Orlando Titusville

⑧ **Canaveral National Seashore**

⑨ **Space Coast**
Cape Canaveral

Melbourne

FLORIDA

Fort Pierce

Okeechobee

Hobe Sound

Lake Okeechobee

West Palm Beach
La Belle

Belle Glade

⑪ ⑩ **Palm Beach**

Delray Beach

Big Cypress National Preserve

⑫ **Fort Lauderdale**

Hollywood

Miami Beach
Miami ⑬ ⑭ **FINISH**
p82

Everglades National Park 30 miles to

Biscayne National Park

remote location, it's not a grand southern mansion, but it does provide a fairly unflinching look at slavery through exhibits and the remains of 23 slave cabins.

The Drive » Follow Hwy 105 inland 15 miles to I-95, then shoot straight south into downtown Jacksonville.

- - - - - - - - - -

③ Jacksonville

With its high-rises, freeways and chain hotels, Jacksonville is a bit of a departure from our coastal theme, but it offers lots of dining options, and its restored historic districts are worth a wander. Check out the **Five Points** and **San Marco** neighborhoods; both are charming, walkable areas lined with bistros, boutiques and bars.

It's also a good chance to work in a little culture at the **Cummer Museum**

LINK YOUR TRIP

5 **Overseas Highway to Key West**

Continuing on down Hwy 1 is a natural; the trip begins 1.5 hours south of Miami.

2 **The Everglades**
Drive one hour southwest to pick up this trip, or go straight west and pick it up at Shark Valley.

of Art (www.cummer.org; 829 Riverside Ave; adult/student $10/6; ☺10am-9pm Tue, to 4pm Wed-Sat, noon-4pm Sun), which has a genuinely excellent collection of American and European paintings, Asian decorative art and antiquities; or the **Jacksonville Museum of Modern Art** (www.mocajacksonville.org; 333 N Laura St; adult/child $8/5; ☺11am-5pm Tue-Sat, to 9pm Thu, noon-5pm Sun), which houses contemporary paintings, sculptures, prints photography, and film.

 p44

The Drive >> Take US 1 southwest for an hour straight into St Augustine, where it becomes Ponce de Leon Blvd.

TRIP HIGHLIGHT

❹ St Augustine

Founded by the Spanish in 1565, St Augustine is the oldest permanent settlement in the US. Tourists flock here to stroll the ancient streets, and horse-drawn carriages clip-clop past townsfolk dressed in period costume. It's definitely tourist-centric, with tons of museums, tours and attractions vying for your attention. Start with the **Spanish Quarter Museum** (33 St George St; adult/child $13/7; ☺9am-6pm), a re-creation of 18th-century St Augustine complete with craftspeople demonstrating trades such as blacksmithing and leather working.

While you're here, don't miss the **Lightner Museum** (☎904-824-2874; www.lightnermuseum.org; 75 King St; adult/child $10/5; ☺9am-5pm) located in the former Hotel Alcazar. We love the endless displays of everything from Gilded Age furnishings to collections of marbles and cigar-box labels.

Stop by the **Visitor Information Center** (☎904-825-1000; www.ci.st-augustine.fl.us; 10 Castillo Dr; ☺8:30am-5:30pm) to find out about your other options, including ghost tours, the Pirate and Treasure Museum, Castillo de San Marcos National Monument, and the Fountain of Youth, a goofy tourist attraction disguised as an archeological park that is purportedly the very spot where Ponce de Leon landed.

✕ ⊨ p44

The Drive >> Take the Bridge of Lions toward the beach then follow Hwy 1A south for 13 miles to Fort Matanzas. To catch the 35-person ferry, go through the visitor center and out to the pier. The ride lasts about five minutes and launches hourly from 9:30am to 4:30pm, weather permitting.

❺ Fort Matanzas National Monument

By now you've seen firsthand that the Florida coast isn't all about fun in the sun; it also has a rich history that goes back hundreds of years. History buffs will enjoy a visit to this tiny Spanish **fort** (www.nps.gov/foma; 8635 Hwy A1A; admission free; ☺9am-5:30pm) built in 1742. Its purpose? To guard **Matanzas Inlet** – a waterway leading straight up to St Augustine – from British invasion.

On the lovely (and free!) boat ride over, park rangers narrate the fort's history and explain the gruesome origins of

---

> ✓ **TOP TIP:**
> **THE ROAD LESS TAKEN**
>
> Despite its National Scenic Byway designation, oceanfront Hwy A1A often lacks ocean views, with wind-blocking vegetation growing on both sides of the road. Unless you're just moseying up or down the coast, Hwy 1 or I-95 are often better choices for driving long distances.

the name. ('Matanzas' means 'slaughters' in Spanish; let's just say things went badly for a couple hundred French Huguenot soldiers back in 1565.)

The Drive » Hopping over to I-95 will only shave a little bit off the hour-long trip; you might as well enjoy putting along Hwy 1A to Daytona Beach, 40 miles south.

- - - - - - - - - - - - -

❻ Daytona Beach

With typical Floridian hype, Daytona Beach bills itself as 'The World's Most Famous Beach.' But its fame is less about quality than the size of the parties this expansive beach has witnessed during spring break, SpeedWeeks and motorcycle events when half a million bikers roar into town. One Daytona title no one disputes is 'Birthplace of NASCAR,' which started here in 1947. Its origins go back as far as 1902 to drag races held on the beach's hard-packed sands.

NASCAR is the main event here. Catch a race at the **Daytona International Speedway** (☎800-748-7467; www .daytonaintlspeedway.com; 1801 W International Speedway Blvd; tickets from $20, tours adult $16-23, child 6-12yr $10-17). When there's no race, you can wander the massive stands for free or take a tram tour of the track and pit area. Racecar fanatics can

**DETOUR:
BISCAYNE
NATIONAL PARK**

Start: ⑭ Miami Beach

About an hour's drive south of Miami Beach, **Biscayne National Park** (☎305-230-7275, 305-230-1100; www.biscayneunderwater.com; 9700 SW 328th St) is a protected marine sanctuary harboring amazing tropical coral reef systems, most within sight of Miami's skyline. It's only accessible by water: you can take a glass-bottomed-boat tour, snorkel or scuba dive, or rent a canoe or kayak to lose yourself in this 300-sq-mile system of islands, underwater shipwrecks and mangrove forests.

indulge in the **Richard Petty Driving Experience** (☎800-237-3889; www .drivepetty.com) and feel the thrill of riding shotgun or even taking the wheel themselves.

✕ 🛏 p44

The Drive » Take South Atlantic Ave 10 miles south along the coast to get to Ponce Inlet.

- - - - - - - - - - - - -

❼ Ponce Inlet

What's a beach road trip without a good lighthouse? About 10 miles south of Daytona Beach is the **Ponce Inlet Lighthouse & Museum** (www.ponceinlet.org; 4931 S Peninsula Dr; adult/child $5/1.50; ☺10am-6pm winter, to 9pm summer). Stop by for a photo op with the handsome red-brick tower built in 1887, then climb the 203 steps to the top for great views of the surrounding beaches.

A handful of historical buildings comprise the museum portion of your tour, including the lightkeeper's house and the **Lens House**, where there's a collection of Fresnel Lenses.

The Drive » Backtrack up Atlantic, then cut over to US 1/FL-5 and head south 20 minutes. Preplanning pays here, because your route depends on where you're heading. One road goes 6 miles south from New Smyrna Beach, and another 6 miles north from the wildlife refuge. Both dead-end, leaving 16 miles of beach between them.

- - - - - - - - - - - - -

TRIP HIGHLIGHT

❽ Canaveral National Seashore

These 24 miles of pristine, windswept beaches comprise the longest stretch of undeveloped beach on Florida's east coast. On the north end is family-friendly **Apollo Beach**,

Classic Trip

DAYTONA

WHY THIS IS A CLASSIC TRIP
MARIELLA KRAUSE, AUTHOR

Who doesn't love cruising down the coast? This trip is a natural for shoreline, seafood and sunshine – but it doesn't rely solely on beach culture. It's a remarkably well rounded drive that culminates in the world-class city of Miami, with diversions along the way that include worthwhile art exhibits, peaceful nature preserves and some of the United States' oldest historical sites.

Top: Daytona International Speedway
Left: Ponce Inlet Lighthouse
Right: Kennedy Space Center

DENNIS K JOHNSON / GETTY IMAGES ©

which shines in a class of its own with gentle surf and miles of solitude. On the south end, **Playalinda Beach** is surfer central.

Just west of (and including) the beach, the 140,000-acre **Merritt Island National Wildlife Refuge** (www.fws.gov/merrittisland; I-95 exit 80; ⊙ park open dawn-dusk, visitor center 8am-4:30pm Mon-Fri, 9am-5pm Sat & Sun, closed Sun Apr-Oct) is an unspoiled oasis for birds and wildlife. It's one of the country's best **birding** spots, especially from October to May (early morning and after 4pm), and more endangered and threatened species of wildlife inhabit the swamps, marshes and hardwood hammocks here than at any other site in the continental United States.

Stop by the visitor center for more information; an easy ¼-mile boardwalk will whet your appetite for everything the refuge has to offer. Other highlights include the **Manatee Observation Deck**, the 7-mile **Black Point Wildlife Drive**, and a variety of **hiking trails**.

The Drive » Although Kennedy Space Center is just south of the Merritt Island Refuge, you have to go back into Titusville, travel south 5 miles on US 1/Hwy 5, then take the Nasa Causeway back over to get there.

41

Classic Trip

9 Space Coast

The Space Coast's main claim to fame (other than being the setting for the iconic 1960s TV series *I Dream of Jeannie*) is being the real-life home to the Kennedy Space Center (p64) and its massive visitor complex. Once a working space-flight facility, Kennedy Space Center is shifting from a living museum to a historical one since the end of NASA's space shuttle program in 2011.

🍴 p45

The Drive » Hop back onto the freeway (I-95) for the 2½-hour drive south to Palm Beach.

10 Palm Beach

History and nature give way to money and culture as you reach the southern part of the coast, and Palm Beach looks every inch the playground for the rich and famous that it is. But fear not: the rest of

us can stroll along the beach – kept pleasantly seaweed-free by the town – ogle the massive gated compounds on A1A or window-shop in uber-ritzy Worth Ave, all for free.

The best reason to stop here is **Flagler Museum** (www.flaglermuseum.us; 1 Whitehall Way; adult/child $18/10; ⏰10am-5pm Tue-Sat, noon-5pm Sun), housed in the spectacular, Beaux-art-styled Whitehall Mansion built by Henry Flagler in 1902. You won't get many details about the railroad mogul himself, but you will get a peek into his opulent lifestyle, including his own personal train car.

The Drive » When you're ready to be back among the commoners, head back inland. West Palm Beach is just a causeway away.

11 West Palm Beach

While Palm Beach has the money, West Palm Beach has the largest art museum in Florida, the **Norton Museum of Art** (📞561-832-5196; www.norton.org; 1451 S Olive Ave; adult/child $12/5; ⏰10am-5pm Tue-Sat, to 9pm Thu, 11am-5pm Sun). The

Nessel Wing features a colorful crowd-pleaser: a cciling made from nearly 700 pieces of handblown glass by Dale Chihuly. Across the street, the **Ann Norton Sculpture Garden** (www.ansg.org; 253 Barcelona Rd; adult/child under 5yr $7/free; ⏰10am-4pm Wed-Sun) is a real West Palm gem.

Come evening, if you're not sure what you're in the mood for, head to **CityPlace** (www.cityplace.com; 700 S Rosemary Ave; ⏰10am-10pm Mon-Sat, noon-6pm Sun), a massive outdoor shopping and entertainment center. Here you'll find a slew of stores, about a dozen restaurants, a 20-screen movie theater and the Harriet Himmel Theater; not to mention free concerts in the outdoor plaza.

🍴🛏 p45

The Drive » Fort Lauderdale is a straight shot down I-95, 45 miles south of Palm Beach. Taking Hwy 1A will add more than half an hour to your trip.

12 Fort Lauderdale

Fort Lauderdale Beach isn't the spring-break destination it once was, although you can still find outposts of beach-bummin' bars and motels in between the swanky boutique hotels and multimillion-dollar yachts. Few visitors venture far inland except maybe to dine and shop along Las Olas Blvd;

3, 2, 1...BLASTOFF!

Along the Space Coast, even phone calls get a countdown, thanks to the local area code: 321. It's no coincidence; in 1999 residents led by Robert Osband petitioned to get the digits in honor of the rocket launches that took place at Cape Canaveral.

most spend the bulk of their time on the coast, frolicking at water's edge. The **promenade** – a wide, brick, palm-tree-dotted pathway swooping along the beach – is a magnet for runners, in-line skaters, walkers and cyclists. The white-sand beach, meanwhile, is one of the nation's cleanest and best.

The best way to see Fort Lauderdale is from the water. Hop on board the **Carrie B** (☏954-642-1601, 888-238-9805; www .carriebcruises.com; tours adult/child $23/13) for a 1½-hour riverboat tour that lets you get a glimpse of the ginormous mansions along the Intracoastal and New River. Or, for the best unofficial tour of the city, hop on the **Water Taxi** (www.watertaxi .com; all-day pass adult/child $20/13), whose drivers offer lively narration of the passing scenery.

✖ 🛏 p45

The Drive ≫ Things are heating up. Miami is just half an hour south of Fort Lauderdale down I-95.

- - - - - - - - - - - - -

⓭ Miami

Miami moves to a different rhythm from anywhere else in the USA, with pastel-hued,

subtropical beauty and Latin sexiness at every turn. Just west of downtown on Calle Ocho (8th St), you'll find **Little Havana**, the most prominent community of Cuban Americans in the US. One of the best times to come is the last Friday of the month during **Viernes Culturales** (www .viernesculturales.org), a street fair showcasing Latino artists and musicians. Or catch the vibe at **Máximo Gómez Park** (SW 8th St, at SW 15th Ave; ◷9am-6pm), where old-timers gather to play dominoes to the strains of Latin music.

Wynwood and the **Design District** are Miami's official arts neighborhoods; don't miss the amazing collection of murals at **Wynwood Walls** (www .thewynwoodwalls.com; NW 2nd Ave, btwn 25th & 26th St; ◷11am-11pm Mon-Sat, noon-6pm Sun), surrounded by blocks and blocks of even more murals that form a sort of drive-though art gallery.

✖ 🛏 p45

The Drive ≫ We've saved the best for last. Cross over the Julia Tuttle Causeway or the MacArthur Causeway to find yourself in art-deco-laden Miami Beach.

TRIP HIGHLIGHT

⓮ Miami Beach

Miami Beach dazzles at every turn. It has some of the best beaches in the country, with white sand and warm, blue-green water, and it's world-famous for its people-watching. Then there's the deco. Miami Beach has the largest concentration of deco anywhere in the world, with approximately 1200 buildings lining the streets around Ocean Dr and Collins Ave. Arrange a tour at the Art Deco Welcome Center (p82) or pick up a walking tour map in the gift shop.

Running alongside the beach, **Ocean Avenue** is lined with cafes that spill out onto the sidewalk; stroll along until you find one that suits your cravings. Another highly strollable area is **Lincoln Road Mall**, a pedestrian promenade lined with stores, restaurants and bars.

Get a taste of everything Miami Beach has to offer with our walking tour (p82).

✖ 🛏 p45

Classic Trip

Eating & Sleeping

Amelia Island ❶

✗ Café Karibo & Karibrew
Fusion, Pub $$

(☎904-277-5269; www.cafekaribo.com; 27 N 3rd St; mains $7-22; ☺11am-9pm Tue-Sat, 11am-8pm Sun, 11am-3pm Mon) With a large and eclectic menu and two separate spaces to choose from – a courtyard cafe or adjacent brewpub – you're bound to find something that's just right.

🛏 Elizabeth Pointe Lodge
B&B $$$

(☎904-277-4851; www.elizabethpointelodge. com; 98 S Fletcher Ave; r $225-335, ste $385-470; ❄🐾) Out at the beach, this Nantucket-style inn looks like a glorious old sea captain's house, with wraparound porches, gracious service and beautifully appointed rooms.

Jacksonville ❸

✗ Aix
Mediterranean $$$

(☎904-398-1949; www.bistrox.com; 1440 San Marco Blvd; mains $10-28; ☺11am-10pm Mon-Thu, to 11pm Fri, 5-11pm Sat, 5-9pm Sun) Dine with the fashionable food mavens on fusion-y Mediterranean dishes that burst with global flavors. Reservations recommended.

✗ Clark's Fish Camp
Southern $$

(☎904-268-3474; www.clarksfishcamp.com; 12903 Hood Landing Rd; mains $13-22; ☺4:30-9:30pm Mon-Thu, 4:30-10pm Fri, 11:30am-10pm Sat, 11:30am-9:30pm Sun) Sample Florida's Southern 'Cracker' cuisine of gator, snake, catfish and frog's legs in this unforgettable swamp shack far south of downtown Jacksonville.

St Augustine ❹

✗ Floridian
New American $$

(☎904-829-0655; www.thefloridianstaug.com; 39 Cordova St; mains $12-20; ☺11am-3pm Wed-Mon, 5-9pm Mon-Thu, 5-10pm Fri & Sat) Though it oozes with locavore earnestness, this farm-to-table restaurant is so fabulous you won't mind. Dine on whimsical neo-Southern creations in a cool eclectic space.

✗ Spanish Bakery
Bakery $

(www.thespanishbakery.com; 42½ St George St; mains $3.50-5.50; ☺9:30am-3pm) This diminutive stucco bakeshop serves empanadas, sausage rolls and other conquistador-era favorites. Don't hesitate; it sells out quick.

🛏 Casa Monica
Historical Hotel $$$

(☎904-827-1888; www.casamonica.com; 95 Cordova St; r $179-379; P❄🐾📶) Built in 1888, this is *the* luxe hotel in town, with turrets, richly appointed rooms and fountains adding to the Spanish-Moorish castle atmosphere.

Daytona Beach ❻

✗ Dancing Avocado Kitchen
Mexican $

(110 S Beach St; mains $6-10; ☺8am-4pm Tue-Sat; 🐾) Fresh, healthful, yummy Mexican dishes dominate the menu at this vegetarian-oriented cafe, but the signature dancing avocado melt is tops.

🛏 Tropical Manor
Resort $$

(☎386-252-4920; www.tropicalmanor.com; 2237 S Atlantic Ave; r $80-315; P❄🐾📶) This beachfront property is vintage Florida, with motel rooms, efficiencies and cottages all blanketed in a frenzy of murals and bright pastels.

Space Coast ⑨

✕ Coconuts on the Beach   Seafood $$
(☎321-784-1422; www.coconutsonthebeach.com; 2 Minutemen Causeway; mains $8-18; ⊙11am-10pm) Coconuts isn't just a name; it's a favored ingredient. The oceanfront 'party deck' hosts regular live music, so head indoors if you're seeking a family atmosphere.

West Palm Beach ⑪

✕ Rhythm Cafe   Fusion $$
(☎561-833-3406; www.rhythmcafe.cc; 3800 S Dixie Hwy; mains $17-30; ⊙5:30-10pm Tue-Sat, to 9pm Sun) There's no lack of flair at this colorful, upbeat bistro located in a converted drugstore. The menu bops happily from goat-cheese pie to tuna tartar to pomegranate-infused catch of the day.

⭰ Hotel Biba   Motel $
(☎561-832-0094; www.hotelbiba.com; 320 Belvedere Rd; r $69-129; ✶🕾⛦) The retro-funky exterior looks like a cute 1950s motel, but the rooms have a modern boutique style that would be right at home in Miami's SoBe.

Fort Lauderdale ⑫

✕ Gran Forno   Italian $
(www.gran-forno.com; 1235 E Las Olas Blvd; mains $6-12; ⊙7am-6pm Tue-Sun) This delightfully old-school Milanese-style bakery and cafe serves warm crusty pastries, bubbling pizzas, and fat golden loaves of ciabatta.

✕ Le Tub   Burgers, American $$
(www.theletub.com; 1100 N Ocean Dr; mains $9-20; ⊙11am-1am Mon-Fri, noon-2am Sat & Sun; 🖟) Decorated exclusively with flotsam collected along Hollywood Beach, this quirky burger joint is routinely named 'Best in America.' Expect a wait, both for seating and cooking time. It's worth it.

⭰ Riverside Hotel   Hotel $$
(☎954-467-0671; www.riversidehotel.com; 620 E Las Olas Blvd; r $129-224; 🅿✶🕾⛦🐾) Fabulously located on Las Olas, with three room types: more modern rooms in the newer tower, restored rooms in the original property and the more old-fashioned 'classic' rooms.

Miami ⑬

✕ Michy's   Fusion $$$
(☎305-759-2001; http://michysmiami.com; 6927 Biscayne Blvd; meals $29-38; ⊙6-10:30pm Tue-Thu, to 11pm Fri & Sat, to 10pm Sun; 🖋) Organic, locally sourced ingredients and a stylish, fantastical decor are what you'll find at Michelle 'Michy' Bernstein's place – one of the brightest stars in Miami's culinary constellation.

⭰ Biltmore Hotel   Historical Hotel $$$
(☎855-311-6903; www.biltmorehotel.com; 1200 Anastasia Ave; r from $209; 🅿✶🕾⛦🖟) This 1926 hotel is a National Historic Landmark and an icon of luxury. Standard rooms are small, but public spaces are palatial; its fabulous pool is the largest hotel pool in the country.

Miami Beach ⑭

✕ 11th St Diner   Diner $
(www.eleventhstreetdiner.com; 1065 Washington Ave; mains $9-18; ⊙24hr except Tue midnight-7am Wed) This deco diner housed inside a gleaming Pullman train car sees round-the-clock activity and is especially popular with people staggering home from clubs.

✕ Joe's Stone Crab Restaurant   American $$$
(☎305-673-0365; www.joesstonecrab.com; 11 Washington Ave; mains $11-60; ⊙11:30am-2pm Wed-Sun Oct-Jun, 6-10pm Wed-Sun year-round) Opened as a 1913 lunch counter, this swanky seafood and chophouse is tops. (Tip: hit the cheaper take-out window for a beach picnic.)

⭰ Clay Hotel   Hotel $
(☎800-379-2529, 305-534-2988; www.clayhotel.com; 1438 Washington Ave; r $88-190; ✶@🕾) Located in a 100-year-old Spanish-style villa – legend has it that Al Capone once slept here – the Clay has clean and comfortable rooms and is located right on Espanola Way.

⭰ Pelican Hotel   Boutique Hotel $$$
(☎305-673-3373; www.pelicanhotel.com; 826 Ocean Dr; r $165-425, ste $295-555; ✶🕾) The name and deco facade don't hint at anything unusual, but the decorators went wild inside with great themes such as 'Best Whorehouse,' 'Executive Zebra' and 'Me Tarzan, You Vain.'

Everglades National Park An ecological wonderland flush with rare species

The Everglades

2

Wade into the Everglades, where gators float through mangrove swamps, birds soar across flooded horizons and endangered manatees perform elegant underwater ballet in the bays.

TRIP HIGHLIGHTS

160 miles
Ochopee
Skunk apes plus a tiny post office are road-trip fun

124 miles
Shark Valley
The breezy tram tour offers up Everglades 101

8

Everglades City

4

Southeastern Everglades

2

37 miles
Flamingo
Kayaking and wildlife make it worth the drive

2–3 DAYS
170 MILES / 274KM

GREAT FOR...

BEST TIME TO GO
December to April for both weather and wildlife.

ESSENTIAL PHOTO
Alligators lounging in the sun at Shark Valley.

BEST FOR FAMILIES
Milkshakes and a petting zoo at Robert is Here.

47

2 The Everglades

The enticing Everglades are what make South Florida truly unique. This ecological wonderland is the USA's largest subtropical wilderness, flush with endangered and rare species, including its star attraction, the alligator (and lots of them). It's not just a wetland, swamp, prairie or grassland – it's all of the above, twisted into a series of soft horizons, long vistas and sunsets that stretch across your entire field of vision.

❶ Southeastern Everglades

Begin your Everglades adventure at **Ernest Coe Visitor Center** (📞305-242-7700; www.nps.gov/ever; Hwy 9336; 🕘9am-5pm), with excellent, museum-quality exhibits and tons of information on park activities. Check ahead for a schedule of ranger-led programs, most of which start 4 miles down at **Royal Palm Visitor Center** (📞305-242-7700; Hwy 9336). You'll also find two short trails here that

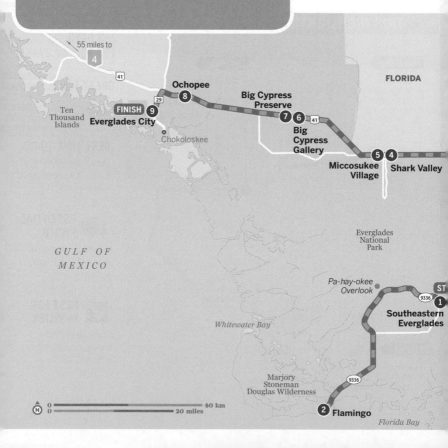

offer easy access to the Everglades, **Anhinga Trail** and **Gumbo-Limbo Trail**.

Heading further into the park, several trails and scenic viewpoints give you a closer look at the park, including **Pa-hay-okee Overlook**, a raised platform that peeks over one of the prettiest bends in the river of grass, and **West Lake Trail**, which runs through the largest protected mangrove forest in the Northern Hemisphere.

The Drive ›› Continue southwest on SR 9336, which

takes you past long fields of marsh prairie, white, skeletal forests of bald cypress and dark clumps of mahogany hammock. The Flamingo Visitor Center is 34 miles south of Royal Palm.

TRIP HIGHLIGHT

② Flamingo

You've come this far, and for your efforts you're rewarded with the opportunity to canoe into the bracken heart of the swamp. Hit the **Flamingo Visitor Center** (☎239-695-2945; ⊙8am-4:30pm) for a map of local canoe trails, such as **Nine Mile Pond**, a 5.5-mile loop that leads you into Florida Bay. You can rent canoes and kayaks at **Flamingo Marina** (☎239-695-3101; ⊙store hours 7am-5:30pm Mon-Fri, from 6am Sat & Sun), and be transported to various trailheads for an additional fee.

🛌 p53

The Drive ›› Head back the way you came in; it's the only way out. Six miles past Ernest Coe Visitor Center, go north on Tower Rd. You'll pass Robert is Here and then Homestead is just a few miles farther up.

---

③ Homestead/ Florida City

Every good road trip needs a kooky tourist attraction, and thus Homestead – in addition to being a good base of operations for the southeastern portion of the Everglades – humbly offers up the **Coral Castle** (☎305-248-6345; www.coralcastle.com; 28655 S Dixie Hwy; adult/child $15/7; ⊙8am-6pm Sun-Thu, to 8pm Fri & Sat), which isn't a castle at all but a monument to both unrequited love and all that is weird and wacky about southern Florida.

In the early 20th century, a Latvian man who had been left at the altar channeled his grief into building a sculpture garden out of more than 1000 tons of coral rock. That he did it by himself, in the dead of night, with no one there to see how he pulled it off, imbues the place with a sense of mystery. At the very least, it's a nifty feat of engineering.

✕ 🛌 p53

LINK YOUR TRIP

1 Highway 1
After driving down the Florida coast, start this Everglades trip just one hour southwest of Miami.

4 Doing Disney & More
Drive 1.5 hours north to Sanibel Island to pick up the end of this trip, then drive it in reverse order.

The Drive » Head 20 miles due north on FL 997/177th Ave until you hit the Tamiami Trail, aka US 41. Shark Valley is 18 miles west. Look out for alligators in the canal that runs alongside the road.

TRIP HIGHLIGHT

❹ Shark Valley

Alligators, alligators and more alligators! If that's what you've come to find, you won't be disappointed at **Shark Valley** (☎305-221-8776; www.nps.gov/ever/planyourvisit/svdirections.htm; 36000 SW 8th St; car/cyclist $10/5; ◷9:15am-5:15pm). Kick back and enjoy the view during an excellent two-hour **tram tour** (☎305-221-8455; www.sharkvalleytramtours.com; adult/child $20/12.75) that follows a 15-mile asphalt trail where you'll see many alligators during winter.

Not only do you get to experience the park from the shady comfort of a breezy tram, but the tour is narrated by knowledgeable park rangers who give a fascinating overview of the Everglades and its inhabitants. Halfway along the trail the tour stops long enough to let you climb a 50ft-high observation tower, an out-of-place concrete structure that offers a dramatic panorama of the park.

The Drive » Exiting the park, turn left onto Tamiami Trail, then immediately turn back off again. The Miccosukee Village is just past the park entrance.

❺ Miccosukee Village

Not so much a quaint little Native American village as it is a handful of commercial ventures, the Miccosukee Village nonetheless offers insight into Native American life in the Everglades. The centerpiece of the village

Everglades National Park Pa-hay-okee boardwalk

is the **Miccosukee Indian Museum** (www.miccosukee .com; MM 70 Hwy 41; adult/ child/5yr and under $10/6/ free; ☺9am-5pm), just half a mile down the road from Shark Valley.

Informative and entertaining, this open-air museum showcases the culture of the Miccosukee via guided tours of traditional homes, a crafts gift store, dance and music performances, and live alligator shows in which a tribal member earns oohs and aahs by provoking a gator and not getting eaten. Afterwards, visitors are invited to have their picture taken holding a wee gator.

Across the road, catch an **airboat ride** that includes a stop at a Miccosukee camp that's more than 100 years old.

The Drive ≫ Continuing west on Tamiami Trail, you'll pass trees, trees and more trees. After about 20 minutes you'll see Big Cypress Gallery on your left.

❻ Big Cypress Gallery

If you're torn as to the relative beauty of the Everglades, stop by the **Big Cypress Gallery** (☎941-695-2428; www .clydebutcher.com; 52388 Tamiami Trail; ☺10am-5pm), featuring the stunning, black-and-white photography of Clyde Butcher. The photographer has been capturing the essence of the Everglades for over 40 years, and there's something about seeing his large-scale prints – some of which are taller than you are – that will make you see the Everglades in a whole new way.

The Drive ≫ The Oasis Visitor Center is on the right, less than a mile west of Big Cypress Gallery.

I always look forward to heading down to Flamingo and getting in a kayak. It's only two hours from Miami city, but it's a world away. It's so soulful and relaxed. If you paddle into the bay, you'll often bump into something – whether a stingray, a shark or a flock of wading birds. Very lucky visitors might see manatees or, if they really go out of their way, a flamingo.

Greg Litten, Everglades National Park ranger

❼ Big Cypress Preserve

North of the Tamiami Trail you'll find this enormous undeveloped preserve that's integral to the Everglades' ecosystem. Encompassing 1139 sq miles, it is indeed big, so where to start? Orient yourself at the **Oasis Visitor Center** (☏941-695-1201; ◷8am-4:30pm Mon-Fri). In addition to trail maps you'll find great exhibits for the kids and an outdoor, water-filled ditch popular with alligators.

Further down Tamiami Trail, but still part of the preserve, you'll find **Kirby Storter Boardwalk**, a 1-mile elevated stroll through a mature cypress dome replete with orchids, bromeliads, and the possibility of wildlife that makes you glad it's elevated.

The Drive ❯❯ Keep going: your next stop is 16 miles west of the Oasis Visitor Center (and 8 miles past Kirby Storter Boardwalk).

TRIP HIGHLIGHT

❽ Ochopee

In tiny Ochopee, you'll find the **Skunk Ape Research Headquarters** (☏239-695-2275; www .skunkape.info; 40904 Tamiami Trail E; animal exhibit adult/ child $5/3; ◷8am-6pm, animal exhibit to 5pm), a tongue-in-cheek endeavor dedicated to finding the southeastern USA's version of Bigfoot. The gift shop stocks all your skunk-ape necessities, and there's even a reptile and bird zoo in back run by a true Florida eccentric, the sort of guy who wraps albino pythons around his neck for fun. While you're there, look into **Everglades Adventure Tours** (EAT; ☏800-504-6554; www.evergladesadventuretours. com; tours from $79, rentals from $60), offering some of the best private tours of the Everglades we've found, and led by some genuinely funny guys with great local knowledge.

Ochopee is also home to the **Smallest Post Office in the United States**, a comically tiny edifice with very limited hours (you try sitting in there for more than a few hours a day). It's a fun photo op, and a great place to mail a postcard.

✕ p53

The Drive ❯❯ Just over 4 miles west of the post office, turn left onto CR-29 and go 3 more miles to reach the not-so-booming town of Everglades City.

❾ Everglades City

One of the best ways to experience the serenity of the Everglades is by paddling the network of waterways that skirt the northwest part of the park. Desolate yet lush, the **Ten Thousand Islands** consist of many (but not really 10,000) tiny islands and a mangrove swamp.

Most islands are fringed by beaches with sugar-white sand, but the water is brackish, and very shallow most of the time. It's not Tahiti, but it's fascinating. **The Wilderness Waterway**, a 99-mile path between Everglades City and Flamingo, is the longest canoe trail in the area. Look for canoe rentals and guided boat trips at the **Gulf Coast Visitor Center** (☏239-695-3311; 815 Oyster Bar Lane; ◷9am-4:30pm mid-Apr–mid-Nov, 8am-4:30pm mid-Nov–mid-Apr).

✕ ⨅ p53

Eating & Sleeping

Flamingo ❷

🏕 Flamingo Campground — Campground $

(☎877-444-6777; www.recreation.gov; tent/RV site $16/30) There are 278 camp sites, some with views of Florida Bay. Get even farther away from it all with backcountry camping; choose between ground sites, beach sites and elevated camping platforms ($10 plus $2 per person).

Homestead/Florida City ❸

✗ Robert is Here — Market $

(www.robertishere.com; 19200 SW 344th St, Homestead; ⊗8am-7pm Nov-Aug) By all means stop at Robert is Here for a milkshake. This roadside fruit stand is Old Florida at its kitschy best. There's a petting zoo for the kids, live music at night and plenty of homemade preserves and sauces.

✗ White Lion Cafe — American $$

(☎305-248-1076; www.whitelioncafe.com; 146 NW 7th St; mains $7-22; ⊗11am-3pm Mon-Sat, from 5pm Tue-Sat) Not just a restaurant but a bit of a social center as well, the always-lively White Lion Cafe has BBQs, patio parties and karaoke. The diverse menu includes a $200 peanut-butter-jelly sandwich served with a complimentary bottle of Dom Perignon.

🏕 Everglades International Hostel — Hostel $

(☎305-248-1122, 800-372-3874; www.evergladeshostel.com; 20 SW 2nd Ave, Florida City; camping $18, dm $28, d $61-75, ste $125-225; P❄☎♨) Located in a cluttered, comfy 1930s boarding house, this friendly hostel has good-value dorms, private rooms and 'semi-privates' with shared baths, and its back yard is a serious garden of earthly delights.

Ochopee ❽

✗ Joannie's Blue Crab Café — American $

(joaniesbluecrabcafe.com; Tamiami Trail; mains $9-17; ⊗9am-5pm) This colorful shack east of Ochopee has open rafters, shellacked picnic tables and alligator kitsch, and serves delicious food of the 'fried everything' variety on paper plates.

Everglades City ❾

✗ Oyster House Restaurant — Seafood $$

(☎239-695-2073; www.oysterhouserestaurant.com; Chokoloksee Causeway, Hwy 29 S, Everglades City; mains $10-27; ⊗11am-9pm Mon-Thu, to 10pm Fri-Sun; 🎯) Pop open a cold beer at the raw bar overlooking the marina or grab a table inside the Oyster House Restaurant for conch fritters, steamed shrimp and fried grouper.

✗ Seafood Depot — Seafood $

(102 Collier Ave; mains $6-20; ⊗10:30am-9pm) Don't totally sublimate your desire for fried food, because the gator tail and frog's legs here offer an excellent way to honor the inhabitants of the Everglades: douse them in Tabasco and devour them.

🏕 Everglades City Motel — Motel $

(☎800-695-8353, 239-695-4244; www.evergladescitymotel.com; 310 Collier Ave; r from $80; ❄☎♨) Large renovated rooms have flat-screen TVs, arctic air-conditioning and a fantastically friendly staff that will hook you up with whatever tours your heart desires at this exceptionally good-value lodge.

🏕 Ivey House — B&B $$

(☎239-695-3299; www.iveyhouse.com; 107 Camellia St, Everglades City; r $99-179; 🎯) A beautifully renovated 1920s lodge with Old Florida atmosphere offers spick-and-span rooms and a hideaway cottage.

Weeki Wachee Springs Its fa
mermaids on show since

North Florida Backwaters & Byways

3

Emerald Coast, Redneck Riviera...call it what you will, but Florida's Gulf Coast beaches are dazzling, and inland you'll find interesting towns to give you a warm Southern welcome.

TRIP HIGHLIGHTS

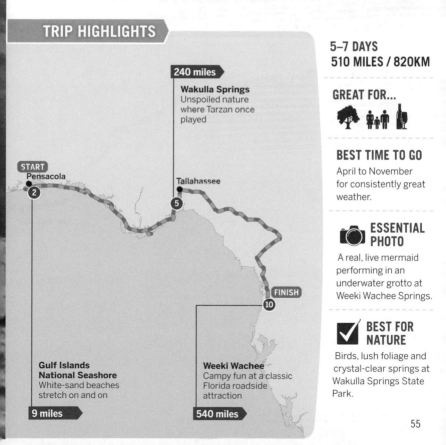

240 miles

Wakulla Springs
Unspoiled nature where Tarzan once played

START
Pensacola
2

Tallahassee
5

FINISH
10

Gulf Islands National Seashore
White-sand beaches stretch on and on
9 miles

Weeki Wachee
Campy fun at a classic Florida roadside attraction
540 miles

5–7 DAYS
510 MILES / 820KM

GREAT FOR...

BEST TIME TO GO
April to November for consistently great weather.

ESSENTIAL PHOTO
A real, live mermaid performing in an underwater grotto at Weeki Wachee Springs.

BEST FOR NATURE
Birds, lush foliage and crystal-clear springs at Wakulla Springs State Park.

55

3

North Florida Backwaters & Byways

Kick off your trip with spectacular white-sand beaches along the Gulf Coast, then meander backroads and byways to discover northern Florida's hidden treasures. Along the way you'll find crystal-clear springs that you can enjoy from an inner tube or glass-bottomed boat, come face to face with a Florida manatee, and end your trip with a classic roadside attraction starring the mermaids of Weeki Wachee.

----

❶ Pensacola

Visitors come here from all over the South for an all-American blue-collar vacation experience: snow-white beaches, jam-packed seafood restaurants, and bars where beer flows like water. Despite its beachy casualness, Pensacola has a more serious side, too, reflecting the town's 300-year history. Get a taste at downtown's **Historic Pensacola Village** (www.historicpensacola.org; Zaragoza St, btwn Tarragona & Adams Sts; adult/child $6/3;

⊙10am-4pm Tue-Sat, tours 11am, 1pm & 2:30pm), a well-preserved collection of 19th-century buildings. A military town at heart, Pensacola is also where you'll find the Pensacola Naval Air Station, home to both the elite Blue Angels squadron (www.blueangels.navy.mil) and a don't-miss collection of jaw-dropping military aircraft at **National Museum of Naval Aviation** (☎850-452-3604; www.navalaviationmuseum.org; 1750 Radford Blvd; admission free; ⊙9am-5pm, from 10am Sat & Sun; 🚹).

✕ 🛏 p61

The Drive >> Take US 98 south across two causeways to get to Pensacola Beach; head west to get to Gulf Islands National Seashore and Fort Pickens.

TRIP HIGHLIGHT

➋ Gulf Islands National Seashore

You'll get your first taste of the area's lovely white sands at Pensacola Beach

LINK YOUR TRIP

21 Gulf Coast
Start with the Gulf Coast trip, then continue on 57 miles to pick this one up in Pensacola.

4 Doing Disney & More
Just one hour south of Weeki Wachi, you can join up with the Disney trip in Tampa.

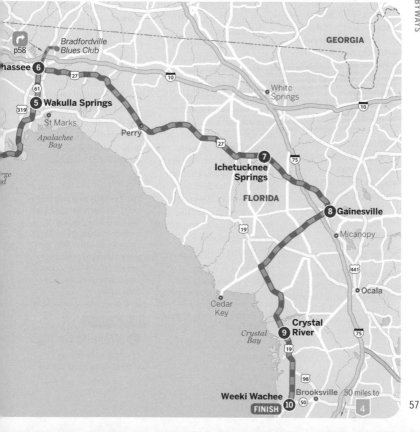

DETOUR: BRADFORDVILLE BLUES CLUB

Start: 6 Tallahassee

After dark, follow rural backroads north of I-10 to **Bradfordville Blues Club** (☎850-906-0766; www.bradfordvilleblues.com; 7152 Moses Lane, off Bradfordville Rd; tickets $5-25; ⏲10pm Fri & Sat, 8:30pm some Thu). Down the end of a dirt road lit by tiki torches, you'll find a bonfire raging under the live oaks at this hidden-away juke joint that hosts excellent national blues acts.

and the neighboring **Gulf Islands National Seashore** (www.nps.gov/guis; 7-day pedestrian & cyclist/car $3/8; ⏲sunrise-sunset), part of a 150-mile stretch of undeveloped beach on Santa Rosa Island. At the western end of the island, poke around **Fort Pickens** (☎850-934-2600; www.nps.gov/guis; Fort Pickens Rd, Pensacola; 👪), a crumbling wreck of a 19th-century fort that sits practically right on the beach – a great compromise for history buffs and beach lovers traveling together. A small museum gives you insight into both the fort's history and the impressive natural surroundings.

✕ 🛏 p61

The Drive » Follow FL-399 to US 98, traveling through Fort Walton Beach and past several oceanfront state parks. Detour on Hwy 30A to reach Seaside, about an hour and a half away.

3 Seaside

Take a breather in almost-too-picturesque Seaside, a tiny pastel town that may feel strangely like a movie set. That's because it was; remember *The Truman Show*? It was about an unwitting star in a reality TV show who lived in a surreally perfect small town.

A handful of eateries and art galleries surround the town square, and right across the street is an absolutely gorgeous beach. A group of vintage silver Airstream trailers form a food court in the center of town, selling everything from fresh-juice smoothies to grilled kabobs for picnicking at the beach.

The Drive » Continue southeast along the coast, passing through the carnivalesqe beach town of Panama City, and the quiet little waterfront town of Mexico Beach.

4 Apalachicola

Apalachicola harbors several historic 19th- and 20th-century buildings, all stationed along a self-guided historical walking tour with stops that include Southern mansions, a former general store and an old-fashioned ships' chandlery.

From Appalachiola, you can cross the causeway into Eastpoint, then head south to the sliver of land that is St George Island, where you'll find 9 miles of glorious beach and sand dunes at the pristine **St George Island State Park** (☎850-927-2111; www.floridastateparks.org/stgeorgeisland; vehicle $6, camping $24; ⏲8am-dusk). Throughout the park, boardwalks lead to shell-sprinkled beaches, where shallow waters are perfect for canoeing and kayaking, and a 2.5-mile nature trail offers exceptional birding.

🛏 p61

The Drive » Head northeast on US 98. After skirting Tates Hell State Forest and crossing Ochlockonee Bay, go north on Spring Creek Hwy (365) then east on Hwy 267 to reach the entrance to Wakulla Springs. The whole drive takes about an hour and a half.

TRIP HIGHLIGHT

5 Wakulla Springs

There's something slightly magical about

Crystal River National Wildlife Refuge Endangered manatees in their natural habitat

Wakulla Springs State Park (☎850-561-7276; www.floridastateparks.org; 465 Wakulla Park Dr; car/bike $6/2, boat tours adult/child $8/5; ⏰8am-dusk); perhaps that's why Walt Disney was once rumored to be considering it for the location of his new theme park. Take a boat tour of the wildlife-filled Wakulla River, which was used as a movie set for several Tarzan movies, as well as *The Creature from the Black Lagoon*. Here, mossy cypress trees and mangroves mingle with manatees, alligators and wading birds. (It wouldn't be a stretch to imagine this serene outing as the inspiration for Disney's Jungle Cruise.) The springs themselves flow from massive underwater caves that are an archeologist's dream, with fossilized bones

including a mastodon that was discovered around 1850.

🛏 p61

The Drive » Tallahassee is just half an hour north up Hwy 61.

- - - - - - - - - - - -
❻ Tallahassee
Closer to Atlanta than Miami, Florida's capital is far more Southern than most of the state it administrates. Downtown, the 1845 **Tallahassee Historic Capitol** (www.flhistoriccapitol.gov; 400 S Monroe St; ♿) is fetchingly draped by candy-striped awnings and topped by a glass dome. Dig deeper into Florida history at **Mission San Luis** (☎850-245-6406; www.missionsanluis.org; 2100 W Tennessee St; adult/child $5/2; ⏰10am-4pm Tue-Sun), the 60-acre site

of a 17th-century Spanish and Apalachee mission that's been wonderfully reconstructed, especially the soaring Council House. Tours provide a fascinating taste of life 300 years ago.

🍴🛏 p61

The Drive » Make your way southeast along US 27 (FL-20), a sleepy, two-lane highway that goes through the town of Perry and not a whole lot else.

- - - - - - - - - - - -
❼ Ichetucknee Springs
After journeying through the land of white-sand beaches, get your freshwater fix at **Ichetucknee Springs State Park** (☎386-497-4690; www.floridastateparks.org/ichetuckneesprings; 12087 SW US 27, Fort White; vehicle admisssion $6, river use per person $5; ⏰8am-sunset). The main reason to

visit? Relaxing in a giant inner tube and floating through gin-clear waters at this popular park on the lazy, spring-fed Ichetucknee River.

The park doesn't rent tubes, but local farmers do, for about $5; find them along the highway on your way in. Admission is limited; arrive early as capacity is often reached midmorning. From May to September the park offers a shuttle service that takes you from the south entrance to the launch points, allowing you to float back down to your car.

The Drive ›› After drying off, keep following US 27 (FL-20) southeast 37 miles to Gainesville.

❽ Gainesville

Gainesville is an energetic, upbeat city, routinely ranked among the country's best places to live and play. It's also home to the nation's second-largest university, the sprawling University of Florida. A student vibe infuses the entire city, with loads of economical eats, cool bars, and indie and punk rock clubs.

While you're there, stop in at the excellent **Florida Museum of Natural History** (www.flmnh.ufl.edu; cnr SW 34th St & Hull Rd; museum admission free, Butterfly Rainforest adult/child $10.50/6; ☺10am-5pm Mon-Sat, 1-5pm Sun), if for no other reason than the Butterfly Rainforest. As you stroll among waterfalls and tropical foliage, hundreds of butterflies flutter freely in the soaring, screened vivarium.

✗ ⊨ p61

The Drive ›› Time to reverse our trajectory and head back to the Gulf Coast. Crystal River is about an hour and a half southwest of Gainesville.

---

❾ Crystal River

Between December and March, **Crystal River National Wildlife Refuge** (☎352-563-2088;www.fws.gov/crystalriver; 1502 SE Kings Bay Dr; ☺visitor center 8am-4pm Mon-Fri) offers your best bet for seeing endangered manatees in the wild. It's an unforgettable thrill to take a glass-bottomed-boat cruise, paddle a kayak or go snorkeling while encountering 'sea cows' in their natural habitat. The refuge is only accessible by boat, but the visitor center can guide you to nearly 40 commercial operators.

For a more casual manatee experience, venture further south to **Homosassa Springs Wildlife State Park** (☎352-628-5343; www.floridastateparks.org/homosassasprings; 4150 S Suncoast Blvd; adult/child 6-12yr $13/5; ☺9am-5:30pm, last entrance 4pm), an old-school outdoor Florida animal encounter. It features a wealth of Florida's headliner species, but the highlight is an underwater observatory where you can go eyeball to eyeball with lettuce-nibbling manatees and enormous schools of fish. Time your visit for the manatee program (11:30am, 1:30pm and 3:30pm).

The Drive ›› Your final stop is a straight shot south down US 19. It's 28 miles from Crystal River, 20 miles from Homosassa Springs.

---

❿ Weeki Wachee

Since 1947, tourists have been lured north down the coast by the kitschy siren song of **Weeki Wachee Springs** (☎352-592-5656; www.weekiwachee.com; 6131 Commercial Way, Spring Hill; adult/child 6-12yr $13/8; ☺9am-5:30pm), one of Florida's original roadside attractions. Guests have flocked here since 1947 to watch glamorous long-haired mermaids perform in their underwater grotto. There's also a wilderness river cruise, plus swimming and waterslides at the adjoining Buccaneer Bay water park.

Eating & Sleeping

Pensacola ❶

✕ Dharma Blue   International $$
(☏850-433-1275; www.dharmablue.com; 300 S Alcaniz St; mains $10-30; ⏱11am-4pm & 5-9:30pm Mon-Sat; 🚼) Many locals consider this the area's best restaurant. The eclectic menu goes from fried green tomatoes to luscious sushi rolls.

🛏 Pensacola Victorian B&B   B&B $$
(☏850-434-2818; www.pensacolavictorian. com; 203 W Gregory St; r $85-125; P ❄ 🛜) This 1892 Queen Anne offers four lovingly maintained guest rooms. We especially like Suzanne's Room, with its hardwood floors, blue toile prints and clawfoot tub.

Gulf Islands National Seashore ❷

✕ Peg Leg Pete's   Seafood $$
(☏850-932-4139; 1010 Fort Pickens Rd; mains $8-20; ⏱11am-10pm; 🚼) Raw? Rockefeller? Casino? Get your oysters any way you like 'em at this popular beach hangout with live music and pirate decor.

🛏 Paradise Inn   Motel $$
(☏850-932-2319; www.paradiseinn-pb.com; 21 Via de Luna Dr; r $80-200; P ❄ 🛜 🛟) Across from the beach, this sherbet-colored motel is a lively, cheery place thanks to its popular bar and grill. Rooms are small and clean, with tiled floors and brightly painted walls.

Apalachicola ❹

🛏 Coombs House Inn   B&B $$
(☏850-653-9199; www.coombshouseinn.com; 80 6th St; r $129-169, ste $149-269; ❄ 🛜) Settle into one of the fabulous rooms in this stunning yellow Victorian and enjoy nightly wine socials in the dining room, where a lavish breakfast is served each morning.

Wakulla Springs ❺

🛏 Wakulla Springs Lodge   Lodge $$
(☏850-926-0700; www.wakullaspringslodge. com; 465 Wakulla Park Dr; r $85-125) The Wakulla Springs Lodge is a grand Spanish-style lodge built in 1937, where an 11ft stuffed alligator named 'Old Joe' keeps an eye on things.

Tallahassee ❻

✕ Catfish Pad   Seafood $
(☏850-575-0053; www.catfishpad.com; 4229 W Pensacola St; mains $8-15; ⏱11am-3pm & 5-9pm Mon-Fri, 11am-9pm Sat) There's no doubt you're in the South at this home-style seafood joint. Go for a plate of cornmeal-battered catfish with a side of grits, chased down with a cup of sweet tea.

🛏 Hotel Duval   Hotel $$
(☏850-224-6000; www.hotelduval.com; 415 N Monroe St; r $109-179; P ❄ 🛜 🛟) Tallahassee's slickest digs, this 117-room hotel goes in for a neo-mod look. A rooftop bar and lounge is open until 2am most nights.

Gainesville ❽

✕ Satchel's Pizza   Pizzeria $
(www.satchelspizza.com; 1800 NE 23rd Ave; menu items $3-15; ⏱11am-10pm Tue-Sat) You eat here as much for the experience as for the build-your-own gourmet pies. Grab a seat at a mosaic courtyard table or in the back of a gutted 1965 Ford Falcon, and enjoy head-scratching collections from Lightnin' Salvage.

🛏 Camellia Rose   B&B $$
(☏352-395-7673; www.camelliaroseinn.com; 205 SE 7th St; r $155-200) Modern upgrades (like Jacuzzi tubs) integrate seamlessly with antique furniture in this fabulously restored 1903 Victorian building featuring a wide, relaxing front porch.

Disney World Family fun and frivolity in the Magic Kingdom

Doing Disney & More

4

Whether you are a kid, have a kid, or ever were a kid, you'll love this adventure-filled trip that absolutely refuses to let you be bored.

TRIP HIGHLIGHTS

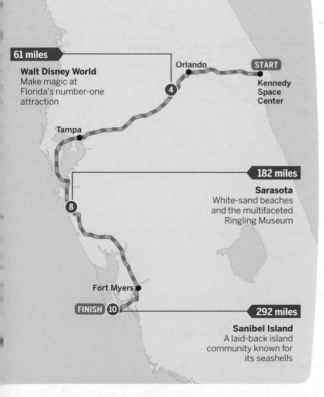

61 miles

Walt Disney World
Make magic at Florida's number-one attraction

4

Orlando

START

Kennedy Space Center

Tampa

182 miles

8

Sarasota
White-sand beaches and the multifaceted Ringling Museum

Fort Myers

FINISH 10

292 miles

Sanibel Island
A laid-back island community known for its seashells

6–10 DAYS
288 MILES / 464KM

GREAT FOR...

BEST TIME TO GO
April to May to avoid peak crowds.

 ESSENTIAL PHOTO

You hugging Mickey Mouse at Walt Disney World.

 BEST FOR LOW-KEY FUN

Searching for seashells on Sanibel Island.

63

4 Doing Disney & More

Let your inner child loose at Mickey's Magic Kingdom, but don't stop there; you'll find plenty more to entertain you in dizzying Orlando. On the east coast, NASA's Kennedy Space Center is a major attraction based on real-world wonder. And on the west coast there are spectacular white-sand beaches and tons of attractions that are family friendly without being too kid-centric.

❶ Kennedy Space Center

Kick off your trip on Florida's Space Coast, where NASA was founded in the 1950s. Here you'll find the **Kennedy Space Center** (☎321-449-4444; www.kennedyspacecenter.com; adult/child $50/40, parking $10; ⏱9am-5pm), from which the first moon landing was launched. Although NASA's space-shuttle program has ended, it's still a gob-stoppingly cool attraction. Devote most

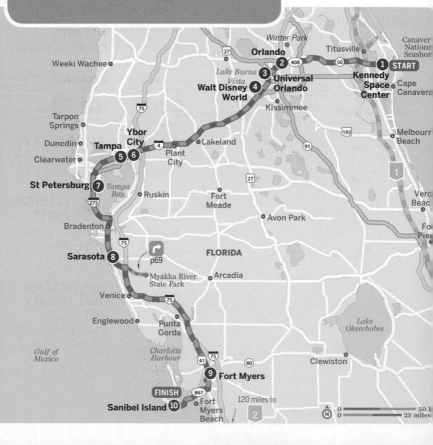

p69

of your day to the science exhibits and historical museum, IMAX theaters, shuttle-launch simulator and **Rocket Garden**, featuring replicas of classic rockets towering over the complex.

But first take the hop-on, hop-off bus tour of working NASA facilities that depart every 15 minutes from 10am to 2:45pm. And don't be surprised if your bus driver points out alligators hanging out by the roadside or bald eagles nesting in nearby trees. That's because NASA is surrounded by Merritt Island National Wildlife Refuge (p41). Want to log some beach time before heading inland? **Canaveral National Seashore** (☎321-267-1110; www.nps.gov/cana; car/bike $5/1; ☺dawn-dusk) protects the longest stretch of undeveloped dunes on Florida's east coast.

LINK YOUR TRIP

1 Highway 1
The first half of the Highway 1 trip is the very best way to get to the first stop on this trip.

2 The Everglades
From I-75 it's only about an hour south to pick up the end of this trip and do it in reverse order.

The Drive >> Make the short hop over to Orlando and its cornucopia of theme parks and attractions, just 52 miles inland.

- - - - - - - - - - - -

② Orlando
While it's quite easy to get caught up in the isolated worlds of Disney or Universal Orlando – squeezing in one more ride, one more parade, one more show – Orlando has so much more. Take the time to explore its lovely neighborhoods, rich performing-arts scene and several fantastic gardens, parks and museums. Picturesque Loch Haven Park, with 45 acres of parkland, huge shade trees and three lakes, is home to several museums that are worth a visit: **Orlando Museum of Art** (☎407-896-4231; www.omart.org; 2416 N Mills Ave; adult/child $8/5; ☺10am-4pm Tue-Fri, from noon Sat & Sun); **Mennello Museum of American Art** (☎407-246-4278; www.mennellomuseum.com; 900 E Princeton St; adult/child 6-18yr $5/1; ☺10:30am-4:30pm Tue-Sat, from noon Sun); and **Orlando Science Center** (☎407-514-2000; www.osc.org; 777 E Princeton St; adult/child 3-11yr $19/13; ☺10am-5pm Thu-Tue).

Just north in Winter Park, a sweet one-hour **Scenic Boat Tour** (www.scenicboattours.com; 1 E Morse Blvd; adult/child 2-11yr $12/6; ☺hourly 10am-4pm) floats through 12 miles of tropical canals and lakes while the enthusiastic tour guide talks about the mansions, Rollins College and other sites along the way. After your tour, wander Winter Park's trendy **Park Ave**, where you'll have a slew of restaurants and bars to choose from.

✕ 📖 p71

The Drive >> Universal Orlando is 10 miles southwest of Downtown Orlando via I-4. Bring quarters; it's a toll road.

- - - - - - - - - - - -

③ Universal Orlando
Just a bit smarter, funnier and faster than dear old Disney, **Universal Orlando** (☎407-363-8000; www.universalorlando.com; 1000 Universal Studios Plaza; single/both parks $92/128, discounts on multi day; ☺daily, hours vary) gets your adrenaline pumping with revved-up rides and entertaining shows. The megaplex features two theme parks, a water park, three hotels and **Universal CityWalk**, an entertainment district that connects the two parks.

The first of the two parks, **Universal Studios**, has a Hollywood backlot feel and simulation-heavy rides dedicated to television and the silver screen, from *The Simpsons* and *Shrek* to *Revenge of the Mummy* and *Twister*.

If you have to choose between the two parks, there's lots to love within the themed 'worlds' that comprise **Islands of Adventure**. You might find yourself riding adrenaline rides on Marvel Super Hero Island, delighting at the whimsy of Seuss Landing, or exploring the ersatz-mystical Lost Continent. But the most magical of all is the **Wizarding World of Harry Potter**, where you can immerse yourself in Hogwarts and Hogsmeade, both brought to life in exquisite, rib-tickling detail.

The Drive ≫ Are we there yet? Are we there yet? Are we there yet? OK fine. We're going there now. The exit for Disney World is another 10 minutes southwest of Universal Orlando. You can't miss it; there's more than a sign or two.

TRIP HIGHLIGHT

4 Walt Disney World

Covering 40 sq miles, **Walt Disney World** (WDW; ☎407-939-5277; http://disneyworld.disney.go.com) is the largest theme park resort in the world. It includes four separate theme parks, two water parks, hotels, restaurants and two shopping and nightlife districts – proving that it's not such a small world, after all. But it's not about size. The park's appeal is in the fact that few visitors can inoculate themselves against Disney's highly infectious enthusiasm and warm-hearted nostalgia.

The centerpiece of it all is the **Magic Kingdom**, land of the iconic Cinderella's Castle and rides such as Space Mountain, the Haunted Mansion and Pirates of the Caribbean. This

Kennedy Space Center Vehicle Assembly Building

is where the fireworks and nighttime light parade illuminate Main St, USA, and as far as Disney mythology goes, it doesn't get better.

But what about those other parks? Park Hopper Passes let you experience them all. **Epcot Theme Park** is a more low-key experience with rides, interactive exhibits and the World Showcase, an interesting toe-dip into the cultures of 11 countries.

Disney Hollywood Studios doesn't bring the magic but it does have the two most exciting rides: the unpredictable elevator in the Twilight Zone Tower of Terror and the Aerosmith-themed Rock 'n' Roller Coaster.

Finally, **Disney's Animal Kingdom** is a sometimes surreal blend of rides, African safari, shows and dinosaurs. It's best at animal encounters and shows, with the 110-acre Kilimanjaro Safaris as its centerpiece.

✕ ⏨ p71

The Drive » From Walt Disney World, it's an easy if uneventful one-hour drive southwest down I-4 to get to Tampa.

5 Tampa

Sprawling and businesslike, Tampa lacks the iconic downtown skyline or cultural buzz that stamps other US cities with an indelible, distinct persona, but it's much more fun and intriguing than first meets the eye. So many new museums, parks and restaurants have popped up recently that the city is dangerously close to becoming stylish. It's also a great family destination, with enough entertainment to last a week.

Florida Aquarium

(📞813-273-4000; www.flaquarium.org; 701 Channelside Dr; adult/child $22/17; 🕙9:30am-5pm) is one of the state's best, with all kinds of activities and programs, and **Lowry Park Zoo** (📞813-935-8552; www.lowryparkzoo.com; 1101 W Sligh Ave; adult/child $25/20; 🕙9:30am-5pm; 🅿 👶) gets you as close to the animals as possible. You can fulfill your adrenaline craving with epic rides woven through an African-theme wildlife park at **Busch Gardens** (📞813-987-5600; www.buschgardens.com; 10165 McKinley Dr; adult/child 3-9yr $85/77, discounts online; 🕙varies by day & season), and across the street is **Adventure Island** (📞813-987-5600; www.adventureisland.com; 10001 McKinley Dr; adult/child 3-9yr $46/42; 🕙hours vary; daily mid-Mar–Aug, weekends Sep-Oct), a massive water park with slides and rides galore.

🛏 p71

The Drive » Your next stop is actually within Tampa, but it has such a distinct flavor we decided to make it its own separate destination. Ybor City is a short car or trolley ride northeast of downtown.

- - - - - - - - - - - -

❻ Ybor City

Historical buildings with wrought-iron balconies, cigar factories lining brick-lined streets, an early 1900s ambiance with a distinctly Latin flavor...what is this place? Welcome to Ybor City, a historical neighborhood established by Don Vicente Martinez Ybor, a cigar factory owner who drew hundreds of immigrant workers to the area.

The main drag is 7th Ave (La Septima), and the **visitor center** (📞813-241-8838; www.ybor.org; 1600 E 8th Ave; 🕙9am-5pm Mon-Sat, noon-5pm Sun) provides an excellent introduction, with walking-tour maps, a small museum and

other info. Just a few blocks away, the **Ybor City Museum State Park** (📞813-247-6323; www.ybormuseum.org; 1818 E 9th Ave; adult/child under 5yr $4/free; 🕙9am-5pm) chronicles the history of cigar-making in interesting if text-heavy exhibits, but the real draw is the excellent historical walking tour.

For true local flavor, don't miss the Columbia Restaurant (p71). Built in 1905, it's Florida's oldest, and its 15 dining rooms sprawl over an entire city block, each decorated in a traditional Spanish style. Reserve ahead to be seated for one of the exuberant, twice-nightly flamenco shows.

✗ p71

The Drive » Across a causeway and out toward the beaches is Tampa's artier and more youthful sibling, St Petersburg. It's about a half-hour drive southwest of downtown Tampa.

- - - - - - - - - - - -

❼ St Petersburg

Breezy and strollable, downtown St Pete's sits right on the waterfront of Tampa Bay, which is lined with spiffy new museums, galleries, restaurants and bars. But the headline attraction here is the **Salvador Dali Museum** (📞727-823-3767; www.thedali.org; 1 Dali Blvd; adult/child 6-12yr $21/7, after 5pm Thu $10; 🕙10am-5:30pm Mon-Sat, to 8pm Thu, noon-5:30pm Sun), with its dazzling new home on the water.

The eccentric Spanish artist painted melting clocks, grew an exaggerated handlebar mustache to look like King Philip, and once filled a Rolls Royce with cauliflower. The largest collection of his work outside of Spain doesn't have *the* melting clocks, but it does have *some* melting clocks, as well as paintings with titles such as *The Ghost of Vermeer of Delft Which Can Be Used as a Table*.

With a collection as broad as the Dalí's is deep, the **St Petersburg Museum of Fine Arts** (☏727-896-2667; www.fine-arts.org; 255 Beach Dr NE; adult/child $17/10; ☺10am-5pm Mon-Sat, to 8pm Thu, from noon Sun) is also worth a stop. The collection traverses world antiquities and follows art's progression through nearly every era, and several large galleries showcase special exhibitions.

✕ p71

The Drive » Heading south on I-275 over the soaring Sunshine Skyway Bridge spanning Tampa Bay, you might feel like you're in a car commercial; several have been filmed here. Sarasota is 45 minutes south of St Petersburg.

TRIP HIGHLIGHT

❽ Sarasota

One of Sarasota's loveliest features is its luscious, white-sand beaches. **Lido Beach** is closest and has free parking, but 5 miles away **Siesta Key** has sand like confectioner's sugar and is one of Florida's best.

The best reason to visit Sarasota is the wonderful, whimsical **Ringling Museum Complex** (☏941-359-5700; www.ringling.org; 5401 Bay Shore Rd; adult/child 6-17yr $25/5; ☺10am-5pm daily, to 8pm Thu; ⊞), a 66-acre complex where one admission gets you into three museums. To begin with, you can tour John and his wife Mabel's Venetian Gothic mansion called **Ca d'Zan**, an over-the-top palace on the water. Also on the grounds is the **John & Mabel Museum of Art**, an excellent art museum that includes a re-created room from the Astor mansion. But the real standout here is the one-of-a-kind **Museum of the Circus**. It has costumes, props, posters, antique circus wagons and an extensive miniature model that let you relive the excitement of the big-top era.

DETOUR: MYAKKA RIVER STATE PARK

Start: ❽ Sarasota

About a half-hour from downtown Sarasota, 57-sq-mile **Myakka River State Park** (www.myakkariver.org; 13208 State Road 72, Sarasota; car/bike $6/2; ☺8am-sunset) is a wildlife preserve starring Florida's oldest resident: the 200-million-year-old American alligator.

Between 500 and 1000 alligators make their home in Myakka's slow-moving river and its shallow, lily-filled lakes, and you can get up close and personal with these toothsome beasts with an airboat or **tram tour** (adult/child $12/6) or by renting a canoe or **kayak** (1st/additional hours $20/5). Check the website for seasonal schedules.

The extensive park's hammocks, marshes, pine flatwoods and prairies are home to a great variety of wildlife, and 38 miles of trails crisscross the terrain. Don't miss the easy, dramatic **Canopy Trail**. The park's 7 paved miles, and various dirt roads, make excellent cycling, and bird-watchers can spot great egrets, flocks of white pelicans and blue herons.

To find out what else Sarasota has to offer, stop by the **Visitor Information Center** (☏941-706-1253; www.sarasotafl.org; 701 N Tamiami Trail; ◷10am-5pm Mon-Sat, 11am-2pm Sun; ☎).

✖ 🛏 p71

The Drive ≫ Head inland a few miles to catch I-75, then go 52 miles south to pick up US 41/Tamiami Trail to the town of Fort Myers. The whole trip takes just over an hour.

- - - - - - - - - - - - - -

❾ Fort Myers

Workaday, sprawling Fort Myers is overshadowed by the region's pretty beaches and upscale, sophisticated towns. However, a recent facelift has spruced up the historical riverfront district (along 1st St between Broadway and Lee St) into an attractive, brick-lined collection of restaurants and bars. Visit www.fortmyers.org for information.

Just a sleepy resort town in 1885, Fort Myers was pretty enough to entice Thomas Edison to build his winter home here. A few decades after Edison moved in, Edison's good friend Henry Ford bought the property next door

(moguls gotta stick together) and now you can see how the early innovators lived at the **Edison & Ford Winter Estates** (☏239-334-7419; www.edisonfordwinterestates.org; 2350 McGregor Blvd; adult/child $20/11; ◷9am-5:30pm).

In addition to Edison's winter home, you'll see his laboratory, gardens and a museum dedicated to his work, as well as the estate Henry Ford bought next door and the largest banyan tree in the continental US. Forty-minute guided tours leave every half-hour until 4pm.

The Drive ≫ With all you've seen and done on this trip, it might be time to downshift a little bit. Luckily, Fort Myers is just a short drive from Sanibel and Captiva Islands, southwest 23 miles down Hwy 867 and over a 2-mile causeway with a $6 toll.

- - - - - - - - - - - - - -

TRIP HIGHLIGHT

❿ Sanibel Island

Ahhhhh, it's island time. Upscale but unpretentious, these two slivers of barrier island have a carefully managed shoreline that feels remarkably lush and undeveloped. Bikes are the preferred mode of travel, and the most

challenging activity you'll engage in will be searching for shells – something Sanibel is particularly known for.

In addition to its fabulous beaches, Sanibel's 6300-acre **JN 'Ding' Darling National Wildlife Refuge** (☏472-1100; www.fws.gov/dingdarling; 1 Wildlife Dr) is a splendid refuge that's home to an abundance of seabirds and wildlife. It has an excellent nature center, a 5-mile Wildlife Drive, narrated tram tours and easy kayaking in Tarpon Bay.

If a sudden afternoon thunderstorm should break out, it's the perfect opportunity to visit the **Bailey-Matthews Shell Museum** (☏239-395-2233; www.shellmuseum.org; 3075 Sanibel-Captiva Rd, Sanibel; adult/child 5-16yr $9/5; ◷10am-5pm). Like a mermaid's jewelry box, this museum is dedicated to shells, yet it's much more than a covetous display of treasures. It's a crisply presented natural history of the sea and its shelled creatures – nearly a must after a day spent combing the beaches.

✖ p71

Eating & Sleeping

Orlando ❷

✖ Ravenous Pig   American $$$
(☏407-628-2333; www.theravenouspig.com;
1234 Orange Ave, Winter Park; mains $13-33;
⊙11:30am-2pm & 5:30-9:30pm Tue-Sat) One of
Orlando's best foodie destinations, this bustling
joint offers designer cocktails, creative shrimp
and grits, and lobster tacos. Reserve ahead.

⌂ Barefoot'n in the Keys   Motel $$
(☏877-978-3314; www.barefootn.com; 2754
Florida Plaza Blvd; ste $89-199; @ ⛌ ⛱) Suites
are bright and spacious in this yellow, six-story
building. Low-key, friendly and close to Disney,
it's an excellent alternative to generic chains.

⌂ Courtyard at Lake Lucerne   B&B $$
(☏407-648-5188; www.orlandohistoricinn.com;
211 N Lucerne Circle E; r $99-225; P ❄ ☎ ⛱)
This historical inn with enchanting gardens has
roomy suites and handsome antiques. It's lovely,
despite sitting under two highway overpasses.

Walt Disney World ❹

✖ California Grill   American $$$
(Disney's Contemporary Resort; mains $15-60;
⊙5-10pm; ⛱) Come for the California fusion
fare, fine wine list and spectacular views of
Disney fireworks shows; reservations essential.

⌂ Disney's
Wilderness Lodge   Resort $$$
(☏407-824-3200; 901 Timberline Dr; r from
$319; P ❄ ☎ ⛌ ⛱; ⛲) One of our favorite
'deluxe' resorts, the 'rustic opulence' theme
here includes erupting geysers, a lakelike
swimming area and bunk beds for the kids.

Tampa ❺

⌂ Tahitian Inn   Hotel $$
(☏813-877-6721; www.tahitianinn.com; 601
S Dale Mabry Hwy; r $79-139, ste $149-199;
P ❄ @ ☎ ⛌ ⛱) This family-owned, full-
service hotel offers fresh boutique stylings at
midrange prices. Nice pool, and airport transfers.

Ybor City ❻

✖ Columbia Restaurant   Spanish $$$
(☏813-248-4961; www.columbiarestaurant.com;
2117 E 7th Ave; mains lunch $9-15, dinner $18-29;
⊙11am-10pm Mon-Thu, to 11pm Fri & Sat, noon-
9pm Sun) Reserve ahead for the exuberant,
twice-nightly flamenco shows, and enjoy robust,
classic Spanish cuisine and heady *mojitos* and
sangria. It's an Old World Iberian time warp.

St Petersburg ❼

✖ Ceviche   Tapas $$
(☏727-209-2299; www.ceviche.com; 10 Beach
Dr; tapas $5-13, mains $15-23; ⊙11am-10pm)
Tapas are flavorful, creative, and generously
portioned. End the evening in the cavernlike
Flamenco Room below, with live flamenco
Thursday and Saturday nights.

Sarasota ❽

✖ Broken Egg   Breakfast $
(www.thebrokenegg.com; 140 Avenida Messina;
mains $7-14; ⊙7:30am-2:30pm; ⛱) This diner-
style breakfast institution on Siesta Key, known
for huge pancakes and cheddary home fries, is a
social hub each morning.

⌂ Hotel Ranola   Boutique Hotel $$
(☏941-951-0111; www.hotelranola.com; 118
Indian Pl; r $109-149, ste $209; P ❄ @) The
nine rooms feel like a designer's brownstone
apartment: free-spirited and effortlessly artful,
but with real working kitchens. It's urban funk,
walkable to downtown Sarasota.

Sanibel Island ❿

✖ Island Cow   Regional $$
(☏239-472-0606; www.sanibelislandcow.com;
2163 Periwinkle Way; mains $8-19; ⊙7am-10pm)
This colorful island cafe has a cheery interior
and tons of options, from paella to po'boys to
steaks – a good choice any time of day.

4 DOING DISNEY & MORE

Seven Mile Bridge A breathtaking drive over stunning Gulf water.

Classic Trip

Overseas Highway to Key West

5

Redefining the road trip, the Overseas Hwy lets you drive straight out into the ocean toward Cuba, surrounded by water as you hop from island to island.

TRIP HIGHLIGHTS

55 miles

Seven Mile Bridge
Giddy views as you drive across the ocean

0 miles

John Pennekamp State Park
Immerse yourself in underwater splendor

START
1

4 Islamorada

6 Marathon

FINISH
9

Key West
A renegade party island that's halfway to Cuba

102 miles

Indian & Lignumvitae Keys
Kayak out to remote deserted islands

25 miles

3–5 DAYS
102 MILES / 164KM

GREAT FOR...

BEST TIME TO GO
December to April, when the weather's at its best.

ESSENTIAL PHOTO
Key West Mile Marker zero (MM 0): proof you made it all the way.

BEST FOR SNORKELING
The coral reef and crystal waters at Pennekamp State Park.

Classic Trip

Overseas Highway to Key West

5

There's no better way — short of hopping on a plane — to enjoy such an utter feeling of escape from the mainland as driving through the Florida Keys. The motto here seems to be 'do whatever the hell you want.' Pull off the highway for biker bars, seafood grills and blissful beaches — wherever and whenever the crazy spirit of these islands moves you.

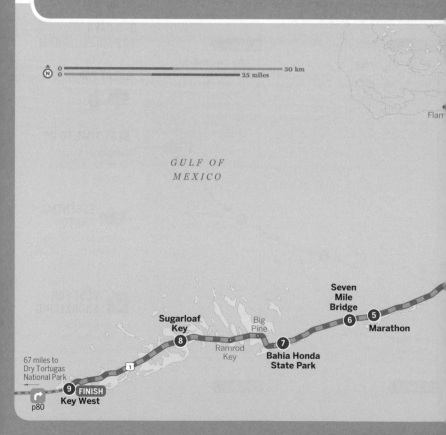

① John Pennekamp Coral Reef State Park

Although the full effect of driving from island to island doesn't kick in until Islamorada, the Keys don't dillydally in delivering an oceanic treat. One of the first things you'll encounter on the Overseas Hwy is **John Pennekamp Coral Reef State Park** (www. pennekamppark.com; MM 102.6 oceanside; car/motorcycle/ cyclist or pedestrian $8/4/2; ⏱8am-sunset, aquarium 8am-5pm; 🛝), the USA's first underwater park.

It's a true jewel box beneath the sea, a vast living coral reef that's home to a panoply of sea life. You never know what you'll see underwater, except for one predictable favorite: the oft-photographed statue **Christ of the Deep**, a sunken 4000lb bronze statue.

Your options for exploring the reef include a popular 2½-hour **glass-bottom boat tour** (📞305-451-6300; adult/child $24/17; ⏱9:15am, 12:15pm & 3:15pm) on a 65ft catamaran from which you can ooh and aah at filigreed flaps of soft coral, technicolor schools of fish, dangerous-looking barracudas and massive sea turtles.

You can also dive in with a **snorkeling trip** (📞305-451-6300; adult/child $30/25) or two-tank **diving trip** (📞305-451-6322; $55), or go DIY and rent a canoe ($20 per hour) or kayak (single/double $12/17 per hour) and journey through a 3-mile network of water trails. Call the park for reservations and departure times.

The Drive » Your instructions for most of this trip will be the same: drive farther southwest along the Overseas Hwy. This first leg is a short one; the park and the town of Key Largo are practically spooning.

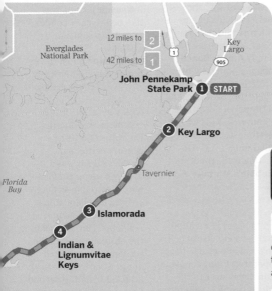

12 miles to ②
42 miles to ①
Everglades National Park
Key Largo
905
John Pennekamp State Park ① START
② Key Largo
Tavernier
Florida Bay
③ Islamorada
④ Indian & Lignumvitae Keys

🔗 LINK YOUR TRIP

Highway 1
Only a 60-mile stretch of Hwy 1 separates these two trips; combining them is a natural.

The Everglades
This trip is the other way out of the Keys, starting on the eastern edge of the Everglades less than an hour from Key Largo.

Classic Trip

❷ Key Largo

We ain't gonna lie: Key Largo (both the name of the town and the island it's on) is slightly underwhelming at a glance, especially given the romantic notions that may have been placed in your head by hearing it mentioned in pop culture references ranging from Humphrey Bogart to the Beach Boys.

As you drive onto the islands, Key Largo resembles a long line of low-lying hammock and strip development. But that's from the highway. Head down a side road and duck into this warm little bar, or that converted Keys plantation house, and the island's idiosyncrasies become more pronounced.

Speaking of pop culture, the actual **African Queen** (☎305-451-8080; www.africanqueenflkeys.com; MM 100 oceanside, at the Holiday Inn Marina; canal cruise $49, dinner cruise $89) – a steamboat used in the 1951 movie starring Humphrey Bogart and Katherine Hepburn – has been restored to her former, er, splendor, and you can relive the movie aboard the tiny vessel on a canal or dinner cruise.

If you behave better than Hepburn's character, the captain might even let you take the helm for a bit.

✗ 🛏 p81

The Drive » Continue south to your next stop, Islamorada, which sounds like an island, but is actually a string of several islands. It is here where the trees open up and you finally start to feel like you're in the islands.

❸ Islamorada

When you reach Islamorada, you'll finally feel like you're in the islands. Here at last are unbroken horizons of sea and sky, one perfect shade of blue mirroring the other. Near mile marker 73.5, sandy **Anne's Beach** opens upon a sky-bright stretch of calm waters for splashing about beside a tunnel of hardwood hammock. Kids will love getting stuck in the tidal mud flats.

Down the road, **Robbie's Marina** (☎305-664-8070; www.robbies.com; MM 77.5 bayside; kayak & canoe rentals from $40; ⊙9am-8pm) is a combo tourist shop, fishing marina and cruise-boat operator. From here you can kayak over to the virgin tropical rain forest of **Lignumvitae Key**, tour Indian Key's historical ruins or get happily buzzed on a party boat. Don't forget to look in on

the fearsome tarpon fish before you leave.

✗ p81

The Drive » You can't drive to your next stop; like many of the keys, these two can only be reached by boat. You can rent a canoe or kayak or catch a charter from Robbie's Marina.

TRIP HIGHLIGHT

❹ Indian & Lignumvitae Keys

Take a boat tour or paddle yourself out to either of these remote islands, both of which are on the National Register of Historic Places and offer a serene glimpse into what Florida was like before cars, condos and cheap souvenir T-shirts.

An island ghost town, **Indian Key** (☎305-664-2540; www.floridastateparks.org/indiankey; MM 78.5 oceanside; per person $2.50; ⊙8am-sunset) contains the ruins of a 19th-century settlement. In the 1830s it was a thriving town, complete with a warehouse, docks, streets, hotel and about 40 to 50 permanent residents. However (cue the ominous music), the settlement was wiped out in a Native American attack during the Second Seminole War, and now all that remains are crumbling foundations. It's a serene if sometimes eerie experience, walking among ruins and paddling around in utter isolation.

On the bay side, the isolated **Lignumvitae Key Botanical State Park** (☎305-664-2540; www.floridastateparks.org/lignumvitaekey; admission $2.50, tour $2; ☺tours 10am & 2pm Fri-Sun) has virgin tropical forests and the 1919-built Matheson House. Douse yourself in bug spray and consider long sleeves – mosquitoes have staged a coup and overtaken the island – to see some beautifully undeveloped island during weekend tours.

The Drive » From Robbie's Marina, settle in for a half-hour drive to Marathon, the halfway point between Key Largo and Key West.

---

⑤ Marathon

Marathon sits right on the halfway point between Key Largo and Key West, and is a good place to stop on a road trip across the islands. It's perhaps the most 'developed' key outside Key West, in the sense that it has large shopping centers and a population of a few thousand.

Stop and stretch your legs at **Crane Point** (www.cranepoint.net; MM 50.5 bayside; adult/child $12.50/8.50; ☺9am-5pm Mon-Sat, from noon Sun;), a nature center with walking trails through a hardwood hammock and wildlife exhibits for

✓ TOP TIP: MILE MARKERS

Many addresses in the Keys are noted by their proximity to mile markers (indicated as MM), which start at MM 126 in Florida City and count down to MM 0 in Key West. They also might indicate whether they're 'oceanside,' which is the south side of the highway, or 'bayside,' which is north.

kids, including marine touch tanks. And if you're ready to hop in the ocean, **Sombrero Beach** (Sombrero Beach Rd, off MM 50 oceanside) is a wonderful park with shady picnic areas, nicer-than-you'd-expect bathrooms, and a playscape for the kiddos. It's one of the few white-sand, mangrove-free beaches in the Keys.

✗ ⌂ p81

The Drive » The almost-aptly-named Seven Mile Bridge starts just past Marathon and continues just on for (shhh, don't tell) just under 7 miles.

TRIP HIGHLIGHT

⑥ Seven Mile Bridge

Take a deep breath because next up on the horizon is the gasp-worthy Seven Mile Bridge. Florida is full of head-spinning causeways, but none longer than this beauty soaring over the Gulf of Mexico. Driving across it provides one of the most memorable stretches of road anywhere.

If you care to stop, you can also walk out onto the parallel **Old Seven Mile Bridge**, a hurricane-battered railway and auto causeway no longer used except as the Keys' longest fishing pier. Below the old bridge, about 2 miles from the mainland, **Pigeon Key** (☎305-743-5999; www.pigeonkey.net; tours leave from MM 47 oceanside; adult/child/under 5yr $12/9/free; ☺tours 10am, noon & 2pm) is a National Historic District. Hop on a ferry over to the island to amble around an early-20th-century railroad workers' village built by real-estate tycoon Henry Flagler, or come just for the snorkeling and sun-splashed beach.

The Drive » Just a couple of miles after the bridge touches down and you're back on land, you'll reach the entrance to Bahia Honda State Park on your left.

---

⑦ Bahia Honda State Park

This park – with its long, white-sand (and

WHY THIS IS A CLASSIC TRIP
MARIELLA KRAUSE, AUTHOR

This is one of my favorite road trips of all time. Leaving the mainland gives you a unique sense of escape, and when you're out there surrounded by ocean, you can't help but feel like you've truly gotten away. It's only fitting that quirky Key West is the last stop – your reward for going all the way to the end.

Top: Lighthouse, Fort Jefferson
Left: *Christ of the Deep* statue, John Pennekamp Coral Reef State Park
Right: Bahia Honda Rail Bridge, Bahia Honda State Park

IMAGE SOURCE / GETTY IMAGES ©

MIKE THEISS / GETTY IMAGES ©

seaweed-strewn) beach is the big attraction in these parts. As Keys beaches go, this one is probably the best natural stretch of sand in the island chain, but we wouldn't vote it the best beach in the continental USA (although Condé Nast did...in 1992). As a tourist, the more novel experience is walking a stretch of the old **Bahia Honda Rail Bridge**, which offers nice views of the surrounding islands. Or check out the nature trails (ooh, butterflies!) and science center, where helpful park employees help you identify stone crabs, fireworms, horseshoe crabs and comb jellies.

The **park concession** (☎305-872-3210; MM 36.8 oceanside) offers daily 1½-hour snorkeling trips at 9:30am and 1:30pm (adult/child $30/25). Reservations are a good idea in high season.

The Drive » Your next stop is another 17 miles along, and you'll need directions to find it. On Sugarloaf Key, turn right at the sign for the Sugarloaf airport, near mile marker 17, then take the right side of the fork in the road.

- - - - - - - - - - - -

❽ Sugarloaf Key

Ready for a little tidbit of randomness? Just off the highway (only about one minute out of your way) you'll find **Perky's Bat Tower**, a 1920s real-estate-developer's vision

BUENA VISTA IMAGES / GETTY IMAGES ©

Classic Trip

gone awry. To eliminate pesky mosquitoes from his planned vacation resort, Richter Perky imported a colony of bats (he'd heard they'd eat mosquitoes) and moved them into a custom-made 35ft tower that resembles an Aztec-inspired fire lookout. The bats promptly flew off, never to return, and the mosquitoes lived happily on. The tower is the only vestige of the development that would have been.

The Drive » Can you feel the excitement? You're only about half an hour away from the end of the road: Key West. Or is that the beginning of the road? US 1 technically begins in Key West,

counting up from mile marker zero. Once you hit town, drive all the way to the edge; that's where the heart of Old Town is located.

TRIP HIGHLIGHT

❾ Key West

Key West has enjoyed a long and colorful history that includes pirates, sunken treasures, literary legends and lots of ghosts. A visit to the **Ernest Hemingway Home and Museum** (☏305-294-1136; www.hemingwayhome .com; 907 Whitehead St; adult/child $13/6; ☻9am-5pm) is practically mandatory, him being the unofficial patron saint of Key West and all. Bearded docents lead tours every half-hour, during which they spin yarns of Papa, his wives, and his famous six-toed cats.

Love a good ghost story? Key West is full of them. You might just find out your guesthouse is haunted during the **Original Ghost Tour** (☏305-294-9255; www. hauntedtours.com; adult/child $15/10; ☻8pm & 9pm), and you'll hear all about the creepy antics that got Robert the haunted doll confined to **Fort East Martello** (☏305-296-3913; www.kwahs.com/martello.htm; 3501 S Roosevelt Blvd; adult/child $7/5; ☻9:30am-4:30pm).

The Keys are home to the only living coral barrier reef in the United States, which means snorkeling here is excellent. Warm, clear water and white sand make conditions ideal, and the fish are vibrant about a half-hour boat ride from the island.

At sunset, crowds fill Mallory Square for the **Sunset Celebration**, a nightly festival where you'll see jugglers, fire-eaters, and street performers of every stripe. And at the end of the day, bar aficionados flock to the **Green Parrot** (www.greenparrot.com; 601 Whitehead St; ☻10am-4am), a fine purveyor of old-school Key West ambiance. Purported to be the oldest bar on the island, it's Key West's tenured local hangout.

🍴 🛏 p81

↱ **DETOUR: DRY TORTUGAS NATIONAL PARK**

Start: ❾ Key West

Seventy miles beyond the end of the Overseas Hwy, **Dry Tortugas National Park** (☏305-242-7700; www. nps.gov/drto; adult/15yr and under $5/free) is a 2¼-hour ferry ride or 40-minute seaplane flight out into the Gulf of Mexico. This small cluster of coral reefs, named 'The Turtles' by Spanish explorer Ponce de León, is a hot spot for diving, snorkeling, bird-watching, fishing and exploring Civil War–era **Fort Jefferson**, a striking hexagonal centerpiece of red brick rising up from the emerald waters. Getting here isn't easy, or cheap, but it's worth it for the middle-of-nowhere experience at American's most inaccessible national park.

Eating & Sleeping

Key Largo ❷

✖ Alabama Jack's   Seafood, Bar $

(http://alabamajacks.com; 58000 Card Sound Rd; mains $7-14; ⏰11am-7pm) On the backroad between Key Largo and Florida City, this funky open-air joint draws an eclectic booze-hungry crowd of genuine Keys characters. Try the rave-worthy conch fritters.

✖ Mrs Mac's Kitchen   American $

(☎305-451-3722; www.mrsmacskitchen.com; MM 99.4 bayside; breakfast & lunch $8-12, dinner $9-22; ⏰7am-9:30pm Mon-Sat) This cute roadside diner bedecked with rusty license plates serves classic highway food such as burgers and fish baskets.

🛏 Largo Lodge   Hotel $$

(☎305-451-0424; www.largolodge.com; MM 102 bayside; cottages $150-265; P) Charming, sunny cottages with their own private beach sit amid palm trees, tropical flowers and lots of roaming birds – a taste of Florida in the good old days.

Islamorada ❸

✖ Island Grill   Seafood $$

(☎305-664-8400; www.keysislandgrill.com; 85501 Overseas Hwy, Islamorada; breakfast $5-10, mains $9-25; ⏰7am-10pm Sun-Thu, to 11pm Fri & Sat) The ramshackle waterfront building may not look like much, but you'll be surprised how damn good the peel-and-eat shrimp and cracked conch are. Casual, contemporary Floribbean fare with breezy ocean views and lotsa live bands.

Marathon ❺

✖ Keys Fisheries   Seafood $

(www.keysfisheries.com; 3502 Gulfview Ave; mains $7-16; ⏰11am-9pm) A rare thing in the islands: a nontouristy, unfussy and authentic seafood spot. Famous for its lobster Reuben sandwiches, Cajun-fried fresh fish and colossal stone-crab claws (in season).

🛏 Lime Tree Bay Resort Motel   Motel $$

(☎305-664-4740, 800-723-4519; www.limetreebayresort.com; MM 68.5 bayside; r $135-175, ste $185-395) A plethora of hammocks and lawn chairs provide front-row seats for the spectacular sunsets at this 2.5-acre waterfront hideaway.

Key West ❾

✖ Blue Heaven   American $$$

(☎305-296-8666; http://blueheavenkw.homestead.com; 729 Thomas St; dinner $17-35; ⏰8am-4pm, to 2pm Sun, 5-10:30pm daily) One of the island's quirkiest venues (and it's a high bar), where you dine in an outdoor courtyard with a flock of chickens. Customers gladly wait, with creative, well-executed dishes as their reward.

✖ Camille's   Fusion $$

(☎305-296-4811; www.camilleskeywest.com; 1202 Simonton St; breakfast & lunch $4-13, dinner $15-25; ⏰8am-3pm & 6-10pm; 🍴) Ditch Duval St and dine with the locals at Camille's; its inventive menu ranges from French toast with Godiva liqueur to tasty chicken salad.

🛏 Cypress House   Hotel $$$

(☎305-294-5229, 800-549-4430; www.cypresshousekw.com; 601 Caroline St; r $169-329; P ❄ 🛜 🏊) This plantationlike getaway has wraparound porches, leafy grounds, a secluded swimming pool and spacious, individually designed bedrooms with four-poster beds.

🛏 Mermaid & the Alligator   Guesthouse $$$

(☎305-294-1894; www.kwmermaid.com; 729 Truman Ave; r winter $258-328, summer $168-228; P ❄ @ 🛜 🏊) Book way ahead: with only nine rooms, this place's charm exceeds its capacity. It's chock-a-block with treasures collected from the owners' travels.

STRETCH YOUR LEGS
MIAMI BEACH

Start/Finish: Ocean Dr

Distance: 3 miles

Duration: Three hours

Greater Miami sprawls, but compact Miami Beach packs in the sights, making it perfect for an afternoon of exploring on foot. Get a taste of its famous art-deco district, as well as its luscious, white-sand beaches.

Take this walk on Trip

1

Ocean Drive

Ocean Dr is the classic Miami strip, where neon-accented art-deco buildings line the way for an endless parade of cars, rollerbladers and pedestrians. Stop at the **Art Deco Welcome Center** (☎305-672-2014; www.mdpl.org; 1001 Ocean Dr, South Beach; ☻9:30am-5pm, to 7pm Thu) if you really want to immerse yourself in the world of decorative finials and cantilevered eyebrows.

The Walk ≫ Head north. To fully appreciate the architecture, stick to the park side of the street. At 13th St, note the Carlyle Hotel, where *The Birdcage* was filmed. Cross Lummus Park to get to the beach.

Lummus Park & South Beach

Take off your shoes and dig your toes into some of the most luscious sand you've ever felt, and stare out at (or run straight toward) the teal-green water that's shallow and warm enough to splash around in for hours. Run up and down if you must – cartwheels in the sand would not be inappropriate – but be sure to notice the six floridly colored lifeguard stands that stretch along this strip.

The Walk ≫ Walk (or wade) up the beach and find the path that takes you to Lincoln Rd just past the Loews Hotel. (If you get to the Sagamore you've gone too far.) Walk two blocks along Lincoln until you reach Washington Ave.

Lincoln Road Mall

Calling Lincoln Rd a mall is technically accurate, but misses the point. Yes, you can shop, and there are sidewalk cafes galore. But this outdoor pedestrian promenade between Alton Rd and Washington Ave is really about seeing and being seen; there are times when it feels less like a road and more like a runway.

The Walk ≫ Head south down busy Collins Ave, another thoroughfare that's lined with deco treasures. At 13th St, hop over one block to Washington Ave.

Miami Beach Post Office

Ahhh, Miami Beach – even its municipal buildings are treasured works of art. A fine example of Streamline Moderne, the **Miami Beach Post Office** (1300 Washington Ave) was built in 1937 as part of the Works Progress Administration. Duck inside to mail some postcards and check out the striking ceiling mural of a stylized night sky.

The Walk » Just two blocks down – and they're not very interesting blocks, so we're tempted to send you back over to Collins – is a vintage dining experience.

11th St Diner

Many art-deco buildings evoke modes of transportation, such as planes, trains or ships. Well, the shiny little 11th St Diner (p45) does more than evoke: it's actually housed in a classic Pullman train car. Pull over for refreshments; the inside is as cute as the outside.

The Walk » Now that you're refreshed, head just a few doors down; your next stop is in the same block.

Wolfsonian-FIU

A fascinating museum that's part of Florida International University, the **Wolfsonian-FIU** (www.wolfsonian .org; 1001 Washington Ave; adult/child 6-12yr $7/5; ⊙ noon-6pm Thu-Tue, to 9pm Fri) showcases artifacts from the height of the Industrial Revolution from the late 19th to mid-20th century. The exhibits span transportation, urbanism, industrial design, advertising and political propaganda, and give some intriguing insight as to what was going on in the world while all that deco was being built.

The Walk » It's just two short blocks along 10th St to get back to Ocean Dr. Between 7th and 8th is a fetching strip of buildings including the Colony Hotel, which you'll recognize instantly if you've ever watched anything set in Miami Beach.

The Carolinas

SPARKLING BEACHES, RUGGED MOUNTAINS AND HAVE-ANOTHER-BISCUIT HOSPITALITY. Yep, the Carolinas share more than just a name and a border.

For a drive on the wild side, North Carolina is the place to start. In the western mountains the Blue Ridge Parkway and Great Smokies serve up wildlife, white water and lofty peaks. In the east, windswept dunes and roaming mustangs keep things wild in the Outer Banks.

South Carolina has its share of adventure, but scenery and history slow the pace. Lowcountry roads meander past plantations and mossy oaks, while Upcountry byways take in battlefields and foothills. And rocking chairs are everywhere – just waiting to ruin your itinerary.

Great Smoky Mountains National Park Fall colors (Trip 7)
GIORGIO FOCHESATO / GETTY IMAGES ©

The Carolinas

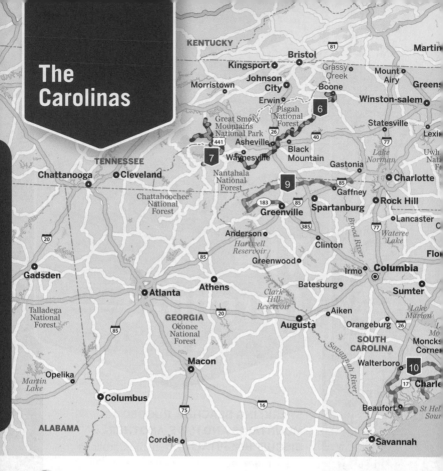

DON'T MISS

Biltmore Legacy

For less of the formality and more of the family, visit the new 'Vanderbilts at Home and Abroad' exhibit on Trip 6

Museum of the Cherokee Indian

Learn about three Cherokee chiefs, who journeyed to England and met with King George III, on Trip 7

Bodie Island Lighthouse

This 1872 lighthouse with an original Fresnel lens is open to visitors for the first time. Visit on Trip 8

Cowpens National Battlefield

Walk the battlefield to witness how terrain, planning and luck propelled Patriot forces to victory on Trip 9

King's Farm Market

You'll spend more time than planned at this roadside market where the conversation is easy and the baked goods delicious. Visit on Trip 10

Grandfather Mountain Springtime flowers (Trip 6)

Blue Ridge Parkway *Wildlife, waterfalls and winsome towns*

Blue Ridge Parkway

6

This drive on America's favorite byway curves through the leafy Appalachians, where it swoops up the East Coast's highest peak and stops by the nation's largest mansion.

TRIP HIGHLIGHTS

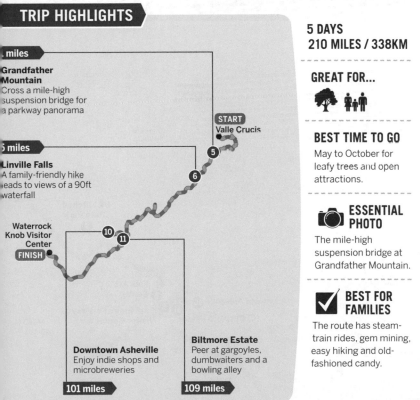

miles

Grandfather Mountain
Cross a mile-high suspension bridge for a parkway panorama

miles

Linville Falls
A family-friendly hike leads to views of a 90ft waterfall

Waterrock Knob Visitor Center
FINISH

START
Valle Crucis

5

6

10 11

Downtown Asheville
Enjoy indie shops and microbreweries

101 miles

Biltmore Estate
Peer at gargoyles, dumbwaiters and a bowling alley

109 miles

**5 DAYS
210 MILES / 338KM**

GREAT FOR...

BEST TIME TO GO
May to October for leafy trees and open attractions.

ESSENTIAL PHOTO
The mile-high suspension bridge at Grandfather Mountain.

BEST FOR FAMILIES
The route has steam-train rides, gem mining, easy hiking and old-fashioned candy.

6 Blue Ridge Parkway

The Blue Ridge Parkway stretches 469 miles, from Shenandoah National Park in Virginia to Great Smoky Mountains National Park in North Carolina. In the Tar Heel State, the road carves a sinuous path through a rugged landscape of craggy peaks, crashing waterfalls, thick forests and charming mountain towns. Three things you'll see? White-tail deer, local microbrews and signs for Grandfather Mountain. And one piece of advice: at breakfast, never say no to a biscuit.

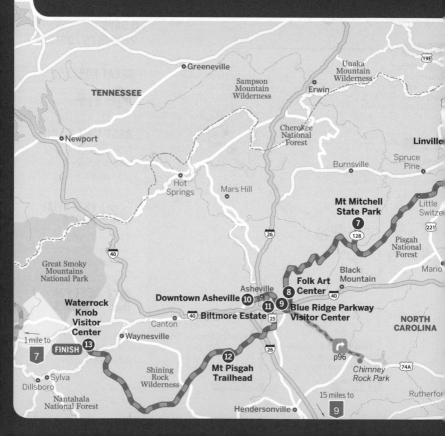

❶ Valle Crucis

How do you start a road trip through the mountains? With a good night's sleep and all the right gear. You'll find both in Valle Crucis, a bucolic village west of Boone. After slumbering beneath sumptuous linens at the Mast Farm Inn (p98), a 200-year-old farmhouse, ease into the day sipping coffee from a rocking chair on the inn's front porch.

Down the road is the **Original Mast General Store** (☎828-963-6511; www.mastgeneralstore.com; Hwy 194, Valle Crucis; ⊙7am-6:30pm Mon-Sat, noon-6pm Sun; 🖘) and its **Annex** (www.mastgeneralstore.com; Hwy 194; ⊙10am-6pm Mon-Sat, noon-6pm Sun). The first of several Mast general stores across the region, the original sells many of the same products that it did when it opened in 1883. Today you'll find bacon and hard candy as well as hiking shoes and French Country hand towels. The Annex building, just south on Hwy 194, sells outdoor apparel and hiking gear.

✗ p98

The Drive » Drive south on Hwy 194, also known as Broadstone Rd, through 3 miles of rural splendor. At Hwy 105 turn left.

----

❷ Boone

If you're traveling with kids or wannabe prospectors, stop at **Foggy Mountain Gem Mine** (☎828-963-4367; www.foggymountaingems.com; 4416 Hwy 105 S, Boone; buckets $17-120; ⊙10am-6pm; 🖘) to pan for semi-precious stones, which are sold by the bucketload. There are several gem-mining spots near the Parkway, but Foggy Mountain, a smaller company, is operated by graduate gemologists who may take their craft a bit more seriously. After sifting your rocks in a miner's flume line, the gemologists will cut and mount your favorite finds in any number of settings.

In downtown Boone, home of Appalachian State, you'll find shopping and dining on **King Street**. Keep an eye out for the bronze statue of local bluegrass legend Doc Watson. He's strumming a Gallagher guitar like nobody's business at the corner of King and Depot Sts.

✗ p98

The Drive » From King St, turn onto Hwy 321 just past the Daniel Boone Inn restaurant. Drive 4 miles then turn right at the theme park.

e Crucis — Boone ❷ [421]
ART ❶ [105]
ses H Cone ❹ [321]
norial Park
❺ ❸ Blowing Rock
Grandfather Mountain [321]

ke
nes Morganton

🔗 LINK YOUR TRIP

7 The Great Smokies
Continue past the last Parkway milepost, Mile 469, to the entrance to the national park.

9 Greenville & Cherokee Foothills Scenic Highway
Drive south on US 25 from Asheville to South Carolina and SC-11.

0 ———— 20 km
0 ———— 10 miles

❸ Blowing Rock

The Parkway runs just above the village of Blowing Rock, which sits at an elevation of 4000ft. On a cloudy morning, drive south on Hwy 321 to the top of the mountain to check out the cloud-capped views of surrounding peaks. The eastern continental divide runs through the bar at the Green Park Inn (p98), a white-clapboard grand hotel that opened in 1891. They say author Margaret Mitchell worked on *Gone with the Wind* while staying here.

A rite of passage for every North Carolina child is the **Tweetsie Railroad** (☎877-893-3874; www.tweetsie.com; 300 Tweetsie Railroad Ln; adult/child $37/23; ☺9am-6pm daily Jun-Aug, 9am-6pm Fri-Sun mid-Apr-May, Sep & Oct; 👶), a theme park where Appalachian culture meets the Wild West. The highlight? A 1917 coal-fired steam locomotive that chugs past marauding Indians and heroic cowboys. Midway rides, fudge shops and family-friendly shows round out the fun.

✕ ⊨ p98

The Drive » The entrance to the Blue Ridge Parkway is in Blowing Rock, 2.3 miles south of the Tweetsie Railroad. Once on the Parkway, drive south 2 miles.

❹ Moses H Cone Memorial Park

Hikers and equestrians share 25 miles of carriage roads on the former **estate** (Mile 294) of Moses H Cone, a wealthy philanthropist and conservationist who made his fortune in denim. His mansion and grounds were given to the national park service in the 1950s. His Colonial Revival mansion, completed in 1901, now houses the **Parkway Craft Center** (☎828-295-7938; www.craftguild.org; Mile 294, Blue Ridge Parkway; ☺9am-5pm mid-Mar–Nov). The shop sells high-end crafts made by members of the Southern Highland Craft Guild. Free tours of the 2nd floor of the mansion, Flat Top Manor, are offered on Saturdays and Sundays June through mid-October at 10am, 11am, 2pm and 3pm. Tours do fill up. To reserve a spot call ☎828-295-3782 on the Friday before your visit.

The Drive » Head south on the Parkway, passing split rail fences, stone walls, streams and meadows. Just south of Mile 304 the Parkway curves across the Linn Cove Viaduct, the last section of the Parkway to be completed, in 1987, because of the terrain's fragility. Exit onto US 221 at Mile 305 and drive 1 mile south.

TRIP HIGHLIGHT

❺ Grandfather Mountain

Don't let a fear of heights keep you from driving up to the famed swinging bridge near the peaks of **Grandfather Mountain** (☎828-733-4337; www.grandfather.com; Blue Ridge Pkwy Mile 305; adult/child 4-12yr $18/8; ☺8am-7pm Jun-Aug). Yes, the 228ft-long bridge is 1 mile above sea level and yes, you can hear its steel girders 'sing' on gusty days, but the ground is just 80ft below the span. Nothing to sneeze at, for sure, but it's not the Grand Canyon, and the views of nearby mountains are superb. The small **Nature Museum** spotlights local flora and fauna as well as regional explorer Daniel Boone. Behind the museum, black bears, deer and otters roam a small animal habitat. Grandfather Mountain is a Unesco Biosphere Reserve.

Park attractions have been privately managed by the Morton family since the 1950s. The North Carolina State Park System purchased the mountain's backcountry lands in 2008, and Grandfather Mountain State Park (www.ncparks.gov) was established the following year. State park trails can be accessed from the Parkway for free, or from parking lots inside the attraction with paid admission. The strenuous but varied **Grandfather Trail** runs 2.4 miles from the suspension bridge parking lot along the mountain's crest, ending atop Calloway Peak; the trail includes cables and ladders.

The Drive » Follow the Parkway south and turn left just south of Mile 316 to reach Linville Falls.

TRIP HIGHLIGHT

❻ Linville Falls

Have time for just one hike? Then hop out of your car for the moderate 1.6-mile **Erwin's View** Trail (round-trip) at popular Linville Falls. Here, the Linville River sweeps over two separate falls before crashing 2000ft through a rocky gorge. The trail crosses the river then follows it downstream. At .5 miles, a spur trail leads to a view of the Upper Falls. The 90ft Lower Falls are visible from the Chimney View and Gorge View overlooks just ahead. At the latter you'll also see the imposing Linville Gorge. Ponder the scope of it all at the trail's last stop, the Erwin's View Overlook.

The Drive » Drive south on the Parkway and turn right, south of Mile 355, onto NC 128. Follow NC 128 into the park.

❼ Mt Mitchell State Park

A trip to **Mt Mitchell** (☏828-675-4611; www .ncparks.gov; 2388 State Hwy 128; admission free; ⊗8am-9pm May-Aug, closes earlier rest of the year) might lead to a fight. Will you drive to the top of the highest mountain east of the Mississippi, or will you hike there? Make your decision at the **park office** (⊗8am-5pm Apr-Oct, closed weekends Nov-Mar), which sits beside a 2-mile trail to the 6684ft summit.

At the top you'll see the grave of the mountain's namesake, Dr Elisha Mitchell. A dedicated professor from the University of

---

BLUE RIDGE PARKWAY TRIP PLANNER

Construction of the Parkway began in 1935, during the Great Depression, after the government harnessed the strength of thousands of out-of-work young men in the Civilian Conservation Corps. The Parkway wasn't fully linked together until 1987, when the Lynn Cove viaduct opened.

Travel Tips

» The maximum speed limit is 45 mph.

» Long stretches of the road close in winter and may not reopen until March. Many visitor centers and campgrounds are closed until May. Check the park service website (www.nps.gov/blri) for the latest information about road closures and the opening dates for facilities.

» The North Carolina section of the Parkway begins at Mile 216.9, between the Blue Ridge Mountain Center in Virginia and Cumberland Knob in North Carolina.

» There are 26 tunnels on the Parkway in North Carolina (and just one in Virginia). Watch for signs to turn on your headlights.

» For more trip planning tools, check the websites for the **Blue Ridge Parkway Association** (www.blueridgeparkway.org) and the **Blue Ridge National Heritage Area** (www.blueridgeheritage.com).

LOCAL VOICE
JENNIFER PHARR
DAVIS, OWNER,
BLUE RIDGE HIKING
CO; AUTHOR OF
CALLED AGAIN, ABOUT
HER 46-DAY TRAVERSE OF THE
APPALACHIAN TRAIL

Past Mt Pisgah you come to a
lookout along the Parkway for
Graveyard Fields. It's a beautiful
area with several different hiking
trails to choose from. There's a
great waterfall right there that's
very close to the Parkway. It's called
Lower Falls, or Second Falls. There's
also an Upper Falls, which is not as
spectacular, but it's a nice walk up.

Top: Bass Lake, Moses H Cone Memorial Park
Left: Horseriding, Moses H Cone Memorial Park
Right: Chimney Rock, Chimney Rock Park

North Carolina, he died after a fall while trying to verify the height of the mountain in 1857. A circular ramp beside the grave leads to panoramic views of the surrounding Black Mountains and beyond.

The Drive >> Return to the Parkway and drive south to Mile 382. During the last two weeks of June look for blooming rhododendrons.

- - - - - - - - - -

❽ Folk Art Center

As you enter the lobby at the **Folk Art Center** (📞828-298-7928; www .craftguild.org; Mile 382; 🕙9am-6pm Apr-Dec, to 5pm Jan-Mar), look up. A row of handcrafted Appalachian chairs hangs from the walls above. They're an impressive calling card for the gallery here, which is dedicated to southern craftsmanship. The chairs are part of the Southern Highland Craft Guild's permanent collection, which holds more than 2400 traditional and modern crafts. Items from the collection – pottery, baskets, quilts, woodcarvings – are displayed on the 2nd floor. The Allanstand Craft Shop on the 1st floor sells a range of fine traditional crafts.

The Drive >> Turn right onto the Parkway and drive south. After crossing the Swannanoa River and I-40, continue to Mile 384.

Classic Trip

9 Blue Ridge Parkway Visitor Center

Sit back and let the scenery come to you at this helpful **visitor center** (☐828-298-5330; www.nps.gov/blri; Mile 384; ☺9am-5pm), where the beauty and wonder of the drive is captured in a big-screen film, *Blue Ridge Parkway – America's Favorite Journey*. A park service representative can provide details about trails along the Parkway at the front desk. For a list of regional sites and activities, slide the digital monitor across the interactive I-Wall map at the back of the main hall. The adjacent regional information desk has brochures and coupons for Asheville area attractions.

The Drive >> Drive north, backtracking over the interstate and river, and exit at Tunnel Rd, which is US 70. Drive west to US 240 and follow it to the exits for downtown Asheville.

TRIP HIGHLIGHT

10 Downtown Asheville

Hippies. Hipsters. Hikers. And a few high-falutin' preppies. This 4H Club gives Asheville its funky charm. Just look around. Intellectual lefties gather at **Malaprops Bookstore and Café** (www.malaprops. com; 55 Haywood St), where the shelves stretch from Banned Books to Southern Cooking. And the hipsters? They're nibbling silky truffles at **Chocolate Fetish** (www.chocolatefetish. com; 36 Haywood St) or sipping homegrown ale at microbreweries like the convivial – and hoppy – **Wicked Weed** (www.wickedweedbrewing. com; 91 Biltmore Ave). At the engaging **Thomas Wolfe Memorial** (www. wolfememorial.com; 52 N Market St; museum free, house tour $5; ☺9am-5pm Tue-Sat), the city celebrates its most famous angsty son, Thomas Wolfe, who penned the Asheville-inspired novel *Look Homeward, Angel*.

Hikers can shop for new boots at impressive **Tops for Shoes** (www .topsforshoes.com; 27 N Lexington Ave) and outdoor gear at **Mast General Store** (www.mastgeneralstore .com; 15 Biltmore Ave). The preppies? They're working at downtown banks and law firms – and checking out the same places as everybody else.

The finishing touch? A sidewalk busker fiddling a lonesome mountain tune. It'll put a spring in your step while maybe just breaking your heart.

The Drive >> Follow Asheland Ave (which becomes McDowell St) south. After crossing Swannanoa River, the entry to Biltmore Estate is on the right.

TRIP HIGHLIGHT

11 Biltmore Estate

The destination that put Asheville on the map is the 175,000-sq-ft **Biltmore Estate** (☐800-543-2961; www.biltmore. com; 1 Approach Rd; adult/ child under 16yr $59/30;

DETOUR: CHIMNEY ROCK PARK

Start: 10 Downtown Asheville

The US flag flaps in the breeze atop this popular park's namesake 315ft granite monolith. The top can be reached by elevator or by stairs – lots and lots of stairs. Once on top, look east for amazing views of **Lake Lure**. Another draw is the hike around the cliffs to 404ft **Hickory Nut Falls**. Scenes from *The Last of the Mohicans* were filmed at the **park** (www.chimneyrockpark.com; Hwy 64/74A; adult/child $15/7; ☺8:30am-5:30pm late Mar-Oct, hours vary rest of the year). There's a small exhibit about the movie inside the Sky Lounge. From Asheville, follow US 74A east for 20 scenic, but very curvy, miles.

🕐 house 9am-4:30pm, restaurants & shops vary). The French Chateau–style mega-mansion, built by shipping and railroad heir George Vanderbilt II, was completed in 1895 after six years of work by hundreds of artists, craftsmen and educated professionals. The Vanderbilt-Cecil family still owns the estate. The entrance fee is steep, so arrive early to get your money's worth, and note that tours of the house are self-guided. The $10 audio tour is worth purchasing for the extra details. For an additional $17 you can take a general guided tour or join a specialized behind-the-scenes guided tour focusing on the architecture, the family or the servants. Children ages 10 to 16 are free June through August with an adult paid admission.

In addition to the mansion there are gardens, trails, lakes, restaurants, an inn and a winery, with complimentary wine tasting. At the estate's Antler Hill Village, don't miss the new **The Vanderbilts at Home & Abroad** exhibit in the Biltmore Legacy building. With a focus on family history and stories, the exhibit includes a family tree – look for Anderson Cooper's name – and a samurai sword owned by George Vanderbilt.

BLUEGRASS & MOUNTAIN MUSIC

For locally grown fiddle-and-banjo music, head deep into the hills of the High Country. Regional shows and music jams are listed on the Blue Ridge Music Trails (www.blueridgemusic.org) and the Blue Ridge National Heritage Area (www.bluerdgeheritage.com) websites. Here are three to get you started, from north to south:

» **Mountain Home Music Concert Series** (www .mountainhomemusic.com) Spring through fall, enjoy shows by Appalachian musicians in Boone on scheduled Saturday nights.

» **Old Fort Mountain Music Jam** (www .mcdowellnc.org) Tap your toes Friday nights from 7pm to 10pm in downtown Old Fort, east of Asheville.

» **Historic Orchard at Altapass** (www .altapassorchard.org) On weekends May through October, settle in for an afternoon of music at Little Switzerland, at Mile 328.

The Drive » After exiting the grounds, turn right onto US 25 and continue to the Parkway, not quite 3.5 miles, and drive south.

- - - - - - - - - - -

⑫ Mt Pisgah Trailhead

For a short hike to a panoramic view, pull into the parking lot beside the Mt Pisgah Trailhead just beyond Mile 407. From here, a 1.6-mile trail (one way) leads to the mountain's 5721ft summit, which is topped by a lofty TV tower. The trail is steep and rocky in its final stretch, but you'll be rewarded with views of the **French Broad River Valley** and **Cold Mountain**, the latter made famous by Charles Frazier's novel of the same name. One mile south are a campground, a general store, a restaurant and an inn.

The Drive » The drive south passes the Graveyard Fields Overlook, which has short trails to scenic waterfalls. The 6047ft Richland-Balsam Overlook at Mile 431.4 is the highest point on the Parkway. From here, continue south another 20 miles.

- - - - - - - - - - -

⑬ Waterrock Knob Visitor Center

This trip ends at the Waterrock Knob Visitor Center (Mile 451.2), which sits at an elevation of nearly 6000ft. With a four-state view, this scenic spot is a great place to see where you've been and to assess what's ahead. Helpful signage attaches a name to the mountains on the distant horizons.

Eating & Sleeping

Valle Crucis ❶

🛏 Mast Farm Inn & Simplicity Restaurant
B&B $$$

(📞828-963-5857; www.themastfarminn.com; 2543 Broadstone Rd; r incl breakfast $209-249, cabins $349-419, restaurant mains $22-34, prix fixe $48-53; 🅿 ❄ 🛜) The farmhouse and adjacent cabins define rustic chic, with hardwood floors and clawfoot tubs. The upscale mountain cuisine at Simplicity is worth a trip in itself. Each guest receives a personalized menu for dinner – 'Slow Chicken NASCAR style but mighty low on points and Ashe County cheese trucked over by Junior Johnson.' Enjoy!

Boone ❷

🍴 Daniel Boone Inn
Southern $$

(📞828-264-8657; www.danlbooneinn.com; 130 Hardin St; breakfast adult $10, child $5-7, dinner adult $17, child $6-10; 🕐11:30am-9pm Mon-Fri, 8am-9pm Sat & Sun Jun-Oct, hours vary rest of the year; 👶) Quantity is the name of the game at this restaurant, and the family-style meals are a Boone (sorry) for hungry hikers. Open since 1959. Cash or check only.

🍴 Hob Nob Farm Cafe
Cafe $$

(www.hobnobfarmcafe.com; 506 West King St; breakfast & lunch $3-12, dinner $8-15; 🕐10am-10pm Wed-Sun; 🍴) Inside a wildly painted cottage, mountain town hippie types gobble up avocado-tempeh melts, Thai curry bowls and sloppy burgers made from local beef. Brunch is served until 5pm.

Blowing Rock ❸

🍴 Six Pence Pub
Pub $$

(www.sixpencepub.com; 1121 Main St; mains $9-18; 🕐restaurant 11:30am-10:30pm Sun-Thu, to midnight Fri & Sat, bar to 2am nightly) The bartenders keep a sharp but friendly eye on things at this lively British pub where the shepherd's pie comes neat, not messy.

🛏 Cliff Dwellers Inn
Motel $$

(📞828-295-3098; www.cliffdwellers.com; 116 Lakeview Terrace; r $99-129, apt $179; 🅿 ❄ 🛜 👶) From its perch above town, this well-named motel lures guests with good service, reasonable prices, stylish rooms and balconies with sweeping views.

🛏 Green Park Inn
Hotel $$

(📞828-414-9230; www.greenparkinn.com; 9239 Valley Blvd, Blowing Rock; r incl breakfast $149-189; 🅿 ❄ 🛜 👶) Under new management, this historical gabled inn serves up history, refreshed Victorian style and made-to-order breakfasts. Pets are $25 per night. The GPS address is 5995 Lenoir Turnpike.

Asheville

🍴 12 Bones
Barbecue $

(www.12bones.com; 5 Riverside Dr; dishes $4-20; 🕐11am-4pm Mon-Fri) Soooooiiieeee, 12 Bones is good. The slow-cooked meats are smoky tender, and the sides, from the jalapeno cheese grits to the buttery green beans, will have you kissing your mama and blessing the day you were born. Order at the counter, grab a picnic table, die happy. Lunch only, closed weekends.

🍴 Admiral
Modern American $$

(📞828-252-2541; www.theadmiralnc.com; 400 Haywood Rd; small plates $10-14, large plates $22-30; 🕐5-10pm) This concrete bunker, which sits beside a car junkyard, looks divey on the outside. But inside? That's where the magic happens. This low-key West Asheville spot is one of the state's finest New American restaurants, serving wildly creative dishes – flat iron steak with soy-sauce mashed potatoes and Vietnamese slaw – that taste divine.

✖ Sunny Point Cafe
Cafe $

(www.sunnypointcafe.com; 626 Haywood Rd; breakfast & lunch $8-12, dinner $8-17; ⏱8:30am-2:30pm Sun & Mon, 8:30am-9pm Tue-Sat) In the morning, solos, couples, and ladies-who-breakfast fill this bright West Asheville spot that's loved for its hearty, homemade fare. The huevos rancheros, with feta cheese and chorizo sausage, is deservedly popular. The cafe embraces the organic and fresh, and even has its own garden. The biscuits are divine.

✖ Tupelo Honey
New Southern $$

(☎828-255-4863; www.tupelohoneycafe.com; 12 College St; breakfast $7-15, lunch & dinner $10-28; ⏱9am-10pm) This long-time favorite is known for New Southern fare like shrimp and grits with goat cheese. Tupelo-born Elvis would have surely loved the nutty fried chicken with milk gravy and smashed sweet potatoes. Breakfasts are superb, but no matter the meal, say yes to the biscuit. And add a drop of honey.

🛏 Aloft Asheville
Hotel $$$

(☎828-232-2838; www.aloftasheville.com; 51 Biltmore Ave; r from $242; P ❄ @ 🛜 🏊 🐾) At first glance this new downtown hotel looks like the 7th ring of hipster – giant chalkboard in the lobby, groovy young staff, a neon lounge with bright retro chairs. The only thing missing is a wool-cap-wearing bearded guy drinking a hoppy microbrew – oh, wait, over there. We jest. Once settled, you'll find the staff knowledgeable, the rooms large with lots of counter space, and the atmosphere convivial. Aloft is also close to the downtown action. Parking is $5 per day; pets are free.

🛏 Campfire Lodgings
Campground $$

(☎828-658-8012; www.campfirelodgings.com; 116 Appalachian Village Rd; tent/RV sites $38/45, yurts from $115, cabins $160; P ❄) All yurts should have flat-screen TVs, don't you think? Sleep like the world's most stylish Mongolian nomad in one of these furnished multiroom tents, on the side of a hill with stunning valley views. Cabins and tent sites are also available.

🛏 Grove Park Inn Resort & Spa
Resort $$$

(☎828-252-2711; www.groveparkinn.com; 290 Macon Ave; r from $269; P ❄ @ 🛜 🏊 🐾) This titanic arts-and-crafts-style lodge, which celebrated its centennial in 2013, has hale-and-hearty decor that conjures an era of adventure. But don't worry modern mavens, the well-appointed rooms come with 21st-century amenities. Look for inspirational quotes scattered across the property. Fees include a $25 daily resort fee and a $5 self-parking fee. The pet fee is $130 per reservation.

🛏 Sweet Peas
Hostel $

(☎828-285-8488; www.sweetpeashostel. com; 23 Rankin Ave; dm/pod/r $28/35/60; P ❄ @ 🛜) This spic-and-span hostel gleams with IKEA-like style. Picture shipshape steel bunk beds and blond wood sleeping 'pods'. Noise can filter up from the bar below, but the hostel's style, sociability and downtown location make it a winner.

The Great Smokies *Hike, camp, mountain-bike and stargaze*

Classic Trip

The Great Smokies

7

Alas, Hobbiton and Narnia don't exist. But the Smokies are a wonderland of their own: home to technicolor greenery, strutting wildlife, whispering waterfalls and the irrepressible Dollywood.

TRIP HIGHLIGHTS

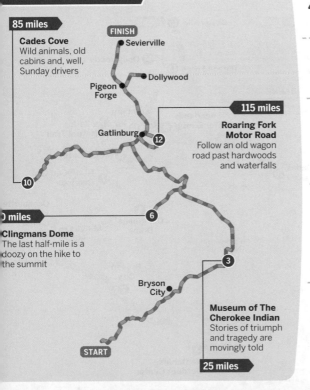

85 miles

Cades Cove
Wild animals, old cabins and, well, Sunday drivers

FINISH
● Sevierville

● Dollywood

Pigeon Forge

Gatlinburg ● 12

115 miles

Roaring Fork Motor Road
Follow an old wagon road past hardwoods and waterfalls

10

0 miles   6

Clingmans Dome
The last half-mile is a doozy on the hike to the summit

Bryson City ●

3

Museum of The Cherokee Indian
Stories of triumph and tragedy are movingly told

START

25 miles

4–5 DAYS
160 MILES / 257KM

GREAT FOR...

BEST TIME TO GO

September to October for fall color; April to June for greenery and waterfalls.

ESSENTIAL PHOTO

The tree-covered slopes snapped from the Newfound Gap Overlook.

BEST FOR OUTDOORS

Cycling the Cades Cove loop on an official 'no-car' morning.

Classic Trip

7 The Great Smokies

While the beauty of the Great Smokies can be seen from your car, the exhilarating, crash-bang, breathe-it-in wonder of the place can't be fully appreciated until you leave your vehicle. Hold tight as you bounce over Nantahala rapids. Give a nod to foraging black bears as you bicycle Cades Cove. And press your nose against windows in downtown Gatlinburg, where ogling short stacks is the best way to choose the right pancake place.

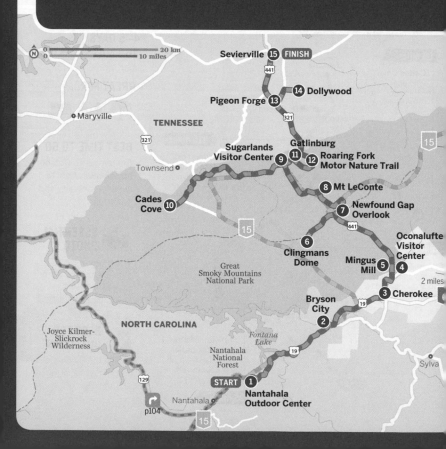

N
0 — 20 km
0 — 10 miles

Sevierville **15** FINISH
441

13 **14** Dollywood
Pigeon Forge **13**
321
TENNESSEE
● Maryville
321
Sugarlands **Gatlinburg** **15**
Visitor Center **9** **11** **12** **Roaring Fork**
Townsend ● **Motor Nature Trail**
8 **Mt LeConte**
Cades **10** **7** **Newfound Gap**
Cove **Overlook**
15 441 **Oconalufte**
Visitor
Center
6 **4**
Clingmans **Mingus** **5**
Dome **Mill**
Great 2 miles
Smoky Mountains
National Park **3** **Cherokee**
Bryson
City 19
2
NORTH CAROLINA
Joyce Kilmer- *Fontana*
Slickrock *Lake* Sylva ●
Wilderness **Nantahala**
National
129 **Forest** 19
START **1**
p104 Nantahala ● **Nantahala**
Outdoor Center
15

1 Nantahala Outdoor Center

Splash, bang, wheeeeee... There's no easing into this trip, which starts in the mountain-fed rivers and rugged valleys of western North Carolina, a region famed for its fantastic kayaking and white-water rafting.

The **Nantahala Outdoor Center** (NOC; ☎828-488-2176, 888-905-7238; www.noc.com; 13077 Hwy 19/74; kayak/canoe rental per day $30/50, guided trips $30-189) launches trips on the class II and III rapids of the Nantahala River from its sprawling outpost near Bryson City. Ride a group raft or a two-person ducky through the wide, brown river gorge. The company also offers white-water trips on six other Appalachian rivers. Experienced paddlers can brave the 9-mile trip

LINK YOUR TRIP

15 Appalachian Trail

The AT crosses US 441 at Newfound Gap Overlook.

6 Blue Ridge Parkway

From Oconaluftee Visitor Center, drive south on US 411 to the entrance of the parkway.

down the roiling class IV-V Cheoah ($169 to $189), launching from nearby Robbinsville.

At the Adventure Center, which is part of the NOC campus, sign up to zipline or to climb an alpine tower. Also on-site are an outdoor store, a year-round restaurant and lodging, which includes campsites, cabins, a hostel and an inn. The Appalachian Trail crosses the property, and the Great Smoky Mountain Railroad stops here.

The Drive » Follow US 19 north about 12.5 miles on a twisty, wooded path that winds past rafting companies and oh-so-many signs for boiled peanuts. Take exit 67 into downtown Bryson City.

2 Bryson City

This friendly mountain town is a great basecamp for exploring the North Carolina side of the Smokies. The marquee attraction is the historic **Great Smoky Mountains Railroad** (☎800-872-4681; www.gsmr.com; 226 Everett St; Nantahala Gorge trip adult/child 2-12yr from $55/31; ☺Mar-Dec), which departs from downtown and plows through the dramatic Nantahala Gorge and across the Fontana Trestle. The former Murphy Branch Line, built in the late 1800s, brought unheard-of luxuries such as books, factory-spun cloth and oil

lamps into town. Trips on the red-and-yellow trains include a Great Pumpkin-themed trip in the fall and the Christmas-time Polar Express, which stops at the North Pole to pick up Santa.

✗ ⛏ p110

The Drive » Continue 10 miles north on US 19.

TRIP HIGHLIGHT

3 Cherokee

The Cherokee people have lived in this area since the last ice age, though many died on the Trail of Tears. The descendants of those who escaped or returned are known as the Eastern Band of the Cherokee. Make time for the **Museum of the Cherokee Indian** (☎828-497-3481; www.cherokeemuseum.org; 589 Tsali Blvd/Hwy 441, at Drama Rd; adult/child 6-12yr $10/6; ☺9am-5pm daily, until 7pm Mon-Sat Jun-Aug). The earth-colored halls trace the history of the tribe, with artifacts such as pots, deerskins, woven skirts and an animated exhibit on Cherokee myths. The tribe's modern story is particularly compelling, with a detailed look at the tragedy and injustice of the **Trail of Tears**. This mass exodus occurred in the 1830s, when President Andrew Jackson ordered more than 16,000 Native Americans be removed

from their southeastern homelands and resettled in what's now Oklahoma. The museum also spotlights a fascinating moment in Colonial-era history: the 1760s journey of three Cherokees to England, where they met with King George III.

The Drive » Drive 3 miles north on US 441, passing the Blue Ridge Parkway.

- - - - - - - - - - -

④ Oconaluftee Visitor Center

If they're offering samples of regional preserves at the **Oconaluftee Visitor Center** (☏865-436-1200; www.nps.gov/grsm; Hwy 441; admission free; ☺8am-7pm Jun-Aug, closing hours vary rest of the year), say yes. But pull out your money because you'll want to take a jar home. Here you'll also find interactive exhibits about the park's history and ecosystems. Helpful guides ($1) about specific attractions are also available. For this trip, the *Day Hikes* pamphlet and the guides to **Cades Cove** and the **Roaring Fork Motor Nature Trail** are helpful supplements.

Behind the visitor center, the pet-friendly **Oconaluftee River Trail** follows the river for 1.5 miles to the boundary of the Cherokee reservation. Pick up a free backcountry camping permit if you plan to go off-trail. The adjacent **Mountain Farm Museum** (☏423-436-1200; www.nps.gov/grsm; ☺9am-5pm mid-Mar–mid-Nov & Thanksgiving weekend) is a 19th-century farmstead assembled from buildings from various locations around the park. The worn, wooden structures, including a barn, a blacksmith shop and a smokehouse, give a glimpse into the hardscrabble existence of Appalachian settlers.

The Drive » Drive half a mile north on US 441. The parking lot is on the left.

- - - - - - - - - - -

⑤ Mingus Mill

Interested in old buildings and 1800s commerce? Then take the short walk to **Mingus Mill** (self-guided tours free; ☺9am-5pm mid-Mar–mid-Nov). This 1886 gristmill was the largest in the Smokies. If the miller is here, he can explain how the mill grinds corn into cornmeal. Outside, the 200ft-long wooden millrace directs water to the building. There's no water wheel here because the mill used a cast-iron turbine.

The Drive » Return to US 441 and turn left, continuing toward Gatlinburg. Turn left and drive 7 miles on Clingmans Dome Rd.

- - - - - - - - - - -

TRIP HIGHLIGHT

⑥ Clingmans Dome

At 6643ft, Clingmans Dome is the third-highest mountain east of the Mississippi. You can drive almost all the way to the top, but the final climb to the summit's Jetsons-like observation tower requires a half-mile walk on a paved trail. It's a very steep ascent, but

---

> ↱ **DETOUR: THE TAIL OF THE DRAGON**
>
> **Start: ① Nantahala Outdoor Center**
>
> A dragon lurks in the rugged foothills of the southwestern Smokies. This particular monster is an infamous drive that twists through Deals Gap beside the national park. According to legend, the 11-mile route, known as the Tail of the Dragon, has 318 curves. From the Nantahala Outdoor Center, drive south on US 19/74 to US 129. Follow US 129 north. The dragon starts at the North Carolina and Tennessee state line. Godspeed and drive slowly. And may you tame the dragon like a Targaryen.

NATIONAL PARK TRIP PLANNER

Established in 1934, **Great Smoky Mountains National Park** (☏865-436-1200; www.nps.gov/grsm) attracts more than nine million travelers per year, making it the most-visited national park in America.

Newfoundland Gap Rd/US 441 is the only thoroughfare crossing the entire 521,000-acre park, traversing 33 miles of deep oak and pine forest, and wildflower meadows. The park sits in two states, North Carolina and Tennessee. The Oconaluftee Visitor Center welcomes visitors arriving on US 441 in North Carolina; Sugarlands Visitor Center is the Tennessee counterpart.

Orientation & Fees

Great Smoky charges no admission fee, nor will it ever; this proviso was written into the park's original charter as a stipulation for a $5 million Rockefeller family grant. Stop by a visitor center to pick up a park map and the free *Smokies Guide* newspaper. The park is open all year although some facilities are only open seasonally, and roads may close due to bad weather. Leashed pets are allowed in campgrounds and on roadsides, but not on trails, with the exception of the Gatlinburg and Oconaluftee River trails.

Camping

The park currently operates seven developed campgrounds. None have showers or hook-ups. **Reservations** (☏877-444-6777; www.recreation.gov) are required at Cataloochee Campground, and they may be made at Elkmont, Smokemont, Cosby and Cades Cove. Big Creek and Deep Creek are first-come, first-served.

Traffic

If you're visiting on a summer weekend, particularly on the Tennessee side, accept that there is going to be a lot traffic. Take a break by following trails into the wilderness.

there are resting spots along the way. The trail crosses the 2174-mile Appalachian Trail, which reaches its highest point on the Dome.

From the tower, on a clear day, enjoy a 360-degree view that sweeps in five states. Spruce- and pine-covered mountaintops sprawl for miles. The **visitor contact station** (⊙10am-6pm Apr-Oct, 9:30am-5pm Nov) beside the parking lot has a bookstore and shop.

The weather here is cooler than at lower elevations, and rain can arrive quickly. Consider wearing layers and bringing a rain poncho. And in case you're wondering, a dome is a rounded mountain.

The Drive » Follow Clingmans Dome Rd back to US 441. Cross US 441 and pull into the overlook parking area.

-----

❼ Newfound Gap Overlook

There's a lot going at the intersection of US 441 and Clingmans Dome Rd. Here, the **Rockefeller Monument** pays tribute to a $5 million donation from The Rockefeller Foundation that helped to complete land purchases needed to create the park. President Franklin D Roosevelt formally dedicated Great Smoky Mountains National Park in this spot in 1940. The overlook sits at the border of North Carolina and Tennessee, within the 5046ft Newfound Gap. Enjoy expansive mountain views from the parking area or hop on the **Appalachian Trail** for a stroll.

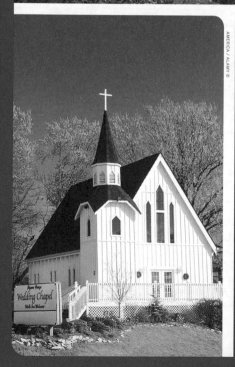

WHY THIS IS A CLASSIC TRIP
AMY C BALFOUR, AUTHOR

As a kid, I loved reading adventure novels set in imaginary kingdoms, those otherworldly places filled with misty mountains, abandoned fortresses and a giant or two. The Great Smokies feel like one of those kingdoms, especially in spring when the forest is a luminous green, the animals are waking up and the trails meander into drifting fog.

Top: Cascades, Great Smoky Mountains National Park
Left: Wedding Chapel, Pigeon Forge
Right: Great Smoky Mountains National Park

AMERICA / ALAMY ©

The Drive » From here, follow US 441 north into Tennessee for about 5 miles to the parking lot.

8 Mt LeConte

Climbing 6593ft Mt LeConte is probably the park's most popular challenge, sure to give serious hamstring burn. The **Alum Cave Trail**, one of five routes to the peak, starts from the Alum Cave parking area on the main road. Follow a creek, pass under a stone arch and wind your way steadily upward. It's a 5.5-mile hike to LeConte Lodge, where you can join the **Rainbow Falls Trail** to the summit.

✕ ⊨ p110

The Drive » Continue on Newfound Gap Rd. Turn left into the parking lot at Little River Rd.

9 Sugarlands Visitor Center

At the juncture of Little River and Newfound Gap Rds is the **Sugarlands Visitor Center** (✆865-436-1291; www.nps.gov/grsm; ⊙8am-7pm Jun-Aug, closing hours vary rest of yr), the park headquarters and main Tennessee entrance. Step inside for exhibits about plant and animal life (there's a stuffed wild boar only a mama boar could love), and a bookstore. Several ranger-led talks and tours meet at Sugarlands.

Classic Trip

The Drive » Turn onto Little River Rd for a gorgeous 25-mile drive beside lively flowing waterways. The road passes Elkmont Campground then becomes Laurel Creek Rd. Watch for cars stopping suddenly as drivers pull over to look at wildlife.

TRIP HIGHLIGHT

⑩ Cades Cove

This secluded valley contains the remnants of a 19th-century settlement. It's accessed by an 11-mile, one-way loop road that has numerous pull-offs. From these, you can poke around old churches and farmhouses or hike trails through postcard-perfect meadows filled with deer, wild turkeys and the occasional bear. For good wildlife viewing, come in the late afternoon when the animals romp with abandon.

The narrow loop road has a speed limit of 10mph and can get crowded (and maddeningly slow) in high season. For a more tranquil experience, ride your bike, or walk, on a Wednesday or Saturday morning from early May through late September when cars are banned from the road between 7am and 10am. Rent a bike at the Cades Cove Campground Store ($4 to $6 per hour). Also recommended is the 5-mile round-trip hike to **Abrams Falls**. Trailhead parking is after the Elijah Oliver Place.

Stop by the **Cades Cove Visitor Center** (📞877-444-6777; ⏰9am-7pm Apr-Aug, closes earlier rest of yr) for ranger talks.

🏠 p110

The Drive » Return to the Sugarlands Vistor Center then turn left onto US 441, which is called Parkway between Gatlinburg and Sevierville. Drive 2 miles to Gatlinburg.

⑪ Gatlinburg

Driving out of the park on the Tennessee side is disconcerting. All at once you pop out of the tranquil green tunnel of trees and into a blinking, shrieking welter of cars, motels, pancake houses, mini-golf courses and Ripley's Believe It or Not Museums. Welcome to Gatlinburg. It's Heidi meets Hillbilly in this vaguely Bavarian-themed tourist wonderland, catering to Smokies visitors since the 1930s. Most of the tourist attractions are within the compact, hilly little downtown.

The **Gatlinburg Sky Lift** (📞865-436-4307; www.gatlinburgskylift.com; 765 Parkway, Parkway light 7; adult/child $14/10.50; ⏰9am-11pm Jun-Aug, varies rest of yr), a repurposed ski resort chair lift, whisks you high over the Smokies. You'll fill up your camera's memory card with panoramic snapshots.

✕ 🏠 p110

From Parkway in downtown Gatlinburg, turn right onto Historic Nature Trail/Airport Rd at the Gatlinburg Convention Center. Follow it into the national park, continuing to the marked entrance for the one-way Roaring Fork Motor Nature Trail.

WATERFALLS OF THE SMOKIES

The Smokies are full of waterfalls, from icy trickles to roaring cascades. Here are a few of the best:

» Grotto Falls You can walk behind these 25ft-high falls, off Trillium Gap Trail.

» Laurel Falls This popular 80ft fall is located down an easy 2.6-mile paved trail.

» Mingo Falls At 120ft, this is one of the highest waterfalls in the Appalachians.

» Rainbow Falls On sunny days, the mist here produces a rainbow.

⑫ Roaring Fork Motor Nature Trail

Built on the foundations of a 150-year-old wagon road, the 6-mile Roaring Fork loop twists through strikingly lush forest. Sights include burbling cascades, abundant hardwoods, mossy boulders and old cabins once inhabited by farming families. The isolated community of Roaring Fork was settled in the mid-1800s, along a powerful mountain stream. The families that lived here were forced to move when the park was established about 100 years later.

For a waterfall hike, try the 2.6-mile round-trip walk to **Grotto Falls** from the Trillium Gap Trailhead. Further down the road, check out the Ephraim Bales cabin, once home to 11 people.

The Roaring Fork Auto Tour Guide, for sale for $1 in the Oconaluftee and Sugarlands visitor centers, provides details about plant life and buildings along the drive. No buses, trailer or RVs are permitted on the motor road.

The Drive » At the end of Roaring Fork Rd turn left onto E Parkway. Less than 1 mile ahead, turn right at US 321S/US 441. Drive 7 miles to Pigeon Forge.

⑬ Pigeon Forge

The town of Pigeon Forge is an ode to that big-haired, big-busted angel of East Tennessee, Dolly Parton – who's known to be a pretty cool chick.

Born in a one-room shack in the nearby hamlet of Locust Ridge, Parton started performing on Knoxville radio at the age of 11 and moved to Nashville at 18 with all her worldly belongings in a cardboard suitcase. She's made millions singing about her Smoky Mountain roots and continues to be a huge presence in her hometown, donating money to local causes and riding a glittery float in the annual Dolly Parade.

Wacky museums and OTT dinner shows line Parkway, the main drag.

Are you an Elvis fan? Step into the low-key **Elvis Museum** (☎865-428-2001; www.elvismuseums.com; 2638 Parkway; adult/child $17/7.50; ⊙10am-6pm Sun-Fri, 10am-8pm Sat), which is chock-full of clothing, jewelry and cars (including a 1967 Honeymoon Cadillac) given away by the generous singer. Tickets are steep, but you can save $5 by pre-purchasing online.

The Drive » Turn right onto Parkway and drive 2 miles southeast. Then turn left onto Dollywood Ln/Veterans Blvd and follow signs to Dollywood, about 2½ miles away.

⑭ Dollywood

Dolly Parton's theme park **Dollywood** (☎865-428-9488; www.dollywood.com; 2700 Dollywood Parks Blvd; adult/child $57/45; ⊙Apr-Dec) is an enormous love letter to mountain culture. Families pour in to ride the country-themed thrill rides and see demonstrations of traditional Appalachian crafts. You can also tour the bald eagle sanctuary or worship at the altar of Dolly in the Chasing Rainbows life-story museum. The adjacent Dollywood's Splash Country takes these themes and adds water.

The Drive » Return to Parkway and follow it north 4½ miles into downtown Sevierville. Turn left onto Bruce St and drive one block to Court Ave.

⑮ Sevierville

On the front lawn of the downtown **courthouse** (125 Court Ave) you might see a few happy folks getting their pictures taken in front of the statue of a young Dolly Parton. Wearing a ponytail, her guitar held loose, it captures something kind of nice. You know where's she's from, where her music is going to take her, and how it all ties in to this tough, but always beautiful, mountain country.

Eating & Sleeping

Bryson City ②

✗ Cork & Bean — Cafe $$

(☎828-488-1934; www.brysoncitycorkandbean.
com; 16 Everett St; breakfast $6-12, lunch
$7-9, dinner $7-25; ☺8am-9pm) Big windows
frame the Cork & Bean, a chic restaurant and
coffee house in downtown Bryson City. With an
emphasis on locally grown and organic fare,
you'll feel less guilty digging into the eatery's
crepes and sandwiches after your local hike.
Look for eggs benedict, huevos rancheros and
Belgian waffles on the weekend brunch menu.
The adjacent coffee house is a welcoming, cozy
place to surf the net.

🛏 Fryemont Inn — Inn $$

(☎828-488-2159; fryemontinn.com;
245 Fryemont St; lodge/ste/cabins from
$110/$180/245, nonguest breakfast $6-9,
dinner $20-29; ☺restaurant 6-8pm Sun-Tue,
6-9pm Fri & Sat mid-Apr–late Nov; P 🤖 🐾)
The view of Bryson City and the Smokies from
the porch of the lofty Fryemont Inn is hard to
beat. This family-owned mountain lodge, which
opened in 1923, feels like summer camp with its
bark-covered main building and a common area
flanked by a stone fireplace. No TVs or AC in the
lodge rooms. Wi-fi is available in the lobby. The
room rate includes breakfast and dinner at the
on-side restaurant, which is open to the public.
Dinner entrees include trout, steak and lamb.

Mt LeConte ⑧

🛏 LeConte Lodge — Cabins $

(☎865-429-5704; www.lecontelodge.com;
cabins per person adult/child 4-12yr $126/85)
These rough-hewn log cabins near the summit
of Mt LeConte are the park's only non-camping
accommodation. There's no electricity, no real
showers, and you have to hike at least 5.5 miles
to get here. But you'll be amply rewarded by

glowing purple sunrises from the eastern-facing
cliffs at Myrtle Point. As for meals, there's beef
and gravy with mashed potatoes for dinner,
scrambled eggs and Canadian bacon for
breakfast.

Elkmont Campground

🛏 Elkmont Campground — Campground $

(☎865-436-1271; information nps.gov/grsm;
Little River Rd; sites $17-23; ☺early Mar-Nov;
🤖) The park's largest campground is on
Little River Rd, 5 miles west of Sugarlands
Visitor Center. Little River and Jakes Creek run
through this wooded site and and the sound of
rippling water adds tranquility. There are 200
tent and RV campsites and 20 walk-in sites. All
are reservable beginning May 15. Like other
campgrounds in the park, there are no showers,
or electrical or water hook-ups. There are
restrooms.

Cades Cove ⑩

🛏 Cades Cove Campground — Campground $

(☎865-448-2472; information www.nps.gov/
grsm; sites $20) This woodsy campground with
159 sites is a great place to sleep if you want
to get a jump on visiting Cades Cove. There's a
camp store, drinking water and bathrooms, but
no showers. There are 29 tent-only sites.

Gatlinburg ⑪

✗ Pancake Pantry — Breakfast, American $

(☎865-436-4724; www.pancakepantry.com;
628 Parkway; breakfast $7-11, lunch $8-10;
☺7am-4pm Jun-Oct, to 3pm Nov-May; 🤖)
This welcoming place is the granddaddy of
Gatlinburg's many pancake houses. Chow

down on a wide variety of pancakes, from wild blueberry to Sugar & Spice, as well as cheese-swollen omelets and whipped-cream-smothered waffles. The building looks like an overgrown Smurf house. Breakfast offered all day.

✕ Smoky Mountain Brewery   Pub $$

(www.smoky-mtn-brewery.com; 1004 Parkway; mains $9-23; ⊗11:30am-1am) For filling pub grub and decent microbrews, head to this busy brewery with lots of TVs and walls covered with dollar bills. Can't make up your mind from the menu? Go with the pizza.

✕ Wild Boar Saloon
& Howard's Steakhouse   Steaks $$

(☑865-436-3600; www.wildboarsaloon.com; 976 Parkway; mains $9-30; ⊗10am-10pm Sun-Thu, until 1:30am Fri & Sat) Since 1947 this dark creekside saloon has been serving burgers, ribs and a tasty pulled pork shoulder drenched in homemade sauce. But it's known for its steaks and for being the oldest joint in town.

🛏 Bearskin Lodge   Lodge $$

(☑877-795-7546; www.thebearskinlodge.com; 840 River Rd; r from $110) This shingled riverside lodge is blessed with timber accents and a bit more panache than other Gatlinburg comers. All rooms have flatscreens and fireplaces, as well as private balconies jutting over the river. And it's an excellent value.

🛏 Hampton Inn   Hotel $$

(☑865-436-4878; www.hamptoninn3.hilton.com; 967 Parkway; r $139-179, ste $219; P @ 🛜 ☒) Yep, it's part of a chain, but the hotel sits in the thick-of-the-action on Parkway. Decor is modern, and furnishings include an easy chair and ottoman. Rooms with king beds have a fireplace. Ahhh.

Cape Hatteras Lighthouse
Climb the 248 steps

North Carolina's Outer Banks

8

This slender chain of barrier islands wears its heart on its fragile sleeve — the windswept dunes, bird-filled marshes and solitary lighthouses are products of a unique, ever-shifting geography.

TRIP HIGHLIGHTS

0 miles

Corolla
Drive on the beach and look for wild mustangs

Kitty Hawk

28 miles

Kill Devil Hills
Learn about the Wright Brothers, first siblings of flight

33 miles

Jockey's Ridge State Park
Watch the sunset from a towering sand dune

Rodanthe

101 miles

Cape Hatteras Lighthouse
Climb 248 steps to the top

Avon

Hatteras Village

FINISH

3 DAYS
112 MILES / 180KM

GREAT FOR...

BEST TIME TO GO
May through October for beach days and outdoor fun.

ESSENTIAL PHOTO
Cape Hatteras Lighthouse for an eye-catching link to the past.

BEST FOR FAMILIES
Taking a wild horse tour on the beach, north of Corolla.

113

8 North Carolina's Outer Banks

Wild mustangs kick off this trip, which starts in the untamed northern reaches of the Outer Banks. From here, the road flows south on a thread of barrier islands, the first line of defense against the roaring Atlantic. Nature is a big draw, with sand dunes, sea oats and coastal views as constant companions. The history impresses too, with lost colonists, flying machines, terrifying shipwrecks and a floating platoon of Doritos.

TRIP HIGHLIGHT

❶ Corolla

Over 100 wild horses, descendants of Colonial Spanish mustangs, graze among the sea oats north of Corolla. There's no paved road north of town, and the main highway is...the beach.

Check out a few exhibits about the horses at the **Wild Horse Museum** (www.corolla wildhorses.com; 1129 Corolla Vilage Rd; admission free; ⏰9:30am-5pm Mon-Fri, 10am-4pm Sat Jun-Aug, 10am-4pm Mon-Fri Sep-May) run by the Corolla Wild Horse Fund. The group also leads two-hour **wild horse tours** (adult/child $45/20).

Numerous commercial outfitters also offer tours, including **Corolla Outback Adventures** (☎252-453-4484; www. corollaoutback.com; 1150 Ocean Trail, Corolla; 2hr tour adult/child $50/25) run by a knowledgeable long-time local, Jay Bender.

Historic Corolla Village is home to the **Currituck Beach Lighthouse** (www .currituckbeachlight. com; adult/child $7/free; ⏰9am-5pm Mar 23-Nov 23), the northernmost of the Outer Banks' six lighthouses. The impressive all-brick sentinel has guided sailors since 1875. The grounds are free, but to appreciate the view, buy a ticket ($7) and climb 214 steps. Learn more about the surrounding marshes at the nearby **Outer Banks Center for Wildlife Education** (www .ncwildlife.org/obx; 1160 Village Ln; admission free; ⏰9am-4:30pm Mon-Sat).

The Drive ›› Hwy 12 starts in Corolla. Follow it south past beach cottages, shopping centers and sand dunes. After Duck and Southern Shores, turn left onto US 158 south. US 158 is also called the Bypass or S Croatan Hwy.

TRIP HIGHLIGHT

❷ Kill Devil Hills

The hilltop monument at Mile 7.5 is a majestic calling card for the **Wright Brothers National Memorial** (☎252-473-2111; www.nps.gov/wrbr; Hwy 158, Bypass Milepost 7.5; adult/child $4/free; ⏰visitor center 9am-5pm) in Kill Devil Hills. It is is NOT, however, the sight of the world's first airplane flight. Nope, the 12-second ride started at the bottom of the hill, and a 6-ton boulder marks the spot. Orville Wright was at the controls during the history-making flight on December 17, 1903. His brother Wilbur steadied the wings as the plane left the ground.

There's a life-size reproduction of the Wright's flying machine in the visitor center plus numerous exhibits about the brothers, who funded their research

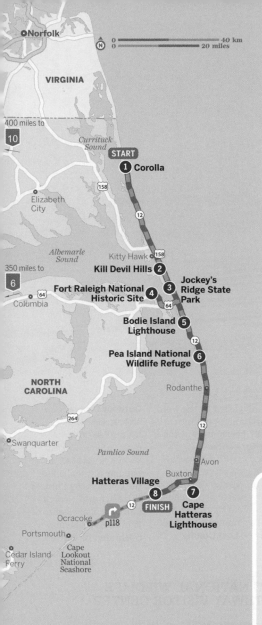

with proceeds from their bicycle shop in Dayton, Ohio. Don't miss the ranger-led 'Flight Room Talk,' a 30-minute talk that describes the brothers' ingenuity and perseverance.

Behind the monument, look for a bronze-and-steel replica of the plane. Scramble across the wing (it's allowed!) to get a feel for its complexity.

✗ 🛏 p119

The Drive >> Continue south on US 158 to Mile 12.

TRIP HIGHLIGHT

3 Jockey's Ridge State Park

Kick off your shoes for a leg-stretching climb up **Jockey's Ridge** (www .ncparks.gov; Hwy 158 Bypass, Mile 12; admission free; ☺8am-9pm Jun-Aug, hours vary rest of year), the largest sand dune on the East Coast. With a 360-degree view that

🔗 LINK YOUR TRIP

10 Lowcountry & Southern Coast

For a mood-drenched look into the past, drive west to I-95 south and Charleston.

6 Blue Ridge Parkway

Leave the beaches for the mountains by taking US 64 west to I-40 west.

JOHN MARCIANO III / GETTY IMAGES ©

sweeps in the Atlantic Ocean and Roanoke Sound, it's a gorgeous spot to watch the sunset. Impress your friends with tales (and video) of your hang-gliding prowess by booking a lesson with **Kitty Hawk Kites** (☏877-359-2447, 252-441-2426; www.kittyhawk.com; 3933 S Croatan Hwy; hang gliding $99, bike/paddleboard rental per day $25/59, kayak rental per day $39-49), which also has a satellite office inside the park.

The Drive » Follow US 12 south through the town of Nags Head to Hwy 64 west, which crosses the sound. On Roanoke Island, turn right to follow Hwy 64 through Manteo to Fort Raleigh Dr.

- - - - - - - - - - - -

❹ Fort Raleigh National Historic Site

Roanoke Island is the site of one of North America's most enduring mysteries. A group of 116 British colonists disappeared from their settlement here in the late 1580s. Were they killed by drought? Did they try to sail home? Or did they leave with a local Native American tribe, as suggested by the word 'Croatan' carved into a tree? Learn more at the **visitor center** (www.nps .gov/fora; 1401 National Park Dr, Manteo; admission free; ⊙grounds dawn-dusk, visitor center 9am-5pm), which has exhibits and a short film.

In summer, sit outside for the **Lost Colony** **Outdoor Drama** (www .thelostcolony.org; 1409 National Park Dr; adult/child $26.50/9.50; ⊙8pm Mon-Sat Jun-late Aug), a popular musical about the colonists by Pulitzer Prize–winning North Carolina playwright Paul Green. The play celebrated its 75th

---

TOP TIP:
COASTAL NC NATIONAL WILDLIFE REFUGE GATEWAY VISITOR CENTER

TOP TIP: This comprehensive **visitor center** (www.fws.gov/ncgatewayvc; 100 Conservation Way, Manteo; ⊙9am-4pm Mon-Sat, noon-4pm Sun), which opened in 2012, provides information about the region's 11 national wildlife refuges and their activities, from a Red Wolf Howling Safari at Alligator River to the Wings over Water Wildlife Festival in October. Multimedia exhibits examine the region's flora, fauna and history.

Corolla Wild horses on the beach

anniversary in 2012. Before the show, wander the 16th-century style **Elizabethan Gardens** (www.elizabethan gardens.org; 1411 National Park Dr; adult/child $9/6; ⏰9am-7pm Jun-Aug, shorter hours fall-spring) next door. Trails pass by flower gardens, the world's largest statue of Queen Elizabeth I and a live oak that was probably alive when the colonists arrived.

The Drive » Return to Hwy 12. Follow it south into Cape Hatteras National Seashore. From here it's 6 miles to Bodie Island Lighthouse Rd and almost 60 miles to Hatteras Village.

⑤ Bodie Island Lighthouse

Cape Hatteras National Seashore (www.nps.gov/caha) is a mesmerizing place. Its boundaries extend some 70 miles across the whisper-thin barrier islands of Bodie, Hatteras and Ocracoke.

Today you can survey the landscape from atop the 156ft **Bodie Island Lighthouse** (☏252-441-5711, ticket reservations 255-475-9417; Bodie Island Lighthouse Rd, Bodie Island; museum free, tours adult/child $8/4; ⏰museum 9am-6pm Jun-Aug, to 5pm Sep-May, tours 9am-5:45pm late Apr-early Oct; 👤), which opened to visitors for the first time in 2013. The 1872 lighthouse has its original Fresnal lens, a rarity. Entry is by guided tour. Tickets can be reserved by phone or purchased on a first-come, first-served basis. In the visitor center a small museum spotlights the lighthouse keepers who tended the light. The island and lighthouse are pronounced 'body.'

The Drive » Oregon Inlet rolls into view just south of the lighthouse. After the marina, Hwy 12 swoops onto Hatteras Island.

TRIP HIGHLIGHT

DETOUR: OCRACOKE

Start: ❽ Hatteras Village

Why take the free Hatteras to Ocracoke ferry? To slow down and escape the modern grind. Gone are the ubiquitous beachwear shops and BrewThru convenience stores of the Carolina coast; instead, you'll find handmade craft stores, organic coffee shops and hemp design boutiques. You can camp by the beach where the wild ponies run, enjoy a fish sandwich in a local pub, bike around the narrow streets of Ocracoke Village or visit the 1823 Ocracoke Lighthouse. For the ferry schedule, see www.ncdot.gov/ferry.

❻ Pea Island National Wildlife Refuge

More than 350 species of migrating birds have landed at this refuge on the northern end of Hatteras Island. To scan for birds, stroll the half-mile, fully accessible North Pond Trail or step inside the **visitor center** (☎252-987-2394; www.fws.gov/peaisland; Hwy 12; ☉visitor center 9am-4pm, trails dawn-dusk) where there's a spotting scope. In summer, check the online calendar for turtle talks and canoe tours. A 90-minute bird walk is offered Friday mornings at 8am; call for for additional dates.

The Drive » Continue south on Hwy 12 passing through the villages of Rodanthe, Waves and Salvo.

❼ Cape Hatteras Lighthouse

What happens when erosion and tidal movement have caused a 4800-ton, 1.25-million-brick lighthouse to end up within almost 100ft of the shorelines? You pick it up and move it, of course. That's what happened to the black-and-white-striped **Cape Hatteras Lighthouse** (www.nps.gov/caha; climbing tours adult/child $8/4; ☉visitor center 9am-5pm Sep-May, to 6pm June-Aug, lighthouse late Apr-early Oct) in 1999. After 60 years of erosion stabilization attempts, the National Park Service authorized this controversial project. Over 23 very slow days, the lighthouse was moved – safely – 2900ft from the shore, completely unscathed.

Today, as you walk up its 248 steps (equal to a 12-story building), imagine being the lighthouse keeper, carrying the 5-gallon, 40lb canister of oil on your back each day. Today, rangers don't advise the climb on an empty stomach. Guided full-moon climbs are offered in summer.

A two-story **museum** in the former double keepers' quarters provides an overview of the island's interesting history.

The Drive » Drive 12 miles south, passing through Frisco and into Hatteras Village. When you see the ferry landing, stay left for museum just ahead.

❽ Hatteras Village

More than 500 ships have met their maker in the battering waves off the coast of the Outer Banks. In Hatteras Village, the **Graveyard of the Atlantic Museum** (☎252-986-2995, www.graveyardoftheatlantic.com; 59200 Museum Dr; admission free, donations appreciated; ☉10am-4pm Mon-Sat Apr-Oct, closed Sat Nov-Mar) displays shipwreck artifacts dating back hundreds of years. One highlight is a WWII enigma (encryption-decryption) machine recovered from a German submarine that sunk in 1942.

✕ 🛏 p119

Eating & Sleeping

Duck

🛏 Sanderling Resort & Spa   Resort $$$

(📞252-261-4111; www.sanderling-resort.com;
1461 Duck Rd; r/ste from $299/539; P ❄ 🛜 🏊)
The Sanderling, fresh off a five-month
renovation, just got posher. Impeccably tasteful
rooms shine with modern but welcoming style
and come with decks and flat-screen TVs.
Weary business travelers should head straight
to the new adults-only tranquility pool. Several
restaurants and a spa are on-site. For a sunset
cocktail, look for the ever-patient Garfield
behind the lobby bar.

Southern Shores

✗ John's Drive-In   Seafood, Ice Cream $

(www.johnsdrivein.com; 3716 N Virginia Dare
Trail; mains $2-13; ⏲11am-5pm Mon, Tue &
Thu, until 6pm Fri-Sun May-Sep) A Kitty Hawk
institution for perfectly fried baskets of 'dolphin'
(mahimahi) and rockfish, to be eaten at outdoor
picnic tables and washed down with a milkshake.
Some folks just come for the ice cream.

Kill Devil Hills ❷

✗ Kill Devil Grill   Seafood, American $$

(📞252-449-8181; www.thekilldevilgrill.com;
Beach Rd, Mile 9¾; lunch $7-11, dinner $9-20;
⏲11:30am-10pm Tue-Sat) Yowza, this place is
good. It's also a bit historical – the entrance is a
1939 diner that's listed in the national registry
of historic places. Pub grub and seafood arrive
with tasty flair, and portions are generous.
Check out the specials, where the kitchen can
really shine.

🛏 Shutters on the Banks   Hotel $$

(📞800-848-3728; www.shuttersonthebanks.
com; 405 S Virginia Dare Trail; r $149-289;
P ❄ 🛜 🏊) Formerly Colony IV by the Sea, this
welcoming seaside hotel now exudes a bright
and sassy joie de vivre. Inviting rooms come
with plantation window, colorful bedspreads, a
flat-screen TV, a refrigerator and a microwave.

Nags Head

✗ Tortugas' Lie   Seafood $$

(www.tortugaslie.com; 3014 S Virginia Dare Trail/
Mile 11; lunch $9-18, dinner $12-24; ⏲11:30am-
9:30pm Sun-Thu, until 10pm Fri & Sat) The
interior isn't dressed to impress – surfboards,
license plates – but who cares? The reliably
good seafood, burritos and burgers go down
well with the beer. And kids will be perfectly fine.
Guy Fieri stopped by in 2012 and scrawled his
signature on the wall. Fills up by 6:30pm.

Cape Hatteras National Seashore

🛏 Campgrounds   Campground $

(📞reservations 800-365-2267, 252-473-2111;
www.nps.gov/caha; tent sites $20-23) The
National Park Service runs four summer-only
campgrounds on the islands, which feature
cold-water showers and flush toilets. They
are located at Oregon Inlet (near Bodie Island
Lighthouse), Cape Point and Frisco (near Cape
Hatteras Lighthouse) and Ocracoke. Sites at
Ocracoke can be reserved; the others are first-
come, first-served.

Hatteras Village ❽

✗ Breakwater Restaurant   Seafood $$$

(📞252-986-2733; www.breakwaterhatteras.
com; 57896 Hwy 12; mains $20-38; ⏲from 5pm
Tue-Sat) This restaurant beside the sound has
been serving food for more than 60 years. Come
here for steamed seafood, fresh fish and and big
daddy crabcakes.

🛏 Breakwater Inn   Motel $$

(📞252-986-2565; www.breakwaterhatteras.
com; 57896 Hwy 12; r/ste inn $159/189, motel
$104/134; P ❄ 🛜 🏊) The end of the road
doesn't look so bad at this three-story inn.
Rooms come with kitchenettes and have private
decks with views of the sound. On a budget?
Book an older 'Fisherman's Quarters' room,
with microwave and refrigerator. The inn is near
the ferry landing.

Greenville Cascades lend a picturesque air to downt...

Greenville & Cherokee Foothills Scenic Highway

9

This trip begins with a Revolutionary battle on a mountaintop, rolls through woodland valleys steeped in legend and ends with dramatic cascades in the center of Greenville.

TRIP HIGHLIGHTS

81 miles

Caesars Head State Park
Watch migrating hawks soar on the thermal breezes

0 miles

Kings Mountain National Military Park
A Revolutionary War turning point

START ①

③

④

7

FINISH

Table Rock State Park
Hike to the top of a mountain famed for its granite face

93 miles

Greenville
The downtown waterfall is a stunning centerpiece

158 miles

---

2 DAYS
172 MILES / 277KM

GREAT FOR...

BEST TIME TO GO
April to November for leafy canopies and hiking; September to November for the Hawk Watch.

ESSENTIAL PHOTO
Table Rock Mountain's huge granite face.

BEST FOR HISTORY
Kings Mountain, where a pivotal battle took place during the Revolutionary War.

9

Greenville & Cherokee Foothills Scenic Highway

Cherokees once roamed the upcountry foothills, which they called 'The Great Blue Hills of God.' Geologically known as the Blue Ridge escarpment, it's the spot where the Blue Ridge Mountains drop dramatically to meet the Piedmont. Frontier patriots, secretive moonshiners and the mighty Duke Energy have all used the region's hills and streams to their advantage. The dynamic heart is Greenville, with its downtown waterfalls and lively city sidewalks.

TRIP HIGHLIGHT

❶ Kings Mountain National Military Park

As Major Patrick Ferguson learned on the summit of Kings Mountain, threatening American patriots is never a good idea. In the fall of 1780, General Lord Cornwallis ordered Ferguson to subdue the frontier militias of the western Carolinas. In a message to the patriots, who were known as the

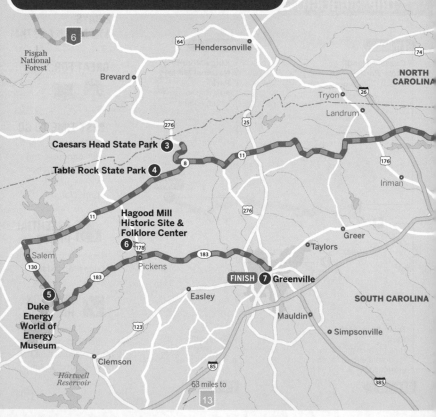

Overmountain Men, Ferguson proclaimed, 'If you do not desist your opposition to the British Arms, I shall march this army over the mountains, hang your leaders and lay waste your country with fire and sword.'

In response, 900 annoyed frontiersmen crossed the mountains, joined forces and surrounded Ferguson and his 1000-man army. Comfortable with close-range combat, the patriots used the mountain's thick trees as cover as they climbed the slopes. After a short period of intense fighting, Ferguson was dead and his troops decimated.

At **Kings Mountain National Military Park** (☎864-936-7921; www.npps.gov/kimo; Hwy 216; admission free; ☺9am-5pm, to 6pm Sat & Sun Jun-Aug) a 1.5-mile paved interpretive trail explores the forested battlefield. At the visitor center, a 26-minute film describes the fight, which was a turning point in the Revolutionary War. A small museum spotlights the battle's major players.

The Drive » Take SC-216 to I-85 south. Follow it to exit 92 and SC-11 south, which is the Cherokee Foothills Scenic Hwy (if you get to giant Peach – aka the peach butt – you've gone too far). The profile of a Cherokee is emblazoned on markers along the byway. Drive 10 miles.

- - - - - - - - - - - -

❷ Cowpens National Battlefield

On January 17, 1781, American commander Daniel Morgan executed a brilliant tactical maneuver (the double envelopment) against a larger, better-equipped British force during the Battle of Cowpens. His success inspired Colonial forces on their path to final victory at Yorktown. At **Cowpens National Battlefield** (☎864-461-2828; www.nps.gov/cowp; 4001 Chesnee Hwy, Gaffney; admission free; ☺9am-5pm, auto loop closes at 4:30pm),

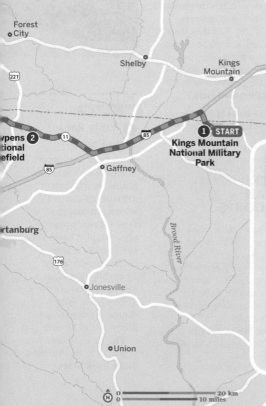

LINK YOUR TRIP

6 **Blue Ridge Parkway**

After ascending Table Rock, take US 25 north for a post-hike microbrew in Asheville.

13 **Hogs & Heifers: a Georgia BBQ Odyssey**

For some old-school BBQ, follow I-85 south toward Lexington.

don't limit yourself to the auto loop, which skirts the central fighting area. Signs scattered across the actual battlefield mark the positions of the different companies and explain Morgan's tactics. Even if you're not fascinated by military history, the strange tranquility of the place makes it worthy of a stroll.

The Drive » From the park, continue south 50 miles on SC-11. The byway passes farms, fields, produce stands and Baptist churches before rolling into the woods. Follow US 276 as it twists upward through the park.

TRIP HIGHLIGHT

❸ Caesars Head State Park

Sometimes you want to earn your stunning view – with a 10-mile hike or an all-day bike ride. Other times you just want to step out of your car, walk 30 steps and say 'Wow!' The overlook at **Caesars Head State Park** (☎864-836-6115; www.southcarolinaparks.com; 8155 Geer Hwy, Cleveland; admission free, trail access $2; ⊙9am-9pm mid-Mar–early Nov, to 6pm rest of year, visitor center hours vary) falls cheerfully into the latter category. This lofty viewpoint atop the Blue Ridge Escarpment offers a sweeping panorama of regional mountains and foothills. From here, Table Rock Mountain juts into view almost dead ahead. During the fall **Hawk Watch** (September to November), migrating hawks catch thermals here – and impress visitors – as they travel south for winter. If you do want to exercise, try the 4.4-mile round-trip hike to a view of 420ft **Raven Cliff Falls**.

The Drive » Take Hwy 8 to SC-11 south then drive 4.6 miles.

AURORA PHOTOS / ALAMY ©

TRIP HIGHLIGHT

❹ Table Rock State Park

Table Rock Mountain is the region's marquee natural attraction. A 3124ft-high mountain with a striking granite face, it's ready-made for photographs. According to Cherokee legend, the mountain served as a table for a giant chieftain, who ate there after a hunt. While dining, he used Stool Mountain as his seat.

The 7.2-mile round-trip hike to its summit at **Table Rock State**

TABLE ROCK STATE PARK: THE CIVILIAN CONSERVATIONS CORPS

In 1933 President Franklin D Roosevelt established the Civilian Conservation Corps (CCC), a workforce of 250,000 young men. Its mission? To conserve and improve America's resources. Within 10 years Roosevelt's 'Tree Army' had laid 28,087 miles of trails and created or improved more than 800 state parks. The CCC built 16 state parks in South Carolina. Construction of Table Rock State Park began in 1935. CCC projects at Table Rock include the concession building, a lodge, most cabins, all trails and the 36-acre Pinnacle Lake.

Table Rock Mountain View from the summit

Park (☎864-878-9813; www.southcarolinaparks .com; 158 Ellison Ln, Pickens; admission adult/child $2/free; ⊙7am-7pm Sun-Thu, to 9pm Fri & Sat, extended evening hours mid-May–early Nov) is a popular local challenge. For a good view of the mountain, take a seat at the park **visitor center**, which is also an information center for the scenic highway.

Visitors can spend the night in one of 14 cabins constructed by the Civilian Conservation Corps. The second Saturday of the month, catch a bluegrass jam here as part of the annual Music on the Mountain Series. Need more options? There's camping, plus swimming and fishing in Pinnacle Lake.

🛏 p127

The Drive ≫ Return to SC-11 south and drive 19 miles to SC-130. Turn left and continue south 10 miles, passing through the town of Salem. SC-130 becomes Rochester Hwy.

- - - - - - - - - - -

❺ Duke Energy World of Energy Museum

After all those trees and waterfalls, it just seems right to stop and stretch your legs at...a nuclear power plant. But hey, why not? The self-guided tour inside the **Duke Energy World of Energy Museum** (☎800-777-1004; www.duke-energy.com/worldofenergy; 7812 Rochester Hwy, Seneca; admission free; ⊙9am-5pm Mon-Fri, noon-5pm Sat) at the Oconee Nuclear Station is a pretty darn interesting look at how electricity has been produced in the region, from the use of water power to coal to uranium. The nuclear plant went online in 1973, and today it can provide electricity for more than 1.7 million average-sized homes.

The Drive » Take SC-130 south to E Pickens Hwy/SC-183. Turn left and drive 14 miles. At US 178, turn left and drive 3 miles. Turn left onto Hagood Mill Rd.

- - - - - - - - - -

❻ Hagood Mill Historic Site & Folklore Center

You'll find more than a historical mill at this streamside **site** (☎864-898-2936; www.co.pickens. sc.us; 138 Hagood Mill Rd; admission free; ☺10am-4pm Wed-Sat) in Pickens County. Several hundred petroglyphs have been discovered in the upcountry, and in 2003 a collection of stick-figure carvings were found on a rock near the mill. These 17 carvings are scheduled to be displayed in a new on-site exhibit hall by the end of 2013. The site's namesake attraction, the 1845 gristmill, has a 20ft

wooden waterwheel. The mill was in continuous commercial operation until 1966. Today it's back in production on the third Saturday of every month, when there's also live bluegrass music. Also on-site are two relocated log cabins, one dating to 1791, as well as an old moonshine still.

The Drive » Return to SC-183 and follow it east 20 miles into downtown Greenville.

- - - - - - - - - - -

TRIP HIGHLIGHT

❼ Greenville

Greenville has one of America's most inviting downtowns. The Reedy River twists through the city center, and its dramatic falls tumble beneath Main St at **Falls Park** (www.fallspark.com). For a photo of the falls, stroll onto the graceful **Liberty Bridge**, a 345ft-long suspension bridge.

Main Street itself rolls past a lively array of boutiques, eateries and craft-beer pubs. Whimsical quotes from notables such as Oscar Wilde, Erma Bombeck and Will Rogers – called 'Thoughts on a Walk' – dot the sidewalk. In the evening, the trees are illuminated by twinkling white lights. Stop by the **visitor center** (☎864-233-0461; www.visitgreenvillesc .com; 206 S Main St; ☺8am-5pm Mon-Fri, 9am-5pm Sat, noon-4pm Sun) for a public art map and clues for Mice on Main.

For exercise, try the **Swamp Rabbit Trail** (http://greenvillerec.com/ swamprabbit), a 17.5-mile path for hikers and cyclists on an old railway line that links downtown to Furman University. Pop into the regionally famed **Mast General Store** (www. mastgeneralstore.com; 111 N Main St; ☺10am-6pm Mon-Thu, 10am-9pm Fri & Sat, noon-6pm Sun) for outdoor gear and old-time candy then sample peach whiskey at **Dark Corner Distillery** (www.darkcornerdistillery.com; 241 N Main St; ☺noon-6pm Mon-Sat). The Dark Corner is the nickname given to the secretive upland corner of Greenville County, which was famed for its bootlegging and hardscrabble Scots-Irish residents.

✗ ⮞ p127

Eating & Sleeping

Table Rock State Park ❹

🛏 Table Rock State Park
Campground & Cabins   Campground $

(📞864-878-9813; www.southcarolinaparks.
com; 158 Ellison Ln, Pickens; campsites $16-21,
cabins $52-181; ❄) The 14 CCC-built cabins
(one to three bedrooms) come with air-
conditioning, kitchenettes and coffeemakers.
Campers have their choice of 93 campsites with
water and hookups, spread across two separate
wooded camping areas. There are also five walk-
in sites ($9 to $13). All sites can be reserved.

Salem

🛏 Sunrise Farm B&B   B&B $$

(📞864-944-0121; www.sunrisefarmbb.com;
325 Sunrise Dr, Salem; incl breakfast r $110-195,
cottage $163-183; P ❄ 🛜 🐾 🐕) Join Cisco the
Bolivian llama and sheep, pygmy goats, cats and
a Lhasa Apso on acres of pastoral lands.

Greenville ❼

🍴 Coffee Underground   Cafe $

(www.coffeeunderground.biz; 1 E Coffee St;
pastries and desserts $2-5, mains $7-11; ⊗7am-
11pm Mon-Thu, 7am-midnight Fri, 8am-midnight
Sat, 8am-10pm Sun) Try the chicken wrap and
the Black Tiger milkshake at this welcoming
indie coffee shop. The chocolate chunk cookies
are darn good too. It's located at the bottom of
the stairs at the corner of Main and Coffee Sts.

🍴 Lazy Goat   Mediterranean $$

(📞864-679-5299; www.thelazygoat.com; 170
River Pl; lunch $5-15, dinner small plates $5-10,
dinner mains $12-25; ⊗11:30am-9pm Mon-Wed,
to 10pm Thu-Sat) Mediterranean-inspired small
plates with influences of Greek, French, Italian
and Southern cuisine. Located beside the Reedy
River, upstream from Main St.

🍴 Lemongrass   Thai $$

(www.lemongrassthai.net; 106 N Main St; lunch
$9-12, dinner $12-16; ⊗11:30am-2:30pm
Mon-Fri, 5:30-10pm Mon-Thu, 5:30-10:30pm Fri
& Sat) Dine on delicious noodle dishes, curries
and Bangkok street dishes, with jazz playing in
the background, at this stylish Thai restaurant
tucked in a narrow space on Main St.

🛏 Drury Inn & Suites   Hotel $$

(📞864-288-4401; www.druryhotels.com; 10
Carolina Point Pkwy; r incl breakfast $108-148;
P ❄ @ 🛜) It's not downtown, but the price
of a room includes a nightly happy hour with a
hearty array of appetizers plus there's a filling
breakfast buffet. Friendly staff to boot. The
hotel is on I-85, 7 miles from downtown. For a
better rate, check the hotel coupon books that
are found at visitor centers, or try the e-saver
rate online.

🛏 Pettigru Place   B&B $$

(📞864-242-4529; www.pettigruplace.com;
302 Pettigru St; r incl breakfast $145-225;
P ❄ 🛜) The five rooms at this downtown B&B
are quaintly Victorian, but they do have modern
conveniences, from Keurig coffeemakers to
wi-fi to flat-screen TVs. Some have jacuzzis and
fireplaces. Helpful host.

🛏 Westin Poinsett   Hotel $$$

(📞864-421-9700; www.westinpoinsett
greenville.com; 120 S Main St; r $209-269;
P ❄ @ 🛜 🐕) This grand hotel, which
originally opened in 1925, is in the heart of
downtown, just steps from Reedy River Falls.
Past guests include Amelia Earhart, Cornelius
Vanderbilt and Bobby Kennedy. Decor is classic
but fresh, and beds come with a pillow-top
mattress. Parking is $6 per day; pets are $75
per stay.

Beaufort Antebellum architecture abounds in this charming town

Lowcountry & Southern Coast

10

Century-old churches, timeless marshes, ancient oaks and Spanish moss: on this Lowcountry loop, the past rises up to say hello. Except on Parris Island, where it yells, 'Move it marine!'

TRIP HIGHLIGHTS

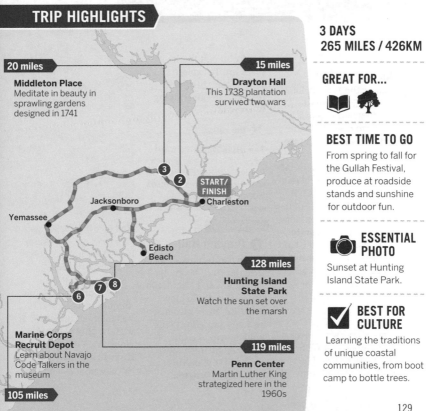

20 miles

Middleton Place
Meditate in beauty in sprawling gardens designed in 1741

15 miles

Drayton Hall
This 1738 plantation survived two wars

Jacksonboro

Yemassee

START/FINISH
Charleston

Edisto Beach

128 miles

Hunting Island State Park
Watch the sun set over the marsh

Marine Corps Recruit Depot
Learn about Navajo Code Talkers in the museum

105 miles

119 miles

Penn Center
Martin Luther King strategized here in the 1960s

3 DAYS
265 MILES / 426KM

GREAT FOR...

BEST TIME TO GO

From spring to fall for the Gullah Festival, produce at roadside stands and sunshine for outdoor fun.

ESSENTIAL PHOTO

Sunset at Hunting Island State Park.

BEST FOR CULTURE

Learning the traditions of unique coastal communities, from boot camp to bottle trees.

129

10 Lowcountry & Southern Coast

The Lowcountry welcomes travelers with a warm embrace – straight from the 1700s. This coastal region, which stretches from Charleston south to Georgia, is a tangle of islands, inlets and tidal marshes. This drive sweeps in plantation life, military history, Gullah culture and a landmark African American school, all set among a moody backdrop of coastal wilds.

Hampton

Yemassee

Ridgeland

95

18 miles to   Bluffton

278

11

❶ Charleston

Charleston is a city for savoring. Stroll past Rainbow Row, take a carriage ride, study the antebellum architecture and enjoy shrimp and grits. Historically, the city is best known for its role in the start of the Civil War. The first shots of the conflict rang out on April 12, 1861, at **Fort Sumter**, a pentagon-shaped island in the harbor. **Boat tours** (boat tour 843-722-2628, park 843-883-3123; www.nps. gov/fosu; 340 Concord St; adult/child $18/11; tours 9:30am, noon & 2:30pm summer, fewer winter) depart from Aquarium Wharf at the eastern end of Calhoun St, and from Patriot's Point in Mt Pleasant. To explore Charleston's historical district, see our walking tour (p136).

✖ 🛏 p135

The Drive » From the wharf, follow Calhoun St west through Charleston to Hwy 61, also known as Ashley River Rd. Follow it north for about 10 miles.

TRIP HIGHLIGHT

❷ Drayton Hall

Three plantations – Drayton Hall, Magnolia Plantation and Middleton Place – border Ashley River Rd, their gardens, swamps and graveyards hidden behind a line of oaks and Spanish moss.

The first plantation on the drive is **Drayton Hall** (843-769-2600; www .draytonhall.org; 3380 Ashley River Rd; adult/child $18/8; 9am-5pm Mon-Sat, 11am-5pm Sun, last tour 3:30pm, built in 1738 and unique for its Georgian-Palladian architecture. It was the only plantation along the Ashley River to survive the Revolutionary and Civil

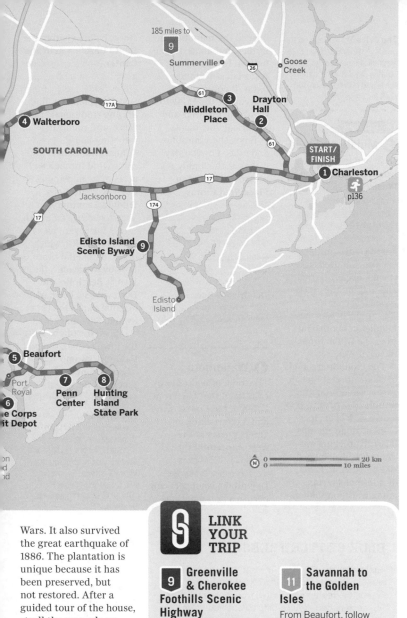

185 miles to
9

Summerville

Goose
Creek

26

61

3

17A

**Drayton
Hall**

**Middleton
Place**

2

4 **Walterboro**

61

SOUTH CAROLINA

START/
FINISH

1 **Charleston**

p136

17

Jacksonboro

17

174

**Edisto Island
Scenic Byway** **9**

Edisto
Island

5 **Beaufort**

Port
Royal

7 **8**

6

**Penn
Center** **Hunting
Island
State Park**

e Corps
t Depot

on
d
nd

0   20 km
0   10 miles

Wars. It also survived
the great earthquake of
1886. The plantation is
unique because it has
been preserved, but
not restored. After a
guided tour of the house,
stroll the grounds on
paths wandering along
the river and around a
marsh.

LINK YOUR TRIP

9 **Greenville
& Cherokee
Foothills Scenic
Highway**

Follow I-28 west to
crashing cascades in
downtown Greenville.

11 **Savannah to
the Golden
Isles**

From Beaufort, follow
Hwy 170 to soak up the
history of Savannah.

The Drive » Continue north on Ashley River Rd/Hwy 61. Pass Magnolia Plantation then drive another 3 miles. After passing the exit to Middleton Inn, turn right for the gardens.

TRIP HIGHLIGHT

❸ Middleton Place

Designed in 1741, the vast gardens at **Middleton Place** (☏843-556-6020; www.middletonplace.org; 4300 Ashley River Rd; gardens adult/child $28/10, house tour add $15; ⏱9am-5pm) are the oldest in the US. One hundred slaves spent a decade terracing and digging the precise geometric canals. The property was the Middleton family seat from the 1700s through the Civil War.

The grounds are a mix of classic formal French gardens and romantic woodland settings – one lonely path leads to a band of stone cherubs blissfully rocking out. There are also flooded rice patties and fields of rare-breed farm animals. Union soldiers burned the main house in 1855, but a guest wing, built in 1755 and later restored, still stands today. It contains a museum with Middleton family furnishings and historical documents.

Enjoy she-crab soup and other Lowcountry dishes at the highly regarded **Middleton Place Restaurant** (☏843-266-7477; www.middletonplace.org; 4300 Ashley River Rd; lunch $13-16, dinner $14-34; ⏱11am-3pm & 6-8pm Tue-Thu & Sun, 6-9pm Fri & Sat).

✗ p132

The Drive » Follow Hwy 61 north to its junction with US 17A. Turn left. Take US 17A south for 24 miles.

❹ Walterboro

The town of Walterboro calls itself the 'The Front Porch of the Lowcountry,' and a red rocking chair greets guests at the **welcome center** (☏843-538-4353; 1273 Sniders Hwy; ⏱9am-5pm Mon-Sat). Downtown, shoppers can peruse a dozen antique stores before visiting the **South Carolina Artisans Center** (www.scartianscenter.com; 318 Wichman St; ⏱9am-5pm Mon-Sat, 1-5pm Sun). Here, folk art, fine art and traditional crafts fill several rooms in a rambling house.

Boardwalks and trails wind through 842 acres of swampland at the new **Walterboro Wildlife Sanctuary** (www.walterborosc.org). One path tracks the Savannah Stage Coach Rd, which dates to Colonial times. Entrances are off Jefferies Blvd at Beach Rd and Detreville St. The park's original name, the Great Swamp Sanctuary, was scrapped in 2013 because the town council thought the word 'swamp' had negative connotations, especially for urban visitors. We beg to differ.

The Drive » From Walterboro, continue south on US 17A to Yemassee. For brochures and history, turn right at US 17 and continue to the Low Country Visitor Center at Frampton Plantation. Otherwise, turn left on US 17 and continue to Beaufort.

❺ Beaufort

The streets are lined with antebellum homes. Magnolias drip with Spanish moss. Boats shimmer on the river. Gobs of cafes and galleries crowd the downtown. The town is so darn charming that it's often the backdrop

BLUE BOTTLE TREES

That tree in the distance? The one with the branches sprouting empty blue bottles? Say hello to your first bottle tree, a tradition that traces back to 9th-century Congo. According to lore, haunts and evil spirits, being of a curious nature, crawl inside the bottles to see what they can find. They become trapped and then are destroyed by the morning sunlight. Stop and listen. On a windy night you might just hear them moan.

Charleston House and grounds at Middleton Place

for Hollywood films set in the South, from *The Big Chill* and *The Prince of Tides* to *Forrest Gump*. Walk, eat, shop...or just nap on the porch at your B&B.

✕ ⊨ p135

The Drive » Take the Sea Island Pkwy over the river then turn right onto US 21N, following it about 5½ miles to Parris Island. Take the first exit toward Malecon Dr. Follow the signs to the museum.

TRIP HIGHLIGHT

❻ Marine Corps Recruit Depot

More than 17,000 men and women endure boot camp each year at the Parris Island recruiting depot (www.mcrdpi.usmc.mil), which has trained marines since 1915. The experience was made notorious by Stanley Kubrick's *Full Metal Jacket*.

The Modern Marine Wing at the **Parris Island Museum** (📞843-228-2951; www.mcrdpi.usmc.mil; 111 Panama St; admission free; ⊙10am-4:40pm) describes marine participation in recent wars. Check out the **Navajo Code Talkers** display – not one of their transmissions was ever compromised during WWII. Another exhibit spotlights famous former marines, including Gene Hackman, Shaggy and George Jones. Check the website for dates for the popular **Friday graduations**. You may be asked to show ID and car registration before driving onto the grounds.

The Drive » Return to the Sea Island Pkwy and turn right. Drive almost 5 miles east to Dr Martin Luther King Jr Dr. Turn right.

TRIP HIGHLIGHT

❼ Penn Center

East of Beaufort is a series of marshy, rural islands including St Helena Island, considered the heart of Gullah Country. The nonprofit **Penn Center** (📞843-838-2432; www.discoversouthcarolina.com; 16 Penn Center Circle W; adult/child $5/3; ⊙11am-4pm Mon-Sat) preserves and celebrates Sea Island culture. Here, the **York W Bailey Museum** traces the history of Penn School, established in 1862, which was one of the nation's first schools for freed slaves. Martin Luther King used the site in the 1960s as a retreat for strategic, nonviolent planning during the Civil Rights movement.

JOHN ELK / GETTY IMAGES ©

GULLAH CULTURE

African slaves were transported across the Atlantic from the Rice Coast (Sierra Leone, Senegal, the Gambia and Angola) to a landscape that was shockingly similar – swampy coastlines, tropical vegetation and hot, humid summers.

These new African Americans retained many of their homeland traditions, even after the fall of slavery and into the 20th century. The resulting Gullah (also known as Geechee) culture has its own language, an English-based Creole with many African words and sentence structures, and many traditions, including fantastic storytelling, art, music and crafts. The Gullah culture is celebrated annually with the energetic **Gullah Festival** (www.gullahfestival. org) in Beaufort on the last weekend in May.

The Drive » Return to the Sea Island Parkway. Follow it east over expansive marshes then cross the Harbor River Bridge.

TRIP HIGHLIGHT

❽ Hunting Island State Park

With its tidal lagoons, maritime forest, bone-white beach, and 3000 acres of salt marsh, **Hunting Island State Park** (📞843-838-2011; www.southcarolinaparks.com; 2555 Sea Island Pkwy; adult/child $5/3, tent sites $17-38, cabins $210; ⏱visitor center 9am-5pm Mon-Fri, 11am-5pm Sat & Sun) is a nature lover's dream. There are also 8 miles of hiking and biking trails. On a rainy day, try climbing the 175 steps inside the **lighthouse** (admission $2; ⏱10am-4:45pm Mar-Oct), with lofty views of the coast as your reward. At the **nature center** (⏱9am-5pm Tue-Sat, open daily Jun-Aug) you can learn about local wildlife. The boardwalk behind the nature center is a great place to catch the sunset. The park was also the setting for the Vietnam War scenes in *Forrest Gump*, which were filmed in the marsh.

🛏 p135

The Drive » Backtrack north on US 21 to its junction with US 17N. Drive almost 30 miles. Turn right onto Hwy 174.

❾ Edisto Island Scenic Byway

With its old churches, grassy marshes, and moss-draped oaks, the 17-mile Edisto Island Scenic Byway is a classic Lowcountry drive. It stretches along Hwy 174 from the Atlantic Intracoastal Waterway south to Edisto Beach State Park.

Swoop over the waterway then take the first right to the **Dawhoo Landing** parking area. A map here lists byway attractions. Turn around for a nice view of the graceful McKinley Washington, Jr Bridge. Continue south to **King's Farm Market** for local produce, baked goods, jams and Cheerwine.

For history, visit the sometimes-open **Edisto Island Museum** and the 1831 **Presbysterian Church**. Next up? The snakey **Edisto Island Serpentarium** (www .edistoserpentarium.com; 1374 Hwy 174; adult/child $15/11; ⏱10am-6pm Mon-Sat Jun–mid-Aug, hours vary Thu-Sat spring & fall, closed winter) followed by the mystery tree – look right, into the marsh, to see its seasonal decorations. Last is **Edisto Beach State Park** (📞843-869-2156; www.southcarolinaparks .com; adult/child $5/3, tent sites from $21, furnished cabins from $80), with camping just steps from the shore. From here, return to Charleston.

🍴 p135

Eating & Sleeping

Charleston ❶

✕ The Ordinary — Seafood $$

(☏843-414-7060; www.eattheordinary.com; 544 King St; small plates $5-25, large plates $24-28; ⏱3pm-close Tue-Sun) Inside a cavernous 1927 bank building, this buzzy seafood hall and oyster bar feels like the best party in town. The menu is short, but the savory dishes are prepared with finesse – from the oyster sliders to the lobster rolls to the nightly fish dishes.

🛏 Ansonborough Inn — Hotel $$$

(☏800-522-2073; www.ansonboroughinn. com; 21 Hasell St; r incl breakfast $209-259; P ✳ @ 🤙) The interior of this intimate hotel looks like an antique sailing ship. Droll neo-Victorian touches like a Persian-carpeted glass lift, closet-sized British pub and formal portraits of dogs add a sense of fun. Huge guest rooms mix old and new, with worn leather couches, high ceilings and flat-screen TVs. Complimentary wine and cheese social from 5pm to 6pm.

Middleton Place ❸

✕ The Inn at Middleton Place — Inn $$

(☏843-556-0500; www.heinnatmiddletonplace. com; 4290 Ashley River Rd; r incl breakfast $169-400; 🤙🤙) In contrast to the antebellum plantation houses on Ashley River Rd, this cool inn is a series of ecofriendly modernist glass boxes overlooking the Ashley River. Rooms have shuttered floor-to-ceiling windows, handcrafted furniture and hardwood floors. Rate includes admission for two to the plantation.

Beaufort ❺

✕ Low Country Produce — Southern $

(www.lowcountryproduce.com; 302 Carteret St; breakfast $5-9, lunch $5-10, small bites under $8, steak & seafood $12-25; ⏱8am-6pm Mon-Wed, to 8:30pm Thu-Sat, to 3pm Sun) At this cafe and market, the decor is glossy while the food is naughty. Take the Oooey Gooey, a grilled pimiento cheese sandwich with bacon and garlic pepper jelly. It is one hot mess. Enjoy a small-bite menu on Thursday and Friday nights, and steak or seafood (with fresh shucked sea island oysters in season) on Saturday nights.

✕ Sgt White's — Southern, Barbecue $

(1908 Boundary St; mains $7-12; ⏱11am-3pm Mon-Fri) For hardcore local flavor, come here. A retired marine sergeant serves up juicy BBQ ribs, collards and cornbread.

🛏 Cuthbert House — B&B $$$

(☏843-521-1315; www.cuthberthouseinn. com; 1203 Bay St; r incl breakfast $179-245; P ✳ 🤙) The most romantic of Beaufort's B&B's, this sumptuously grand white-columned mansion is straight out of *Gone with the Wind II*. Antique furnishings are found throughout, but monochromatic walls add a fresh, modern feel. Some rooms have a river view. On his march through the South in 1865, General William T Sherman slept at the house.

Hunting Island State Park ❽

🛏 Hunting Island State Park Campground — Campground $

(☏reservations 866-345-7275, office 843-838-2011; www.southcarolinaparks.com; 2555 Sea Island Pkwy; tent/RV sites from $19/31, cabin $210; ⏱6am-6pm, to 9pm early Mar-early Nov) At South Carolina's most-visited park, you can camp under pine trees or palm trees, with several sites just steps from the beach. All are available by walk-up or reservation, but reservations are advisable in summer.

Edisto Island Scenic Byway ❾

✕ King's Farm Market — Fresh Produce $

(2559 Hwy 174, Edisto Island; ⏱9:30am-6pm Mon-Thu, to 6:30pm Fri & Sat, to 5pm Sun, closed Jan) It's not just about the fresh produce, the macadamia nut cookies, the key lime pie, the blackberry cobbler, the breakfast quiche, or the sandwiches and casseroles. It's also about the easy-going friendliness. C'mon already, come in.

STRETCH YOUR LEGS
CHARLESTON

Start/Finish: Husk

Distance: 1.8 miles

Duration: Three to four hours

Few cities evoke the same storied romanticism as Charleston. But the romance can overshadow the darker elements of the city's past. This stroll, which includes a slave mart, a dungeon and a city park, examines the city's compelling but contradictory history.

Take this walk on Trip

10

Husk

Every great walking tour begins with just the right lunch, which is always a sure thing at **Husk** (☎843-577-2500; www.huskrestaurant.com; 76 Queen St; brunch & lunch $10-16, dinner $27-30; ⊘11:30am-2:30pm Mon-Sat, 5:30-10pm Sun-Thu, 5:30-11pm Fri & Sat, brunch 10am-2:30pm Sun). The creation of acclaimed chef Sean Brock, Husk is one the South's most buzzed-about restaurants. Everything on the menu is grown or raised in the South, and the menu changes daily. The setting, in a two-story mansion, is elegant but unfussy.

The Walk » Follow Queen St east to Meeting St. Turn right. Walk one block south to Chalmers St, the city's red light district in the 1700s. Cross Church St. The museum is ahead on the left.

Old Slave Mart

Charleston was a major marketplace for the African slave trade. In 1856 the city banned the selling of slaves on the streets, which drove merchants indoors. The **Old Slave Mart Museum** (www.nps.gov/nr/travel/charleston/osm.htm; 6 Chalmers St; adult/child $7/5; ⊘9am-5pm Mon-Sat) sits inside one of the resulting auction houses. Text-heavy exhibits illuminate the slave experience and slave trading; the few artifacts, such as leg shackles, are especially chilling. For first-hand stories, listen to the oral recollections of former slave Elijah Green, born in 1853.

Save $2 with a combination ticket to the Old Exchange.

The Walk » Continue east on Chalmers St to State St and turn right. Walk south to Broad St. Turn left. The Old Exchange is one block ahead.

Old Exchange & Provost Dungeon

This 1771 Georgian-Palladian **custom house** (www.oldexchange.org; 122 E Bay St; adult/child $8/4; ⊘9am-5pm; 🚶) is certainly impressive, but it's the brick dungeon underneath that wows the crowds. On the docent-led tour of this basement space, you'll learn about the

pirates imprisoned here in 1718 when it was part of a battery guard house. The British kept American patriots captive in the space during the Revolutionary War. After the war, several of them returned to the building to ratify the United States Constitution.

The Walk » Follow E Bay St south. As you climb onto the promenade, grab your camera for photos of Rainbow Row, a line-up of candy-colored townhouses.

The Battery & White Point Gardens

Soak in more history at The Battery, the southern tip of the Charleston peninsula that is buffered by a seawall. Fortifications and artillery were here during the Civil War. In the gardens, stroll past cannons and statues of military heroes, and ponder the risk-filled lives of the pirates who were hanged here. From the promenade, look for Fort Sumter. The island fortress was fired upon by Confederates on April 12, 1861 – the first shots of the Civil War.

The Walk » From the gardens, walk north on Meeting St.

Nathaniel Russell House

Built in 1808, the Federal-style **Nathaniel Russell House** (www .historiccharleston.org; 51 Meeting St; adult/child $10/5; ⊙10am-5pm Mon-Sat, 2-5pm Sun, last tour 4:15pm) is noted especially for its spectacular, self-supporting spiral staircase and its English garden. Russell, a merchant from Rhode Island, was known in Charleston as The King of the Yankees. The home underwent major renovations in 2013, which added exhibits and preserved architectural features.

The Walk » Continue north on Meeting St. Its junction with Broad St is known as the Four Corners of the Law, with a post office, a state courthouse, City Hall and a church each occupying one of the corners. Broad St here is known as Gallery Row. Follow Meeting St to Queen St for a cocktail at the speakeasy-style bar at Husk.

Georgia & Alabama

GEORGIA AND ALABAMA ARE A MICROCOSM OF THE SOUTH – on the one hand, they're home to jet-set cities and urban glitterati, and on the other, a slow lifestyle steeped in tradition and history. In Georgia, Atlanta tempts visitors with slick design hotels, hipster bars, sensational restaurants and world-class cultural attractions. There's wine-drenched Dahlonega in the north; prim Savannah, a gorgeous Southern belle with an edge in the south; and tempting barbecue throughout. Alabama, immersed in captivating civil rights history, is also home to two iconic sports venues, and offers Birmingham, an endearing up-and-coming city, and a progressive example of the new South.

Savannah Gracious antebellum architecture at every turn (Trip 11)
LILLISPHOTOGRAPHY / GETTY IMAGES ©

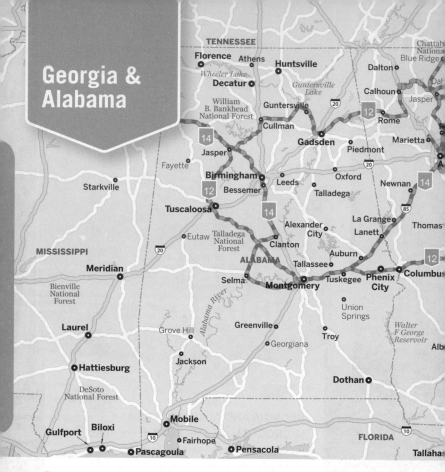

Georgia & Alabama

☑ DON'T MISS

Savannah

Savannah has European elegance, a Southern spirit, shady squares, tasty cafes and a historical core that is as inviting as it is pedestrian-friendly. Experience it on Trips 11 13

Sweet Auburn

A historical corner of downtown Atlanta that gifted us Martin Luther King, a pastor's son who became the ultimate humanitarian and world leader. Explore it on Trip 14

Westside Provisions

Atlanta's new and tasteful complex of gourmet delis, burger joints, imaginative diners, fine-dining rooms and one rather cavernous, bustling pub, not far from Midtown. Taste it all on Trip 12

Birmingham

Unlike Alabama's other cities and towns scarred by oppressive history, Birmingham deftly balances its progressive present with its dark past. See it on Trip 14

Great Smoky Mountains National Park The heart of the Appalachian Trail (Trip 15)

141

Savannah Plantation oaks, elegant homes and leafy squares

Classic Trip

Savannah to the Golden Isles

11

Georgia's Golden Isles are a 100-mile stretch of maritime forests, wildlife-rich estuaries, wild beaches and coastal towns that evoke a bygone era. Georgia's best-kept secret is out.

TRIP HIGHLIGHTS

0 miles

Savannah
Antebellum architecture, leafy streets and squares

1 START

47 miles

Jekyll Island
Turn-of-the-century lore, good cycling, stunning beaches

Sunbury Crab Company

6

122 miles

Little St Simons Island
Empty beaches, raw nature, silence

St Simons Island

8

St Mary's

FINISH

4 DAYS
165 MILES / 266KM

GREAT FOR...

BEST TIME TO GO
From March to May for warm weather but tolerable humidity.

ESSENTIAL PHOTO

Driftwood Beach, where full grown oaks end up as driftwood, roots and all.

BEST FOR OUTDOOR ACTIVITIES

Little St Simons Island for days on the beach and amazing kayaking.

Classic Trip

11 Savannah to the Golden Isles

Georgia has one of America's most diverse and interesting shorelines. Its barrier islands are (mostly) pristine jewels and it's home to one-third of the entire East Coast's salt marshes, and preserved 18th- and 19th-century Southern architecture. Plus it's just a damn fine place to get away from it all. And when you begin in artsy and elegant Savannah, this trip becomes even more breathtaking.

TRIP HIGHLIGHT

1 Savannah

Like a Southern belle with a wild side, this grand historical town revolves around formal antebellum architecture and the revelry of local students from Savannah College of Art & Design. With its gorgeous mansions, and wonderfully beautiful squares, Savannah preserves its past with pride and grace, but she has ample grit and soul.

Here, even an aimless wander is life-affirming. Make sure to visit **Forsyth Park**, and the **Owens-Thomas House** (www.telfair.org; 124 Abercorn St; adult/child $15/5; ☺noon-5pm Mon, 10am-5pm Tue-Sat, 1-5pm Sun), a 19th-century villa which exemplifies English Regency–style architecture, known for its symmetry. Modernists will appreciate the striking, and ambitious, SCAD Museum of Art (p191). The Jepson Center for the Arts (p191) makes for another fun peek. The shopping on Broughton St is underrated. Handbag obsessives should duck into **Satchel** (☎912-233-1008; www.shopsatchel.com; 311 W Broughton St), owned and operated by the designer herself. She also manufacturers her goods, and there is no better photo op in town than the Avenue of the Oaks at the Wormsloe Plantation Historic Site (p168).

To sip coffee with the unshaven, it's all about Sentient Bean; start your day here and follow our walking tour through this charming city (p190).

✗ 🛏 p152

The Drive » The gateway to Brunswick and the Golden Isles is US 17, which rolls south from Savannah through several tiny, picturesque Georgia towns. It's about 40 miles from Savannah to Midway Pass, then take a 15-minute detour east on US 84 past Fort Morris until the road ends.

2 Sunbury Crab Company

This **restaurant** (☎912-884-8640; 541 Brigantine Dunmore Rd; mains $8-27; ☺5-10pm Wed-Fri, noon-10pm Sat, noon-7:30pm Sun) is one of

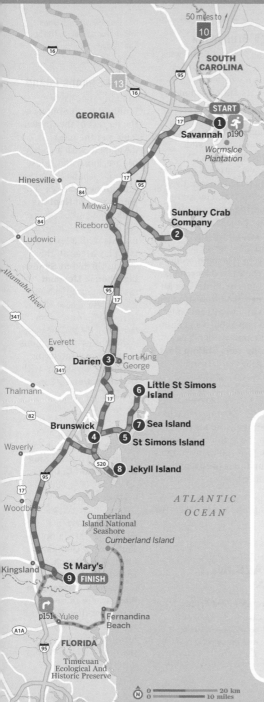

SOUTH
CAROLINA

GEORGIA

START
① 🏃
Savannah p190

Wormsloe
Plantation

Hinesville

Midway

Riceboro

Ludowici

Sunbury Crab
Company ②

Altamaha River

Everett

Darien ③ Fort King
George

Thalmann

Little St Simons
Island ⑥

Brunswick
④ ⑤ St Simons Island

Sea Island ⑦

Waverly

⑧ Jekyll Island

Woodbine

ATLANTIC
OCEAN

Cumberland
Island National
Seashore
Cumberland Island

Kingsland

St Mary's
⑨ FINISH

p151 Yulee

Fernandina
Beach

FLORIDA

Timucuan
Ecological And
Historic Preserve

Ⓝ 0 ⸺ 20 km
0 ⸺ 10 miles

those truly special finds
that elude most travelers.
Here you'll find a Key
West–style treehouse
built with reclaimed
wood from old barns
and department stores.
The menu is whatever is
fresh that day: blue crab
caught that morning by
the son, shrimp caught
by the neighbor and
oysters brought in by the
uncle. All of it is steamed
and chased by cold beer
overlooking the gorgeous
St Catherine's Sound.

The Drive » Head back to US
17 and follow it south for another
40 miles into the small town of
Darien.

③ Darien

Darien is a simple,
relatively sprawling yet
quiet town sheltered by
trees and surrounded by
marsh, with a middling

🔗 LINK YOUR TRIP

13 Hogs & Heifers: a Georgia BBQ Odyssey

Savannah includes a stop on
this decadent, carnivorous
jaunt into the pit-smoked
soul of Georgia's spiciest,
juiciest kitchens.

10 Lowcountry & Southern Coast

Hop across the border,
from one historical town to
another, where the food only
gets better.

historical core dotted with middle- and working-class homes, but there is one remarkable site. **Fort King George** (☎912-437-4770; www.gastateparks.com; 1600 Wayne St; adult/senior/youth 6-18yr/child under 5yr $7/6.50/4/free; ⏲9am-5pm Tue-Sat, 2-5:30pm Sun; 👪) is a remarkably reconstructed version of Georgia's first fort, a British outpost dating back to 1721. The fort overlooks a vast estuary, and is surrounded by mossy oaks. Expect to spot egrets and storks and to be serenaded by songbirds. It's a beautiful scene. There are also two restaurants of note here.

✕ p152

The Drive » Thus far, US 17 has often felt like it was hugging the interstate, nothing more than a glorified frontage road. For the next 19 miles, however, the roads diverge, and US 17 begins snaking through the estuary and courting the sea breeze.

4 Brunswick

The town of Brunswick is a vaguely historical town worth a stroll for its antique shops and potpourri of architectural styles along its main drag, Newcastle St, and throughout its Old Town National Register Historic District. Even better is the pleasant marina where egrets and pelicans soar and dive and weathered old shrimp boats bob on the canal. The land seems to be carved by rivers, canals and inlets on all sides. An interesting way to kill an afternoon is to hop aboard a genuine shrimp trawler. The **Lady Jane Shrimp Boat** (☎912-265-5711; www.shrimpcruise.com; 1200 Glynn Ave; adult/child under 6yr $40/25; ⏲3:45pm Wed & Fri-Sun; 👪) takes tourists out trawling for shrimp in the St Simons Sound. Before you know it, the shrimp is peeled and served.

The Drive » Brunswick is separated from the Golden Isles by a causeway, which leads rather dramatically to the St Simons isles

5 St Simons Island

Roughly the size of Manhattan, St Simons is the largest of the Golden Isles and the most developed, with a clutch of cute shops and cafes and an L-shaped pier that juts out over the sea. The pier is part of **Neptune Park** (www.glynncounty.org; 550 Beachview Dr), which unfurls with a lawn and two play areas all the way to the old **St Simons Lighthouse Museum** (www.saintsimonslighthouse.org; 101 12th St; adult/child 5-11yr $10/5; ⏲10am-5pm Mon-Sat, 1:30-5pm Sun).

Activities on St Simons range from a satisfying two-hour kayak trip with **Ocean Motion** (☎800-669-5215, 912-638-5225; www.stsimonskayaking.com; 1300 Ocean Blvd; per person $45), through the island's marshes, or you could head over to **King & Prince Golf Course** (☎912-634-0255, 800-342-0212; www.kingandprince.com; 201 Arnold Rd; resort guests/public per person $75/115; ⏲8am-5pm) at Hampton Club, one of Georgia's finest. **East Beach**, the island's best, can be accessed at **Massengale Park**, where there is ample parking. Here white sand rolls south for more than a mile to a point backed by scrubby dunes.

TOP TIP: FIRST FRIDAYS IN BRUNSWICK

If you happen to be in Brunswick for **First Friday** (www.brunswickgeorgia.net; Newcastle St; ⏲5-8pm), held the first Friday of the month, you'll enjoy perusing the local art and antique galleries, and enjoy wine and bites with the locals.

LOCAL KNOWLEDGE: WHY I LOVE SAVANNAH

After graduation from SCAD, Elizabeth Seeger decided to stay in Savannah and pursue a design career under her own steam. These days, her company, Satchel (p144), is growing rapidly. Here's why she chose to stay in town after graduation to launch her business.

Savannah offers me the pleasure to be able to do what I love in a picturesque location, and the fact that it's affordable is key to my being able have a boutique and a workshop on the best shopping street in the city. The lifestyle is laid back – I walk less than a mile to work everyday, and stroll back with a beer in hand every evening – and the Lowcountry scenery is spectacular. The bright green marsh grass on the drive to **Tybee Island** in the summer is truly breathtaking. All 12 years I've been here (since starting SCAD in 2001) I've lived in the historic district, in homes as old as General Oglethorpe himself! On the weekends I go to the **Forsyth Park Farmers Market** (www.forsythfarmersmarket.com; Forsyth Park; ⊙9am-1pm Sat) for some fresh local goodies, so I can always make dinner for friends at the drop of a hat. Here in Savannah, we love entertaining in our homes and on our porches, which is why I love all of our consignment stores, like **Habersham Antiques Market** (☏912-238-5908; www.habershamantiquesmarket.com; 2502 Habersham St; ⊙9:30am-5:30pm Mon-Fri, 10am-5pm Sat) and **Clutter** (☏912-354-7556; www.facebook.com/ClutterFurnishingsAndInteriors; 1100 Eisenhower Dr; ⊙10am-5:30pm Tue-Sat). This weekend alone I found a set of Limoges Pot de Creme & Baccarat Coupe Champagne Glasses. But if sitting on your porch with a libation isn't your thing, there's always something going on. **Connect Savannah** (www.connectsavannah.com) is a great place to start if you're looking for some nightlife. I love having drinks at Circa and Pinkies, and if you're into live music you have to come to **Savannah Stopover** (www.savannahstopover.com), our new local indie music festival that's held the weekend before South by Southwest (SXSW), and is kind of a warm-up for bands en route to Austin. It's held over four days, in over 10 locations and features 75-plus bands. Come for a weekend, stay for a week, rent a house here next summer – and before you know it, you may move here. After all, life here is just a little more enjoyable than everywhere else.

While the coast is obviously lovely, inland residential neighborhoods draped in regal, mossy oaks are likewise magical. Wandering the quiet clean streets beneath those mighty trees can be positively Savannah-like.

✖ ⊨ p152

The Drive » The soothing drive to the end of the island passes stables and seaside estates along Hampton Point

Dr. That's where you'll find the marina with transport to the island next door, if you have a reservation, of course.

`TRIP HIGHLIGHT`

❻ Little St Simons Island

This unhurried, 10,000-acre island is an unspoiled jewel. Four successive stages of vegetation (dune meadow, wax myrtle and sweet grass, pine forest and climax maritime forest) make it a haven for kayaking, interpretive nature tours and birding, all of which are led by naturalists who are intimately knowledgeable about the local ecosystem. It's a miraculous getaway – full of European fallow deer, sea turtles and gators – that is preciously undeveloped. But access is an issue, as the only way to enjoy it

Classic Trip

DENNIS K JOHNSON ©

KEN HOWARD / ALAMY ©

WHY THIS IS A CLASSIC TRIP
ADAM SKOLNICK, AUTHOR

Savannah is seldom mentioned when considering America's great cities, but there are few – if any – that are more beautifully planned. It's a city elegant with plazas, shady with oaks and colored with art, modern and antiquated. South Georgia's charm grows and deepens as you visit humble shrimping ports, vast estuaries, pristine islands and one spectacular driftwood beach.

Top: Forsyth Park, Savannah
Left: Driftwood Beach, Jekyll Island
Right: St Simons Island Lighthouse

is by booking with the all-inclusive Lodge on Little St Simons (p152), or by joining one of its day trips, which includes passage to the island, an island tour, a gourmet lowcountry lunch, and an afternoon to explore its 7 miles of pristine beach. Trips depart from St Simons Island at 10:30am and return at 4:30pm. You probably won't want to leave, but you have to. Book at least a month in advance for day trips.

🛏 p152

The Drive » Once you're back on St Simons head for the traffic circle on Federica Rd where you'll find the well-signed turn to Sea Island Rd. A bridge will lead over the narrow inlet to this gated isthmus of an 'island'.

7 Sea Island

Little St Simons it is not. Sea Island, the Golden Isles' other private 'isle,' is much less about raw nature and much more about the game of golf. Billed as a five-star golf retreat, it features several restaurants, a 65,000-sq-ft spa and fitness center, tennis and squash courts, and it does have three 18-hole golf courses, which is why it was named one of America's top 75 golf resorts. If you do want to get into nature, join one of its kayaking or fishing trips, go horseback riding, or simply wander

Classic Trip

down to the beach club, which accesses 5 miles of private beach.

📑 p152

The Drive » Departing Sea Island, head back to St Simons where you can cross the evocative Sydney Lanier Bridge to the Jekyll Island Causeway, the gateway to Jekyll Island.

TRIP HIGHLIGHT

8 Jekyll Island

This glorious island was once the stamping ground for America's rich and famous, and it's not hard to see why. Sixty-five percent undeveloped,

woodlands and marshlands dominate the landscape here, peppered with some of the most interesting architecture this side of Charleston. The winter cottages, built between 1884 and 1929, are now the highlight of the **Jekyll Island National Historic Landmark District**. You may peek inside a few of the fancier buildings on a **Jekyll Island Museum** (📞912-635-4036; www .jekyllisland.com; 100 Stable Rd; museum entry free, trolley tour adult/child 6-12yr $16/7; ⏰9am-5pm; 👶) trolley tour. Alternatively, rent a bike from the hotel. The entire island lends itself to cycling and features more than 20 miles of paved bike paths. Sign up for an

after-dark turtle walk at **Georgia Sea Turtle Center** (📞912-635-4444; www.georgiaseaturtlecenter .org; 214 Stable Rd; adult/ child $7/5; ⏰9am-5pm Sun-Tue, 10am-2pm Mon; 👶), a rehabilitation and research facility working to save Georgia's sea turtles. We love the wide beach and scrubby dunes accessible off Borden Lane. It's empty, breezy and perfect, but **Driftwood Beach** is Jekyll's sweet spot. On the island's northeast point, it's saturated with enormous washed-up oak trees and is magical at dawn.

🍴 📑 p153

The Drive » Make your way back over the causeway – absorb the last of those

---

BEST BEACHES

Georgia's coastline is long and languid, with ample beaches fringing oak woodlands and rambling estuaries. Unfortunately, not all of said beaches are created equal. If you're craving that idyllic stretch of Georgian sand, one (or more) of these will do.

» Cumberland Island One of the two most pristine of Georgia's barrier islands, the beaches on the west coast are lovely, with views of the nearby estuary. You'll see ample birdlife, and, on its southern tip, south of the Dungeness Ruins, you can often find shark teeth in the sand. But the east coast is where you'll want to swim and camp. Find **Stafford Beach**, one long, unbroken strip of sand accessible by pedal and boot, road and trail.

» Little St Simons Island This private, 10,000-acre island includes an unbroken and pristine **7-mile Beach**, which unfurls along its east coast.

» Jekyll Island For a comfortable stretch of sand, where you can lay out and enjoy a day at the beach, find **Borden Lane** on the east coast and follow it to pay dirt. For something otherworldy fantastic, it's all about **Driftwood Beach** at dawn.

» St Simons Island With the village occupying the south end of the island, and the Hampton-like estates walling off access to the beaches in the north, you'll head to Massengale Park where you'll have access to the wide and inviting **East Beach**.

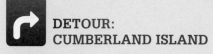

DETOUR: CUMBERLAND ISLAND

Start: St Mary's

Cumberland Island (www.nps.gov/cuis), Georgia's largest and southernmost barrier island, is the belle of the ball. Isolated, rugged and hauntingly pristine, this 57-sq-mile island is brimming with wild marshes, unspoiled beaches and a population and infrastructure lost in time. Think: cultural ruins and ancient oak trees dripping in Spanish moss. John Kennedy Jr was married on the island at the **First African Baptist Church**.

In all, there are 18 miles of roads, best explored on two wheels. You can rent your bike on the ferry for $16 per day, but unless you're on the island for several days of trekking (not a bad idea), the only way to see the whole thing is by booking a van tour (adult/child $15/12) at the Visitor Center in St Mary's. Of course, the one drawback of a van tour is that you don't actually visit the beach. If you wish to spend time on the sand, it's best to pedal or stroll. And no matter where or how you travel, be sure to bring food. There are no public restaurants on the island. Book **passage** (☎912-882-4335; www.nps.gov/cuis; round-trip adult/senior/child $20/18/14; ⊗departures 9am & 11:45am, returning 10:15am & 4:45pm) well in advance. Walk-in tickets are difficult to wrangle, as there is a limit of 300 visitors per day.

If you'd like to experience Cumberland with a bit more style, continue south on I-95 to Fernandina Beach, FL, where ferries operated by the **Greyfield Inn** (☎904-261-6408; www.greyfieldinn.com; r incl meals $425-635) – the island's only hotel – leave three times a day.

supreme estuary and inlet views (for now) and head inland on GA-520 to the I-95 south. Exit on Laurel Island Pkwy and follow the signs to St Mary's.

- - - - - - - - - - - - - -

❾ St Mary's

This is is a cute little harbor enclave whose raison d'être is really to get guests over and back to and from Cumberland Island, but it's attractive in its own right and worthy of at least a night. Sprinkled with historical B&Bs, there is a dynamite Greek restaurant here too, and, most importantly, St Mary's is home to the **Cumberland Island National Seashore** (www.nps.gov/cuis; admission $4) visitor center, where you can book camp sites, van tours and transport to and from the island.

✗ ⊨ p153

Eating & Sleeping

Savannah ❶

✗ Wilkes' House — Southern $$
See Trip 🔟 (p216).

🛏 East Bay Inn — Inn $$$
See Trip 🔟 (p216).

Darien ❸

✗ B & J's Steaks & Seafood — Seafood $
(☎912-437-2122; 901 Hwy 17; mains $5-17; ⏰7am-9pm Mon-Sat, 9am-2pm Sun) A humble roadside diner, and the working man's (or woman's!) choice for local shrimp. It does half-pound baskets and full-pound shrimp dinners, fried of course. It also cracks oysters and steams crab in the evenings when in season.

✗ River House — Continental $$
(☎912-437-2510; www.darienriverhouse.com; 306 Fort King George Dr; mains $16-27; ⏰5-10pm Wed-Sat) Set in a converted whitewashed home, steps from the shrimping harbor, this destination restaurant attracts regulars from Savannah for chef Eric Lynch's three-course tasting menus, which come paired with three wines ($45). You may also order mains like the roast duck glazed in bourbon barbecue sauce, and classic wild Georgia shrimp and grits, à la carte.

St Simons Island ❺

✗ Crab Trap — Seafood $$
(☎912-638-3552; www.thecrabtrapssi.com; 1209 Ocean Blvd; dishes $11-25) A funky, stripped-down seafood house, with pebbled concrete floors, a dark-beamed wooden interior and vintage diving and fishing gear on display. Shrimp, oysters, scallops, crab and a fresh catch of the day are grilled, steamed or fried. Its crab soup (not bisque!) is locally beloved.

✗ Palm Coast — Cafe $
(www.palmcoastssi.com; 318 Mallery St; mains $8-12) For simple and affordable eats in the village, choose among the wraps, sandwiches and entree salads at this tasty coffee house set in a cottage on the main drag. Its cozy bar gets a crowd, it has a rather expansive dining patio out back and rockers on the concrete front porch.

🛏 St Simons Inn By The Lighthouse — Inn $$
(☎912-638-1101; www.saintsimonsinn.com; 609 Beachview Dr; r incl breakfast from $179; 🅿❄🖥🏊) Cute and comfortable, accented with white wooden shutters, it's well located next to the downtown drag and a short pedal from East Beach. Continental breakfast included.

Little St Simons Island ❻

🛏 Lodge on Little St Simons Island — Lodge $$$
(☎912-638-7472; www.littlessi.com; 1000 Hampton Pt; all-inclusive d from $475; ⏰May-Sep; 👪) An isolated historical lodge on the pristine and private Little St Simons. Book a month ahead for day trips.

Sea Island ❼

🛏 The Cloister — Resort $$$
(☎855-714-9201; www.seaisland.com; Sea Island Dr; d from $425) Horse stables, a 56,000-sq-ft spa, 54 holes of golf – no luxurious stone is left unturned at this Mediterranean-inspired resort.

Jekyll Island ❽

✕ Lattitude 31
Restaurant & Rah Bar   Seafood $

(☎912-635-3800; www.latitude31jekyllisland
.com; One Pier Rd; mains $8-26; ⏱11am-late
) The casually elegant Rah Bar is best for
Lowcountry boils. Think: crab legs, shrimp,
crawdaddies, corn, pork sausage and red
potatoes. Best paired with beer. Lattitude 31,
the dressed-up dining room, is dinner only, and
also specializes in local seafood.

🛏 Jekyll Island Club Hotel   Hotel $$

(☎800-535-9547; www.jekyllclub.com;
371 Riverview Dr; d/ste from $179/279;
🅿❄@🛜🏊) Sleep in a bygone era in this
grand historical landmark hotel that once
hosted folks with names like Rockefeller,
Goodyear, Macy, Vanderbilt and Pulitzer. It
was built in 1886, and its rooms are decorated
with Victorian flair. The cottages are the most
romantic choice here.

🛏 Villas By The Sea   Condos $$

(☎912-635-2521, 800-841-6262; www
.villasbythesearesort.com; 1175 N Beachview Dr;
condos from $149) A nice choice on the north
coast, close to Driftwood Beach. Villas are
decent, one and two bedroom condos, set in
a complex of lodge buildings sprinkled over a
garden. Not fancy but plenty comfy. Expect flat
screens, queen beds and full kitchens.

St Mary's ❾

✕ Riverside Cafe   Greek $$

(www.riversidecafesaintmarys.com; 106 St Marys
Rd; mains $8-18; ⏱11am-9pm Mon-Fri, from
8:30am Sat & Sun) A Greek cafe that does a take
on the gyro called the Riverside Wrap. Pork,
lamb and beef are mixed, seasoned, pounded
into gyro like strips (it doesn't have a rotisserie),
piled with lettuce, feta, tzatziki and folded into a
fresh pita. The spanakopita looks tremendous,
as well. Come before the ferry and they'll pack
a lunch to go.

🛏 Spencer House Inn   Inn $$

(☎912-882-1872; www.spencerhouseinn.com;
200 Osborne St; r $135-245) A historical inn
c 1872, brushed up pink, there are 14 spacious
rooms on three floors, with slightly less
personality and clutter than other local comers.
It's also more up to date with flat screens
and top-end bath products. Staff book ferry
reservations, pack lunches for day trippers and
serve a full gourmet breakfast each morning.

Dahlonega Mountainous w
region with 10 vineyards to v

Georgia & Alabama Backroads

12

If you crave life beyond the common stops and exits, it's best to avoid the interstate. Especially in Georgia and Alabama, where unearthed treasures await.

TRIP HIGHLIGHTS

59 miles

Dahlonega
An undercover wine region in the splendid Georgia mountains

Carters Lake

2

Gadsden

Jasper

Atlanta **START**

5

658 miles

Fort Valley
Because everybody loves peaches!

8
FINISH

6

Tuscaloosa
A picturesque college town with a football obsession

398 miles

Tuskegee
African American advancement started here

539 miles

**4–5 DAYS
748 MILES /
1204KM**

GREAT FOR...

BEST TIME TO GO
March to May for the best mix of weather, prices and crowds.

 ESSENTIAL PHOTO

Breathtaking mountain views from a Daholnega vineyard.

BEST FOR OUTDOOR ACTIVITIES
The backroads for many hiking, paddling and boating options.

155

12 Georgia & Alabama Backroads

Have you ever tried to take a road trip sans interstates? It's rather difficult. When President Dwight D Eisenhower hatched the interstate system in 1956, several towns, big and small, and their once-popular attractions, were suddenly off the cross-country map. Yet being left to languish kept things sweet, real and homegrown, while interstate towns often suffered corporate and fast-food overload. Time to get real.

❶ Atlanta

Begin in Atlanta where you can catch a breath of urban culture before heading into the Georgia and Alabama backwoods. Midtown is one of Atlanta's most vibrant neighborhoods, and home to the **High Museum of Art** (www.high.org; 1280 Peachtree St NE; adult/child $19.50/12; ◷10am-5pm Mon-Sat, noon-5pm Sun), with a truly excellent collection of early American modern art from the likes of George Morris and Albert Gallatin, not to mention post-war work from Mark Rothko. For dinner, venture a bit off center to **Decatur** – which is technically still part of the Atlanta metro area, yet feels like its own leafy small town. There's the lovely courthouse square, with a gazebo in its heart, dotted with cute shops and special restaurants, imagined by top level gourmet brains. After dinner, head to **Brick Store Pub** (www.brickstorepub.com; 125 E Court Sq), which draws a cute young crowd midweek, who come for their seven pages of beers! Downstairs serves American craftsman brews; the intimate Belgian beer bar is upstairs.

🍴 🛏 p161

The Drive » Drive north from Atlanta on GA-400, and you'll soon find yourself in a layered landscape of blue mountains, studded with oaks and pines, and laced with vineyards.

TRIP HIGHLIGHT

❷ Dahlonega

Here's a super-charming mountain town with a courthouse square dotted with tasting rooms, representing 10 vineyards nestled in the

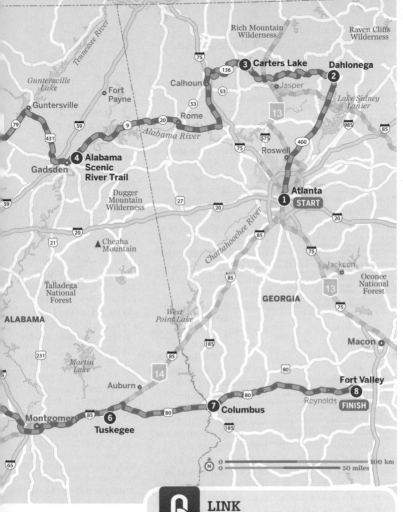

surrounding mountains.
Our favorite is Naturally
Georgia (p184). They
pour dry whites and
robust, Portuguese-
style reds. Dahlonega
has gold-mining roots
and the town prospered
with each strike. In 1838
the federal government
opened a mint in the
town square, where

LINK YOUR TRIP

14 Civil Rights Tour

Delve into the impact
of Tuskegee on African
American history,
and the Civil Rights
movement on Atlanta,
Alabama and beyond.

13 Hogs & Heifers: A Georgia BBQ Odyssey

Drive the backroads
then taste Georgia's pit
smoking, juicy, spicy,
backcountry barbecue.

more than $6 million in gold was coined before the operation was closed at the dawn of the Civil War. You can absorb some of that history at the **Dahlonega Courthouse Gold Museum** (⚬706-864-2257; www.dahlonega.org; Public Sq; adult/senior/child $6/5.50/3.50; ⊙9am-5pm Mon-Sat, 10am-5pm Sun). Of course, the most fun to be had here is driving past spectacular mountain scenery on the mountain roads between wineries. We're big fans of **Frogtown Cellars** (⚬706-878-5000; www.frogtownwine.com; 700 Ridge Point Dr; tastings $15; ⊙noon-5pm Mon-Fri, to 6pm Sat, 12:30-5pm Sun) – a massive stone lodge where you can taste seven wines for $15. Behind it, Three Sisters (p184) is a wonderfully unpretentious vineyard where Cheetos, overalls and bluegrass tunes pair just fine with the wine. And if you still can't get enough mountain magic, hit the trail in **Amicalola Falls State Park** (⚬706-265-4703; www.amicalolafalls.com; per vehicle $5).

🛏 p161

The Drive ≫ The road gets increasingly lonely and luscious as you wind your way west on GA-52 to GA-136 and Carters Lake.

---

❸ Carters Lake

An emerald lake nestled in the southern end of the Blue Ridge Mountains, Carters Lake is a haven for boating, birdwatching, hiking and mountain biking. Stop at the **Carters Lake Marina** (⚬706-276-4891; www.carterslake.com; 575 Marina Rd, Chatsworth; day use per vehicle $4, r from $100; ⊙10am-6pm Apr-Oct; 👶🐾), where you can rent a pontoon boat (no experience necessary) or settle into one of the roomy pine log cabins with expansive decks overlooking the lake. The most popular hiking trail in the area is the **Amadahy Trail** (3.5 miles, two hours round-trip) offering scenic lake views. For cyclists, the **Ridgeway Mountain Bike Trail** (6 miles, 40 minutes) is a mixture of single-track and narrow logging roads with creek crossings and technical descents.

This area has a bit of sad history. In 1838, during the height of the Georgia gold rush, local Cherokee families were rounded up and held near the present day dam. They were forced north, and eventually onto the famed Trail of Tears.

The Drive ≫ There are several backroad options that connect Carters Lake with Gadsden, Alabama. We suggest heading west on GA-136, veer south on GA-225, jog left on US 41 then make your way to GA-20 which becomes AL-9 as you cross the border. AL-9 leads to the Alabama Scenic River Trail in Gadsden.

---

❹ Alambama Scenic River Trail

River rats can paddle part of the Piedmont Section of the 631-mile **Alabama Scenic River Trail** (www.alabamascenicrivertrail.com), which begins at the Alabama–Georgia border and winds its way south towards Gadsden along the Upper Coosa River. You can put in for a half-day paddle on Terrapin Creek, one of the Upper Coosa's tributaries. The **Terrapin Outdoor Center** (⚬256-447-6666; www.canoeshop.net; 4114 County Rd 175; ⊙9am-5pm) rents kayaks and canoes, and it has Stand Up Paddle (SUP) boards too.

The Drive ≫ Head east on US 278 back toward Gadsen then veer north on US 431 over Guntersville Lake. Take the AL-79 south then the AL-74 west to Jasper, where you can pick up AL-69 south to Tuscaloosa.

TRIP HIGHLIGHT

❺ Tuscaloosa

Tuscaloosa is just an hour from Birmingham but it feels a million miles from everywhere, as if farmland and the woods were cleared and a college town dropped into the gap. Local life revolves around the

Fort Valley Peach capital of the Peach State

University of Alabama (www.ua.edu) – and Crimson Tide football. The campus is lovely and leafy: pebbled concrete sidewalks lead past attractive brick buildings to a beautiful quad, featuring an expansive lawn and stand-alone bell tower. Pre-game festivities begin here, before the hordes move en masse to Bryant-Denny Stadium (p300): most recently expanded in 2010, it seats more than 101,000 people. Real football fanatics – many of whom converge from across the state on football Saturdays –

will want to explore the **Paul W Bryant Museum** (☎205-348-4668; www. bryantmuseum.com; 300 Paul W Bryant Dr; adult/senior & child $2/1; ☺9am-4pm). Named in honor of the legendary coach 'Bear' Bryant, this is the Crimson Tide Football Hall of Fame.

✗ ⊨ p161

The Drive » Arguably the prettiest stretch of highway since you left Dahlonega, the narrow US 82, shaded by pines, rolls over foothills and past small farming towns. This is the quintessential backroad. In Montgomery, rejoin I-85N for 32 miles, into Tuskegee.

TRIP HIGHLIGHT

6 Tuskegee

School yourself on African American history at **Tuskegee Institute National Historic Site**, which is home to the **George Washington Carver Museum** (☎334-727-6390; www.nps.gov/tuai; University Campus Ave; ☺9am-4:30pm), devoted to the iconic agricultural pioneer and educator. Don't miss **The Oaks** (☎334-727-6390; www.nps.gov/tuin.com; University Campus Ave; ☺9am-4:30pm, tours 10am, 11am, 1pm & 3pm Sat & Sun),

MOTORCYCLES, MOTORCYCLES AND MORE MOTORCYCLES...

If you love motorcycles, or even if you (think you) don't, the **Barber Vintage Motorsports Museum** (📞205-699-7275; www.barber.museum.org; Exit 140, I-20, Leeds, Alabama; adult/child $15/10; ⏰10am-5pm Mon-Sat, noon-5pm Sun Oct-Mar, to 6pm Apr-Sep) is an absolute must. Especially, if you're swerving these backroads on two wheels. The museum's collection includes 1200 motorcycles dating from today all the way back to 1902, and at least 600 of them are on display at all times. It was launched by George Barber, a local businessman who loved restoring and racing vintage Porsches. Once his attention turned to motorcycles in 1989, he assembled a restoration team and began collecting in earnest. The sheer range of his collection is mental. Here is a 1912 Indian, there a 1953 Victoria Bergmeister; there are Harleys, Ducatis and BMWs all from decades long gone, along with plenty of obscure models and brands you may not have heard of. Barber also races these bikes and has a team that wins national championships on the vintage racing circuit. His museum is located on the 740-acre Barber Sports Motorpark, which includes a speedway.

the home of Booker T Washington. Born into slavery, he went on to found the institute and become the university's first president. Five miles outside of town, the Tuskegee Airmen National Historic Site (p173) has been restored to its former glory as the training grounds and airfield for the first African American pilot candidates in the US military. Several of the original training planes are on display here. The Tuskegee Airmen were among the original desegregation pioneers.

The Drive » Head east out of Tuskegee on US 80 past the Tuskegee National Forest (the smallest in the USA) and into Columbus.

⑦ Columbus

The main attraction here is the fascinating **National Civil War Naval Museum** (📞706-327-9798; www.portcolumbus.org; 1002 Victory Dr; adult/senior/child $7.50/6.50/6; ⏰10am-4:30pm Tue-Sat, from 12:30pm Sun & Mon; 🚻) dedicated to the Confederate navy. Check out the CSS *Jackson*, an 1862 ironclad Confederate navy ship that was hauled up after 95 years underwater; and the stunning collection of mid-18th-century American and Confederate flags, unearthed from an attic in – funnily enough – Massachusetts.

The Drive » Skedaddle out of Columbus and stay eastbound on US 80 into a land of peaches and pecans.

TRIP HIGHLIGHT

⑧ Fort Valley

Fort Valley is the beating heart of Peach County (no, really), the peach capital of the peach state. Your nose, and ample signage, should lead you to **Lane Southern Orchards** (📞800-277-3224; www.lanepacking.com; 50 Lane Rd; tours adult/senior/child 3-12yr $6/5/4; ⏰9am-6pm; 🚻), where more than 3000 acres are dedicated to the cultivation of peaches and pecans. You can stock up on the fruits and nuts themselves, but you may also wish to explore the peach salsa, peach cobbler jam (yum!), peach ice cream, and the peach hot sauce. Learn to embrace the peach! Farm tours are available in June and July when the pickings are at their peak.

Eating & Sleeping

Atlanta ❶

✗ Leon's Full Service   Fusion $$

(📞404-687-0500; www.leonsfullservice.com; 131 E Ponce de Leon Ave; mains $11-24; ⏰5pm-1am Mon, 11:30am-1am Tue-Thu & Sun, to 2am Fri & Sat) No pretense, just a gorgeous concrete bar and an open floor plan that spills out of a former service station and onto a groovy heated deck with floating beams. Everything, from the beer, wine and cocktails (its spirits are all craftsman, small-batch creations) to its menu (think: pan roasted trout served over spiced bulgar wheat with roasted cauliflower and an apple curry broth or house made chicken sausage in green curry with baby bok choi) is crafted with care. No wonder this place is packed. No reservations.

🛏 Hotel Artmore   Boutique Hotel $$

See Trip 🔟 (p179).

Dahlonega ❷

🛏 Hall House Hotel   Inn $$

(📞706-867-5009; www.hallhousehotel.com; 90 Public Square; r $100-175) A charming historical nest on the square dating to 1881. There are five bright and charming rooms, each uniquely decorated, some with four post beds.

Lake Guntersville

🛏 Lodge at Lake Guntersville State Park   Lodge $

(📞256-571-5440; www.alapark.com/lakeguntersville; 1155 Lodge Dr; r from $96, sites from $17.44; 🚹) This bluff-side resort boasts rooms, lakeside cottages and a 321-site campground.

Tuscaloosa ❺

✗ Nick's Original Filet House   Steaks $

See Trip 🔢 (p306).

🛏 Hotel Capstone   Hotel $$

See Trip 🔢 (p306).

Georgia barbecue Ribs, pork, chicken, turkey — take your pick

Hogs & Heifers: A Georgia BBQ Odyssey

13

There's brisket in Texas and dry rub in Memphis, but in Georgia the term BBQ is synonymous with chopped or pulled pork: pit-roasted, tender, juicy and simmering in succulent sauce.

TRIP HIGHLIGHTS

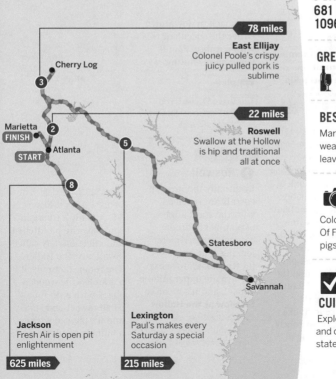

78 miles

East Ellijay
Colonel Poole's crispy juicy pulled pork is sublime

Cherry Log

3

22 miles

Marietta
FINISH

2

Roswell
Swallow at the Hollow is hip and traditional all at once

5

Atlanta

START

8

Statesboro

Savannah

Jackson
Fresh Air is open pit enlightenment

625 miles

Lexington
Paul's makes every Saturday a special occasion

215 miles

**3 DAYS
681 MILES /
1096KM**

GREAT FOR...

BEST TIME TO GO

March to May for mild weather, new green leaves and wildflowers.

ESSENTIAL PHOTO

Colonel Poole's Hill Of Fame, packed with pigs of all sizes.

BEST FOR SOUTHERN CUISINE

Exploring, comparing and devouring the state's signature meal.

163

Hogs & Heifers: A Georgia BBQ Odyssey

The Deep South's contributions to the American culinary landscape are well documented – fried green tomatoes, fried chicken, collard greens and pecan pie among them – but perhaps no food is more inherently Southern than a juicy plate of smoked meat. Get to know what good is.

❶ Atlanta

Don't leave the Atlanta city limits until you sample **Fat Matt's Rib Shack** (www.fatmatts ribshack.com; 1811 Piedmont Ave NE; mains $6-21; 11:30am-11:30pm Mon-Fri, to 12:30am Sat, 1-11:30pm Sun). Although it does serve chopped pork we suggest a slab of ribs (though a half slab will probably suffice). Take special note of the Brunswick stew, a delicious side dish best described as barbecue soup. And the best part? It has live blues nightly. Another classic Atlanta haunt is Daddy Dz (p179), a juke joint of a BBQ shack, consistently voted tops in town, and

set smack in downtown. Order the succulent ribs with cornbread, and you'll leave smiling.

🛏 p169

The Drive » Take US 85 northeast and then take GA-140 northwest to Roswell.

TRIP HIGHLIGHT

❷ Roswell

Eventually the Roswell corrals are replaced with the stark angles of planned bedroom community perimeter fencing...but it's plenty enough to sense the urbane upper middle appeal, and it's home to **Swallow at the Hollow** (678-352-1975; www .swallowatthehallow.com; 1072 Green St; sandwiches $9-10,

plates $16-23; 11am-9pm Wed, Thu & Sun, to 10pm Fri & Sat), many a Georgian son's favorite pit kitchen, and affectionately called 'Swaller At the Haller.' The room – actually, it's a double wide wooden shack with a tin roof – smells sweet and smoky and it's blessed with a humble bandstand

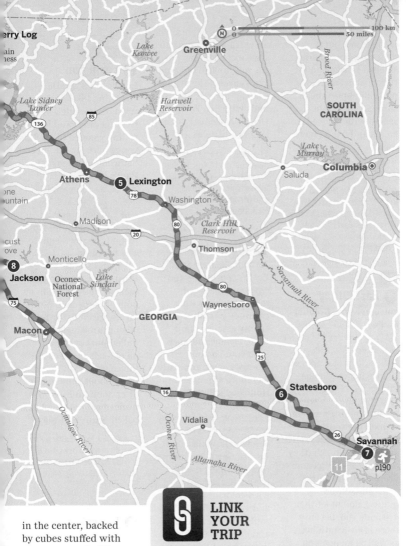

in the center, backed by cubes stuffed with vintage records. There are modern accents – the stainless steel bar (with craftsman beer on tap), two flat screens for ballgames and ample outdoor seating. All tables are blessed with the spicy house sauce and house mustard

LINK YOUR TRIP

11 Savannah to the Golden Isles

Follow the coast down to the shrimping town of Brunswick and across the causeway to the captivating Golden Isles.

12 Georgia & Alabama Backroads

Now that you've sampled Georgia's downhome cuisine, swerve more of her backroads and soak up the local culture.

too. The chopped pork is the thing, but it does ribs, homemade smoked sausage and turkey platters. It even pit smokes portabella shrooms for veg-heads, served with smoked gouda and fried green tomatoes. Hey, it's the suburbs!

The Drive ≫ Take US 140 west to the GA-515, head north to I-575 north and you'll find yourself on a gorgeous stretch of road that winds high into wooded Appalachia toward Tennessee.

TRIP HIGHLIGHT

❸ East Ellijay

You can't miss **Colonel Poole's** (☎706-635-4100; 164 Craig St; mains $3.50-9.50; ⏰11am-6pm Thu, to 8pm Fri & Sat, to 7pm Sun; 🚻), a right-wing roadhouse known as the Taj-Ma-Hog. Yes, there is still a Buchanan for President sign on the wall, and they still harbor a grudge against the French (they call their fries Freedom Fries); but bleeding-heart BBQ-lovers (guilty), do not let that dissuade you, because there is a warmth here, as well as an open pit that conceives some deliciously crispy pulled pork, and meaty, fatty ribs. It does pulled or bone-on chicken plates, and brisket too. The beans are special, the best we had in the state, and they're swimming with chunks of pork. For an extra $5 you too can have a colorful pig on the nearby Hill of Fame! Who cares if the original Colonel Poole is best buds with Tea Party icon Grover Norquist? OK, that is a little weird.

The Drive ≫ Head about 10 miles north on GA-515, where the foothills give rise to fully formed mountains, rolling prairies and historical towns ripe for antiquing.

❹ Cherry Log

Just up the road from Poole's, pork, ribs and chicken are served in a log cabin with a chimney pumping out smoky essence of pit BBQ. Democrats, such as devout customer Jimmy Carter, generally feel more at home in **Holloway's Pink Pig** (☎706-276-3311; www.budspinkpig.com; 824 Cherry Log St; sandwiches $5-6, plates $10-15; ⏰11am-9pm Thu-Sun; 🚻), a fun dining room with exposed beams decked out with colorful signs. In addition to BBQ, it does soul food like chicken and dumplings, chicken livers, cured ham, and fried green tomatoes, but the pit is the thing.

The Drive ≫ It's quite a pretty drive southeast down GA-136, via the lovable college town of Athens to the historical antiquing village of Lexington.

TRIP HIGHLIGHT

❺ Lexington

Lexington is a rather charming historical town, surrounded by Georgia pines and lovely rolling wooded hills. But you're here for the special Saturday-only feast at **Paul's** (☎706-338-5099; Hwy 78, Main St; mains $5-11; ⏰9am-2:30pm Sat & July 4; 🚻), which starts at 9:30am at his store front, just off the town square. The tradition started in 1929, and Jimmy Paul, a third-generation smoker, reckons he cooks 50lb to 60lb of barbecued pork on any given Saturday (about three hogs). The pulled pork is served on old-school checkered tablecloths. Don't even think about showing up after noon unless you want to eat nothing but baked beans and 'slaw.

The Drive ≫ The nearly three hour drive south down GA-80 and US 25 takes you through foothills from Lexington to Statesboro.

❻ Statesboro

A civil rights case was once fought over the integration of **Vandy's** (☎912-764-2444; 22 W Vine St; mains $8-14; ⏰6am-3pm Mon-Sat; 🚻), a Satesboro institution since the '30s. Simplicity wins here. Its chopped pork sandwich is served with a vinegar and mustard sauce on

The taste of Georgia Classic pulled pork sandwich

two slices of white bread baked next door. The hog is smoked overnight in a massive block-and-brick pit out back to beat the Georgia heat. Statesboro itself is charming and historical, with a jolt of contemporary life thanks to the nearby Georgia Southern University. You're far east at this point, so it's a good place to crash for the night.

🛏 p169

The Drive » From Statesboro stay on GA-26 east for about 55 miles and you'll wind up in Savannah, Georgia's most charming and beautiful city.

7 Savannah

There are few cities in America as glorious as Savannah, a southern charmer that blends the European architectural influence of New Orleans with the spreading oaks and hospitable smiles of Charleston. It's artsy, progressive, walkable (check it out on our walking tour, p136) and one of those cities you simply must visit at least once – which means you'll probably be back at least twice. Although food isn't generally Savannah's strong suit,

there is a transcendent hole in the wall tucked down a back alley, hidden away among her shady squares and elegant mansions. **Angel's BBQ** (www.angels-bbq.com; 21 West Oglethorpe Lane; sandwiches/ plates $6/8; ⏰11:30am-3pm Tue, to 6pm Wed-Sat) has a perpetually smoldering smoker that roasts beef brisket, chicken and pork – of course. As elsewhere across the state, the pulled pork is its specialty. It's moist and juicy, dazzled with its vinegary but not-too-sweet house sauce. It also has a Memphis sweet

DON'T MISS: WORMSLOE PLANTATION HISTORIC SITE

On the beautiful Isle of Hope, an island connected to Savannah proper by a low-slung causeway that spans the wetlands and is surrounded by intercostal waterways, the **Wormsloe Plantation Historic Site** (www.gastateparks.org; 7601 Skidaway Rd; adult/senior/youth 6-17yr/child 1-5yr $10/9/4.50/1; ⏰9am-5pm Tue-Sun) is one of the most photographed sites in Savannah, and with good reason. The dreamy entrance leads you past the iron gates and beneath a 1.5 mile road that is sheltered by ancient, mossy oaks that appear to be holding hands over the road. Also on-site are 4 miles of trails, an existing antebellum mansion, home to descendants of Noble Jones, and the last colonial ruins in Georgia, along with a colonial site where you can see folks demonstrate blacksmithing, and other long-gone trades. Jones arrived in Savannah with General James Oglethorpe, the city's founder in 1733.

sauce and a cayenne mustard worth trying. Get your meat on a sandwich or plate. It has Mexican coke here too.

📖 p169

The Drive ≫ From Savannah, the I-16 leads west back up into the foothills, where after 200 miles and three hours you'll find Jackson, and one of our favorite open pits in the state.

TRIP HIGHLIGHT

⑧ Jackson

Jackson is where you'll find **Fresh Air** (✆770-775-3182; 1164 Hwy 42; mains $6-7; ⏰8am-8pm Mon-Thu, to 9pm Fri & Sat, to 8:30pm Sun; ⊞),

the Holy Grail of Georgia BBQ, a glorious warm and friendly pioneer-style, wooden roadside shack. The outdoor seating area in front is covered in sawdust. Fresh Air only does three things: chopped pork, Brunswick stew and coleslaw. No ribs. No shoulder. The hams spend a full 24 hours in the smoker, which is the way it's been done since 1929. The result is transcendent, vinegary BBQ that is even better with a dash of that hot sauce. Congratulations, you have reached swine nirvana.

The Drive ≫ If you depart late afternoon, the drive from Jackson through Georgia's gentle foothills to the Atlanta area is rather glorious, what with the pale sun flickering through slender stands of feathery pines along I-75.

⑨ Marietta

This culinary odyssey ends in Marietta, just north of Atlanta, at **Sam's BBQ1** (✆770-977-3005; www.bbq1.net; 4944 Lower Roswell Rd; mains $5-13; ⏰11am-7:30pm Mon-Thu, to 8pm Fri & Sat, to 3pm Sun; ⊞), run by grill master Sam Huff, who makes pork so tender, sweet and satisfying he has been immortalized in song (and on the Food Network). He smokes pork, chicken, brisket, ribs, sausages and turkey. But like elsewhere, pork is king, and he has the awards to prove it. If you can't bear to leave the Georgia flavor behind as you head out of state, make sure you sign up for Huff's **Pork U** (as in university), a one-day open pit cooking intensive where you will learn how to roast a whole hog and craft a damn fine sauce, to boot. You've had the rest, now learn to make the best.

Eating & Sleeping

Atlanta ❶

🛏 Highland Inn　　　　　　Inn $$
(📞404-874-5756; www.thehighlandinn.com;
644 N Highland Ave; r from $81; 🅿 ❄ 📶)
Walking distance to Carter Center, rooms
aren't huge and that carpet is a bit threadbare,
but there is a good vibe here, it's as affordably
nice as Atlanta gets, and it's well located in the
desirable Virginia Highlands area.

🛏 Stonehurst Place　　　　B&B $$$
(📞404-881-0722; www.stonehurstplace.com;
923 Piedmont Ave NE; r $159-399; 🅿 ❄ @ 📶)
Built in 1896 by the Hinman family, this elegant,
almost Parisian B&B has all the modern
amenities one could ask for and is fully updated
with ecofriendly water treatment and heating
systems, and it has original Andy Warhol
illustrations on the wall! Smack in the middle
of Midtown, this is truly an exceptional place to
stay if you have the budget.

Statesboro ❻

🛏 Statesboro Inn　　　　　Inn $
(📞912-489-8628; www.statesboroinn.com;
106 S Main St; r $80-125; 🚹) The homey
and historical choice, walking distance from
Vandy's. An Allman Brothers song was said to
have been written here.

Savannah ❼

🛏 Mansion on Forsyth Park　　Hotel $$$
(📞912-238-5158; www.mansiononforsythpark.
com; 700 Drayton St; r weekend/weekday
$249/199; ❄ @ 📶 🏊) A choice location and
chic design highlight the luxe accommodations
on offer at the 18,000-sq-ft Mansion – the sexy
bathrooms alone are practically worth the
money. The best part of the hotel-spa is the
amazing local and international art that crowds
its walls and hallways, over 400 pieces in all.
Parking costs $20 per day.

Martin Luther King Jr Birthp...
See where a legendary leader was

Civil Rights Tour

14

Absorb the history of the American Civil Rights movement as you follow in the nonviolent footsteps of the legendary Dr Martin Luther King Jr from Atlanta to Memphis.

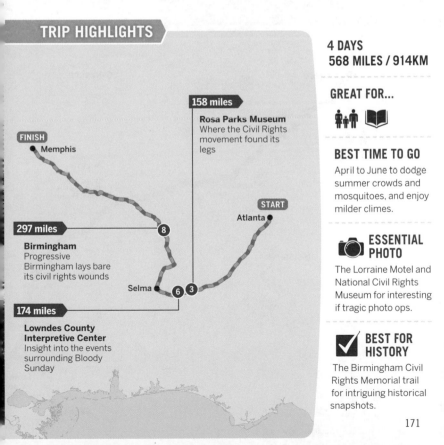

TRIP HIGHLIGHTS

158 miles

Rosa Parks Museum
Where the Civil Rights movement found its legs

FINISH
Memphis

297 miles — 8

Birmingham
Progressive Birmingham lays bare its civil rights wounds

Selma — 6 3

174 miles

Lowndes County Interpretive Center
Insight into the events surrounding Bloody Sunday

START
Atlanta

4 DAYS
568 MILES / 914KM

GREAT FOR...

BEST TIME TO GO
April to June to dodge summer crowds and mosquitoes, and enjoy milder climes.

ESSENTIAL PHOTO
The Lorraine Motel and National Civil Rights Museum for interesting if tragic photo ops.

BEST FOR HISTORY
The Birmingham Civil Rights Memorial trail for intriguing historical snapshots.

171

PEGAZ / ALAMY ©

14 Civil Rights Tour

To trace the solemn, sad, yet triumphant road of American civil rights activists is to explore the very worst and incomparable best of America. Martin Luther King Jr's journey from his Atlanta birth and biblical upbringing to his assassination in Memphis visits the stages of Montgomery, Selma and Birmingham and reveals within the human experience an infinite capacity to love, endure and cultivate strength and faith, no matter what.

❶ Atlanta

The story begins in Atlanta, where the **Sweet Auburn** neighborhood was already a bustling, affluent, middle-class beacon of African American advancement in the oppressive, segregated South when a preacher's son, Martin Luther King Jr, was born here on January 15, 1929. You can visit the **Martin Luther King Jr Birthplace** (www.nps .gov/malu; 501 Auburn Ave; admission free; ⊘ tours 10am, 11am, 2pm, 3pm, 4pm &

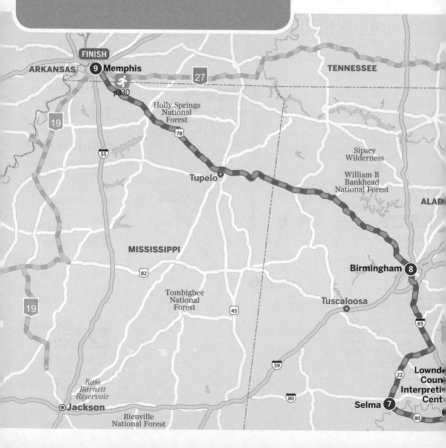

4:30pm) on a guided tour, one of several sights that form the **Martin Luther King Jr National Historic Site** (📞404-331-5190, 404-331-6922; www.nps.gov/malu/index.htm; 450 Auburn Ave; ⊙9am-5pm), Atlanta's civil rights nexus. First, get a powerful civil rights primer at the **Visitor Center** (📞912-944-0455; www.savannahvisit.com; 301 Martin Luther King Jr Blvd; ⊙8:30am-5pm Mon-Fri, 9am-5pm Sat & Sun), where dehumanizing segregation era laws are etched into glass. Across the street is

the **First Ebeneazor Baptist Church** (www.historicebenezer.org; 407 Auburn Ave NE; ⊙tours 9am-6pm Mon-Sat, 1:30-6pm Sun), where King's father led the congregation, and his mother directed the choir. Sit on a wooden pew and listen to Dr King's voice echo through the serene sanctuary of a 1963 time capsule. Nearby, King is entombed in the courtyard behind the nonprofit **King Center for Nonviolent Social Change** (www.thekingcenter.org; 449 Auburn Ave NE;

⊙9am-5pm, to 6pm summer), where there's a small gallery on the 2nd floor worth seeing.

⚒ 🛏 p179

The Drive ≫ It's a two hour drive south on I-85 across the state line and into Alabama.

② Tuskegee

Before the Civil Rights movement of the 1950s and 1960s, there were the **Tuskegee Airmen**. Also known as the Red Tails, these African American fighter pilots – America's first – shattered the glass ceiling and received their training at what is now the **Tuskegee Airmen National Historic Site** (📞334-724-0922; www.nps.gov/tuai/index.htm;

LINK YOUR TRIP

The Blues Highway
19 From Memphis, get on Hwy 66 and delve into the Mississippi Delta, where like a diamond from coal, Mississippi's institutionalized poverty, segregation and oppression birthed the blues and American popular music.

Memphis to Nashville
27 After getting a taste of the blues, head east to Nashville and enjoy some honky-tonk enlightenment.

RADIUS IMAGES / ALAMY ©

1616 Chappie James Rd;
admission free; 9am-
4:30pm;) in July 1941.
The first graduating
class had 13 cadets, but
eventually over 300
African American pilots
were trained here and
served overseas. Their
legacy is important
because African
American soldiers who
had served in Europe
enjoyed freedoms there
that they were denied at
home, and many began
to work diligently for
desegregation upon
returning to the South
after the war. Tuskegee
is also the home of
Booker T Washington's

Tuskegee Institute,
which was America's
first African American
teacher's college, as well
as a noted agricultural
institute. George
Washington Carver –
the famed agricultural
pioneer who developed
alternative crops to
cotton such as peanuts
and soy – taught and
published here for 47
years; there is a museum
(p159) dedicated to him.

The Drive >> Continue
southwest on I-85 for
another 45 minutes to reach
Montgomery, Alabama's capital
city.

TRIP HIGHLIGHT

3 Rosa Parks Museum

It was in Montgomery
where the Civil Rights
movement truly found
its footing in 1955 when
a secretary for the local
chapter of the National
Association for the
Advancement of Colored
People (NAACP), Rosa
Parks, refused to give
up her seat to a white
passenger on a city bus.
This iconic moment is
recreated at the **Rosa
Parks Museum** (www
.trojan.troy.edu/community/
rosa-parks-museum/; 251

Selma Edmund Pettus Bridge

Montgomery St; adult/child 4-12yr $7.50/5.50; ⊙9am-5pm Mon-Fri, 9am-3pm Sat; 🚹), located in the former spot of the Empire Theater, in front of which Parks took her defiant stand. Parks wasn't the first to engage in this sort of civil disobedience. In fact she was well trained in the discipline along with some of her NAACP colleagues at a retreat not long before her admirable defiance. Yet her actions and subsequent arrest became national news when they sparked the Montgomery Bus Boycott, led by an as yet unknown, 26-year-old preacher named Martin Luther King Jr.

The Drive ≫ You can just as easily walk the two blocks northeast on Montgomery to the traffic circle, and hang a right on Dexter Ave. Continue for five blocks.

---

❹ Dexter Avenue King Memorial Church

King had only recently presided over the **Dexter Avenue congregation** (☎334-263-3970; www.dexterkingmemorial.org; 454 Dexter Ave; adult/child 3-12yr $10/6; ⊙10am-4pm Tue-Fri, to 2pm Sat), when he was chosen to lead the boycott precisely because he was a relative unknown. He also happened to be a highly intelligent seminary graduate, with passionate views about the power of nonviolence and civil disobedience. Under his leadership, the boycott was unanimous and well organized. Overnight, African Americans abandoned the city buses and utilized a complex system of carpools to get to and from work. During that time, King's modest home, today the **Dexter Parsonage Museum**, was bombed, and King was arrested for the first time along with 88 others when local authorities attempted to outlaw the boycott. But the movement would not be deterred and on November 13, 1956 the Supreme Court ruled segregation of city buses unconstitutional. King had scored his first major victory, and the leadership behind this boycott would soon form the Southern Christian Leadership Council (SCLC), a major engine driving a movement that would grow in scope and power.

The Drive » Take Dexter Ave to Decatur St. Make a right, walk one block to Washington Ave, and make another right.

---

❺ Civil Rights Memorial Center

Closer to the Alabama Capitol steps is the **Civil Rights Memorial Center** (www.civilrightsmemorialcenter. org; 400 Washington Ave; adult/ child $2/free; ⏰9am-4:30pm Mon-Fri, 10am-4pm Sat). The memorial is a circular fountain designed by Maya Lin – who also designed the Vietnam Veterans Memorial – and a haunting remembrance of 40 martyrs of the movement, all activists or citizens murdered for their convictions, deeds

or simply their color. Some of the names like Emmet Till and Medgar Evers are relatively well known, others are much less heralded and their stories just as tragic. Inside the center are interactive displays that provide context for each victim. The museum is a project of the **Southern Poverty Law Center**, the legendary nonprofit credited with bankrupting the Ku Klux Klan after it was held responsible for a racially motivated murder in 1987.

The Drive » US 80 is a straight shot west into Alabama's old cotton country. You are now traveling one of the Civil Rights movement's darkest and most divisive roads, and it leads to Selma.

TRIP HIGHLIGHT

❻ Lowndes County Interperative Center

The **Selma to Montgomery National Historic Trail** (www .nps.gov/semo; US 80) commemorates the 1965 Voting Rights March, one of the most violent and contentious of Alabama's civil rights confrontations. During voting rights activities in nearby Dallas County, a young activist, Jimmie Lee Jackson, was shot and killed at point-blank range while attempting to shelter his mother from police batons during a peaceful

march. In his memory, the Dallas County Voting Rights League decided to walk from Selma to Montgomery to highlight police brutality, and invited King and the SCLC to join them. But another violent police crackdown in Selma halted the march. A second attempt was made, but King turned the marchers back fearing for their safety. Finally, the march succeeded on its third attempt. Halfway between Montgomery and Selma, the **Lowndes County Interpretive Center** (www.nps.gov/ semo; 7002 US 80; ⏰9am-4:30pm) is a wonderfully done museum, where a 25-minute documentary delves into the march in detail. This site was also integral to the next phase of the movement. The seeds of Black Power were sown here after the march was over.

The Drive » Stay on US 80 east into Selma.

---

❼ Selma

On March 7, 1965, aka 'Bloody Sunday,' Alabama State troopers and recently deputized local white men attacked 500 peaceful marchers on the **Edmund Pettus Bridge** (Broad St & Walter Ave) with clubs and tear gas. The whole thing was captured on video, marking one of the

LOWNDES COUNTY & BLACK POWER

The march from Selma to Montgomery was a watershed moment in the Civil Rights movement. As well as the violence that turned stomachs around the world, it also sparked a rupture between the Student Nonviolent Coordinating Committee (SNCC) and Martin Luther King's Southern Christian Leadership Conference (SCLC).

SNCC was first on the ground in Selma, and was supporting the Dallas County Voting Rights League when Jimmie Lee Jackson was shot and killed. It invited the SCLC to join them because King's stature allowed them to raise money and receive maximum media attention. Yet some younger SNCC activists, including Stokley Carmichael who would go on to be a founding member of the Black Panther Party, bristled at what they saw as a takeover of their organizing work, and were especially peeved when King turned the marchers around during their second attempt to cross the Edmund Pettus Bridge. When they eventually passed through Lowndes County on their way to Montgomery, Carmichael promised local folks that SNCC would be back. He kept his promise, and their ensuing voter registration drive saw the number of Lowndes County blacks registered to vote increase from 70 to 2600 – 300 more than white registered voters. The new party, the Lowndes County Freedom Organization, was the first to employ a black panther as its logo.

The success of Carmichael's registration drive had a ripple effect. Locally, about 40 share-cropping families were evicted from their land by their white landlords after the ensuing election. So they set up a tented camp and lived on what is now home to the Lowndes County Interpretive Center. On a national level, within a year, the existing SNCC leadership – closely allied with Dr King – was ousted in favor of Carmichael, who made more waves when he delivered his first 'Black Power' speech in Greenwood, Mississippi in 1966.

first times Americans outside the South had witnessed the horrifying images of the struggle. Shock and outrage was widespread, and support for the movement grew. Eventually President Lyndon Johnson ordered the Alabama National Guard to protect what became over 8000 marchers (Joan Baez famously walked among them) who poured in from across the country to walk the 54 miles in four days, beginning on March 16

and culminating with a classic King speech on the capitol steps. The **National Voting Rights Museum** (☎334-327-8218; www.nvrm.org; 1012 Water Ave; adult/senior & student $6/4; ☺10am-4pm Mon-Thu & by appointment) is near the base of the bridge. The bulk of the organizing took place at the striking brick-red Victorian church, **Brown Chapel** (410 Martin Luther King St).

The Drive ⟫ From Selma, head east on AL-22, skirt the pine dappled lake at Paul M Grist State Park, then veer

north on AL-191 before merging with US 31 and I-65 north into Birmingham.

- - - - - - - - - -

TRIP HIGHLIGHT

❽ Birmingham

Progressive Birmingham was not always so inviting. When Bull Conner was the sheriff, civil rights activists, led by Dr King, embarked on a desegregation campaign downtown. Their strategy was to flood the city jails with students, many of them high school students who became known as 'foot soldiers' within the movement. After weeks of restraint, police set attack dogs upon the kids and firemen blasted them with water canons in **Kelly Ingram Park** (1600 5th Ave N), and on the city streets. The campaign also gave us King's famed 'Letter from Birmingham Jail'. All this history is on display at the superb **Birmingham Civil Rights Institute** (www.bcri.org; 520 16th St N; adult/senior/child $12/5/3, Sun free; ☉10am-5pm Tue-Sat, 1-5pm Sun). The seven-block **Birmingham Civil Rights Memorial Trail** (www.bcri.org; 520 16th St N), installed in 2013 for the 50th anniversary of the campaign, depicts 22 moving scenes with statues and photography.

It begins at the BCRI. The saddest and most enduring memory of the campaign remains the murder of four little girls when the **16th Street Baptist Church** (www.16thstreetbaptist.org; cnr 16th St & 6th Ave N; donation $5; ☉ministry tours 10am-4pm Tue-Fri, 10am-1pm Sat) was bombed by the Klan during Sunday School.

✗ ⌂ p179

The Drive ≫ From Birmingham take the US 78 west for 219 miles through the Holly Springs National Forest and merge onto I-240, which snakes into Memphis.

- - - - - - - - - - - - -

❾ Memphis

It was here that King's crusade was abruptly halted in April 1968, when he visited in support of the black sanitation workers' strike. The visit was tense, and King's entourage noticed he was more nervous than usual. On April 4, while standing on the balcony of room 306 at the Lorraine Motel, James Earl Ray shot him in the neck and face. King collapsed, one foot hanging off the railing, and died. Both the Lorraine Motel and the boarding house from where the shot was allegedly fired are part of the National Civil Rights Museum (p330); see our walking tour (p330).

✗ ⌂ p179

Eating & Sleeping

Atlanta ❶

✖ Daddy Dz   Barbecue $$

(📞404-222-0206; www.daddydz.com; 264 Memorial Dr; sandwiches $6-12, plates $13-20; **P**) This juke joint of a BBQ shack, consistently voted tops in town, is smack in downtown Atlanta, and has soul to spare, from the graffiti murals on the red, white and blue exterior to the all-powerful smoky essence and the reclaimed booths on the covered patio. Order the succulent ribs or a pulled pork plate. You'll leave smiling.

🛏 Hotel Artmore   Boutique Hotel $$

(📞404-876-6100; www.artmorehotel.com; 1302 W Peachtree St; r $134-274; **❄ @ 🛜**) This fun art-deco gem in Midtown combines excellent service with sizeable rooms and suites and a superb location across the street from Arts Center MARTA station. The 1924 Spanish-Mediterranean architectural landmark was completely revamped in 2009, resulting in a satisfying boutique hotel that's become an urban sanctuary for those who appreciate their trendiness with a dollop of discretion. Parking is $18.

Montgomery

✖ Farmer's Market Cafe   Southern $

(www.farmersmarketcafe.net/; 315 N McDonough St; meals $6.75-8.75; ⏰5:30am-2pm Mon-Fri) This oversized downtown cafeteria serves up God-fearing Southern home cooking at recession-friendly prices according to the meat/veggie combo of your choice. Don't skip the grits casserole.

Birmingham ❽

✖ Bottega   Italian $$$

(📞205-939-1000; www.bottegarestaurant. com; 2240 Highland Ave S; lunch mains $13-19, dinner $25-42; **P**) Enjoy a spot of Birmingham posh at this fine Italian bistro in the Highlands. It impresses with creative pizzas like fried oyster and pancetta or the Persian piadine with watercress, mint, dill, walnuts and radish. It also does a nice pasta with pork meatballs and a popular hangar steak, not to mention a pan-roasted venison.

🛏 Redmont Hotel   Historical Hotel $$

(📞205-324-2101; 2101 5th Ave N; r/ste from $89/129; **❄ @ 🛜**) A historical hotel built in 1925, the piano and chandelier in the lobby lend a certain old-world feel throughout and all deluxe rooms have been renovated, giving it a modern edge. The spacious rooftop bar doesn't hurt, either. It's walking distance to the civil rights sights.

Memphis ❾

✖ Cozy Corner   Barbecue $$

See Trip 🔢 (p275).

🛏 Talbot Heirs   Guesthouse $$

See Trip 🔢 (p316).

Amicalola Falls State Park Tum
cascades and hiking an

Classic Trip

Appalachian Trail

15

Georgia, Tennessee and North Carolina each claim a section of the 2175-mile Maine-to-Georgia trail. On this journey you'll get a taste of the trail and the charming towns alongside it.

TRIP HIGHLIGHTS

3 miles

Springer Mountain
Here it begins

301 miles

Carvers Gap
A panoramic 10-mile stretch of the AT

Laurel Fork **FINISH**
Gorge & Falls

11

Max Patch **8**
Mountain

Great Smoky
Mountains
National Park

5

Hot Springs
Submerge into the welcome heat on the riverside

242 miles

2

START
hicalola Falls   Dahlonega
State Park

138 miles

Nantahala Outdoor Center
Paddle class III rapids

5–7 DAYS
343 MILES / 552KM

GREAT FOR...

BEST TIME TO GO

April to October, when the AT is open for long-distance and day hikers.

ESSENTIAL PHOTO

Max Patch Mountain for signature views of the lower part of the AT.

BEST FOR OUTDOORS

The AT – the original long-haul trail and a mecca for outdoors enthusiasts.

181

Classic Trip

15 Appalachian Trail

Originally the idea of one man, Benton MacKaye, as an antidote to the busy, urban lifestyle of the East Coast in the 1920s, the Appalachian Trail (known as the AT) was completed in 1937. The entire route is marked by a series of 2in x 6in white blazes, and is for foot traffic only. Our trip will allow you to experience the trail with a minimum of sufferance.

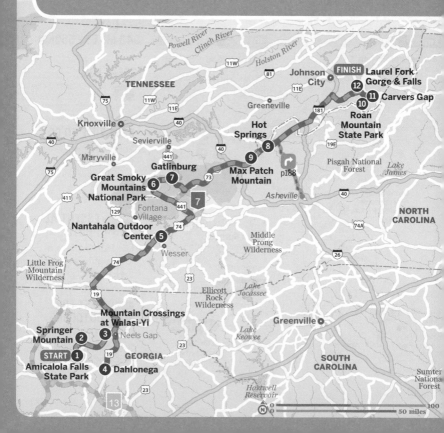

❶ Amicalola Falls State Park

There is no better way to get a feel for the grandeur of the Appalachian Trail than at its Georgian gateway, Amicalola Falls State Park. Amicalola, a Cherokee Indian word meaning 'tumbling waters,' is an appropriate name for these 729ft falls – the tallest cascade east of the Mississippi River. The park offers more than 12 miles of hiking trails, including the 8.5 mile **Approach Trail**, past the falls to Springer Mountain, where the Appalachian Trail officially begins.

Get set up with maps and local hiking tips at the **Amicalola Falls State Park Visitors**

LINK YOUR TRIP

7 The Great Smokies

If you want still more mountain madness, further explore the glory of the Smoky Mountains.

13 Hogs & Heifers: A Georgia BBQ Odyssey

Take a detour from Dhalonega and explore the soulful, smokey sustenance that is Georgia barbecue.

Center (☎706-265-4703; www.gastateparks.org/info/amicalola; 418 Amicalola Falls State Park Rd, Dawsonville, GA; ⏱7am-10pm), which also offers exhibits and a gift shop.

🛏 p189

The Drive ≫ Thru-hikers can trek here from Amicalola Falls State Park, but if the 604-step staircase freaks you out, take GA-52E to Winding Stair Gap Rd, and you'll find some nice views of Springer Mountain.

TRIP HIGHLIGHT

❷ Springer Mountain

The Appalachian Trail officially starts on top of this mountain, marked with a plaque: 'A footpath for those who seek fellowship with the wilderness.'

Most thru-hikers (or '2000 milers,' as those who walk the Appalachian Trail in a single journey are known) usually start here, at the Georgia terminus (about two hours north of Atlanta), in the late spring, and finish five to seven months later on Mt Katahdin in Maine, 2175 miles to the north. About 400 to 600 registered hikers complete the journey each year, about a quarter of those who set out. Altogether, only a little over 10,000 brave and hearty trekkers have ever completed the journey. A few of those

thru-hike the entire route in one go, but many hike the trail in sections – a few months, or weeks, at a time.

The Drive ≫ Thirty miles north of Springer Mountain by foot is your first stop in civilization, but if you're on wheels, it's 65 miles by car down graded roads. Take Service Road 42, make a right on GA-60 and a left on GA-19. Always check road conditions before starting off. Sometimes roads are closed or impassable due to weather.

---

❸ Mountain Crossings at Walasi-Yi

Mountain Crossings at Walasi-Yi (☎888-MT-XINGS; www.mountaincrossings.com; 9710 Gainesville Hwy, Blairsville, GA; hostel per person per night $15; ⏱9am-5pm Mon-Thu, to 6pm Fri-Sun) is the one and only man-made intrusion on the trail. Of course, parched and sore hikers will be happy it isn't a mirage, as they follow the AT directly through the store, which has served as an outfitter to AT hikers since it was completed by the New Deal's Civilian Conservation Corps in 1937. There are hostel beds for those who'd like to do the first part of the trail and then hike (or hitchhike) back to Springer Mountain. And if you're a thru-hiker and already blown through gear or forgot something vital, they'll have it here.

Classic Trip

The Drive » Take US 19 from Mountain Crossings to Dahlonega.

---

④ Dahlonega

In the 1820s the Dahlonega area was the site of the country's first gold rush. Its story is told inside the oldest courthouse in Georgia, built in 1836, and home of the Dahlonega Courthouse Gold Museum (p158). But the new boom can be seen in the thousands of acres of vineyards that lace the surrounding mountainsides.
Naturally Georgia (www.naturallygeorgia.com; 90 Public Sq North; ⏱noon-5pm Mon-Thu, to 8pm Fri-Sun), on the courthouse square, is a combined tasting room and art gallery where they pour surprisingly good dry whites and Portuguese reds from Tiger Mountain (you can find them in Whole Foods) and Crane Creek (a vintner who only sells locally). Or you could simply head to one of 10

nearby vineyards for a tasting. Frogtown Cellars (p158) is a beautiful winery and has a killer deck on which to sip libations and nibble cheese.

Nearby **Three Sisters** (☏706-865-9463; www .threesistersvineyards.com; tastings $15; ⏱1-5pm Thu-Sun) is as unpretentious as it is quirky, where fine wine is paired with bluegrass, overalls and Cheetos.

✕ 🛏 p189

The Drive » It's yet another gorgeous drive up GA-19 through Vogel State Park and the Blue Ridge Mountains into North Carolina. Hang a right on US 74 to Bryson City.

`TRIP HIGHLIGHT`

⑤ Nantahala Outdoor Center

Go wild at your next stop, the **Nantahala Outdoor Center** (NOC; ☏828-488-2176, 888-905-7238; www.noc .com; 13077 Hwy 19/74; kayak/canoe rental per day $30/50, guided trips $30-189), where the Appalachian Trail and Nantahala River meet. Nestled in a steep gorge, the river offers 8 miles of easy class II rapids before splashing through exciting class III whitewater at **Nantahala**

Falls. (For more on the NOC, see p103.) The AT cuts through the parking lot beside the outdoor store then crosses the river on the pedestrian bridge. From the NOC it's a 4-mile (strenuous!) hike to **Jump Up**, a rocky outcrop boasting outstanding views, or a 6.5-mile hike to the top of **Wesser Bald** (4627ft) and the former fire tower, now an observation deck, offering panoramic views of the Great Smoky Mountains. Hiking north, it's a longer, more strenuous hike (8.1 miles) to the summit of **Cheoah Bald** (5062ft), which offers splendid panoramas of the Southern Appalachians. There are AT sleeping shelters all along the trails for overnight hikers.

The Drive » It's a lovely 65 miles up US 74E to US 441N into Tennessee and the Great Smoky Mountains National Park.

---

⑥ Great Smoky Mountains National Park

This 815-sq-mile park is America's most visited but studies have shown that 95% of visitors never venture further than 100 yards from their cars, so it's easy to leave the teeming masses behind. In total there are 842 miles of trails in the Great Smoky Mountains National

---

WARNING

Always check road conditions before starting off. Sometimes roads are closed or impassable due to weather, especially in the winter and spring.

Park, including 73 miles of the Appalachian Trail which acts as a natural border between North Carolina and Tennessee. **Clingmans Dome** (6643ft) is almost dead center in the park, and is its highest point. The easiest way to get here is to take US 441 to Clingmans Dome Rd – a 7-mile spur road that ends in a paved parking lot. From there it's a mere half-mile walk to the peak. The **Sugarlands Visitor Center** (www.nps.gov/grsm; Hwy 441; ⏲6am-7pm summer, hours vary off-season) is a great resource for travellers. You can get backcountry permits ($4 per night) and reserve your camp site here. It has loads of maps and advice, and behind the visitor center is a mile-long nature trail to the modest but lovely Cataract Falls.

TOP TIP: CLINGMANS DOME

Although it may be tempting to take the lazy man's alternative (ie drive), it is much sweeter to sweat your way to the summit. Especially since you'll be hiking a 7.7-mile slice of the Appalachian Trail, which begins in Newfound Gap. Sure, it parallels the road in sections, but don't let that dissuade you, and if you'd rather not walk down the mountain, you can easily hitch a ride back.

The Drive » It's just 3 quick miles down US 441 from the Sugarlands Visitor Center to downtown Gatlinburg.

7 Gatlinburg

Wildly kitschy Gatlinburg hunkers at the entrance of the Great Smoky Mountains National Park, waiting to stun hikers with the scent of fudge and cotton candy. Tourists flock here to ride the gondola, shop for Confederate-flag undershorts, get married at the many wedding chapels and play hillbilly mini-golf. Love it or hate it, the entire village is a gin-u-wine American roadside attraction. The best activity here is the **Ober Gatlinburg Aerial Tramway** (www.obergatlinburg.com; 1001 Parkway; adult/child $11/8.50; ⏲7:30am-6:20pm Sun, to 10:40pm Mon, Fri & Sat, 9:30am-9:49pm Tue-Thu). A ski or snow tube area in the winter and an alpine slide in the summer time, families love the ride to the lodge at the top of the mountain in the glassed-in gondola, and enjoy coming down even more. **Ole Smoky Moonshine Holler** (☎865-436-6995; www.olesmokymoonshine.com; 903 Parkway; ⏲10am-10pm) is a stone-and-wood moonshine distillery where you may peer over oak barrels and copper boilers then taste that fiery hooch. Don't bother with the flavored varietals. It's all about the White Lightening.

✕ 🛏 p189

The Drive » Take TN-73 east to the TN-32 into Newport where you'll turn onto the US 70 east into the Cherokee National Forest and back over the North Carolina state line.

TRIP HIGHLIGHT

8 Hot Springs

Hot Springs is known for its steaming, frothing mineral water upwelling from the earth to heal you. **Hot Springs Spa & Mineral Baths** (☎828-622-7676; www.nchotsprings.com; 315 Bridge St; mineral hot tubs $15-45, massage $50-100; ⏲noon-10pm Mon-Thu, 10am-midnight Fri-Sun) has 17 outdoor riverfront hot tubs fed by natural springs that range from 100°F to 104°F, plus massage rooms and a pre- or post-massage fire pit for relaxing. Want to hit the river? **Huck Finn Rafting** (☎877-520-4658; www.huckfinnrafting.com; 158 Bridge St; trips adult/child from $35/25; ⏲8.30am-6pm) will set you up. Take a 5-mile guided trip down the French Broad River on class IIs and IIIs,

IAN DAGNALL / ALAMY ©

PAT & CHUCK BLACKLEY / ALAMY ©

LOCAL VOICE
ANDREW DOWNS, APPALACHIAN TRAIL CONSERVANCY

The Appalachian Trail is maintained by volunteers, and more than 6000 people work to protect it each year. Volunteers meet at a base camp ready for adventure and the ATC provides the food, tools, safety equipment and leadership necessary for crews to get the job done. Want to meet some great folks, live on the AT for a week and paint a blaze? Join the Konnarock, Rocky Top or Mid-Atlantic crews and bust some trail! Check it out at www.appalachiantrail.org/crews.

Top: Main Square, Dahlonega
Left: View From Grassy Ridge, Roan Mountain State Park
Right: White-tailed deer buck, Great Smoky Mountains National Park

or brave a 9-mile trip with class IVs. To float at your own pace, hop into a kayak (adult/child $35/30) or inner tube ($15).

✕ ⌂ p189

The Drive » It's a brilliant 45-minute mountain drive from the springs to a bald peak. Take NC-209 south for about 7 miles from Hot Springs, turning west on NC-1175 for 5.3 miles then turn onto Max Patch Rd (NC-1182). The parking area at the foot of the bald is 3 miles down Max Patch Rd.

❾ Max Patch Mountain

While there is pleasant hiking both north and south, the 1.6-mile round trip hike, accessed from a trailhead on Max Patch Rd, offers the best pay off for the least amount of sweat. The **Short Loop Trail** winds up the Appalachian Trail's southernmost bald, Max Patch Mountain. From atop the grassy summit there are panoramic views of the Blacks, Balds, Balsams and the Great Smoky Mountains, of course. On a clear day you can even see the highest point in the eastern US – **Mount Mitchell** (6684ft). Add another mile, pick up the peak, and enjoy even more scenic beauty on the **Long Loop Trail**.

The Drive » Hop over the border to Tennessee, then continue another 50 miles on

Classic Trip

TN-352 and I-26. Take exit 32 to reach Roan Mountain State Park.

- - - - - - - - - - - -

⑩ Roan Mountain State Park

This **park** (☎800-250-8620; www.state.tn.us/environment/parks/roanmtn/; 1015 Hwy-143, Roan Mountain; ⊗8am-4:30pm) encompasses 2006 acres of southern Appalachian forest at the base of 6285ft Roan Mountain. On the top of Roan Mountain, straddling the Tennessee–North Carolina border, are the ruins of the old **Cloudland Hotel** site. The 300-room hotel was built in 1885 by Civil War General John T Wilder. Legend has it that North Carolinian sheriffs would hang out in the saloon, waiting for drinkers

from the Tennessee side to stray across the line, as North Carolina was a dry state back then. There's also a great 4.6-mile round-trip hike to **Little Rock Knob** (4918 ft) through hardwood forests, with epic clifftop views into Tennessee.

🛏 p189

The Drive » Just 8 miles past Roan Mountain State Park on NC-143 you'll reach Carvers Gap.

- - - - - - - - - - - -

TRIP HIGHLIGHT

⑪ Carvers Gap

Carvers Gap is where a set of log steps leads to a section of the Appalachian Trail which crosses a 10-mile series of so-called grassy balds – treeless mountains with unobstructed views over Tennessee's Blue Ridge Mountains. Theories for their evolution include everything from extensive grazing to their creation by aliens. Uh huh. To the south, the AT climbs to the high point

of the Roan Mountain ridge, the 6285ft **Roan High Knob**.

The Drive » It's just a 27 mile drive through the Cherokee National Forest between trailheads. Take NC-143 north and turn left on TN-37 north.

- - - - - - - - - - - -

⑫ Laurel Fork Gorge & Falls

Two moderately taxing hikes lead to Laurel Fork Gorge & Falls. The vertical walls of the gorge rise 100ft on either side of the AT, the only trail through the gorge. You can access it, and the 40ft falls, on one of two feeder trails. The first is a 5-mile round trip, and the other, a 2.6-mile round trip. To hike the former, access the blue-blazed **Hampton Blueline Trail** where I-321 crosses Laurel Fork in Hampton, TN (there's a parking lot for hikers here). The shorter hike can be reached by taking TN-67 from Hampton to Braemar, where you can pick up USFS 50 (Dennis Cove Rd) for the 3 miles to the parking area on the left. Both hikes use the Appalachian Trail and with the exception of the steep and quite rocky descent to the falls – which can be treacherous – it's quite flat and easy.

↱ **DETOUR: ASHEVILLE**

Start: ⑧ **Hot Springs**

With its homegrown microbreweries, decadent chocolate shops and stylish New Southern eateries, Asheville is one of the trendiest small cities in the east. Glossy magazines swoon for the place, but don't be put off by the hipsters and the flash. At heart, Asheville is still an overgrown mountain town, an oasis for hikers, musicians and artists, and more than a few hard-core hippies.

Eating & Sleeping

Amicalola Falls State Park ❶

🛏 Amicalola Falls Lodge — Lodge

(📞706-265-8888; www.amicalolafalls.com; 418 Amicalola Falls State Park Rd, Dawsonville, GA; campsites $50, r & cottages $54-249) The lodge is a full-service hotel with beautiful views from every room, while the rustic cottages sleep four to 10. You can eat buffet-style at its **Maple Restaurant**.

🛏 Len Foote Hike Inn — Lodge

(📞800-581-8032; www.hike-inn.com; 240 Amicalola Falls State Park Rd, Dawsonville, GA; r $97-140; ⊘year-round) You will be far, far from the rat race at this hike-in-only lodge, 5 miles from the nearest road. You'll need to carry in everything, haul out your own trash and reserve in advance. It serves three meals a day.

Dahlonega ❹

✗ Back Porch Oyster Bar — Seafood $$

(📞706-864-8623; www.facebook.com/ BackPorchOysterBar; 19 North Chestatee St; mains $9-30; ⊘11:30am-8pm) Oysters, ahi and clams are among the bounty flown in fresh daily to be shucked, seared and steamed at this neighborhood fish house. Everything about it is homey and inviting, and the food delivers.

🛏 Hiker Hostel — Hostel $

(📞770-312-7342; www.hikerhostel.com; 7693 Hwy 19N; dm/r $18/42; 🅿 ❄ @ 🛜) This converted log cabin is owned by a couple of avid cycling and outdoors enthusiasts. Each bunk room has its own bath and is wonderfully neat and clean. It even has espresso.

Gatlinburg ❼

✗ Wild Boar Saloon & Howard's Steakhouse — Steaks $$

See Trip 🔟 (p111).

🛏 Bearskin Lodge — Lodge $$

See Trip 🔟 (p111).

Hot Springs ❽

✗ Smoky Mountain Diner — Diner $

(📞828-622-7571; www.mokymountaindiner hotsprings.com; 70 Lance Ave, Hot Springs, NC; mains $5-13; ⊘6am-8pm Mon-Sat, to 4pm Sun) Located directly on the Appalachian Trail running through town, fuel up for a day of hiking with one of the giant egg dishes. Re-energize with burgers, meatloaf or fried chicken when you return. Save room for pie.

🛏 Mountain Magnolia Inn — Inn $$

(📞828-622-3543; www.mountainmagnoliainn. com; 204 Lawson St; r incl breakfast $100-230, ste $175-185) Built in 1868, and featured in *This Old House*, HGTV and *Southern Living*, this upscale inn gives guests an opportunity to enjoy the health-giving properties of the springs, while its restaurant completes the experience with pricey organic fare. Some rooms are in buildings off-site.

Roan Mountain State Park ❿

🛏 Roan Mountain State Park Lodge — Lodge $

(📞800-250-8620; www.state.tn.us/ environment/parks/RoanMtn/; 1015 Hwy 143, Roan Mountain; campsites $11-20, r from $67, cabins $80-120; ⊘year-round, tent camping Apr-Nov) Book a camp site or cabin amid one of the trail's most beautiful locations.

STRETCH YOUR LEGS
SAVANNAH

Start/Finish: Sentient Bean, Forsyth Park

Distance: 3.3 miles

Duration: Three hours

Savannah is a living museum of Southern architecture and antebellum charm. Gorgeous and full of Old South charisma, its historical heart is freckled with pleasant squares shaded by spreading oaks dripping with Spanish moss. This town was made for walking.

Take this walk on Trips

11 13

Sentient Bean

Savannah is a coffee-loving town, and there's no better place to start your morning than **Sentient Bean** (www.sentientbean.com; 13 E Park Ave; ☉7am-10pm; 🛜), a fabulous bohemian cafe with terrific coffee, gourmet scones, a hipster clientele and baristas with attitude (the good kind). Plus, it's just across the street from Forsyth Park.

The Walk » Step across the street and stroll through Savannah's most central, and most beautiful, park.

Forsyth Park

Gushing with fountains, draped with mossy oaks, unfurled with vast lawns and basketball and tennis courts, this is one dynamite city park. The Visitor Center has a number of brochures and maps that delve into local architecture and history and is worth stopping by. You also might consider staying the night at the hip and swanky Mansion on Forsyth Park (p169).

The Walk » From the north end of the park continue straight to elegant Monterey Sq, your first of many such rectangular oases of charm.

Mercer-Williams House

The location of an infamous homicide, the **Mercer-Williams House** (www.mercerhouse.com; 429 Bull St; adult/child $12.50/8) was bought and restored by eccentric art dealer Jim Williams in 1969. Inside you'll find the room in which Danny Hansford was murdered in 1981. That story is at the heart of *Midnight in the Garden of Good and Evil*, the book and subsequent film that put Savannah on the map.

The Walk » From Monterey Sq, take Bull St north for four blocks, past a row of historical homes to E Charlton St on Madison Sq.

Shop SCAD

Creative impulses charge through Savannah's veins, thanks in large part to the Savannah College of Art & Design (SCAD). SCAD students are legion, its

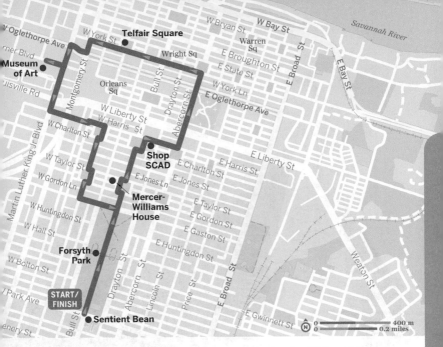

graduates often settling in town to paint or open flower shops, textile depots or design businesses. All the wares – throw pillows, art books, jewelry and T-shirts – on sale at **ShopSCAD** (www.shopscadonline. com; 340 Bull St; ☺9am-5:30pm Mon-Wed, to 8pm Thu-Fri, 10am-8pm Sat, noon-5pm Sun) were imagined by SCAD students, alumni or faculty.

The Walk » Make a right on Harris St and meander through Laffayette Sq (one of our favorites) then make a left on Abercorn St and another on York St.

Telfair Square

Two of Savannah's most popular museums are set around this leafy residential plaza. The **Telfair Academy of Arts & Sciences** (www.telfair.org; 121 Barnard St; adult/child $12/5; ☺noon-5pm Mon, 10am-5pm Tue-Sat, 1-5pm Sun) is filled with 19th-century American art and silver, and a smattering of European pieces. Nearby, **Jepson Center for the Arts** (JCA; www.telfair.org; 207 W York St; adult/child $12/5; ☺10am-5pm Mon, Wed, Fri & Sat, 10am-8pm Thu, noon-5pm Sun; [⬇]) has 20th- and 21st-century art.

The Walk » Take York St west to Montgomery, head south to Oglethorpe and west again. Cross Martin Luther King Jr Blvd, one of town's major streets, and walk two long blocks to Turner Blvd.

SCAD Museum of Art

More than the sum of its parts, the **SCAD Museum of Art** (www.scadmoa .org; 601 Turner Blvd; adult/child under 14yr $10/free; ☺10am-5pm Tue, Wed & Fri, to 8pm Thu, noon-5pm Sat & Sun) is a new brick, steel, concrete and glass longhouse carved with groovy sitting areas inside and out, and filled with fun rotating exhibitions – like an installation of video screens strobing various karaoke interpretations of Madonna's *Lucky Star*. It has intriguing mixed-media pieces and an inviting cafe.

The Walk » Your mile-and-a-quarter walk back to the start follows MLK to Harris St. Make a left to Barnard, and head south, through Pulaski and Chatham Sqs. Make a left on Gaston to enter Forsyth Park.

Mississippi, Louisiana & Arkansas

VENTURE INTO THESE THREE DISTINCT, ALLURING STATES and you may just fall in love. Arkansas flaunts granite bluffs, scenic rivers, quirky mountain towns and narrow trails that lead to the edge of heaven. In sultry Mississippi, juke joints hum until the wee hours, historical Oxford is the kind of fun-yet-refined college town that reels you in, and the Natchez Trace Parkway is the most beautiful highway in the South. Then let Louisiana satiate you with the naughty flavor, period architecture and addictive soundtrack of New Orleans. Outside Crescent City, explore a fertile maze of plantations, misty bayous and swamps, and tasty Cajun towns. The complex, tortured, musical, joyful Southern soul is laid bare here, and you'll leave inspired.

Natchez Trace Parkway French Camp Museum (Trip 16)
DANITA DELIMONT / GETTY IMAGES ©

193

Mississippi, Louisiana & Arkansas

Buffalo River View from Steel Creek overlook (Trip 22)

Classic Trip

16 **Natchez Trace Parkway 3 days**
The journey south from Nashville stuns with natural beauty and American history.

17 **Southern Gothic Tour 7 days**
Trace the backstories of the South's most revered literary legends.

18 **Historical Mississippi 3 days**
Mississippi's complex history is on display from Oxford to Vicksburg to Natchez.

Classic Trip

19 **The Blues Highway 3 days**
A soulful ramble to the root of American popular music.

20 **Cajun Country 4 days**
Explore bayous, dance halls, crawfish boils and folk ways in Louisiana's idiosyncratic Acadiana region.

21 **Gulf Coast 4 days**
Glimpse the Gulf from Louisiana wetlands, Mississippi beaches, and industrial Alabama ports.

22 **Backroads Arkansas 4 days**
Hike, paddle, zip and drive through Arkansas' soul-stirring countryside.

✔ **DON'T MISS**

French Quarter
Wrought-iron balconies, brick-covered ivy, and Creole, Spanish and Caribbean architecture: the timeless French Quarter is an adult Disneyland. Explore it on Trips **18** **22** **27**

Rowan Oak
William Faulkner spent years on this peaceful Oxford estate, and to see his home is to glimpse his soul. See it on Trips **18** **19**

Clarksdale
The hub of the Delta has the Crossroads, a spectacular juke joint and comfortable digs from which to explore the blues. Visit it on Trips **19** **20** **27**

Natchez
This laid-back river town is an antebellum time capsule, and a charming respite for a few days of strolling and contemplation. See it on Trips **17** **19** **27**

Buffalo River
Scenic and protected, the crystaline Buffalo wends between majestic bluffs. Paddle the river on Trip **22**

195

Natchez Trace Parkway *Stirring history and natural beauty*

Classic Trip

Natchez Trace Parkway

16

With emerald mounds, opulent mansions and layers of history, the Natchez Trace Parkway winds 444 gorgeously wooded miles from Nashville all the way to southern Mississippi.

TRIP HIGHLIGHTS

START
Nashville ●
● Franklin

0 miles

6

Tishomingo State Park
Stunning nature, indigenous history

9

178 miles

Tupelo
A little Elvis always livens things up

1 miles

11

Jeff Busby Park
One of the best views on the parkway

● Jackson

433 miles

14
Natchez ●
FINISH

Emerald Mound
An ideal stop for a shot of peaceful contemplation

3 DAYS
444 MILES / 714KM

GREAT FOR...

📖

BEST TIME TO GO
September to November and April to June to dodge the sweltering heat.

📷 ESSENTIAL PHOTO
Emerald Mound for magical sunset views.

✓ BEST FOR HISTORY
The whole route for glimpses of indigenous ways, echoes of a pioneering past, and the birthplace of Elvis.

197

16 Natchez Trace Parkway

America grew from infancy to childhood then adolescence in the late 18th and 19th centuries. That's when settlers explored and expanded, traded and clashed with Native Americans, and eventually confronted their own shadows during the Civil War. Evidence of this drama can be found along the Natchez Trace, but before you begin, hit the honky-tonks and enjoy a little night music.

❶ Nashville

Although this leafy, sprawling southern city – with its thriving economy and hospitable locals – has no scarcity of charms, it really is all about the music. Boot-stomping honky-tonks lure aspiring stars from across the country in the hopes of ascending into royalty, of the type on display at the Country Music Hall of Fame, which you can visit on our walking tour (p328). Don't miss Bluebird Cafe (p315): tucked into a suburban strip mall, this singer-songwriter haven was made famous in the recent television series *Nashville*. No chit chat or you will get bounced. Enjoy a less-controlled musical environment at Tootsie's Orchid Lounge (p328), a glorious dive smothered with old photographs and handbills from the Nashville Sound glory days, although the music (still country) has evolved with the times. Bluegrass fans will adore Station Inn (p329), where you'll sit at one of the small cocktail tables, swill beer (only), and marvel at the lightning fingers of fine bluegrass players.

✗ ⊨ p206

The Drive » The next day head south, and you will traverse the Double-Arch Bridge, 155ft above the valley, before settling in for a pleasant country drive on the parkway. You'll notice dense woods encroaching and arching elegantly over the baby-bottom-smooth highway for the next 444 miles.

❷ Franklin

Although it's just 10 miles outside of Nashville, it's worth stopping in the tiny historical hamlet of Franklin. The Victorian-era downtown is charming and the nearby artsy enclave of **Leiper's Fork** is fun and eclectic. But you're in the area to check out one of the Civil War's bloodiest battlefields. On November 30, 1864, 37,000 men (20,000 Confederates and 17,000 Union soldiers) fought over a 2-mile stretch of Franklin's outskirts. Nashville's sprawl has turned much of that

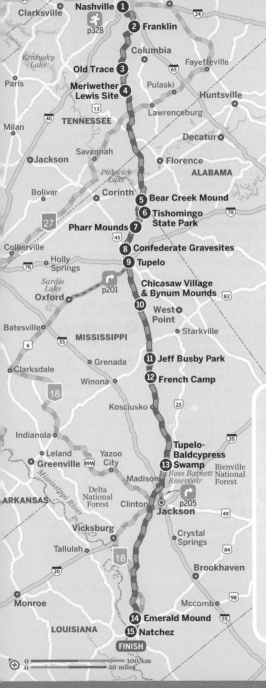

battlefield into suburbs, but the **Carter House** (☎615-791-1861; www.carter-house.org; 1140 Columbia Ave; adult/senior/child $8/7/4; ⏰9am-5pm Mon-Sat, 1-5pm Sun; 👶🐾) property is a preserved 8-acre chunk of the Battle of Franklin. The house is still riddled with 1000-plus bullet holes.

The Drive » The Parkway carves a path through dense woodland as you swerve past another historical district at Leiper's Fork before coming to the first of several Old Trace turnouts.

❸ Old Trace

At Mile 403.7 (don't mind the 'backward' mile markers, we think a north–south route works best) you'll find the first of several sections of the Old Trace. In the early 19th century, Kaintucks

🔗 LINK YOUR TRIP

18 Historical Mississippi

From Oxford to Vicksburg, don't abandon the past in Natchez, continue your odyssey through the deep roots of Mississippi's complex history.

27 Memphis to Nashville

Follow this trip in reverse, start in Nashville and make your way to Beale St.

Classic Trip

(boatmen from Ohio and Pennsylvania) floated coal, livestock and agricultural goods down the Ohio and Mississippi Rivers aboard flat-bottom boats. Often their boats were emptied in Natchez, where they disembarked and began the long walk home up the Old Trace to Nashville, where they could access established roads further north. This walking path intersected Choctaw and Chicasaw country, which meant it was hazardous. In fact, indigenous travellers were the first to beat this earth. You can walk a 2000ft section of that original trail at this turnout.

The Drive » There's beaucoup beauty on a 20-mile stretch of road, as the Parkway flows past Jackson Falls and the Baker Bluff overlook, which offers views over the Duck River.

- - - - - - - -

❹ Meriwether Lewis Site

At Mile 385.9, you'll come to the Meriwether Lewis Site, where the famed explorer and first governor of the Louisiana territory died of mysterious gunshot wounds at nearby Grinders Inn. His fateful journey began in September, 1809. His plan was to

travel to Washington DC to defend his spending of government funds. Think of it as an early-days subpoena before a Congressional committee. At Fort Pickering, a remote wilderness outpost near modern day Memphis, he met up with a Chicasaw agent named James Neely. Neely was to escort the Lewis party safely through Chicasaw land. They traveled north, through the bush, and along the Old Trace to **Grinder's Stand**, and checked into the inn run by the pioneering Grinder Family. Mrs Grinder made up a room for Lewis and fed him, and after he retired, two shots rang out. The legendary explorer was shot in the head and chest and died at 35. Lewis' good friend, Thomas Jefferson, was convinced it was suicide. His family disagreed.

The Drive » Continue on and you will cross into Alabama at Mile 341.8, and Mississippi at Mile 308.

- - - - - - - -

❺ Bear Creek Mound

Just across the Alabama state line and in Mississippi, at Mile 308.8, you'll find Bear Creek Mound, an ancient indigenous ceremonial site. There are seven groups of Indian mounds found

along the parkway, all of them in Mississippi. They varied in shapes from Mayan-like pyramids to domes to small rises and were used for worship, to bury the dead, and some were seen as power spots for local chiefs who sometimes lived on top of them. That was arguably the case at Bear Creek, which was built between 1100 and 1300 AD. Archaeologists who did the 1965 excavation work here are convinced that there was a temple and/ or a chief's dwelling on the top of the rise.

The Drive » The highway bisects Tishomingo State Park at Mile 304.5.

- - - - - - - -

TRIP HIGHLIGHT

❻ Tishomingo State Park

Named for the Chicasaw Indian Chief Tishomingo, if you're taking it slow, you may want to **camp** (📞662-438-6914; www.mississippistateparks.reserveamerica.com; mile-marker 304.5 Natchez Trace Parkway, Tishomingo; campsite $16; 👫🐾) here, among the evocative, moss-covered sandstone cliffs and rock formations, fern gullies and waterfalls of Bear Creek canyon. Hiking trails abound, canoes are available for rent if you wish to paddle Bear Creek, and spring wildflowers bloom once the weather warms. It's a special oasis, and one that was utilized by the Chicasaw and their Paleo Indian antecedents. There is proof of their civilization in the park dating back to 7000BC.

The Drive » Just under 20 miles of more wooded beauty leads from Tishimongo State Park to the next in a series of Native American mounds at Mile 286.7

❼ Pharr Mounds

The Pharr Mounds is a 2000-year-old, 90-acre complex of eight indigenous burial sites. Four of them were excavated in 1966 and found to have fireplaces and low platforms where the dead were cremated. Ceremonial artifacts were also found, along with copper vessels, which raised some eyebrows. Copper is not indigenous to Mississippi, and its presence here indicated an extensive trade network with other nations and peoples.

The Drive » About 17 miles on, at Mile 269.4, you'll come across a turnout that links up to another section of the Old Trace and offers a bit more recent history.

❽ Confederate Gravesites

Just north of Tupelo, on a small rise overlooking the Old Trace, lies a row of 13 graves of unknown Confederate soldiers.

DETOUR: OXFORD

Start: ❾ Tupelo

If you plan on driving the entire Natchez Trace from Nashville to Natchez, you should make the 50-mile detour along Hwy 6 to Oxford, Mississippi, a town rich in culture and history. This is Faulkner country, and Oxford is a thriving university town with terrific restaurants and bars. Don't miss the catfish dinner at Taylor Grocery (p216), 15 minutes south of Oxford.

What led to their fate has been lost in time, but theories range from their having died during the Confederate retreat from Corinth, Mississippi, following the legendary **Battle of Shiloh**. Others believe they were wounded in the nearby **Battle of Brices Cross Roads**, and buried by their brothers, here. Today they rest as reminders of the ultimate cost of war in any time and place.

The Drive » Less than 10 miles later you will loop into the comparatively large hamlet of Tupelo, at Mile 266, where you can gather road supplies for the southward push.

TRIP HIGHLIGHT

❾ Tupelo

Here, the **Natchez Trace Parkway Visitors Center** (☏800-305-7417; www.nps.gov/natr; mile-marker 286.7 Natchez Trace Parkway; ☺8am-5pm, closed Christmas; 🚻🎠) is a fantastic resource with well-done natural and American history displays, and detailed parkway maps. You should pick the brains of local rangers behind the counter, who may know a secret or two. Of course, music buffs will know that Tupelo is world famous for its favorite son. Elvis Presley's Birthplace (p270) is a pilgrimage site for those who kneel before the king. The original structure has a new roof and furniture, but no matter the decor, it was within these humble walls that Elvis was born on January 8, 1935, where he learned to play the guitar and began to dream big. His family's church, where Elvis first was bit by the music bug, has been transported and restored here, as well.

The Drive » Just barely out of Tupelo, at Mile 261.8, is Chicasaw Village. The Bynum Mounds are another nearly 30 miles south. You'll see the turn off just after leaving the Tombigbee National Forest.

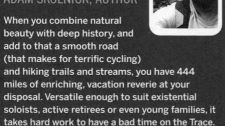

WHY THIS IS A
CLASSIC TRIP
ADAM SKOLNICK, AUTHOR

When you combine natural beauty with deep history, and add to that a smooth road (that makes for terrific cycling) and hiking trails and streams, you have 444 miles of enriching, vacation reverie at your disposal. Versatile enough to suit existential soloists, active retirees or even young families, it takes hard work to have a bad time on the Trace.

Left: Emerald Mound
Right: Confederate gravesites

---

⑩ Chicasaw Village & Bynum Mounds

South from Tupelo, the Trace winds past the Chickasaw Village Site, where displays document how the Chickasaw lived and traveled during the fur-trade heydays of the early 19th century. It was 1541 when Hernan De Soto entered Mississippi under the Spanish flag.

FRANKE KEATING / GETTY IMAGES ©

PAT CANOVA / ALAMY ©

They fought a bitter battle, and though De Soto survived, the Chickasaw held strong. By the 1600s the English had engaged the Chickasaw in what became a lucrative fur trade. Meanwhile, the French held sway just west in the massive Louisiana territory. As an ally to England, the Chickasaw found themselves up against not only the French, but their Choctaw allies. That was the state of affairs when this now leveled village and fort compound was built in the 18th century. Further down the road are the site of six 2100-year-old Bynum Mounds. Five of them were excavated just after WWII, and copper tools and cremated remains were found. Two of the mounds have been restored for public viewing.

The Drive » Between Miles 211 and 205 this gold and green riverine parkway turns post-apocalyptic thanks to an April 2011 tornado that decimated the forest, with hundreds of trees snapped like so many toothpicks. This profound and astonishing dead zone is a sight to behold. Jeff Busby Park can be found at Mile 193.1.

⓫ Jeff Busby Park

Don't miss this hilltop park with picnic tables and a fabulous overlook taking in low-lying, forested hills that extend for miles, all the way to the horizon. Exhibits at the top include facts and figures about local flora and fauna, as well as a primer on indigenous tools. **Little Mountain Trail**, a ½-mile loop that takes 30 minutes to complete, descends from the parking lot into a shady hollow. Another ½-mile spur trail branches from that loop to the campground below.

The Drive ›› Thirteen miles down the road, at Mile 180, the forest clears and an agrarian plateau emerges, jade and perfect, as if this land has been cultivated for centuries.

LOCAL KNOWLEDGE: KAYAKING THE OLD RIVER

According to Keith Benoist, a photographer, landscaper and co-founder of the **Phatwater Challenge** marathon kayak race, the Mississippi has more navigable river miles than any other state in the union. Natchez-born Benoist trains for his 42-mile race by paddling 10 miles of the Old River, an abandoned section of the Mississippi fringed with cypress and teeming with gators. If you're lucky enough to meet him at Under the Hill, he may just take you with him.

⓬ French Camp

The site of a former French pioneer settlement, here you can tour a cute antebellum two-story home, built by Revolutionary War veteran Colonel James Drane. An end table is set for tea, aged leather journals are arranged on the desk and Drane's original US flag is in an upstairs bedroom along with an antique loom. Even more noteworthy is the ornate stagecoach of Greenwood LeFlore, which carried the last chief of the Choctaw nation east of the Mississippi on his two trips to Washington to negotiate with President Andrew Jackson, a route that demanded the navigation of a hazardous piece of the Old Trace known as the Devil's Backbone. For more recent French camp history you can peruse the **French Camp Museum**. Set in a vintage log cabin, there are a number of historical photos on the porch, as well as framed newspaper articles and maps in the museum itself.

🛏 p207

The Drive ›› As you head south, the forest clears for snapshots of horses in the prairie, before the trees encroach again and again.

⓭ Tupelo-Baldcypress Swamp

At Mile 122, you can examine some of these trees up close as you tour the stunning Tupelo-Baldcypress Swamp. The 20-minute trail snakes through an abandoned channel and continues on a boardwalk over the milky green swamp shaded by water tupelo and bald cypresses. Look for turtles on the rocks and gators in the murk.

The Drive ›› The swamp empties into the Ross R Barnett Reservoir, which you'll see to the east as you speed toward and through the state capital of Jackson. The next intriguing sight is just 10.3 miles from Natchez, accessible by graded road that leads west from the Parkway.

⓮ Emerald Mound

Emerald Mound is by far the best of the indigenous mound sites. Using stone tools, pre-Columbian ancestors to the Natchez people graded this

8-acre mountain into a flat-topped pyramid. It is now the second-largest mound in America. There are shady, creekside picnic spots here, and you can and should climb to the top where you'll find a vast lawn along with a diagram of what the temple may have looked like. It would have been perched on the secondary and highest of the mounds. A perfect diversion on an easy spring afternoon just before the sun smolders, when birdsong rings from the trees and co-mingles with the call of a distant train.

The Drive >> As you approach Natchez, the mossy arms of southern oaks spread over the roadway, and the air gets just a touch warmer and more moist. You can almost smell the river from here.

- - - - - - - - - - - -

⑮ Natchez

When the woods part, revealing historical antebellum mansions, you have reached Natchez, Mississippi. In the 1840s, Natchez had more millionaires per capita than any city in the world (because the plantation

DETOUR: JACKSON

Start: ⑬ Tupelo-Baldcypress Swamp

Twenty-two miles south of the swamp, and just a bit further along the the interstate, is Mississippi's capital. With its fine downtown museums, and artsy-funky **Fondren District** – home to Mississippi's best kitchen – Jackson offers a blast of Now if you need a pick-me-up. The city's two best sites are the Mississippi Museum of Art (p223), which promotes home-grown artists and offers rotating exhibitions, and the Eudora Welty House (p214). This is where the literary giant, and Pulitzer Prize winner, crafted every last one of her books. And do not leave town without enjoying lunch or dinner at Walker's Drive-In (p216).

owners didn't pay their staff). Yes, old cotton money built these homes with slave labor, but they are graced all the same with an opulent, *Gone With the Wind* charm. 'Pilgrimage season' is in the spring and fall, when the mansions open for tours, though some are open year-round. The brick-red **Auburn Mansion** (☎601-446-6631; www .natchezpilgrimage.com; Duncan Park; ⊙11am-3pm Tue-Sat, last tour 2:30pm; ⊕) is famous for its freestanding spiral staircase. Built in 1812, the architecture here influenced countless

mansions throughout the South.

Natchez has dirt under its fingernails too. When Mark Twain came through town (and he did on numerous occasions), he crashed in a room above the local watering hole. **Under the Hill Saloon** (☎601-446-8023; www.underthehillsaloon. com; 25 Silver St; ⊙9am-late), across the street from the mighty Mississippi River, remains the best bar in town, with terrific (and free) live music on weekends.

✕ ⊨ p207

Eating & Sleeping

Nashville ❶

✕ City House   New Southern $$$

(☎615-736-5838; www.cityhousenashville.
com; 1222 4th Ave N; mains $15-24; ⏱5-10pm
Mon, Wed-Sat, to 9pm Sun) This signless brick
building in Nashville's gentrifying Germantown
hides one of the city's best restaurants.
The food, cooked in an open kitchen in the
warehouselike space, is a crackling bang-up
of Italy-meets–New South. They do tangy kale
salads, a tasty chickpea and octopus dish
flavored with fennel, onion, lemon and garlic,
and pastas feature twists like rigatoni rabbit,
or gnocchi in cauliflower ragu. They cure their
own sausage and salamis, and take pride in their
cocktail and wine list. Save room for dessert.
Sunday supper features a stripped down menu.

✕ Monell's   Southern $$

(☎615-248-4747; www.monellstn.com; 1235 6th
Ave N; all-you-can-eat $13-19; ⏱10:30am-2pm
Mon, 10:30am-2pm & 5-8:30pm Tue-Fri, 8:30am-
3pm & 5-8:30pm Sat, 8:30am-4pm Sun) In an old
brick house just north of the District, Monell's is
beloved for down-home Southern food served
family-style. This is not just a meal, it's an
experience. Especially at breakfast when platter
after platter of sausage, bacon, bone in ham,
skillet-fried chicken, hominy, corn pudding,
baked apples and potatoes are served along
with baskets of biscuits and bowls of sugary
cinnamon rolls.

✕ Prince's Hot Chicken   Fried Chicken $

(www.facebook.com/pages/Princes-Hot-
Chicken/166097846802728; 123 Ewing Dr;
quarter/half/whole chicken $5/9/18, cash only;
⏱noon-10pm Tue-Thu, noon-4am Fri, 2pm-
4am Sat; P) Cayenne-rubbed 'hot chicken,'
fried to succulent perfection and served on a
piece of white bread with a side of pickles, is
Nashville's unique contribution to the culinary
universe. Tiny, faded Prince's, in a gritty,
northside strip mall, is a local legend that's
gotten shout-outs everywhere from the New
York Times to Bon Appétit. In mild, medium,
hot and death-defying extra hot, its chicken
will burn a hole in your stomach and you'll be
begging for more.

⌂ Hutton Hotel   Hotel $$$

(☎615-340-9333; www.huttonhotel.com; 1808
West End Ave; r from $289; P ❋ @ ☎) Our
favorite Nashville boutique hotel riffs on mid-
century Modern design with bamboo-paneled
walls and grown-up beanbags in the lobby. Rust-
and chocolate-colored rooms are sizable and
well appointed with marble rain showers, glass
wash basins, king beds, ample desk space, fat
flat screens, high-end carpet and linens, and top
level service.

⌂ Indigo Nashville Downtown   Hotel $$

(☎877-846-3446; www.ichotelsgroup.com;
301 Union St; r from $139; P ❋ ☎) Most of
downtown's midrange hotels are corporate
behemoths catering to conventioneers. Not
so the Indigo, with its mod high-ceiling lobby,
space-age violet-and-lime color schemes, and
arty floor-to-ceiling photomurals of Nashville
landmarks. Parking is $20.

⌂ Union Station Hotel   Hotel $$$

(☎615-726-1001; www.unionstationhotel
nashville.com; 1001 Broadway; r from $359;
P ❋ ☎) Set in the old grey stone, church-like
edifice that was once the Nashville train station.
The lobby is especially glorious with an arced,
stained-glass ceiling, and roaring fireplace.
Rooms are elegant, modern and Marriott
approved.

French Camp �12

🛏️ French Camp B&B   B&B $

(📞662-547-6835; www.frenchcamp.org; Mile
180.7 Natchez Trace Parkway; r $85; 🚹) Stay
the night in a log cabin built on a former French
pioneer site that was further developed by a
Revolutionary War hero.

Natchez 🕧

🍴 Cotton Alley   Cafe $$

(www.cottonalleycafe.com; 208 Main St; mains
$10-15; ⏱11am-10pm Mon-Sat) This cute
whitewashed dining room is choc-a-block with
knickknacks and artistic touches and the menu
borrows from local tastes. Think: grilled chicken
sandwich on Texas toast and jambalaya pasta,
but it does a nice chicken Ceasar and a tasty
grilled salmon salad too.

🍴 Magnolia Grill   Southern Fusion $$

(📞601-446-7670; www.magnoliagrill.com; 49
Silver St; mains $13-20; ⏱11am-9pm, to 10pm Fri
& Sat; 🚹) Down by the riverside, this attractive
wooden storefront grill with exposed rafters
and outdoor patio is a good place for a pork
tenderloin po'boy, or a fried crawfish spinach
salad.

🛏️ Historic Oak Hill Inn   Inn $$

(📞601-446-2500; www.historicoakhill.com; 409
S Rankin St; r incl breakfast from $125; 🅿️❄️📶)
Staying at classic Natchez B&B Historic Oak Hill
Inn you'll get a taste of antebellum aristocratic
living, from period furniture to china. A
high-strung staff makes for an immaculate
experience.

🛏️ Mark Twain
Guesthouse   Guesthouse $

(📞601-446-8023; www.underthehillsaloon.
com; 33 Silver St; r without bath $65-85; ❄️📶)
Riverboat captain Samuel Clemens used to
drink till late at the saloon and pass out in one
of three upstairs bedrooms (room 1 has the
best view) with shared baths. Can be noisy until
after 2am.

Columbus *Childhood home*
Tennessee Willia...

Southern Gothic Literary Tour

17

Serve regional drama (obscene riches, crippling poverty, racial oppression), garnished with sweltering nights and powerful storms, and become a giant in the South's own literary genre.

TRIP HIGHLIGHTS

750 miles

Oxford
Visit the estate that fed William Faulkner's tortured soul

450 miles

Monroeville
Capote, Harper Lee and Atticus Fitch's home town (kind of)

5

Jackson

Natchez

4

START
1

Columbus

8 FINISH

New Orleans
Because it's always fine to be sipping in New Orleans

1200 miles

Savannah
Arts, architecture and oak trees

0 miles

7 DAYS
1336 MILES / 2150KM

GREAT FOR...

BEST TIME TO GO
March to June for nature in bloom and a perfect mild climate.

ESSENTIAL PHOTO
Faulkner's wooded lair on a gorgeous Oxford estate.

BEST FOR ARTS & ARCHITECTURE
Discovering the roots of some of America's finest authors.

Southern Gothic Literary Tour

The South has produced some of America's most glorious writers, novels and characters. William Faulkner, Tennessee Williams, Carson McCullers and Flannery O'Connor have roots in Southern soil, as do the unforgettable Vampire Lestat, the brave Atticus Fitch, and wily Huckleberry Finn and his friend Jim. The Great American Novel was invented here, and the Southern Gothic genre has flourished. There have been countless bestsellers, Pulitzers and one Nobel Prize.

TRIP HIGHLIGHT

❶ Savannah

Our journey begins at *Midnight in the Garden of Good and Evil*, also known as Savannah, Georgia. This opulent, historical town is nestled on the Savannah River. Lowcountry swamps and massive oaks heavy with Spanish moss surround countless antebellum mansions and Colonial relics; explore it on our walking tour (p190). It's a beautiful place, and you're here because of

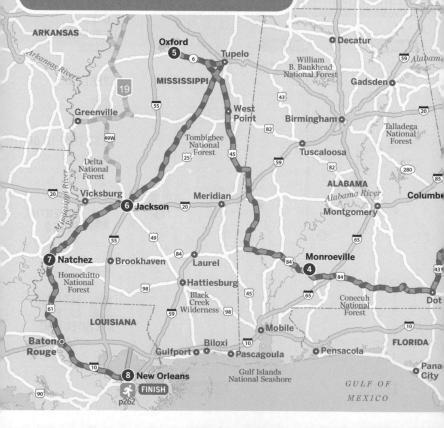

one of the more recent books on our list. *Midnight* was written by John Berendt in 1994, and though it's classified as nonfiction, it reads like a novel. Written in the Southern Gothic tone, this tale revolves around the murder of a local hustler, Danny Hansford, by respected art dealer Jim Williams – an event that triggered four murder trials. Williams lived in the Mercer-Williams House (p190), where Hansford was killed. Williams died in 1990 and the house opened for tours in 2004. The 'garden of good and evil' refers to Savannah's **Bonaventure Cemetery** (www.savannahga.gov; 330 Bonaventure Rd; ☺8am-5pm). Serious lit buffs should also stop by the **Flannery O'Connor Childhood Home** (☎912-233-6014; www.flanneryoconnorhome.org; 207 E Charlton St; adult/student $6/5; ☺1-4pm Fri-Wed, closed Thu) on beautiful Laffayette Sq.

🍴 🛏 p216

The Drive ›› Take I-16W for 112 miles to GA-19 north for 3 miles to US 441N for 44 miles.

❷ Andalusia

Flannery O'Connor was raised on the 544-acre estate, **Andalusia** (☎800-653-1804; www.andalusiafarm.org; Greene St, Milledgeville; admission by donation; ☺10am-4pm Mon, Tue & Thu-Sat; ♿), when her family moved from Savannah. After attending the Writers Workshop at the University of Iowa, she returned here to write. Her acclaimed short story collection, *A Good Man is Hard to Find,* was published in 1955. Like her father, she died of lupus. She was just 39. Before she passed she published two novels and two short story collections. She won the National Book Award for her compilation, *The Complete Stories,*

🔗 LINK YOUR TRIP

19 The Blues Highway
An easy adjunct to the literary tour would be to follow Hwy 61 from Jackson into Clarksdale – the beating heart of the Mississippi Delta, the birthplace of the blues and American popular music.

11 Savannah to the Golden Isles
From Savannah follow the coast to a host of wild and beautiful beaches.

published posthumously. Set amid beautiful wooded, rolling hills, her home is open for walk-in tours five days a week

The Drive » From Andalusia, McCullers fans should make their way back to the I-16W, merge onto the I-75S and exit onto GA-22/US 80W which you'll follow to GA-208W which leads to GA-315W into Columbus.

PETER JOHANSKY / GETTY IMAGES ©

❸ Columbus

Carson McCullers, Tennessee Williams' favorite protégé, was born here and her home town served as inspiration for the mill town depicted in her first and greatest novel, *The Heart is a Lonely Hunter*. It's a beautifully sad yet ultimately hopeful tome about an enlightened deaf mute and his various friends and confidantes (including an adolescent girl, an African American doctor, a business owner and a hard-drinking communist) during the Great Depression. These days, her **childhood home** (☎(706) 565-4021; www.mccullerscenter.org; 1519 Stark Ave; admission $5; ⊙ by appointment) is open for tours, and it's the base of operations for the Carson McCullers Center which runs a McCullers-based archive and offers fellowships to aspiring writers and artists. Call at least a day ahead to tour the home.

The Drive » Take US 431S for 99 miles to the small town of Dothan, where you'll catch the US 84 and take it 22 miles until it meets the AL-36. Hang a right and you'll reach Monroeville.

TRIP HIGHLIGHT

❹ Monroeville

Monroeville is a small Alabama town that gave us both Truman Capote, the progenitor of the nonfiction novel, and his childhood friend, Harper Lee. *To Kill a Mockingbird*, written by Lee, in the Southern Gothic style, takes aim at the institutional racism of the South. A runaway hit, it earned her the 1961 Pulitzer Prize, and takes place in the fictional town of Maycomb, a mirror image of Monroeville. The plot revolves around

Bonaventure Cemetery The original 'garden of good and evil'

the trial of a young black man who is wrongfully accused of raping a white woman during the Great Depression. It's narrated by six-year-old Scout Finch, whose dad, Atticus, risks his and his family's safety to defend his railroaded client. If you've never read it, this book is an absolute must. Each May, curtains rise on a production of *To Kill A Mockingbird* at the **Old Courthouse Museum** (251-575-7433; www.tokillamockingbird.com; 31 N Alabama Ave; admission free; ⏰8am-4pm Mon-Fri, 10am-2pm Sat; ♿), which also has permanent exhibits on both Lee and her pal, Capote.

The Drive » When the curtain drops, find US 45N and take the long drive to MS-6 and Oxford, Mississippi.

TRIP HIGHLIGHT

⑤ Oxford

Nobel Prize winner William Faulkner may be long dead, but he still owns this town, home to the lovely University of Mississippi (p220). **Rowan Oak** (www.rowanoak. com; Old Taylor Rd; adult/child $5/free; ⏰10am-4pm Tue-Sat, 1-4pm Sun), Faulkner's fine, 33-acre estate, nurtured many novels, but required him to slum in Hollywood as a studio-owned screenwriter to pay it off. Ninety-percent of Rowan Oak's original furnishings are in tact – you'll see Faulkner's prized typewriter, rusted golf clubs, and an outline for a never-written fable written on the walls. His 1950 Nobel Prize is on permanent display at the Center for Southern Culture (p221). It also has a copy of his acceptance speech, which became an instant classic. Oxford isn't all about the past.

Square Books (✆662-236-2262; www.squarebooks.com; 160 Courthouse Sq; ◷9am-9pm Mon-Thu, to 10pm Fri & Sat, 9am-6pm Sun) is one of the very best indie bookstores in America. Visiting authors read from their newly published works on the regular, and autographed copies of hot novels abound.

There's a Faulkner section upstairs, next to the cafe.

✕ 🛏 p216

The Drive » After enjoying Oxford, detour through Tupelo, the birthplace of King Presley, and hop on the Natchez Trace Parkway through a glorious oak-and-swamp-studded countryside, before buzzing east on I-20 to Jackson.

---

⑥ Jackson

Mississippi's capital is clean, historical and resolute. Eudora Welty, one of the state's great writers and a Pulitzer Prize winner, lived here all her life. She moved into what is now the **Eudora Welty House** (✆601-353-7762; www.mdah.state.ms.us/welty; 1119 Pinehurst St; ◷tours 9am, 11am, 1pm & 3pm Tue-Fri) when she was 16 and penned every one of her books in the study, where readers and visitors would descend unannounced (and were always welcomed). She cut and pinned up her manuscripts, in what was her own (pre-Nabokov) revision system. Noted author, traveler and thinker Richard Wright was also a Jackson native. Best known for his story collection *Uncle Tom's Children*, based in part on lynchings in Mississippi, he was an important writer and devoted communist living in New York by the time he was 30. Eventually he moved to Europe, where he mingled with Sartre and Camus and died too soon at 52. Wright was the valedictorian of Jackson's first African American School (p223). Wright's and Welty's insightful words grace the eaves at the worthwhile Mississippi Museum of Art (p223).

✕ 🛏 p216

The Drive » Merge back onto I-20 west to the Natchez Trace Parkway, and follow that green band of historical beauty until it ends in Mark Twain's old haunt.

---

⑦ Natchez

Natchez is one of the only antebellum towns left standing in the South. Mostly because when Sherman and his Union troops marched in, the local ladies served them sweet tea and Southern hospitality. A hundred and fifty years later and Natchez attracts visitors

SOUTHERN GOTHIC EXPOSED

Gothic literature was born in England, when writers took on the moral blindness of the medieval era through supernatural tales. Southern writers, for the most part, muted the supernatural in their work. Instead they plumbed the characters and communities damaged by a regional history of white Christian supremacy, frosted with an 'everything-is-just-fine-as-it-is' veneer. Writers knew that such social tension led to years of brutality, as well as economic and moral bankruptcy, because they lived it. Which makes their stories more dramatic and poignant.

from around the world to its historical antebellum mansions. Especially during pilgrimage season. But if slaver wealth leaves you cold (or angry, or both), head down to the riverside.

The Mississippi River forms a natural border, dividing Mississippi and Louisiana, and is another of Natchez's main attractions. Back when Mark Twain was steamboat pilot Samuel Clemens, he cruised through town countless times and did his drinking at the Under the Hill Saloon (p205) (still a local hot spot with live music on weekends). And when he'd had enough, he often crashed upstairs.

Of course, Mark Twain moved on from the riverboat to become the inventor of the Great American Novel (or so he has been credited) with the publication of *The Adventures of Huckleberry Finn*, which followed Huck and Jim as they floated downriver on a raft, searching for freedom.

✗ ⛏ p217

The Drive » Eventually, all southern roads pass through New Orleans, and the literary one is no exception. From Natchez drive south on US 61 until it merges with I-110E in Baton Rouge and then I-10E towards New Orleans.

ADAPTATION

The book is always better, but that doesn't mean we don't love movies. Here are three Southern Gothic dramas that made the leap with style:

» *A Streetcar Named Desire* (1951) Brando's Stanley Kowalski loves STELLA! Four Oscars, Marlon becomes a star.

» *To Kill a Mockingbird* (1962) Best actor, Gregory Peck, is Atticus Finch.

» *Interview With a Vampire* (1994) An unintentional comedy. Tom Cruise and Brad Pitt vamp around New Orleans in wigs and makeup.

TRIP HIGHLIGHT

❽ New Orleans

This is the town of Tennessee Williams, Anne Rice and Ignatius J Reilly (explore its history on our walking tour, p262). Many of the city's literary sites are concentrated in the French Quarter. Lafitte's Blacksmith Shop (p248), a stone shack on the corner of Bourbon St, claims to be the oldest bar in the USA. Williams used to party here with fellow artists while a pianist played whatever sheet music Williams brought in that day. Nearby **Napoleon House** (☎504 524 9752; www .napoleonhouse.com; 500 Chartres St; ⊙11am-late), an attractive bar set in a courtyard building erected in 1797, was another drinking haunt of Williams; on hot days you can sit in the courtyard, order a scoop of shrimp remoulade in a half avocado and dream sultry literary dreams.

If you prefer sexed-up vampires who are into rock'n'roll and a bit of evil, check out **Lafayette Cemetery No 1** (Washington Ave at Prytania St; ⊙9am-2:30pm; ☒11 or 12). Shaded by magnificent groves of lush greenery, this Garden District landmark was a favorite haunt (pun intended) of Anne Rice, and has featured prominently in many vampire and witches of Mayfair novels. You'll notice many German and Irish names on the above-ground graves, testifying that immigrants were devastated by 19th-century yellow-fever epidemics. Not far from the entrance is a tomb containing the remains of an entire family that died of that plague.

✗ ⛏ p217

Eating & Sleeping

Savannah ❶

✕ 11 Ten Local New American $$$

(☎912-790-9000; www.local11ten.com; 1110 Bull St; mains $24-32; ☺6-10pm Mon-Sat) Upscale, sustainable, local, fresh: a combination of elements that creates a monumental experience in an elegant, well-run restaurant, and it's hands down the best food in Savannah. Start with a spring roll salad. The roll is unfurled and speckled with ginger dressing. Then move onto the big eye tuna, seared perfectly and plated with kim chi and green pea puree. Or just pick a grilled protein – filet, fresh catch, scallops, or chicken breast, and one or three of its awesome sauces and sides like brussels with walnuts and sausage or a historically good mac and cheese.

✕ Wilkes' House Southern $$

(www.mrswilkes.com; 107 W Jones St; lunch $16; ☺11am-2pm Mon-Fri) The line outside can begin as early as 8am at this first come, first served, Southern comfort food institution. Once the lunch bell rings and you are seated family-style, the kitchen unloads on you: fried chicken, beef stew, meatloaf, collard greens, black-eyed peas, mac 'n' cheese, rutabaga, candied yams, squash casserole, creamed corn *and* biscuits. It's like Thanksgiving and the Last Supper rolled into one massive feast chased with sweet tea.

🛏 East Bay Inn Inn $$$

(☎912-238-1225; www.eastbayinn.com; 225 E Bay St; r from $235) Wedged between corporate rivals this brick behemoth offers just 28 huge rooms all with original double wide wood floors, exposed brick walls, soaring ceilings, slender support columns and flat screens, along with much charm and warmth to spare.

Oxford ❺

✕ City Grocery New Southern $$

(☎662-232-8080; www.citygroceryonline.com; 152 Courthouse Sq; mains $9-22; ☺10am-2pm & 6-10pm Mon-Sat) Eclectic Southern cuisine is served on the south side of the square. Writers and students congregate at the stylish, funky upstairs bar. It does a well-documented and beloved shrimp and grits and a Southern-style crudo where gulf tuna is chopped and served with pickled onions and preserved okra drenched in Georgian olive oil. Its desserts rock.

✕ Taylor Grocery Seafood $$

(www.taylorgrocery.com; 4 County Rd 338 A; dishes $9-15; ☺5-10pm Thu-Sat, to 9pm Sun) Be prepared to wait (and to tailgate in the parking lot) at this splendidly rusticated catfish haunt. Get your cat fried or grilled, and bring a marker to sign your name on the wall. It's about 7 miles from downtown Oxford, south on Old Taylor Rd.

🛏 Inn at Ole Miss Hotel $$

(☎662-234-2331; www.theinnatolemiss.com; 120 Alumni Dr; r from $129; P ❄ @ 🛜 🚐) Unless its a football weekend, in which case, you'd be wise to book well ahead, you can usually find a nice room at this 180-room hotel and conference center right on the Ole Miss Grove. Although less personal than the local inns, it's comfortable, well-located and walkable to downtown.

Jackson ❻

✕ Walker's Drive-In Southern $$$

(☎601-982-2633; www.walkersdrivein.com; 3016 N State St; lunch mains $10-17, dinner mains $25-35; ☺11am-2pm Mon-Fri & from 5:30pm Tue-Sat) This retro diner has been restored

th love and infused with new southern foodie
hos. Lunch is diner 2.0 fare with grilled redfish
ndwiches, tender burgers and BBQ oyster
boys, as well as a seared, chili crusted tuna
lad, which comes with spiced calamari and
aweed salad, and is exceptional. Things get
en more gourmet at dinner. Think: lamb
rterhouse, wood grilled octopus and miso
arinated seabass. There's an excellent wine
t and service is impeccable.

🍴 Mayflower Seafood $$$

(☎601-355-4122; 123 W Capitol St; mains
21-29; ⏱11am-2:30pm & 4:30-9:15pm Mon-Fri,
30-9:30pm Sat) It looks like just another
wntown dive, but it's a damn fine seafood
use. Locals swear by the broiled red fish, and
e Greek salad, which becomes a meal when
u add pan seared scallops (sensational!).
erything is obscenely fresh.

🛏 Fairview Inn Inn $$

(☎601-948-3429; www.fairviewinn.com;
34 Fairview St; r incl breakfast $129-329;
| ❄ @ 🢅) For a colonial estate experience,
e 18-room Fairview Inn, set in a converted
storical mansion, will not let you down. The
tique decor is stunning. It also has a full spa.

atchez ❼

🍴 Magnolia Grill Southern Fusion $$

ee Trip 🔟 (p207).

🛏 Historic Oak Hill Inn Inn $$

ee Trip 🔟 (p207).

ew Orleans ❽

🍴 Sylvain Contemporary $$

(☎504-265-8123; 625 Chartres St; mains
2.50-25; ⏱5:30-11pm Mon-Thu, to midnight
Fri & Sat, to 10pm Sun, 11:30am-2:30pm Fri &
Sat, 10:30pm-2:30pm Sun) Sylvain is the sort
of exciting new New Orleans restaurant the
French Quarter is sorely in need of. This rustic
yet elegant gastropub draws inspiration from
the dedication to ingredients and localvore love
demonstrated by chefs like Thomas Keller. The
duck confit served on a bed of black-eyed peas
is indicative of the gastronomic experience: rich,
refined and delicious. They also mix some mean
cocktails if you need to tie one off before dinner.

🛏 Hotel

Maison de Ville Historical Hotel $$$

(☎504-561-5858; www.hotelmaisondeville.com;
727 Toulouse St; ❄ 🢅 🛏) The Maison greets
with a quintessentially French Quarter facade of
twirling wrought iron and candy-colored plaster
shell. The Audubon Cottage suites (where artist
John J Audubon stayed and painted while in
town) surround a lushly landscaped courtyard;
the pool is rumored to be the oldest in the
Quarter (from the late 1700s).

🛏 Hotel Monteleone Hotel $$$

(☎504 523 3341, 800 535 9595; www.
hotelmonteleone.com; 214 Royal St; r from $250)
Perhaps the city's most venerable old hotel,
the Monteleone is also the French Quarter's
largest. (Not long after the Monteleone was
built, preservationists put a stop to building on
this scale below Iberville St.) Since its inception
in 1866, the hotel has been the local lodging of
choice for writers, including luminaries such as
William Faulkner, Truman Capote and Rebecca
Wells. The Carousel Bar, a New Orleans classic,
has appeared in numerous films and TV shows.
Rooms throughout exude an old-world appeal
with French toile and chandeliers.

Rowan Oak *A scenic insight* the life of William Faulk

Historical Mississippi

Over the course of her history, Mississippi has proven to be beautiful and wild, serene and violent, complex yet simple. To explore her turbulent past is to discover Mississippi now.

TRIP HIGHLIGHTS

64 miles

Clarksdale
Home of Red's, a classic Mississippi Delta juke joint

272 miles

Vicksburg
Gravitas and Mississippi River beauty

FINISH Natchez

Jackson

Oxford
Our favorite town in Mississippi for good reason

0 miles

① START
②
⑥

3 DAYS
354 MILES / 570KM

GREAT FOR

BEST TIME TO GO

September and October for a respite from the summer heat; April to June for fresh blooms.

ESSENTIAL PHOTO

The gorgeous grounds of Rowan Oak.

BEST FOR HISTORY

The entire route, from Indian mounds and the birth of the blues to the civil rights movement.

18 Historical Mississippi

Stroll in the footsteps of literary masters and civil rights heroes, consider the origins of American popular music, and hear gun shots ring and crosses burn in the mind as you stroll blood-soaked battlefields and consider the state's once-impenetrable segregation stranglehold. Her history will never be easy to reconcile, but her stories — her people — are forever compelling.

TRIP HIGHLIGHT

❶ Oxford

Oxford is one of those rare towns that seeps into your bones and never leaves. Local life revolves around the quaint-yet-hip square, where you'll find inviting bars, wonderful food and decent shopping, and the rather regal **University of Mississippi** (www.olemiss.edu), aka Ole Miss. All around and in between are quiet residential streets, sprinkled with antebellum homes and

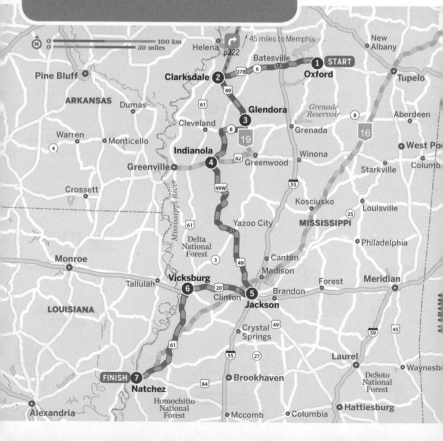

shaded by majestic oaks. Oh, and there's history to spare. Begin at The Grove, the heart of Ole Miss, and home to one of the Civil Rights movement's iconic scenes. The **Center for Southern Culture** (☎662-915-5855; 1 Library Loop; admission free; ⏱8am-9pm Mon-Thu, to 4pm Fri, to 5pm Sat, 1-5pm Sun; 🅿) archive, on the 3rd floor of the JD Williams Library, displays William Faulkner's correspondence along with his 1950 Nobel Prize. A half-mile trail leads from the **University of Mississippi Museum** (www.museum.olemiss .edu; University Ave, at 5th St; admission $5; ⏱10am-6pm Tue-Sat), where you'll find a collection of early astronomical marvels,

LINK YOUR TRIP

16 Natchez Trace Parkway

The 444-mile Natchez Trace Parkwayis one of the most beautiful roads in America, and offers even more history if you're still hungry for stories.

19 The Blues Highway

Jump from the history book to the origins of American popular music on this journey through the Mississippi Delta.

Choctaw lacrosse sticks, Confederate soldier gear, and original Man Ray and Georgia O'Keefe canvasses, through the woods to **Rowan Oak** (www.rowanoak.com; Old Taylor Rd; adult/child $5/ free; ⏱10am-4pm Tue-Sat, 1-4pm Sun). This 33-acre estate is the former home of Faulkner. Ninety per cent of the original furnishings are intact, including his prized typewriter. For more on Rowan Oak, see (p213).

✕ 🍴 p225

The Drive » It's just over an hour east on MS-6/US 278 through rolling hills into Clarksdale and the Delta.

❷ Clarksdale

You can't explore Mississippi history without paying homage to the birthplace of American music. Blues legend Robert Johnson is said to have sold his soul to the devil down at **the Crossroads** (cnr Hwy 61 & Hwy 49; admission free; 🅿🎫), the junction of Hwy 61, the Blues Highway, and Hwy 49 in Clarksdale. Clarksdale is the hub of Delta blues country and its most comfortable and vibrant base. Here you can visit Muddy Water's childhood cabin at the Delta Blues Museum (p231), and see modern-day blues men howl at Red's (p231). WC Handy was the first songwriter

who finally put the 12-bar blues down on paper, several years after he first heard a nomadic guitar man strumming in tiny Tutwiler in 1903. Their convergence is remembered with a mural along the Tutwiler Tracks (p233).

The Drive » From Clarksdale, take Hwy 49 south for 13 miles to 49 east, which diverges from 49 west for 13 miles, though both run north and south. Yes, it's confusing, but 16 miles later you will land in Glendora.

❸ Glendora

Sixteen miles south of Tutweiler is another small Delta town, but Glendora's legacy is much darker. It was here on August 28, 1955, that Emmett Till was kidnapped and murdered following a brief encounter with a white woman in a local store. Born in Chicago and just 13 years old, he was ignorant of the local racial mores, and supposedly said, 'Bye Baby,' to a white woman on a dare. Days later he was murdered by the woman's husband and half brother-in-law who were swiftly acquitted of the crime, though there was never an argument that they did it. After Till's mother ordered an open casket at his funeral, so all could see how badly he had been beaten, his case became national news, and a rallying cry for civil rights activists throughout the South. You can learn more about the case at the **Emmett Till Museum** (📞662-375-9304; www.glendorams.com/cultural-heritage-tourism/emmett-till-museum/; 33 Thomas St; admission $5; 🕒10am-5pm Mon-Fri, to 2pm Sat), which also has a wing dedicated to local blues legend and BB King's mentor, Sonny Boy Williamson.

The Drive ›› Take Hwy 49E south for 8 miles to MS-8 west to Hwy 49W, which runs south through the plains until it intersects with Hwy 82 in Indianola.

GETTY IMAGES ©

❹ Indianola

Indianola is a rather prosperous middle class town in the delta with a corporate bloom on highway 82, and wide, lovely leafy streets dotted with well-kept single family homes around downtown, where BB King used to play guitar for passers by. BB King is Indianola's favorite son, and you'll see his likeness on murals, and on a plaques on his favorite street corner, and you'll learn all about his difficult, triumphant life at his brand new BB King Museum & Delta Interpretive Center (p234). The region's very best museum offers engaging interactive exhibits that illuminate the various musical influences on the Delta blues sound, and on King's music in particular. It's a must see for music geeks.

The Drive ›› Drive south on US 49 to Jackson.

↪ DETOUR: MEMPHIS

Start: ❷ Clarksdale

Easily accessible to both Oxford and Clarksdale, Memphis is a thriving city with a blues history to match Mississippi. Set right on the river, the musical roots here (Stax Records, Sun Studios, Graceland) are what attract the tourists, but the warmth and hospitality of the locals is why you'll fall in like or love.

❺ Jackson

Mississippi's capital and largest city has plenty of history to explore, and the **Old Capitol Museum** (www.mdah.state.ms.us/museum; 100 State St; 🕒9am-5pm Tue-Sat, 1-5pm

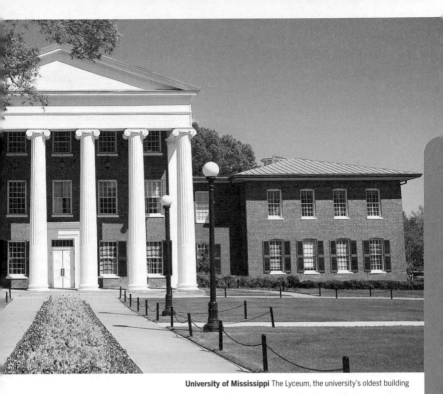

University of Mississippi The Lyceum, the university's oldest building

Sun) is a good place to start. It tells the story of the Greek Revival building itself, and in so doing touches on Mississippi history. You'll learn that 15 lawmakers opposed secession in the run-up to the Civil War, and there are some interesting exhibits on reconstruction and what were the nation's harshest 'Black Codes,' the gateway to full segregation.

The **Mississippi Museum of Art** (www.msmuseumart.org; 380 South Lamar St; permenant collections free, special exhibitions $5-12; ☺10am-5pm Tue-Sat, noon-5pm Sun) includes 200 works from Mississippi artists. Our favorites were the photographs of literary scions Eudora Welty and William Faulkner, and another of Quincy Jones and Elvis crooning at a Tupelo concert. Housed in Mississippi's first public school for African American kids is the **Smith Robertson Museum** (www.jacksonms.gov/visitors/museums/smithrobertson; 528 Bloom St; adult/child $4.50/1.50; ☺9am-5pm Mon-Fri,10am-2pm Sat, 2-5pm Sun), the alma mater of author Richard Wright. It offers insight and explanation into the pain and perseverance of the African American legacy in Mississippi. And then there's the Eudora Welty House (p214), a must for literature buffs.

✕ 🛏 p225

It's 44 quick miles west from Jackson to Vicksburg on I-20.

- - - - - - - - - - - - -

TRIP HIGHLIGHT

❻ Vicksburg

Vicksburg is famous for its strategic location in the Civil War, thanks to its position on a high bluff overlooking the Mississippi River, and history buffs dig it. General Ulysses S Grant

JAMES MEREDITH

The generally peaceful and serene Grove was the site of a riot on September 21, 1962, when a violent mob of segregationists descended to prevent James Meredith, the school's first ever African American student, from enrolling for the semester. With the Mississippi governor siding with the mob, the Kennedy administration called in 500 federal marshals and federalized the national guard to tamp down the rioters and ensure Meredith's safety. Those troops remained on campus when Meredith and state NAACP chairman, Medgar Evers (who would later be assassinated), marched through thousands of vitriolic segregationists to break the Ole Miss color barrier on October 1, 1962. Meredith went on to march 220 miles across the state, from Memphis to Jackson, in a 1966 protest against racial violence. Some of his correspondence is on display at the Center for Southern Culture (p221).

besieged the city for 47 days, until its surrender on July 4, 1863, at which point the North gained dominance over North America's greatest river. The **Vicksburg National Military Park** (www.nps .gov/vick; Clay St; per car/ individual $8/4; ☺8am-5pm Oct-Mar, to 7pm Apr-Sep) honors that battle. You can drive, or pedal (if you're travelling with bicycles), along the 16-mile **Battlefield Drive**, which winds past 1330 monuments and markers – including statues, battle trenches, a restored Union gunboat, and a National Cemetery. Vicksburg's historical riverside core is rather pretty, and worth a look. You'll find

regal old homes lined up on terraced bluffs with views of slender wooded islands forming natural inlets, which loom at arms length along with those riverboat casinos. As long as you're downtown don't miss the Attic Gallery (p323). It features virtuoso regional artists, and a funky collection of folk art and jewelry.

🛏 p225

Hop on US 61, which follows the Mississippi River (though not always so closely) down to Natchez.

- - - - - - - - - - -

❼ Natchez

Adorable Natchez stews together a wide variety of humans, from gay

log-cabin republicans to intellectual liberals and down-home folks. Perched on a bluff overlooking the Mississippi, it attracts tourists in search of antebellum history and architecture – 668 antebellum homes pepper the oldest civilized settlement on the Mississippi River (beating New Orleans by two years). Although most such towns were torched by Union troops, Natchez was spared thanks to what legend has it were some rather hospitable local ladies who invited the troops in for rest and relaxation. The **visitor and welcome center** (☎601-446-6345; www. visitnatchez.org; 640 S Canal St; tours adult/child $12/8; ☺8:30am-5pm Mon-Sat, 9am-4pm Sun) is a large, well-organized tourist resource with little exhibits of area history and a ton of information on local sites. During the 'pilgrimage' seasons in spring and fall, local mansions are opened to visitors, though some properties, such as the Auburn Mansion (p205), are open year-round. Natchez is also the end (or is it the beginning?) of the scenic 444-mile Natchez Trace Parkway (see p197).

✗ 🛏 p225

Eating & Sleeping

Oxford ❶

✕ City Grocery   New Southern $$
See Trip 🔟 (p216).

🛏 (5) Twelve   B&B $$
(☎662-234-8043; www.the12oxford.com; 512
Van Buren Ave; r from $115; P ❄ 🛜) This six-
room B&B has an antebellum-style exterior and
modern interior (think: tempurpedic beds and
flat screens). Room rate includes full Southern
breakfasts to order, it's an easy walk from shops
and restaurants, and we cannot say enough
good things about the innkeepers. They make
you feel like family.

Clarksdale ❷

✕ Yazoo Pass   Cafe $$
(www.yazoopass.com; 207 Yazoo Ave; lunch
mains $6-10, dinner mains $13-26; ⏱7am-9pm
Mon-Sat; 🛜) A contemporary new space
in town with exposed brick walls, polished
concrete floors, rattan furnishings and leather
booths where you can enjoy fresh scones
and croissants in the mornings, a salad bar,
sandwiches and soups at lunch, and pan seared
ahi, filet mignon, burgers and pastas at dinner.

🛏 Shack Up Inn   Inn $
(☎662-624-8329; www.shackupinn.com;
Hwy 49; d $75-165; P ❄ 🛜) Guests stay
in refurbished sharecropper cabins or the
creatively renovated cotton gin. The whole place
reeks of down-home dirty blues and Deep South
character – possibly the coolest place you'll
ever stay.

Jackson ❺

✕ Walker's Drive-In   Southern $$$
See Trip 🔟 (p216).

🛏 Old Capitol Inn   Boutique Hotel $$
(☎601-359-9000; www.oldcapitolinn.com;
226 N State St; r incl breakfast from $135;
P ❄ @ 🛜 🌡) A heck of a deal, this 24-room
boutique hotel, near museums and restaurants,
has up-to-date rooms that are comfortably and
uniquely furnished. The rooftop deck, complete
with hot tub, overlooks a courtyard and pool. A
full Southern breakfast and early-evening wine
and cheese are included.

Vicksburg ❻

🛏 Corners Mansion   B&B $$
(☎601-636-7421; www.thecorners.com; 601
Klein St; r incl breakfast from $125; P ❄ 🛜)
The best part of this Old South 1873 B&B could
be looking over the Yazoo and Mississippi
Rivers from your porch-swing vantage point.
The gardens and Southern breakfast don't hurt
either.

Natchez ❼

✕ Magnolia Grill   Southern Fusion $$
See Trip 🔟 (p217).

Clarksdale *The ideal base*
Mississippi blues

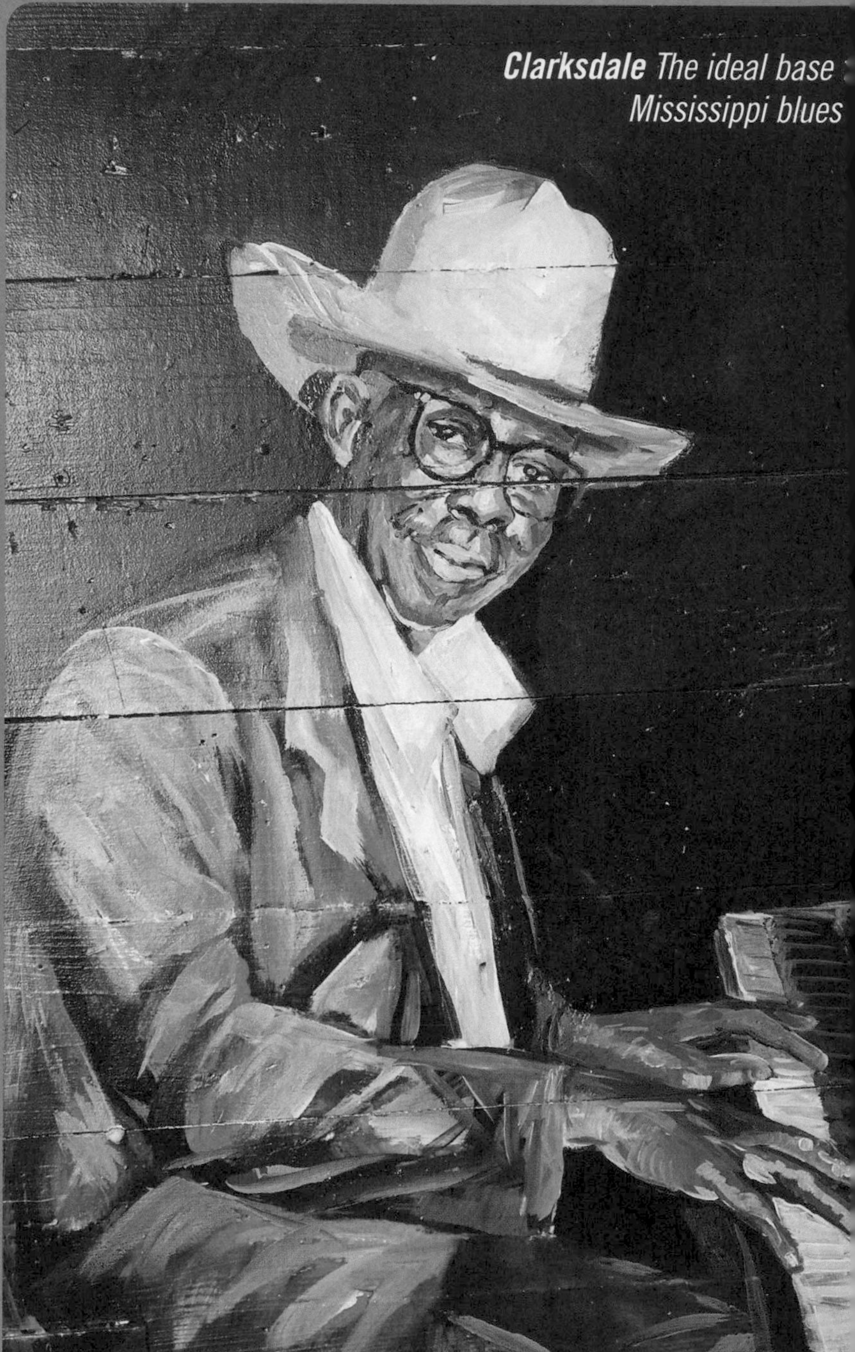

Classic Trip

The Blues Highway

19

Listen to living blues legends howl their sad enlightenment and pay homage to the music that saturated northern Mississippi for a century, and bloomed rock'n'roll.

TRIP HIGHLIGHTS

START
● Memphis

Helena

0 miles — 4

larksdale
he inviting hub of
elta blues country

5 — **110 miles**

Tutwiler
Pay homage to the tiny
town that sprouted the
blues

0 miles — 7

dianola
ome to our favorite
useum in the Delta

● Greenwood

● Bentonia
FINISH

3 DAYS
350 MILES / 563KM

GREAT FOR...

BEST TIME TO GO
May and June for blues
festivals in the Delta.

ESSENTIAL PHOTO
Red's smoky, burgundy
glow when a bluesman
is wailing on stage.

BEST FOR MUSIC
The music and soul
of the Mississippi
Delta – a cultural
immersion with an epic
soundtrack.

227

Classic Trip

19 The Blues Highway

In the plains, along Hwy 61, American music took root. It arrived from Africa in the souls of slaves, morphed into field songs, and wormed into the brain of a sharecropping troubadour waiting for a train. In Clarksdale, at the Crossroads, legend has it that Robert Johnson made a deal with the devil and became America's first guitar hero. But to fully grasp its influence, start in Memphis.

① Memphis

The Mississippi Delta and Memphis have always been inextricably linked. Memphis was a beacon for the Delta bluesmen, with its relative freedoms, African American–owned businesses and the bright lights and foot-stamping crowds of Beale St, which is still rocking (check it out as part of our walking tour, p330). **Rum Boogie Cafe** (📞912-528-0150; www.rumboogie.com; 182 Beale St) is a Cajun-themed blues bar with a terrific house band. The original **BB King's** (📞901-524-5464; www.bbkingclubs.com; 143 Beale St; 🕐 noon-1am, kitchen open until 11pm) is a living monument to

the Mississippi genius who made good here. And it was in Memphis where WC Handy was first credited with putting the blues to paper when he wrote 'Beale Street Blues' in 1916. You can visit the house (p330) where he lived. The Mississippi Delta legacy bubbles up at Sun Studio (p271), where you can tour the label that launched Elvis, whose interpretation of the blues birthed rock'n'roll. And it's running through the veins of the wonderful Stax Museum of American Soul Music (p311). Those connections are explained perfectly at the Memphis Rock 'n' Soul Museum (p274).

🍴 🛏 p236

The Drive » US 61 begins in Memphis, where it is a wide avenue snaking through the city's rough seam. Eventually urbanity gives way to flat farmland, and the highway goes rural as you enter Mississippi

② Tunica

A gathering of casinos rests near the riverbanks in Tunica, Hwy 61's most prosperous and least authentic town. Nevertheless, it is the gateway to the blues and home to their juke-joint mock-up of a **Tunica Visitors Center** (📞662-363-3800; www.tunicatravel.com; 13625 US 61; 🕐9am-6pm), where a cool interactive digital guide comes packed with information on famed blues artists and the

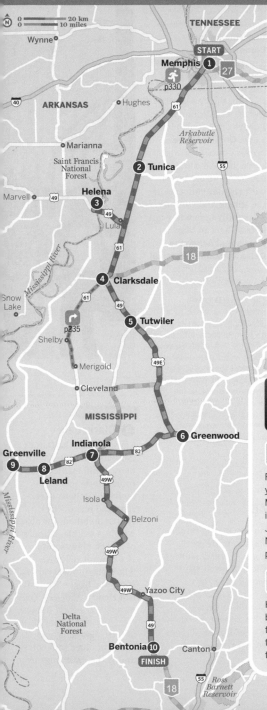

Mississippi Blues Trail itself. It's a good place to get inspired about what you are about to experience, and perhaps do some plotting and planning. Unless you play cards, however, Tunica is not otherwise noteworthy.

The Drive >> Continue on the arrow-straight road for 19 miles, then veer west on US 49 and over the Mississippi River into Helena, Arkansas.

❸ Helena

Helena, Arkansas, a depressed mill town 32 miles north and across the Mississippi River from Clarksdale, was once the home of blues legend Sonny Boy Williamson. He was a

LINK YOUR TRIP

18 Historical Mississippi

From the Delta, continue your journey through the Mississippi mind by taking in the towns of Oxford, Jackson, Vicksburg and Natchez and exploring the past and present all at once.

27 Memphis to Nashville

Head from the rhythm and blues haunts of Beale St to the down-home honky-tonks that put Nashville on the map.

Classic Trip

regular on *King Biscuit Time*, America's original blues radio show. It still broadcasts out of the **Delta Cultural Center** (☎870-338-4350; www.deltaculturalcenter.com; 141 Cherry St; admission free; ☺9am-5pm Tue-Sat), a worthwhile blues museum. Down the street you'll find the Delta's best record store, **Bubba's Blues Corner** (☎870-995-1326; 105 Cherry St; admission free; ☺9am-5pm Tue-Sat; ♿). Delightfully disorganized, it's supposedly a regular stop on Robert Plant's personal blues pilgrimages. Bubba himself is warm and friendly and a wealth of knowledge. If the shop isn't open when you fall by, give him a ring, and he'll happily open up. Helena hosts

two festivals of note. The **King Biscuit Blues Festival** (www.kingbiscuitfestival.com; tickets $45; ☺Oct) is held over three days each October. In 2013, the headliners were Greg Allman and Robert Cray. It also hosts a **Live On The Levee** (www.kingbiscuitfestival.com/live-on-the-levee; adult/child $30/free) concert series, with regular concerts in the spring and summer. Rockabilly fans will want to land here in May, for the annual **Arkansas Delta Rockabilly Festival** (www.deltarockabillyfest.com; tickets $30; ☺May).

The Drive » US 49 converges with the US 61 in Mississippi, and from there it's 30 miles south until you reach the Crossroads. Peeking out above the trees on the northeast corner of US 61 and US 49, where the roads diverge once again, is the landmark weathervane of three interlocking blue guitars. You have arrived in the Delta's beating heart.

DAVID LYONS / ALAMY ©

KING BISCUIT TIME

Sonny Boy Williamson was the host of *King Biscuit Time* when BB King was a young buck. He recalls listening to the lunch-hour program, and dreaming of possibilities. When he moved to Memphis as a teenager and began playing Beale St gigs, Williamson invited King to play on his radio show, and a star was born. Williamson remained an important mentor for King as his career took off. The radio show, which begins weekdays at 12:15pm, is still running, and has been hosted by Sunshine Sonny Payne since 1951.

TRIP HIGHLIGHT

❹ Clarksdale

Clarksdale is the Delta's most useful base – with more comfortable hotel rooms and modern, tasteful kitchens here than the rest of the Delta combined. It's also within a couple of hours of all the blues sights. If you want to know who's playing where, come see Roger Stolle at **Cat Head** (☎662-624-5992; www.cathead.biz; 252 Delta Ave; ☺10am-5pm Mon-Sat; ♿). He also sells a good range of blues souvenirs, and is the main engine

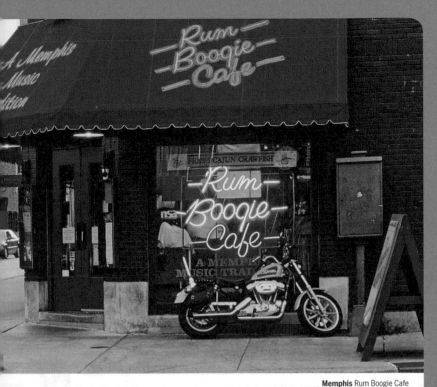

Memphis Rum Boogie Cafe

behind the annual **Juke Joint Festival** (www.jukejointfestival.com; tickets \$15). Wednesday through Saturday live music sweeps through Clarksdale like a summer storm. Morgan Freeman's **Ground Zero Blues Club** (www .groundzerobluesclub.com; 0 Blues Alley; ⊗11am-2pm Mon-Tue, to 11pm Wed & Thu, to 1am Fri & Sat) has the most professional bandstand and sound system, but it will never compare to **Red's** (☑662-627-3166; 395 Sunflower Ave; cover \$10; ⊗live music 9pm Fri & Sat), a funky, red-lit, juke joint run with in-

your-face charm by Red himself. He'll fire up his enormous grill outside on special occasions. The **Delta Blues Museum** (www.deltabluesmuseum .org; 1 Blues Alley; adult/senior & student \$7/5; ⊗9am-5pm Mon-Sat), set in the city's old train depot, has a fine collection of blues memorabilia, including Muddy Waters' reconstructed Mississippi cabin. The creative, multimedia exhibits also honor BB King, John Lee Hooker, Big Mama Thornton and WC Handy.

✕ 🛏 p236

The Drive » From Clarksdale, take US 49 south from the Crossroads to the tiny town of Tutwiler.

- - - - - - - - - -

TRIP HIGHLIGHT

❺ Tutwiler

Sleepy Tutwiler is where WC Handy heard that ragged guitar man in 1903. Handy, known as the 'father of the blues,' was inspired to (literally) write the original blues song, in 12 bars with a three chord progression and AAB verse pattern, in 1912, though he wasn't widely recognized as an originator until 'Beale Street Blues' became a hit

Classic Trip

WHY THIS IS A CLASSIC TRIP
ADAM SKOLNICK, AUTHOR

The story of America is one of arrival from elsewhere, suffering at the mercy of nature – or an oppressor or time – and it's also a story of rebirth. The blues is America's soundtrack. Beautiful and wild, it thrums up in those darkest hours and explodes like catharsis. It's a painkiller, a purification. In the moment, it feels like liberation. It's a sound that revolutionized America. And it happened here.

Top: Instrument display, Delta Blues Museum
Left: Tunica Visitors Center
Right: James 'Chicken' Dooris, Ground Zero Blues Club

Gateway
TO THE
BLUES
— TUNICA, MS —
★

VISITORS
CENTER **ENTRAN**

in 1916. That way-back divine encounter, which birthed blues and jazz, is honored along the **Tutwiler Tracks** (off Hwy 49; 🚶), where the train station used to be. The mural also reveals the directions to **Sonny Boy Williamson's Grave** (off Hwy 49; 🚶🚻). He's buried amid a broken-down jumble of gravestones. Williamson's headstone is set back in the trees. Rusted harmonicas, candles and half-empty whiskey bottles have been left here out of respect.

The Drive ❯❯ Continue on the other Blues Highway, US 49 south through more farmland, across the Yazoo River, and into the rather charming and tony town of Greenwood.

⑥ Greenwood

Greenwood is the Delta's most prosperous town that doesn't involve slot machines. The financial backbone here is the Viking Range corporation which build its magnificent ranges in town and whose wares you can buy in upmarket showrooms. There is also a fantastic cafe and a fine hotel – the best in the Delta – within these city limits. And each May, the town gets behind the local music scene, with its annual **River to the Rails** (📞662-453-7625; www.rivertotherails.org; 325 Main St) festival. Along with two days of live blues, there is a barbecue

Classic Trip

and an art competition. As far as history goes, Greenwood happens to be the hometown of Byron de la Beckwith, the presumed murderer of Medgar Evers.

✕ ⎧═ p237

The Drive » From Greenwood, take US 82 east, over the Yazoo River, through leafy horse country, and through an ugly commercial bloom of big chain stores and kitchens, into Indianola.

- - - - - - - - - - - -

TRIP HIGHLIGHT

⑦ Indianola

You have reached the home town of arguably the Delta's biggest star. When BB King was still a child, Indianola was home to **Club Ebony** (📞662-887-3086; www

.clubebony.biz; 404 Hannah St; no cover; ⊙noon-late daily, live music 6-10pm Sun), a fixture on the so-called 'chitlin circuit.' Ebony gave BB his first steady work, and hosted legends like Howlin' Wolf, Muddy Waters, Count Basie and James Brown. The corner of Church and 2nd is where BB used to strum his beloved guitar, Lucille, for passers-by. Nearby, the **BB King Museum & Delta Interpretive Center** (📞662-887-9539; www.bbkingmuseum.org; 400 Second St; adult/child 5-12yr/under 5yr $12/$5/free; ⊙10am-5pm Tue-Sat, noon-5pm Sun & Mon) is set in a complex around the old Indianola cotton gin. The experience starts with a 12-minute film covering his life's work. Afterward you are free to roam halls packed with interactive exhibits, tracing King's

history and his musical influences – African, gospel and country. Other interactive exhibits demonstrate his influence on the next generation of artists, including Jimmie Hendrix and the Allman Brothers. Oh, and his 12 Grammy awards are here too. King returns to Indianola for a free annual show as part of his annual **BB King Homecoming** (www .bbkingmuseum.org; Fletcher Park; advance purchase/day of $12/18) festival.

The Drive » From Indianola, go west through the fast-food jumble along US 82 into Leland.

- - - - - - - - - - - -

⑧ Leland

Leland is a small, down-on-its-luck town, but one with a terrific museum. **Highway 61 Blues Museum** (📞662-686-7646; www.highway61blues.com; 400 N Broad St; admission $7; ⊙10am-5pm Mon-Sat; 🚸) offers details on local folks like Ruby Edwards and David 'Honeyboy' Edwards. It also puts on a lauded blues festival each October, held in Warfield Point Park, right on the Mississippi River.

Local luminary Jim Henson, the creator of the Muppets, is also from Leland, and his life and work are celebrated at the **Jim Henson Exhibit** (📞662-686-7383; www .birthplaceofthefrog.com; 415 S Deer Creek Dr; donations

---

BB KING'S BLUES

BB King grew up in the cotton fields on the outskirts of Indianola, a leafy middle-class town, and it didn't take long before he learned what it meant to have the blues. His parents divorced when he was four. His mother died when he was nine. His grandmother passed away when he was 14. All alone, he was forced to leave Indianola – the only town he ever knew – to live with his father. He quickly became homesick, and made his way back. As a young man he was convinced he would become a cotton farmer. There weren't many other possibilities to consider. Or so he thought. When he went to Memphis for the first time in the 1940s, his world opened. From there he drifted into West Memphis, Arkansas, where he met Sonny Boy Williamson, who put the young upstart on the radio for the first time, launching his career.

encouraged; ⊙10am-4pm Mon-Sat) on the bank of Deer Creek.

The Drive » Head west on US 82 for 25 miles until it ends near the river.

- - - - - - - - - -

❾ Greenville

The Mississippi River town of Greenville was a fixture on the riverboat route and has long been a gambling resort area. For years it supported blues and jazz musicians who played the resorts, and some – including BB King – make appearances to this day. Although it's scruffy around the edges, Greenville can be pleasant along the river. But the real reason to visit is to try the steaks, tamales and chili at **Doe's Eat Place** (☑662-334-3315; 502 Nelson St; ⊙5-9pm Mon-Sat), a classic hole-in-the-wall joint you may never forget.

The Drive » Return to Indianola then drive south on US 49W to humble Bentonia.

- - - - - - - - - -

❿ Bentonia

Bentonia, once a thriving farming community, now has fewer than 100 people and the downtown is gutted, but it's still home to one of Mississippi's most historical jukes. The Holmes family opened **The Blue Front** (☑662-755-2278; www.facebook.com/BentoniaBluesFestival; downtown Bentonia; ⊙hours vary, call ahead) during

DETOUR: PO MONKEYS

Start: ❹ Clarksdale

Take US 61 south from Clarksdale for about 27 miles and head west on Dillon Rd through farmland. Po Monkeys, in Merigold, Mississippi, is one of the Delta's most beloved juke joints. It only has live music about once a month, but there's sweet trouble to be found here on Mondays when naked Shack Dancers prowl, and on Thursdays when college kids dance to DJ sets till the wee hours. Being a night-time venue, you'll be doubling back to Clarksdale after partying here.

the Jim Crow period, when African Americans weren't even allowed to sip Coca-Cola. They sold house-stilled corn liquor (to blacks and whites) during Prohibition and welcomed all the Delta blues artists of the day: Sonny Boy, Percy Smith and Jack Owens among them. The joint still opens in the evenings, but live blues only blooms during Bentonia's annual **festival** (www.facebook.com/BentoniaBluesFestival; Downtown Bentonia; tickets $10; ⊙mid-Jun) when the town comes back to life, if ever so briefly.

FAVORITE BLUES FESTS

To make the most of your music-loving dollar, hit the Delta during one of its many blues festivals. Rooms can be scarce. Book well in advance.

» Juke Joint Festival (www.jukejointfestival.com; tickets $15) Clarksdale, mid-April

» King Biscuit Blues Festival (www.kingbiscuitfestival.com; tickets $45) Helena, October

» BB King Homecoming (www.bbkingmuseum.org; Fletcher Park; tickets $18) Indianola, early June

» Highway 61 Blues Festival (www.highway61blues.com; Warfield Point Park) Leland, early June

» Bentonia Blues Festival (www.facebook.com/BentoniaBluesFestival; Downtown Bentonia; tickets $10) Bentonia, mid-June

» Sunflower River Blues & Gospel Festival (www.sunflowerfest.org) Clarksdale, August

Eating & Sleeping

Memphis ❶

✕ Arcade
Diner $

(www.arcaderestaurant.com; 540 S Main St; mains $8-10; ⏰7am-3pm, plus dinner Fri) Elvis used to eat at this ultra-retro diner, Memphis' oldest. Crowds still pack in for sublime sweet-potato pancakes and greasy-spoon cheeseburgers. It's walking distance from downtown and Beale St.

✕ Charlie Vergos' Rendezvous
Barbecue $$

(☎901-523-2746; www.hogsfly.com; 52 S 2nd St; mains $10-20; ⏰4:30-10:30pm Tue-Thu, 11am-11pm Fri, from 11:30am Sat) Tucked in an alleyway off Union Ave, this subterranean institution sells an astonishing 5 tons of its exquisite dry-rubbed ribs weekly. The ribs don't come with any sauce, but the pork shoulder does, so try a combo and you'll have plenty of sauce to enjoy. The beef brisket is also tremendous. With a superb, no-nonsense waitstaff, and walls plastered with historical memorabilia, eating here is an event. Expect a wait.

✕ Gus's World Famous Fried Chicken
Chicken $

(☎901-527-4877; www.facebook.com/pages/Guss-World-Famous-Fried-Chicken-Memphis-TN/103867756323858; 310 S Front St; mains $6-9; ⏰11am-9pm Sun-Thu, to 10pm Fri & Sat) Fried-chicken connoisseurs across the globe twitch in their sleep at night, dreaming about the gossamer-light fried chicken at this downtown concrete bunker with the fun, neon-lit interior and vintage juke box. On busy nights, waits can top an hour. So worth it.

🛏 Heartbreak Hotel
Hotel $$

(☎877-777-0606, 901-332-1000; www.elvis.com/epheartbreakhotel; 3677 Elvis Presley Blvd; d from $120; P ❄ @ 🛜 🖙) At the end of Lonely St (seriously) across from Graceland, this basic hotel is tarted up with all things Elvis. Ramp up the already palpable kitsch with one of the themed suites, such as the red-velvet monstrosity that is the Burnin' Love room.

🛏 Madison Hotel
Boutique $$$

(☎901-333-1200; www.madisonhotelmemphis.com; 79 Madison Ave; r from $264; P ❄ @ 🛜 🖙) If you're looking for a sleek treat, check in to this swanky, boutique sleep. The rooftop garden is one of the best places in town to watch a sunset, and rooms have nice touches, like high ceilings, Italian linens and whirlpool tubs.

Clarksdale ❹

✕ Abe's
BBQ $

(☎662-624-9947; 616 State St; sandwiches $4-6, plates $6-14; ⏰10am-9pm Mon-Thu, 10am-10pm Fri & Sat, 11am-2pm Sun; 🖙) In business at the crossroads since 1924, the slow-burning, chili-smothered tamales and melt-off-the-bone ribs are dynamite, and it does brisket and pulled pork sandwiches and plates too.

✕ Delta Donuts
Donuts $

(☎662-627-9094; 610 N State St, Clarksdale; doughnuts $2; ⏰6am-11am; 🖙) Forget calories, and enjoy one of these delectably warm doughnuts stuffed with chocolate and vanilla cream.

✕ Oxbow
Deli $

(115 3rd St; ⏰10am-6pm Mon-Fri, to 5pm Sat) Self-caterers will want to stop by this fresh gourmet market and art gallery with some produce and a selection of specialty deli meats, cheeses, artisan breads, and an array of house-made salads including a tasty-looking quinioa salad and citrus ginger slaw.

✕ Rust   Southern $$

(www.rustclarksdale.com; 218 Delta Ave; mains $12-36; ⊘6-9pm Tue-Thu, to 10pm Fri & Sat) Upscale comfort food done with some degree of aplomb. The crawfish cakes (seasonal) are nice and the grilled asparagus with balsamic reduction is a winner. The burger is decent too. Overall, it's good, not great, unless you count the atmospherics. Think: wood floors, intimate booths and cozy corners. It's definitely a nice spot for a dinner out before a blues show.

✕ Yazoo Pass   Cafe $$

See Trip 🖫 (p225).

⚏ Lofts at the Five & Dime   Lofts $$

(☏888-510-9604; www.fiveanddimelofts. com; 211 Yazoo St; lofts $150-175) Set in a 1954 building are six plush, loft-style apartments with molded concrete counters in the full kitchen, massive flat screens in living room and bedroom, exposed rafters, terrazzo showers and free sodas and water throughout your stay. Units sleep up to four people comfortably.

⚏ Shack Up Inn   Inn $

See Trip 🖫 (p225).

Greenwood ❻

✕ Delta Bistro   Southern fusion $$

(☏662-455-9575; www.deltabistro.com; 117 Main St; mains $9-24; ⊘11am-9pm Mon-Sat) A tasty upmarket cafe serving southern treats like fried catfish and barbecue shrimp po' boys and crab bisque, as well as fine departures like the tender elk brisket, and a seared duck breast served with pork belly and grilled baby asparagus. This is the best kitchen in the Delta.

⚏ Alluvian   Boutique Hotel $$$

(☏662-453-2114; www.thealluvian.com; 318 Howard St; r $200-215; Ⓟ ❋ @ ⧠) A stunning four-star boutique hotel done up by the Viking corporation, with a gushing fountain in the courtyard and spacious rooms and suites with all the trimmings: soaker tubs, high ceilings, granite wash basins and checkerboard parlor floors in the bath. Some rooms have courtyard views. Others overlook the antiquated downtown. Book ahead, especially on weekdays. This is a business hotel, after all.

Breaux Bridge *Steamy swamp*
and outstanding Cajun cu

Cajun Country 20

Enter a maze of bayous, lakes, swamps and prairies where the crawfish boils, and all-night jam sessions and dance parties don't end.

TRIP HIGHLIGHTS

160 miles

Chicot State Park
Wander between bayous and cypress stands

105 miles

Breaux Bridge
Dine on decadent Cajun fare

3 Mamou

2

6 **FINISH**

New Iberia

Morgan City · Thibodaux **START**

230 miles

Lafayette
Split time between live music and Cajun cuisine

---

4 DAYS
370 MILES / 595KM

GREAT FOR...

BEST TIME TO GO

March to June for festivals in Acadiana, plus warm weather and lots of parties.

 ESSENTIAL PHOTO

Cajun concerts rocking Fred's Lounge every Saturday morning.

 BEST FOR CULTURE

The unique folkways of Acadiana permeating south Louisiana.

20 Cajun Country

Cross into south Louisiana, and you venture into a land that's intensely, immediately unique. You will drive past dinosaur-laced wetlands where standing water is uphill from the floodplain, through villages where French is still the language of celebration (and, sometimes, the home) and towns that love to fiddle, dance, two-step and, most of all, eat well. *Bievenue Louisianne, cher*: this is Cajun Country, a waterlogged, toe-tapping nation unto itself.

❶ Thibodaux

Thibodaux (tib-ah-doe), huddled against the banks of Bayou Lafourcge, is the traditional gateway to Cajun country for those traveling from New Orleans. Thanks to a city center lined with historical homes, it's a fair bit more attractive than nearby Houma, which is often also cited as a major Cajun country destination but is in reality more of a charmless oil town. The main attraction in Thibodaux is the **Wetlands Acadian Cultural Center** (☎985-448-1375; www.nps.gov/jela; 314 St Mary St; admission free; ❃9am-8pm Mon, to 6pm Tue-Thu, to 5pm Fri & Sat, closed Sun Jun-Aug, plus Christmas & Mardi Gras; 🚻🐾), part of the **Jean Laffitte National Park** system. NPS rangers lead boat tours from here into the bayou during spring and fall; you can either chug to the **ED White Plantation** (❃10am-noon; admission $5) on Wednesday or the **Madewood Plantation** (❃10am-2:30pm; admission $28.25) on Saturday, where you're given a house tour and lunch. The Center also hosts an excellent onsite museum and helpful staff who provide free walking tours of Thibodaux town (2pm, Monday, Tuesday and Thursday). If you're lucky, you'll land here on a Monday evening, when Cajun musicians jam out (5:30pm to 7pm).

✖ p245

The Drive ❯❯ Get on Hwy 90 and drive to Breaux Bridge. It's about two hours nonstop, but don't be afraid to occasionally peel off and check out some side roads.

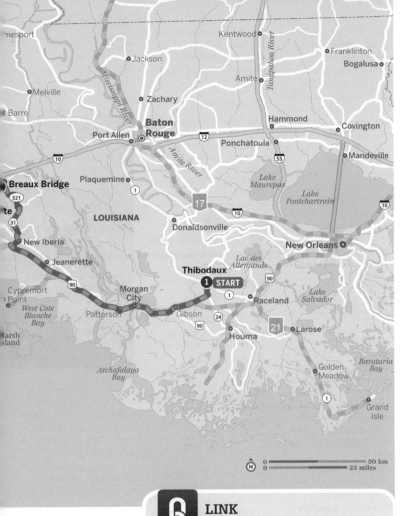

LINK YOUR TRIP

TRIP HIGHLIGHT

❷ Breaux Bridge

Little Breaux Bridge boasts a pretty 'downtown' of smallish side streets, Cajun hospitality and a silly amount of good food. Your main objective is to eat at the ridiculously

17 **Southern Gothic Literary Tour**

Search for stories amidst the storied streets of New Orleans while night falls over her gothic neighborhoods.

21 **Gulf Coast**

Go to Grand Isle and follow the Gulf Coast, from Louisiana's wetland-speckled shores to sugar sand beaches.

delicious Café des Amis (p245), where sinfully good Cajun fare is often served alongside local live music. The shows are scheduled for Wednesday nights and Sunday mornings (zydeco brunch!), but performers have a habit of dropping in unexpectedly. Otherwise there's not a lot to do in Breaux Bridge but stroll around the handsome town center and, if you're here during the first weekend in May, check out the **Breaux Bridge Crawfish Festival** (www.bbcrawfest.com).

Three miles south of Breaux Bridge is **Lake Martin** (Lake Martin Rd), a bird sanctuary that hosts thousands of great and cattle egrets, blue heron and more than a few gators. A small walkway extends over the algae-carpeted black water and loops through a pretty cypress swamp, while birds huddle in nearby trees.

Stop by Henderson, 8 miles northeast of Breaux Bridge. On Sunday afternoons, **Angelle's Whiskey River** (☏337-228-8567; 1006 Earlene Dr; cover varies; ☺call for opening hours) rocks to zydeco and Cajun tunes. It's a small house, and it gets packed. Locals dance on tables, on the bar and in the water. Nearby **Pat's** (☏337-228-7512; www.patsfishermans wharf.com; 1008 Henderson Levee Rd; mains $12-24; ☺11am-10pm, to 10:30pm Fri-

Sun; P ♿) serves decent seafood of the fried variety, and dancing of the two-step and Cajun genre.

✕ 🛏 p245

The Drive » From Breaux Bridge you can take Hwy 49 north for about 24 miles, then US 167 north to Ville Platte, then LA-3042 to Chicot State Park, a total trip time of about 80 minutes.

- - - - - - - - - - - - -

TRIP HIGHLIGHT

❸ Chicot State Park

Cajun country isn't just a cultural space – it's a physical landscape as well, a land of shadowy, moss-draped pine forest and slow-water bayous and lakes. Sometimes it can be tough seeing all this from the roadways, as roads have understandably been built away from floodable bottomlands. **Chicot State Park** (☏888-677-2442, 337-363-2403; www.crt.state.la.us/parks/ichicot.aspx; 3469 Chicot Park Rd; per person $1; P ♿ 🐾) is a wonderful place to access the natural beauty of Cajun Country. An excellent interpretive center is fun for kids and informative for adults, and deserves enormous accolades for its open, airy design. Miles of trails extend into the nearby forests, cypress swamps and wetlands. If you can, stay for early evening; the sunsets over the Spanish moss–draped

JOHN ELK III / ALAMY ©

trees that fringe Lake Chicot are superb. There are camp sites ($16 per night October to March, $20 April to September), six- and 15-person cabins ($85/120) and boat rentals (per hour/day $5/20) all available.

The Drive » Head back towards Ville Platte, then turn onto LA-10 west. After 7 miles turn south onto LA-13; it's about 4 miles more to Mamou.

- - - - - - - - - - - - -

❹ Mamou

Deep in the hart of Cajun Country, Mamou is a typical south Louisiana small town six days of the week, worth a peek

Lafayette La Chapelle des Attakapas, Vermilionville

and a short stop before rolling to Eunice. But on Saturday mornings, Mamou's hometown hangout, little **Fred's Lounge** (420 6th St; ⏰8am-1:30pm Sat), becomes the apotheosis of a Cajun dancehall.

OK, to be fair: Fred's is more of a dance shack than hall. It's a little bar and it gets more than a little crowded from 8:30am to 2pm-ish, when owner 'Tante' (auntie) Sue and her staff host a Francophone-friendly music morning, with bands, beer, cigarettes and dancing (seriously, it gets smoky in here. Fair

warning). Sue herself will often take to the stage to dispense wisdom and song in Cajun French, all while taking pulls off a bottle of brown liquor she keeps in a pistol holster.

The Drive » Eunice is only 11 miles south of Mamou; just keep heading straight on LA-13.

- - - - - - - - - - - -

⑤ Eunice

Eunice lays in the heart of the Cajun prairie, its associated folkways, and music. Musician Mark Savoy builds accordions at his **Savoy Music Center** (📞337 457 9563; www.savoymusiccenter.com; Hwy 190; ⏰9am-5pm Tue-Fri,

9am-noon Sat), where you can also pluck some CDs and catch a Saturday morning jam session. Saturday night means the Rendez-Vous Cajuns are playing the **Liberty Theater** (📞337-457-7389; 200 Park Ave; admission $5), which is just two blocks from the **Cajun Music Hall of Fame & Museum** (📞337-457-6534; www .cajunfrenchmusic.org; 230 S CC Duson Dr; admission free; ⏰9am-5pm Tue-Sat) – a small affair, to be sure, but charming in its way. The NPS-run **Prairie Acadian Cultural Center** (📞337-457-8499; www.nps .gov/jela; 250 West Park Ave;

243

CAJUNS, CREOLES AND...CREOLES

A lot of tourists in Louisiana use the terms 'Cajun' and 'Creole' interchangeably, but the two cultures are different and distinct. 'Creole' refers to descendants of the original European settlers of Louisiana, a blended mix of mainly French and Spanish ancestry. The Creoles tend to have urban connections to New Orleans and considered their own culture refined and civilized. Many (but not all) were descended from aristocrats, merchants and skilled tradesmen.

The Cajuns can trace their lineage to the Acadians, colonists from rural France who settled Nova Scotia. After the British conquered Canada, the proud Acadians refused to kneel to the new crown, and were exiled in the mid-18th century – an act known as the *Grand Dérangement*. Many exiles settled in south Louisiana; they knew the area was French, but the Acadians ('Cajun' is an English bastardization of the word) were often treated as country bumpkins by the Creoles. The Acadians-cum-Cajuns settled in the bayous and prairies, and to this day self-conceptualize as a more rural, frontier-stye culture.

Adding confusion to all of the above is the practice, standard in many post-colonial French societies, of referring to mixed-race individuals as 'creoles.' This happens in Louisiana, but there is a cultural difference between Franco-Spanish Creoles and mixed-race creoles, even as these two communities very likely share actual blood ancestry.

admission free; ⊘8am-5pm Tue-Fri, to 6pm Sat) is another worthy stop, and often hosts music nights and educational lectures.

The Drive >> Head east on US 190 (Laurel Ave) and turn right onto LA-367. Follow LA-367 for around 19 miles (it becomes LA-98 for a bit), then merge onto I-10 eastbound. Follow I-10 for around 14 miles, then take exit 101 onto LA-182/ N University Ave; follow into downtown Lafayette.

- - - - - - - - - - - - -

TRIP HIGHLIGHT

❻ Lafayette

Lafayette, capital of Cajun Country and fourth-largest city in Louisiana, has a wonderful concentration of good eats and culture for a city of its size (around 120,000). On most nights you can catch fantastic zydeco, country, blues, funk, swamp rock and even punk blasting out of the excellent **Blue Moon Saloon** (www .bluemoonpresents.com; 215 E Convent St; cover $5-8); the crowd here is young, hip and often tattooed, but they'll get down to a fiddle as easily as drum-and-bass. During the last weekend in April Lafayette hosts **Festival International de Louisiane** (www .festivalinternational.com), the largest Francophone musical event in the Western Hemisphere.

Vermilionville (📞337-233-4077; www.vermilionville .org; 300 Fisher Rd; adult/ student $8/6; ⊘10am-4pm Tue-Sun; 👪), a restored/ re-created 19th-century Cajun village, wends its way along the bayou near the airport. Costumed docents explain Cajun, Creole and Native American history, local bands perform on Sundays and boat tours of the bayou are offered. The not-as-polished **Acadian Village** (📞337 981 2364; www.acadianvillage.org; 200 Greenleaf Dr; adult/student $7/4; ⊘10am-4pm) offers a similar experience, minus the boat tours. Next to Vermilionvile, the NPS runs the **Acadian Cultural Center** (www .nps.gov/jela; 501 Fisher Rd; ⊘8am-5pm), containing exhibits on Cajun life; it's a little dry compared to the above, but still worth a visit.

✕ 🛏 p245

Eating & Sleeping

Thibodaux ➊

✖ Fremin's
Cajun $$

(☎985-449-0333; 402 West Third St; mains $11-23; ☷11am-2pm Tue-Fri, 5-9pm Tue-Thu, to 10pm Fri & Sat) Fremin's is one of the great granddaddies of high-end, classic Cajun cuisine. The menu doesn't change much, and while there are some items that could use an update, overall this is a solid menu. Case in point: soft-shell crab served over pasta with a meltingly good mushroom brandy sauce.

Breaux Bridge ➋

✖ Café des Amis
Cajun $$$

(www.cafedesamis.com; 140 E Bridge St; mains $17-26; ☷11am-2pm Tue, to 9pm Wed & Thu, 7:30am-9:30pm Fri & Sat, 8am-2pm Sun) What's better than the Creole and Cajun menu at this joint? Not much really, but there's a strong case to be made for the surreal folk art on the walls and the live zydeco breakfast that goes off every Saturday morning.

▦ Bayou Cabins
Cabin $

(☎337-332-6158; www.bayoucabins.com; 100 W Mills Ave; cabins $60-125) Each of the 14 cabins on the Bayou Teche is completely individual. Cabin 1 has 1949 newspapers as wallpaper (aka insulation), and cabin 7 has fine Victorian antiques and a claw-foot tub. Your full, hot breakfast is served at 9am and the on-site store sells homemade cracklings and boudin.

Lafayette ➏

✖ Artmosphere
American $

(☎337-233-3331; 902 Johnston St; mains under $10; ☷11am-2am Mon-Sat, to midnight Sun) Your place if you're jonesing for vegan/vegetarian food, or even just a hookah, plus a lovely selection of beer on offer. Live music every night and a crowd that largely consists of the student and artist set.

✖ Dwyer's
Diner $

(☎337-235-9364; 323 Jefferson St; mains $5-12; ☷7am-3pm; ⧉) This family-owned joint is especially fun on Wednesday mornings when local Cajuns shoot the breeze in their old-school French dialect.

✖ French Press
Breakfast $$$

(www.thefrenchpresslafayette.com; 214 E Vermillion; breakfast $6-$10.50, dinner mains $29-38; ☷7am-2pm Tue-Thu, 7am-2pm & 5:30-9pm Fri, 9am-2pm & 5:30-9pm Sat, 9am-2pm Sun; ☏) This French-Cajun hybrid is the best culinary thing going in Lafayette. Breakfasts are mind blowing, with a sinful Cajun benedict (boudin instead of ham), cheddar grits (that will kill you dead) and organic granola (offset the grits). Dinner is wonderful as well; that rack of lamb with the truffled gratin is a special bit of gastronomic dreaminess.

▦ Blue Moon Guest House
Guesthouse $

(☎877-766-2583, 337-234-2422; www.bluemoon guesthouse.com; 215 E Convent St; dm $18, r $73-94; ﾈ❄@☏) There's a backyard nightclub and hostel environs (dorms and some private rooms) in this tidy old Lafayette home. Does it get loud? Hell yes, but the music is great.

▦ La Maison de Belle B&B
B&B $$

(☎337-235-2520; 608 Girard Park Dr; r $110-150) Overnight where John Kennedy Toole dreamed up Confederacy of Dunces. The grounds and adjacent park are lovely.

Gulf Islands National Seashore
Remote islands and deserted beaches

Gulf Coast **21**

Explore a labyrinthian coast of wetlands and gulf harbors, shrimp boats, pine forests, bayous and white-sand beaches in three states.

TRIP HIGHLIGHTS

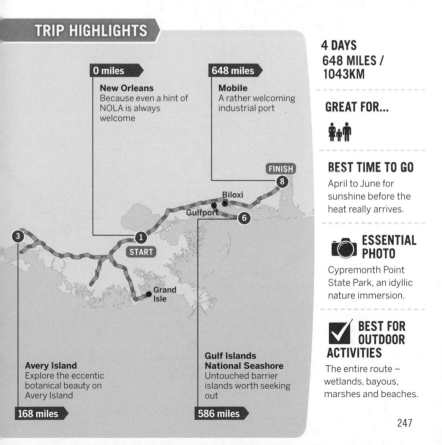

0 miles

New Orleans
Because even a hint of NOLA is always welcome

648 miles

Mobile
A rather welcoming industrial port

FINISH
8

Biloxi

Gulfport

6

3

1
START

Grand Isle

Avery Island
Explore the eccentic botanical beauty on Avery Island

168 miles

Gulf Islands National Seashore
Untouched barrier islands worth seeking out

586 miles

4 DAYS
648 MILES /
1043KM

GREAT FOR...

BEST TIME TO GO
April to June for sunshine before the heat really arrives.

ESSENTIAL PHOTO
Cypremonth Point State Park, an idyllic nature immersion.

BEST FOR OUTDOOR ACTIVITIES
The entire route – wetlands, bayous, marshes and beaches.

247

21 Gulf Coast

Florida gets all the good press when it comes to southern coastline, but the Gulf laps the beaches of Louisiana, Mississippi, and, ever so briefly, Alabama too. And while she has been used and abused and even ended up in the (bad) news more than once during the past decade, there are plenty of overlooked pockets of charm, beauty and history to occupy you.

TRIP HIGHLIGHT

❶ New Orleans

Few destinations have as many ways to creatively kill time as the Crescent City. It's deep in history and architecture, there's sensational food, and more great free live music here than anywhere else. Begin with a tipple at **Lafitte's Blacksmith Shop** (☎504 523 0066; 941 Bourbon St; ⊙noon-late), set in one of the few 18th-century cottages to survive the French Quarter fires during the

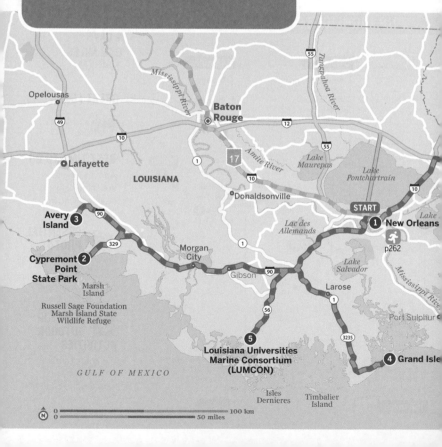

Spanish era. Then quickly seek some cleansing night music. **Preservation Hall** (www.preservationhall.com; 726 St Peter St; Cover $15; ⊘8-11pm) is the place to hear authentic New Orleans jazz played by local masters. When night falls, head to **Frenchman Street** in the Fauborg Marigny District – a haven for terrific live jazz with a more evolutionary bent. The **St Charles Avenue Streetcar** (per ride $1.25; 🚻) will take you up and down this famous avenue, through the CBD, to the **Garden**

District and **Uptown** mansions. Out in Mid City, by scenic Bayou St John, you can peruse the **New Orleans Museum of Art & Besthoff Sculpture Gardens** (📞504-658-4100; www.noma.org; 1 Collins Dibol Circle; adult/senior/child $8/7/3, out-of-state admission $16/15/10; ⊘10am-5pm Thu-Sun, noon-8pm Wed, closed Mon & Tue; 🚻) or just stroll beneath the old, mossy oaks in **City Park** (www.neworleanscitypark.com). Explore the city further with our walking tour, p262.

🍴 🛏 p253

The Drive »» Take Avery Island road (LA-329) to New Iberia town, then hop on LA-83 and take that south. After about 15 miles you'll take a right in LA-319; from here it's about 5.5 miles to Cypremont Point.

----

❷ Cypremont Point State Park

You can't get more end of the road than **Cypremont Point** (📞888-867-4510, 337-867-4510; 306 Beach Lane, Cypremort Point; adults/ senior & child under 3yr $1/ free; ⊘7am-9pm, to 10pm Fri & Sat; 🅿🚻🎎), a lonely, windswept promontory of land buffeted by foam spray off the Gulf of Mexico. There's a little man-made beach and some picnic tables, but we mainly like coming

🔗 LINK YOUR TRIP

3 North Florida Backwaters & Byways

Why turn away from the beach when you can keep going? On this trip you will traverse Mobile Bay into Pensacola and follow the coastline as it arcs and bends southward.

17 Southern Gothic Literary Tour

Explore the south's literary landscape as you investigate the roots and admire the legacy of some of America's finest scribes.

Map labels:
Lucedale
Wiggins
SSIPPI
90 miles to 3 (65)
FINISH Mobile ❽
DeSoto National Forest
Pascagoula River
Ocean Springs ❼
Mobile Bay
ALABAMA
Gulfport Biloxi
Pascagoula
Bon Segour Bay
❻
Gulf Islands National Seashore
Chandeleur Islands
Chandeleur Sound
GULF OF MEXICO
Garden Island Bay
East Bay

21 GULF COAST

249

here for the long, slightly surreal drive over miles and miles of breeze-bent marshland and still piney woods.

The Drive › From I-90 or LA-83, take the exit for LA-329 towards Avery Island. The exit is essentially attached to the cute town of New Iberia, which boasts a handsome historical center and **Shadows-on-the-Teche**, a plantation home that is as beautiful as it sounds.

TRIP HIGHLIGHT

❸ Avery Island

Tabasco, the most famous hot sauce in the world, is produced here on **Avery Island** (🕿337-365-8173; www.tabasco.com/avery-island; Jungle Gardens adult/child $8/5; ⏱9am-5pm; **P ⊞**), known for its red chili peppers and natural salt deposits. A dollar gets you onto the island and into the Tabasco factory for a (very) brief tour, which includes a creepily optimistic promotional video hosted by (seemingly) a Tabasco-swag wearing Laura Bush. More interesting are the gardens: in 1890, EA McIlhenny, son of the founder of Tabasco, started a bird sanctuary now known as **Jungle Gardens**. Here you can drive or walk through 250 acres of subtropical flora and view an amazing array of water birds (especially snowy egrets, which nest here in astounding numbers), turtles and alligators.

Watch for turtles and peacocks crossing the road and an enormous, centuries-old Buddha meditating serenely over the wetlands, a gift acquired by EA McIlhenny himself.

🛏 p253

The Drive › From I-90, take LA-1 southbound; at Larose, get off of 1 and onto LA-3235. From here it's about a 46-mile drive down to Grand Isle (you'll re-merge with LA-1 after about 16 miles), past miles of marshy lowlands and the ever-present hump of the levee.

❹ Grand Isle

The end of the road down bayou way is 70 miles southeast of Houma, in Grand Isle. The windswept barrier-island town seems to consistently take a beating from hurricanes and disasters like the BP Gulf oil spill, yet this beach village retains charm and character. In addition to seafood shacks and fishing camps, boat charters are the big business here. Watching the waves lap ashore at **Grand Isle State Park** (www.crt.state.la.us; Admiral Craik Dr; admission $1; ⏱7am-10pm), it's easy to imagine the power of mother nature. Rent canoes ($20 per day) to explore the inland canals or just watch as the brown pelicans, the state bird, dive for fish offshore.

JOHN ELK III / GETTY IMAGES ©

The Drive › From I-90, take exits for LA-56/Little Caillou Rd, which will run through the not particularly impressive heart of Houma. From Houma it's about a 35-mile drive south to Lumcon (look for Chauvin, LA, if you have a GPS) over a patchwork quilt of water, marsh and partially flooded plains.

❺ Louisiana Universities Marine Consortium (Lumcon)

Lumcon? Sounds like something out of a science fiction novel, right? Well, there is science here, but it's all fact, and still fascinating. **Lumcon** (🕿985-851-2800;

Avery Island Tabasco factory

www.lumcon.edu; 8124 Hwy 56; ⊘8am-4pm; 🚻) is one of the premier research facilities dedicated to the Gulf of Mexico; if you want to dig deeper into the region's ecosystems, you shouldn't pass this place up. There are nature trails running through hairy tufts of grassy marsh, nine small aquariums and an observation tower that gives visitors an unbeatable view (short of climbing into a helicopter) of the great swathes of flat, fuzzy wetlands that makes up the south Louisiana coast.

The Drive » Work your way back to the I-90 to New Orleans, and hop the I-10 to the Gulfport exit.

- - - - - - - - - - -

TRIP HIGHLIGHT

❻ Gulf Islands National Seashore

A maze of wetlands, beaches and five off-shore barrier islands, it's not tremendously accessible, but if you plan ahead, you will experience the migrating birds, scrubby dunes and empty white-sand beaches. The three wilderness islands, **Horn**, **Petit Bois** and **East Ship Island**, are open to camping, but you'll need to charter a boat to get there. During the osprey nesting season some parts of the island will be off limits to nurture the nesting flocks. **West Ship Island** is the most accessible island in the archipelago. There's a twice daily **ferry** (📞228-864-1014; www.msshipisland.com/; 1022 23rd Ave, Gulfport Ferry Pier, Gulfport; round trip adult/child $27/17) to and from the island all summer, and ferries run Wednesday to Sunday in the spring and fall. In addition to snorkeling, body boarding, swimming and beachcombing, you can

251

visit **Fort Massachusetts**, a brick fort built in 1868, right on the beach.

The Drive ≫ Hug the coastline on Beach Blvd through Biloxi and take the Bienville Blvd Bridge into Ocean Springs.

- - - - - - - - - - - - - -

❼ Ocean Springs

Ocean Springs remains charming with a romantic line-up of shrimp boats in the harbor alongside recreational sailing yachts, a historical downtown core, and a powdery fringe of white sand on the gulf. The highlight is the **Walter Anderson Museum** (www.walterandersonmuseum.org; 510 Washington St; adult/child $10/5; ⊘9:30am-4:30pm Mon-Sat, 12:30-4:30pm Sun). A consummate artist and lover of Gulf Coast nature, Anderson suffered from mental illness, which spurred his solitary, almost monastic, existence

that fueled his life's work. After he died, the beachside shack where he lived on Horn Island was discovered to be painted in mind-blowing murals, which you'll see here. You can also access the **Davis Bayou**, part of **Gulf Islands National Seashore** (www.nps.gov/guis; camping $16-20).

✖ p253

The Drive ≫ Stay off the interstate a while, and stay on the US 90, a causeway with alternating gulf and wetland views, through the port of Pascagoula, skirt the Grand Bay Wildlife Refuge, then hop on I-10 and buzz into Alabama.

- - - - - - - - - - - - - -

TRIP HIGHLIGHT

❽ Mobile

The city that spawned Hammerin' Hank Aaron, with its impressive industrial port, the nation's 13th biggest, and homey, historical downtown, Mobile is a surprisingly fun and

friendly place. The stroll down Dauphin St from the waterfront to its inner heart is pocked with green squares and fountains, and more than a few pubs, bars, cafes and restaurants bustling with young people, thanks to Mobile's three universities. The biggest attraction is the striking and modern **Gulf Coast Exploreum** (www.exploreum.com; 65 Government St; admission $10; ⊘9am-5pm Tue-Sat, noon-5pm Sun), a science center with 150 interactive exhibits and displays in three galleries, an IMAX theater and live demonstrations in its chemistry and biology labs. War geeks will want to tour the **USS Alabama** (www.ussalabama.com; 2703 Battleship Pkwy; adult/child $15/6; ⊘8am-6pm Apr-Sep, 8am-5pm Oct-Mar), a 690ft behemoth famous for escaping nine major WWII battles unscathed. Baseball historians should stop by **Hank Aaron Stadium** (📞251-479-2327; www.hankaaronstadium.com; 755 Bolling Brothers Blvd; adult/child $3/2; ⊘9am-5pm Mon-Fri, 10am on game weekends), home of the Mobile Bay Bears, where there is a museum, set in his old childhood home (moved to this location). It documents his incredible life from obscure Alabama poverty to home-run king.

✖ 🛏 p253

DISASTER ENDURANCE

In the backyard of New Orleans, the Mississippi Gulf Coast's economy, traditionally based on the seafood industry, got a shot of adrenaline in the 1990s when big Vegas-style casinos muscled in alongside the sleepy fishing villages. And then a double whammy of disasters descended. Just when the casinos in Biloxi had been rebuilt following Hurricane Katrina in 2005, the *Deepwater Horizon* oil spill in the Gulf in 2010 dealt the coast another blow. However, Mississippi's barrier islands helped divert much of the oil problems toward New Orleans and Alabama, and Mississippi's coastline is surprisingly serene in places – especially on those hard-to-access barrier islands.

Eating & Sleeping

New Orleans ❶

✕ Dante's Kitchen — Louisianan $$$

(☎504-861-3121; www.danteskitchen.com; 736 Dante St; mains $19-26, brunch $9-12.50; ⊘5:30-10pm Wed-Mon, 10:30am-2pm Sat & Sun) Dante's specializes in melding French, American and Louisiana traditions: pork shoulder with red *boudin* (Cajun sausage) dirty rice and maple-glazed chicken with potato-bacon hash cake are good examples, but it's the Sunday brunch we enjoy most. Debris and poached eggs on a caramelized onion biscuit, topped with a demi-glacé hollandaise sauce, is a pretty unbeatable way to start your day, unless you opt for the bread pudding French toast.

🛏 Bywater Bed & Breakfast — B&B $

(☎504-944-8438; www.bywaterbnb.com; 1026 Clouet St; r without bathroom $100) An artsy B&B, Bywater is particularly popular with lesbians, and is about as homey and laid-back as it gets. It's a restored double-shotgun, very colorful, with a kitchen and parlors in which guests can cook or loiter. The walls double as gallery space, showcasing a collection of vibrant outsider and folk art. The four guest rooms are simple and comfortable with more cheery paint and art. The owners enjoy steering guests in the right direction, whether you're looking for a great po'boy, live music or gay bars. Two-night minimum usually required.

Avery Island ❸

🛏 Estorage-Norton House — B&B $

(☎337-365-7603; www.estorge-nortonhouse.com; 446 E Main St; r incl breakfast $85-110) Located in a historical district, this is a comfortable 100-plus-year-old bungalow home with four comfortable bedrooms decked out in frilly, if cozy, accoutrement. Two of the rooms can sleep three or more. *Pain perdu* ('lost bread,' or French toast) topped with marmalade is a breakfast special.

Ocean Springs ❼

✕ Government Street Grocery — Pub $

(www.facebook.com/pages/The-Government-Street-Grocery/288438943516; 1210 Government St; mains $7-10; ⊘4pm-1am Mon, from 11am Tue-Thu, 11am-2:30am Fri & Sat) It does an array of burgers, fried shrimp baskets and po'boys, gyro and falafel. It gets a nice bar crowd at night, especially Thursdays through Saturdays, thanks to its live-music calendar.

✕ Leo's — Pizza $$

(www.facebook.com/pages/Leos-Wood-Fired-Pizza/207257882651589; 1107 Government St; mains $9-13; ⊘11am-9pm Sun-Thu, to 1am Fri & Sat) A wood-fired pizzeria with an upmarket sensibility. Its trendy dining room spills onto the shady patio with ample bar space. It pours two dozen beers from the tap, and makes its pizzas, wraps, salads and sandwiches in an open kitchen, which closes at 10pm on Fridays and Saturdays.

Mobile ❽

✕ Wintzell's — Seafood $$

(☎251-432-4605; www.wintzellsoysterhouse.com; 605 Dauphin St; mains $11-23; ⊘11am-10pm Sun-Thu, 11am-11pm Fri & Sat) A Mobile classic since 1938, and the first of an Alabama chain. It specializes in oysters raw, char-grilled or fried but it also does an excellent broiled fish of the day, and serves succulent shrimp and scallops too, in brew-house, blue-jean environs.

🛏 Battle House — Hotel $$

(☎251-338-2000; www.marriott.com/hotels/travel/mobbr-the-battle-house-renaissance-mobile-hotel-and-spa/; 26 N Royal St; r from $159; P ❋ @ 🛜 🏊 🐾) By far the best address in Mobile, you want to stay in the original historical wing with its ornate domed marble lobby, though the striking new tower is on the waterfront. Rooms are spacious, luxurious, four-star chic.

Buffalo River Kayak and hike
through sublime landscapes

Backroads Arkansas

22

From the Capitol steps, head north and veer off the interstate into layered mountains laced with streams and rivers, studded with quirky towns and blessed with magnificent vistas.

TRIP HIGHLIGHTS

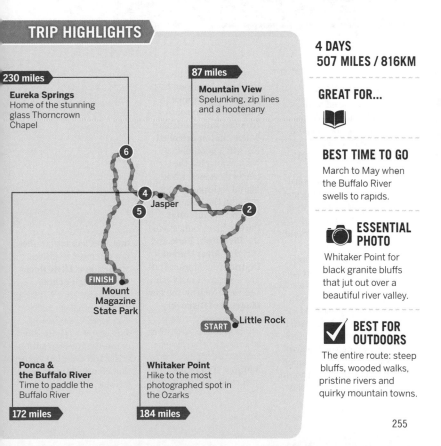

230 miles

Eureka Springs
Home of the stunning glass Thorncrown Chapel

87 miles

Mountain View
Spelunking, zip lines and a hootenany

6

4
Jasper

5

2

FINISH
Mount Magazine State Park

START   Little Rock

Ponca & the Buffalo River
Time to paddle the Buffalo River

172 miles

Whitaker Point
Hike to the most photographed spot in the Ozarks

184 miles

4 DAYS
507 MILES / 816KM

GREAT FOR...

BEST TIME TO GO
March to May when the Buffalo River swells to rapids.

ESSENTIAL PHOTO
Whitaker Point for black granite bluffs that jut out over a beautiful river valley.

BEST FOR OUTDOORS
The entire route: steep bluffs, wooded walks, pristine rivers and quirky mountain towns.

255

Backroads Arkansas

Arkansas offers dry counties and left-wing history, folk music and hot springs. Her two-lane country backroads roll by tucked-away cattle ranches, magically disintegrating barns, cathedral caverns and the life-affirming Buffalo River. Frequently tree shaded and generally spectacular, you will see a snapshot of Americana far off the beaten track.

Eureka S

Beaver Lake

Rogers

Springdale

Huntsv

Fayetteville

540 71

23

Arkansas River

30

Pa

10   FII
Booneville   **Mount M**
71   **St**

Wil

❶ Little Rock

It would be easy to dismiss this leafy, attractive state capital on the Arkansas River as quiet, maybe a little dull, and certainly conservative. But you'd be wrong. Little Rock is young, up-and-coming, gay- and immigrant-friendly, and just friendly in general. Start at the **William J Clinton Presidential Center** (☎501-748-0419; www.clintonlibrary. gov; 1200 President Clinton Ave; adult/reduced/child $7/5/3, with audio $10/8/6; ◷9am-5pm Mon-Sat, 1-5pm Sun), where you'll learn that, at 32, Bill became the youngest governor in US history. The display

commemorating his unlikely, victorious 1992 presidential campaign includes a video clip from the famous debate when Clinton defended his wife's good name. Next, walk past the perfectly rusted Rock Island Railroad Bridge, through the 30-acre **Clinton Presidential Park**, which connects to the **Riverfront Park**, and thriving **River Market District** (the Market Hall has a range of tasty ethnic eateries). Nearby, the new **Museum of Discovery** (www.museumofdiscovery .org; 500 President Clinton Ave; adult/child $10/8; ◷9am-5pm Tue-Sat, 1-5pm Sun) is a proper science and natural history museum

that's perfect for families. But the most riveting attraction is **Little Rock Central High School** (www.nps.gov/chsc; 2125 Daisy Bates Dr; ◷9:30am-4:30pm, tours 9am & 1:15pm Mon-Fri mid-Aug–early Jun), the site of the 1957 desegregation crisis and eventual victory that changed the country forever.

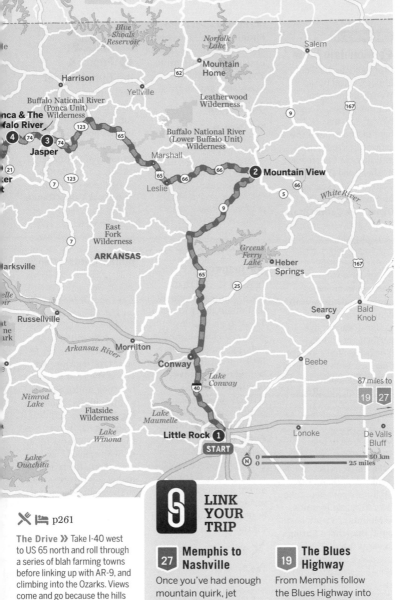

87 miles to
19 27

X 🛏 p261

The Drive ›› Take I-40 west
to US 65 north and roll through
a series of blah farming towns
before linking up with AR-9, and
climbing into the Ozarks. Views
come and go because the hills
are draped in velvety trees. After
threading a mountain pass you
will descend into a wide valley.

🔗 **LINK YOUR TRIP**

27 Memphis to Nashville

Once you've had enough
mountain quirk, jet
into some nightlife on
this trip linking two of
America's best night
music towns.

19 The Blues Highway

From Memphis follow
the Blues Highway into
the Mississippi (and
Arkansas!) Delta, and get
a whole different kind of
country flavor.

② Mountain View

Promoted as the 'Folk Music Capital of the World,' impromptu hill music, gospel and bluegrass jams are held in and around the attractive sandstone buildings of Courtsquare by the Stone County Courthouse (especially on Saturday night). The **Ozark Folk Center State Park** (☎800-264-3655; www .ozarkfolkcenter.com; 1032 Park Ave; auditorium adult/ child $12/7; ◷10am-5pm Tue-Sat Apr-Nov), just north of town, hosts ongoing old-timey craft demonstrations, as well as frequent live performances (folk, bluegrass, Shakespeare) that lure an avid, older crowd. The park's newest concession, **LocoRopes** (☎870-269-6566; www .locoropes.com; 1025 Park Ave; per zip line $7.50; ◷10am-5pm Mar 1-Nov 30) offers a ropes course, slack lining, a free fall, a climbing wall and three zip lines. From here take Hwy 87 north 14 miles to Mountain View's best sight, **Blanchard Springs Caverns** (☎870-757-2211; www.blanchardsprings.org; NF 54, Forest Rd, off Hwy 14; adult/child Drip Stone Tour $10.50/5.50, Wild Cave Tour $75; ◷10:30am-4:30pm; ⓘ), where you can opt for the rather staid, one-hour Drip Stone Tour, or sign up for three to four hours

of genuine spelunking. Shimmy through a crawl space, and emerge into an underground cathedral. You'll return filthy, exhausted and smiling.

✖ ⤶ p261

The Drive ❯❯ AR-66 winds west through gorgeous pasture land, rolling green hills, and some stunning pastoral villages. In quaint Leslie turn onto US 65 and head north. Cross the Buffalo River and take AR-123 south past gorgeous views of granite bluffs to the AR-74 west into Jasper.

---

③ Jasper

Here's a simple rustic town that leans heavily on Buffalo River tourism. There are a couple of good eateries, affordable lodgings and a fabulous little adventure boutique selling pocket knives, hammocks, quick-dry T-shirts, water bottles, camp stoves and kayaks, of course. **The Floating Buffalo** (www.thefloating buffalo.com; Church St; ◷noon-6pm Mon-Fri, from 10am Sat & Sun) is set in an old saddlery-turned-service station; it'll have everything you may need for the river or campsite.

✖ p261

The Drive ❯❯ Take AR-74 west from Jasper, wrap around the horseshoe canyon where you can see more river bluffs, and drop into Low Gap. From here, take the hairpin before the Steel Creek put-in, where there are still more bluff views, meet the AR-43 and buzz into Ponca.

④ Ponca & the Buffalo River

Ponca is an early-20th-century mining camp–turned–ranch town whose current perch makes it the best launch point for a day's paddle on the Buffalo. Rent canoes or kayaks from **Lost Valley Canoe** (☎870-861-5522; www .lostvalleycanoe.com; Hwy 43, Ponca; kayaks per day $40, shuttle service $27) or **Buffalo Outdoor Center** (BOC; ☎800-221-5514; www .buffaloriver.com; cnr Hwys 43 & 74, Ponca; kayak/canoe per day $58/60, car shuttle from $18, zip line tour $89; ◷8am-5pm; ⓘⓘ) in Ponca. Both will shuttle your car to your landing spot. From Ponca the river snakes between multicolored granite bluffs. Those at **Big Bluff** are a mind-boggling 525ft, the highest rock faces in mid-America. Once you pass them, the river makes a 90-degree bend to the right, where you'll find a thumb. Pull into it, and find the **Goat Trail** on the left bank. It leads to a sublime lookout 350ft above the river. A few miles downstream, three bluffs after the well-marked **Jim's Bluff**, the river makes a hard right. Stay left, and stop on the gravel bar in the center of that curve. Follow the unmarked

Buffalo River region Whitaker Point

spur trail to **Hemmed-in-Hollow**, the Ozarks' tallest waterfall. Paddle on to **Kyle's Landing**, a campground 10 miles downstream from Ponca, and pull out.

🛏 p261

The Drive ›› Take AR-43 past the AR-21 turn-off, and go over two small bridges. Just before the third, make a right onto a graded dirt road. In 6 miles, just past Cave Mountain Church, you'll find a trailhead.

TRIP HIGHLIGHT

❺ Whitaker Point

You can't leave the Buffalo River area until you've hiked this easy 1.5-mile trail (one way) to a granite table-top jutting out from streaked bluffs, draining rainwater 500ft above the lush river valley. Pristine, verdant ridges roll to the horizon in all directions. It's simply spectacular. No wonder it's the most photographed location in the Ozarks.

The Drive ›› Double back to AR-21 and head north past still more stunning countryside until you get to the forgettable commercial sprawl of Berryville. From here follow US 62 west to Eureka Springs.

THE LITTLE ROCK 9

Despite the landmark 1954 *Brown v Board of Education* ruling by the US Supreme Court, which unanimously determined segregation in public schools to be unconstitutional, by 1957 blacks were still being barred from Little Rock's public schools. A handful of educators and members of the local school board, some of whom were well-meaning white Southerners, were determined to change this. They identified nine pioneering African American students to enroll that fall, but they were not prepared for the vitriolic backlash when over 1000 white people – including several local students, as well as agitators from across the state – descended on the school to deny their entry. Police escorted the nine students inside, but as violence spread, they were secretly shuttled home. The next day, President Eisenhower federalized the Arkansas National Guard and ordered the 101st Airborne Battalion to escort the students into school. For the remainder of the year, the students were shadowed by soldiers who watched their back (and flirted with local girls).

TRIP HIGHLIGHT

❻ Eureka Springs

Artsy, quirky and gorgeous, Eureka Springs, near Arkansas' northwestern corner, perches in a steep valley and is one of the coolest towns in the South. Restored Victorian buildings line crooked, hilly streets and a crunchy local population welcomes tourists with an abundance of kitschy shops and galleries.

Thorncrown Chapel (☏479-253-7401; www .thorncrown.com; 12968 Hwy 62 West; donation suggested; ☉9am-5pm Apr-Nov, 11am-4pm Mar & Dec) is the top attraction. A magnificent sanctuary made of glass, with its 48ft-tall wooden skeleton holding 425 windows (crafted with 6000 sq ft of glass), there's not much between your prayers and God's green earth majesty here. It's in the woods on the lip above town. Our favorite shop is **Meteorites & More** (www.arnoldmeteorites.com; 28 1/2 Spring St; ☉10am-5pm) owned by Steve Arnold, the Science Channel's *Meteorite Man*. He sells space rocks, including glassy stone pieces sourced from the American desert, the Sahara and (relatively recently) Russia. **Chelsea's Pizzeria** (☏479-253-8231; www.chelseascornercafe. com; 10 Mountain St; mains $10-20; ☉noon-10pm Sun-Thu, to midnight Fri & Sat) has consistent food, but is better known for its frequent jams, held in its cavernous downstairs bar on any given night. It's always worth a peek.

✕ 🏠 p261

The Drive » Take the AR-23 south to Harrison, where blue mountains rise and the road snakes along fingerling valleys, shallow aquamarine rivers, elegantly disintegrating barns and weather-beaten log cabins. Cross under the I-40 to the AR-309 south through the impoverished mid-century town of Paris, before climbing Mount Magazine.

---

❼ Mount Magazine State Park

The magnificent vistas begin immediately after entering **Mount Magazine State Park** (☏479-963-8502; www .mountmagazinestatepark .com; 16878 Hwy 309 S). The lodge and visitor center is across the street from an excellent lookout over the Arkansas River Valley. The 2753ft **Signal Hill**, Arkansas' highest point, looms just behind. The visitor center is useful for maps, as there are 14 miles of hiking trails to explore. The park is also popular with rock climbers and paragliders, who ride and glide the thermals. From here it's an easy two-hour drive back to Little Rock.

Eating & Sleeping

Little Rock ❶

✕ House
Pub $

(www.facebook.com/TheHouseInHillcrest; 722 N Palm St; mains $8-11; ⊙11am-2pm & 5pm-late Mon-Sat; 🛜) Arkansas' first gastropub, run by Hillcrest hipsters, is really all about its excellent burgers. Get yours with a turkey or veggie patty if you must.

🛏 Capital Hotel
Boutique Hotel $$

(📞888-293-4121, 501-374-7474; www. capitalhotel.com; 111 W Markham St; r from $160; P ✳ @ 🛜) Renovated into the stately Capital Hotel, this 1872 former bank building with a cast-iron facade – a near-extinct architectural feature – is top digs in Little Rock. There is a wonderful outdoor mezzanine for cocktails, and massive elevators, the largest hydraulic lifts in Arkansas.

Mountain View ❷

✕ Tommy's Famous Pizza and BBQ
Pizza, BBQ $

(cnr Carpenter & W Main Sts; pizza $7-26, mains $7-13; ⊙from 3pm) Run by the friendliest bunch of backwoods hippies you could ask for. The BBQ pizza marries Tommy's specialties indulgently. The affable owner, a former rocker from Memphis, plays great music, has a fun vibe, and just two conditions: no attitude and no loud kids.

🛏 Wildflower Inn
Inn $

(📞870-269-4383; www.wildflowerbb.com; 100 Washington; r incl breakfast from $89; P ✳ 🛜) Set right on the Courtsquare with a rocking chair–equipped wraparound porch and cool folk art on the walls. If you can, get the front room upstairs. It's flooded with afternoon light, has a queen bed and a joint sitting room with TV. Booking online is best.

Jasper ❸

✕ Arkansas House
Cafe $$$

(📞870-446-5900; www.thearkhouse.com; 215 E Court St; mains $8-35; ⊙11am-7pm Sun-Tue & Thu, to 9pm Fri & Sat, closed Wed; 🛗) It specializes in artisinal meats, like organic beef, wild caught razorback (pork), elk, buffalo and local trout too. Its elk chili is popular, as is its crawfish etouffee.

Ponca & the Buffalo River ❹

🛏 River Wind Lodge & Cabins
Cabins $$

(📞800-221-5514; www.buffaloriver.com; cnr Hwys 43 & 74, Ponca; cabins $129-299; 🛗🐾) Choose from among 18 immaculate, well-appointed log cabins, built from local hardwoods, that sleep up to eight people comfortably (depending upon the cabin), and have outrageous mountain and valley views.

Eureka Springs ❻

✕ Mud Street Café
Cafe $$

(www.mudstreetcafe.com; 22 G S Main St; mains $9-13; ⊙8am-3pm Thu-Tue) Here are simple, tasty options like gourmet sandwiches, wraps and entree salads. The coffee drinks and breakfasts cultivate a devoted local following.

🛏 Treehouse Cottages
Cottages $$

(📞479-253-8667; www.treehousecottages.com; 165 W Van Buren St; cottage from $149-169; P ✳ 🛜) Sprinkled amid 33 acres of pine forest, these cute, kitschy and spacious stilted wooden cottages in the trees are worth finding. There's lovely accent tile in the baths, a jacuzzi tub for two overlooking the trees, a private balcony with a grill at the ready, a flat screen and a fireplace.

STRETCH YOUR LEGS
NEW ORLEANS

Start/Finish: New Orleans African American Museum

Distance: 2.6 miles

Duration: Three hours

Few destinations have as many sensational ways to kill time as the Crescent City. Its history runs deep, the colonial architecture is exquisite, and there's mouthwatering Cajun and Creole food, historical dive bars, a gorgeous countryside, and lashings of great free live music.

Take this walk on Trips

New Orleans African American Museum

We'll start in the Treme (pronounced truh-may), one of the country's oldest African American neighborhoods, at the **New Orleans African American Museum** (www.thenoaam.org; 1418 Governor Nicholls St; adult/student/child $7/5/3; ⊙11am-4pm Wed-Sat), a window into the African American experience in Louisiana, which stands out from the rest of the country due to the French-colonial connection.

The Walk » Go southeast along Governor Nicholls St and turn right onto Henriette Delille St.

Backstreet Cultural Museum

New Orleans is often described as both the least American city in America and the northernmost city in the Caribbean. This is due to a unique colonial history that preserved the bonds between black New Orleanians and Africa and the greater black diaspora. Learn about this deep culture at the **Backstreet Cultural Museum** (www.backstreetmuseum .org; 1116 St Claude Ave; admission $8; ⊙10am-5pm Tue-Sat), a small but fascinating peek into the street-level music, ritual and communities that underlie the singular New Orleans experience.

The Walk » Return to Governor Nicholls St and continue southeast. Once you cross busy Rampart St, you've entered the French Quarter. Turn right onto Royal St, a pretty lane with cute art galleries, antique shops and wonderful architecture.

Historic New Orleans Collection

The **Historic New Orleans Collection** (www.hnoc.org; 533 Royal St; admission free, tours $5; ⊙9:30am-4:30pm Tue-Sat, 10:30am-4:30pm Sun) is an interesting museum, spread over several exquisitely restored buildings and packed with well-curated exhibits. Rotating exhibitions are inevitably fascinating. Separate home, architecture/courtyard and history tours run at 10am, 11am, 2pm and 3pm, the home being the most interesting.

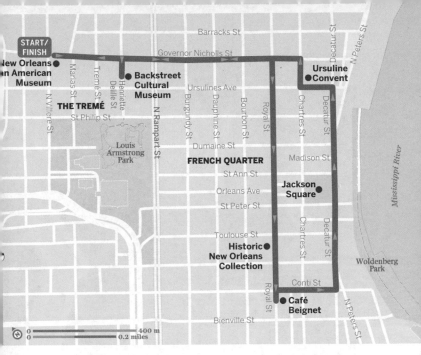

The Walk >> Continue in a southerly direction on Royal St; at the 400 block, you'll pass the marbled magnificence of the Louisiana State Supreme Court. It's only about 500ft to the next stop.

Café Beignet

You've likely heard about the beignets (fired, sugar-covered doughnuts) at Café du Monde. They're good, but the place is horribly crowded. Instead, head to **Café Beignet** (☏504 524 5530; 334B Royal St; meals $6-8; ◷7am-5pm) on Royal St. Watch pedestrians stroll by, drink your espresso in peace and try a beignet; they're delicious.

The Walk >> Turn around and turn right on Conti St, follow it for two blocks, then turn left on Decatur St. To your right, over the levee, is the Mississippi River. Walk north four blocks to get to Jackson Sq.

Jackson Square

Stroll over to Jackson Sq, the city green of New Orleans. Lovers' lanes and trimmed hedges surround a monument to Andrew Jackson, the hero of the Battle of New Orleans and the seventh

president of the USA. But the real star is the magnificent, French-style St Louis Cathedral, flanked by the Cabildo and Presbytere. The former houses a Louisiana state history museum; the latter an exhibition on Mardi Gras.

The Walk >> Continue north on Decatur St for three blocks, then turn left onto Ursulines Ave. After one block, turn right onto Chartres St.

Ursuline Convent

In 1727, 12 Ursuline nuns arrived in New Orleans to care for the French garrison's 'miserable little hospital' and educate the colony's young girls. Between 1745 and 1752 the French army built the **Ursuline Convent** (1112 Chartres St; adult/child $5/3; ◷tours 10am-4pm Mon-Sat), now the only remaining French building in the Quarter. A self-guided tour takes in various rotating exhibits and the beautiful St Mary's chapel.

The Walk >> Walk up Chartres St and turn left on Govenor Nicholls St. From here it's a half-mile back to the African American Museum and your starting point.

Tennessee & Kentucky

BOURBON AND BLUES, BLUEGRASS AND HONKY-TONKS, and some of the finest cities in America: welcome to an undercover wonderland. Tennessee has three distinct regions, represented by the three stars on the state flag. In the east you'll hike through the heather-colored Great Smokies. In the middle you'll check out the glittering honky-tonks of Nashville, and in the Delta lowlands of the west, you'll dig barbecue and blues.

Kentucky is stitched together with bluegrass pastures and jutting seams of limestone. Lonely two-lane roads link distilleries on the Bourbon Trail, and skirt the breeding grounds of million-dollar thoroughbreds in the countryside surrounding Lexington and Louisville.

Beale Street Neon guitars (Trips 23 and 27)
TETRA IMAGES / GETTY IMAGES ©

Tennessee & Kentucky

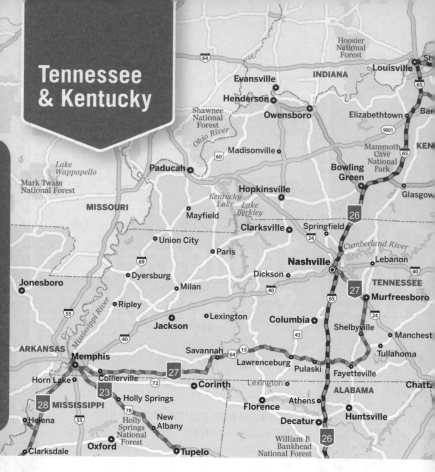

23 Elvis Presley Memorial Highway
3 days

Rejoice in the king, from humble Tupelo to glittering Graceland.

24 Kentucky Bluegrass & Horse Country 4 days

Watch throroughbreds gallop at sunrise on this picturesque journey through Kentucky bluegrass.

25 The Bourbon Trail 3 days

Taste and tour your way through America's finest whiskey distilleries.

Classic Trip

26 Tailgate Tour 6 days

A wild ramble linking iconic sports venues and the parties they inspire.

27 Memphis to Nashville 3 days

From Soulsville juke joints to beer soaked honky-tonks, music reigns supreme.

28 Big Muddy 5 days

Follow the mighty Mississippi River from Memphis to the river mouth.

DON'T MISS

Graceland

If you only make one stop in Memphis, make it the sublimely kitschy, gloriously bizarre home of the king of rock'n'roll. Visit it on Trips 23 27

Churchill Downs

On the first Saturday in May, the upper-crust don pinstripe suits and flamboyant hats for the Kentucky Derby. Join them on Trips 24 26

Woodford Reserve

A gorgeous setting and some damn fine bourbon await at this historical site along a Versailles creek. Take a taste on Trips 24 25

Stax Museum of American Soul Music

The legendary Stax studio is now a museum documenting the rise of '60s soul music. Explore it on Trips 19 27

Sun Studio

Guided tours explain how Johnny Cash, Roy Orbison andElvis became stars. See it on Trips 19 23 27 28

Churchill Downs Running of the Kentucky Derby (Trips 24 and 26)

267

Beale Street Blues
wr

Elvis Presley Memorial Highway

23

Trace the journey of a king from his humble Tupelo origins to his nouveau-riche castle in the Memphis suburbs. Along the way drive the 109-mile Elvis Presley Memorial Hwy.

TRIP HIGHLIGHTS

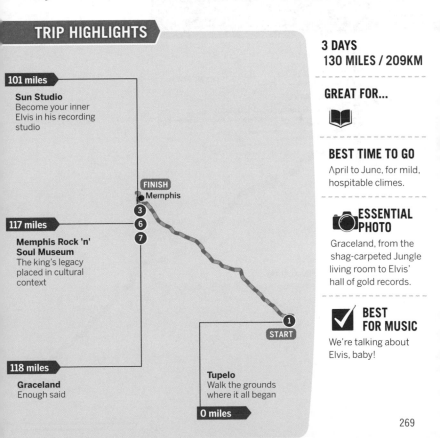

101 miles

Sun Studio
Become your inner Elvis in his recording studio

FINISH
Memphis

117 miles

Memphis Rock 'n' Soul Museum
The king's legacy placed in cultural context

START

118 miles

Graceland
Enough said

Tupelo
Walk the grounds where it all began

0 miles

---

3 DAYS
130 MILES / 209KM

GREAT FOR...

BEST TIME TO GO
April to June, for mild, hospitable climes.

ESSENTIAL PHOTO
Graceland, from the shag-carpeted Jungle living room to Elvis' hall of gold records.

BEST FOR MUSIC
We're talking about Elvis, baby!

23 Elvis Presley Memorial Highway

When Elvis wriggled his hips, women fainted, preachers raged about damnation and hell-fire, and the National Guard stormed in to keep the peace. But before all that, he was just another working-class kid from Tupelo. When his family moved to Memphis, the seed of a dream blew into the fertile soil of a musical mind. And a king bloomed.

TRIP HIGHLIGHT

❶ Tupelo

Two hours southeast of Memphis in Tupelo, MS, is **Elvis Presley's Birthplace** (📞662-841-1245; www.elvispresleybirthplace .com; 306 Elvis Presley Blvd; adult/senior/child $15/12/6; ⏰9am-5:30pm Mon-Sat, 1-5pm Sun). His 18-year-old father, Vernon, built the two-room shotgun shack in a feverish rush just before his son was born. Elvis was actually a twin, but his brother was stillborn just a half-hour

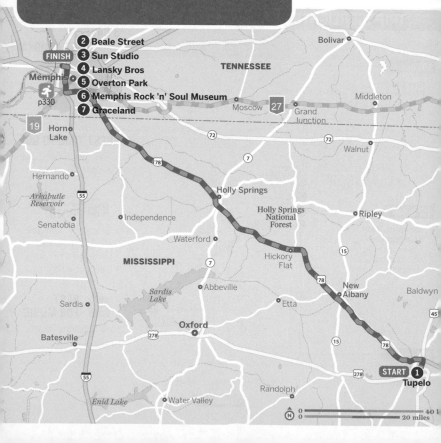

❷ Beale Street
FINISH ❸ Sun Studio
❹ Lansky Bros
Memphis ❺ Overton Park
p330 ❻ Memphis Rock 'n' Soul Museum
❼ Graceland

TENNESSEE
Bolivar
Middleton
Moscow 27 Grand Junction
19 Horn Lake
72
72
Walnut
Hernando
78
Arkabutla Reservoir
55
Holly Springs
Independence
Holly Springs National Forest
Ripley
Senatobia
Waterford
7
15
Hickory Flat
MISSISSIPPI
7
78
Sardis Lake
New Albany
Baldwyn
Sardis
Abbeville
Etta
45
Oxford
278
15
78
Batesville
55
278 START ❶ Tupelo
Randolph
Enid Lake
Water Valley
N 0 ____ 40 km
0 ____ 20 miles

before Elvis arrived on January 8. The family was soon on government assistance and money was scarce. When Elvis was just three, his father was jailed for eight months and the family lost their home. Elvis and his mother, Gladys – just 22 when she gave birth to her son – attended the Assembly of God church in Tupelo, and Elvis often hopped off mama's lap and ran to the pulpit when the choir was rocking, letting the music flow through him. You can visit his childhood church on a tour of his Birthplace site, which includes a dated section of downtown Tupelo known as the Walk of Life. It includes a mock-

up of the hardware store where he got his first guitar.

The Drive » US 78, aka the Elvis Presley Memorial Hwy, bisects the Holly Springs National Forest and Wall Doxey State Park as it rambles into Memphis in just under two hours.

----

❷ Beale Street

With a gospel base rooted in the fertile ground of his mind, Elvis Aaron Presley and his family moved to Memphis, this sultry, gritty city on the banks of the Mississippi River, when he was 13 years old, and a whole new world opened. The hallelujahs of Pentecostal Holiness choirs blended with the rhythms of the blues singers in the Beale St clubs, sounds that would later inform his genre-bending rock'n'roll.

Beale St began to form into the walking street filled with nightclubs and good times in the 1890s. WC Handy penned 'Beale Street Blues' in 1916, and from the 1920s to the 1940s greats such as Muddy Waters, Memphis Minnie and BB King all cut their teeth and honed their craft here. Elvis did the same. These days, it's less hip and more kitsch, but BB King's (p228), the guitar great's first ever blues club, remains a Beale St staple. Rum Boogie (p228) is also good for live music nightly, and

WC Handy's home (p330) is a museum. Beale St is also the start of our walking tour (p330).

🍽 🛏 p275

The Drive » Once you've been bitten by the Beale St bug (theoretically), make like Elvis and walk for a mile down Beale to Myrtle. Make a left and you'll find Sun Studio.

TRIP HIGHLIGHT

❸ Sun Studio

Welcome to ground zero for rock'n'roll. An 18-year-old Elvis reportedly walked into **SunStudio**(☎800-441-6249; www.sunstudio.com; 706 Union Ave; adult/child $12/ free; ⊙10:30am-5:30pm) and, when asked what famous musician he most sounded like, replied (cue the warbling accent) 'I don't sound like nobody.' The best part of the fact-filled tour is the old studio itself, where you can pose for pictures on an 'X' marking the spot where Elvis stood while recording his breakout single, 'That's All Right.'

Starting in the early 1950s, Sun's Sam Phillips also recorded blues artists such as Howlin' Wolf, BB King and Ike Turner, followed by the rockabilly dynasty of Jerry Lee Lewis, Johnny Cash and Roy Orbison. Forty-minute tours through the tiny studio offer a chance to hear original tapes of historic recording sessions.

LINK YOUR TRIP

27 Memphis to Nashville

Now that you're steeped in Elvis lore, and in touch with the bluesy, soulful roots that made him the king, head east to Tennessee's other music mecca, and feel that country twang.

19 The Blues Highway

Now that you've indulged in the king of rock, trace his musical roots back into the funky soil of the Mississippi Delta.

Guides are witty and full of anecdotes; many are musicians themselves. Don't leave without grabbing a CD of the 'Million Dollar Quartet,' Sun's 1956 jam session between Elvis, Johnny Cash, Carl Perkins and Jerry Lee Lewis.

The Drive » It's less than a mile down Union from Sun Studio to Memphis' long-running fashion depot.

❹ Lansky Brothers

The posh **Lansky Brothers** (📞901-529-9070; www.lanskybros.com; 149 Union Ave; ⏰9am-6pm Sun-Wed, to 9pm Thu-Sat) department store once supplied Elvis with his hi-boy collar shirts and gold lamé suits. After years of admiring their threads from afar, Elvis

began to rock them in his senior year in high school, before he could afford them. By then he had already grown out his sideburns and coated and combed his hair in Vaseline. These days, you can buy your own pink-and-black-striped 'speedway' shirt, sequined button-up, or Humes High School (Elvis' alma mater) tee.

Graceland Elvis' gold and platinum records

The Drive » From here, jog over to Poplar Ave, and take it for 3 miles through Midtown and into Memphis' signature green space.

- - - - - - - - - - -

❺ Overton Park

After recording with Sam Phillips, Elvis and his trio performed live for the first time at the Bon Air Club on July 17, 1954. At the end of the month he booked his first stage show at **Overton Park** (Poplar Ave) in leafy Midtown. It is said that the large crowd made him so nervous that his normal rhythmic stage movements became even more exaggerated. His legs and hips quaked and the women in the audience began shrieking with delight.

In recent years the band shell decayed and was narrowly saved from demolition. It reopened as **Levitt Shell** (www .levittshell.org) in 2008, with a full concert schedule.

✖ p275

The Drive » Double back to Beale St down Poplar Ave, to a museum which places Elvis' career in cultural context.

THE KING IS DEAD, LONG LIVE THE KING

Elvis died at home, face-down in the bathroom, on August 16, 1977, felled by heart failure likely brought on by chronic prescription drug abuse. He was 42. He's buried behind the house, with his parents and grandmother in the Meditation Gardens, next to the kidney-bean-shaped pool.

His passing and his life are celebrated across Memphis during **Elvis Week** (www.elvisweek.com) in mid-August, when tens of thousands of shiny-eyed pilgrims descend for seven days of festivities. *This* is Weird America. Attend a *Viva Las Vegas* or *Aloha From Hawaii* screening and dance party, an International Elvis Tribute Artist competition, or run an Elvis 5K – sideburns not included. The signature event, held on August 16, is a spooky, solemn candlelight march to his grave.

TRIP HIGHLIGHT

❻ Memphis Rock 'n' Soul Museum

Elvis didn't just drive the ladies wild, he also helped invent youth culture as we know it. That's certainly the position of the **Memphis Rock 'n' Soul Museum** (☎901-205-2533; www .memphisrocknsoul.org; cnr Lt George W Lee Ave & 3rd St; adult/child $11/8; ⊘10am-7pm), part of downtown's massive **FedEx Forum** (☎box office 901-205-2640; www.fedexforum.com; 191 Beale Street). It also further explains how gospel and the blues fed rock'n'roll and soul music. You'll hear the low, lonely howls of sweet Delta bluesmen, and the skit-skat of early

rock'n'roll on the song-packed audio tour.

The Drive » If you opt not to hop the free shuttle between this museum, Sun Studio and Graceland, make your way to I-69 south and exit on Elvis Presley Blvd. You're going to Graceland, Graceland in Memphis, Tennessee!

TRIP HIGHLIGHT

❼ Graceland

The white-columned Colonial-style mansion that is **Graceland** (☎901-332-3322; www.elvis.com; Elvis Presley Blvd/US 51; house tour adult/child $33/30, full tour $37/33; ⊘9am-5pm Mon-Sat, to 4pm Sun, shorter hours & closed Tue winter) is smaller than one might have imagined and sees 600,000 visitors a year. A then-22-year-old Elvis bought it for

about $100,000 in 1957, the year after his self-titled debut record was released by RCA.

Press play on the free audio tour and enter a shrine to both Elvis and his ostentatious 1970s style. Highlights include a wood-panelled kitchen where housekeepers once fixed vats of banana pudding; a stairwell covered entirely – ceiling included – in pea-green shag carpet; the tiki-styled Jungle Room, with its faux waterfall and leopard-print furniture, and an epic hall of gold (and platinum) records. Despite never learning to read music, Elvis made 149 top-100 records, and had 90 albums in the top 100. He sold over a billion records overall, and produced each one himself.

Out back, you'll find the movie-memorabilia-filled Trophy Room, the racquetball court, and Elvis' old office. The Platinum admission includes tours of Elvis' private planes, the Elvis jumpsuit collection and the **Graceland Automobile Museum** (☎901-332-3322; www.elvis .com; 3765 Elvis Presley Blvd; Graceland admission plus museum adult/child $29/15; ⊘9am-5pm summer, 10am-4pm winter; 🛏).

🛏 p275

Eating & Sleeping

Beale Street ❷

✕ Arcade
Diner $

See Trip ⑲ (p236).

✕ Cozy Corner
Barbecue $$

(www.cozycornerbbq.com; 745 N Pkwy; mains $7-12; ⏰11am-9pm Tue-Sat) Slouch in a torn vinyl booth and devour an entire barbecued Cornish game hen, the house specialty at this pug-ugly cult favorite. Ribs and wings are spectacular too, and the fluffy, silken sweet-potato pie is an A-plus specimen of the classic Southern dessert.

⌬ Lauderdale Courts
Inn $$$

(☎901-523-8662; www.lauderdalecourts .com; 252 North Lauderdale St; Elvis Suite $250) Sleep in the Elvis Suite, part of a Depression-era public housing complex where the Presley family lived at number 328 from 1949 through 1953.

⌬ Westin Memphis Beale Street Hotel
Hotel $$$

(☎901-334-5900; www.westinmemphis bealestreet.com; 170 Lt George W Lee Ave; r from $189) Directly across from the FedEx Forum and the gateway to Beale St, this is Memphis' newest and flashiest hotel. Spacious rooms have all the four-star trimmings and excellent service.

Overton Park ❺

✕ Bar DKDC
Gastropub $

(www.facebook.com/bardkdc; 964 S Cooper St; dishes $3-8; ⏰5pm-3am Wed-Sun) It's all

tapas here, and the food is cheap and flavorful. Per the menu's suggestions, 'begin' with sugar cane shrimp, 'continue' with an island jerk fish club sandwich and 'keep going' with jerk chicken or lamb chops or a guava glazed pork chop. The space is groovy too, with a eclectic decor, chalkboard wine list, wood floors and friendly bartenders.

✕ Beauty Shop
Fusion $$$

(☎901-272-7111; www.thebeautyshoprestaurant .com; 966 S Cooper St; mains $15-24) All the many strands that make a contemporary restaurant appealing are here. There's a sleek design, excellent lighting and soundtrack, and a creative menu. We love the Thai steak or the grilled pear salad to start. Mains include a mustard crusted brisket, and crispy Peking duck served with muddled blackberries and butternut squash.

Graceland ❼

⌬ Heartbreak Hotel
Hotel $$

See Trip ⑲ (p236).

⌬ Memphis Graceland RV Park & Campground
Campground $

(☎901-396-7125; www.elvis.com; 3691 Elvis Presley Blvd; tent sites/cabins from $27/51; P🛜🐾) Next to Graceland and owned by Elvis Presley Enterprises. Keep Lisa Marie in business when you camp out or sleep in one of no-frills log cabins (with shared bathrooms).

Rural byways Visit thoroughbred e.
climbing hot spots and historical

Kentucky Bluegrass & Horse Country

24

Drive the scenic byways from Louisville to Lexington and beyond, stopping to tour storybook country estates, horseride through the poplar forests and sip the region's famous bourbon.

TRIP HIGHLIGHTS

242 miles

Louisville
A touch of progressive hipster panache

172 miles

Versailles
Classic Kentucky horse country

FINISH
9

Frankfort

Keeneland Association

Lexington
6

Winchester

START

3

4

Shaker Village at Pleasant Hill
A blast from the stagecoach past

30 miles

Natural Bridge State Resort Park
Rock climbing Red River Gorge

110 miles

---

4 DAYS
264 MILES / 425KM

GREAT FOR...

BEST TIME TO GO

April to June for running horses; July to September for lush bluegrass pastures.

ESSENTIAL PHOTO

Churchill Downs, home of the Kentucky Derby.

BEST FOR OUTDOOR ACTIVITIES

The entire route for rural roads, backcountry trails and horses pounding the turf.

277

24 Kentucky Bluegrass & Horse Country

This trip leads from the cradle, or stud ranches, surrounding Lexington, to the ultimate winners' circle at Churchill Downs in Louisville. The secret to the state's unparalleled success in breeding and training champions is found underground, in Kentucky's rich limestone deposits. The limestone not only filters water, but its natural fertilizers also feed the lush meadows that, in turn, nourish grazing thoroughbreds.

1 Lexington

Lexington was once known as the 'Athens of the West' for its architecture and culture, and remains a mecca for thoroughbred racing fans. The 1200-acre **Kentucky Horse Park** (www.kyhorsepark.com; 4089 Iron Works Pkwy; admission adult/child $16/8, horseback riding $25; ⏲9am-5pm daily mid-Mar–Oct, Wed-Sun Nov–mid-Mar; 👪), on its outskirts, has a daily Parade of Breeds; its **Museum of the Horse** has life-sized displays on horses

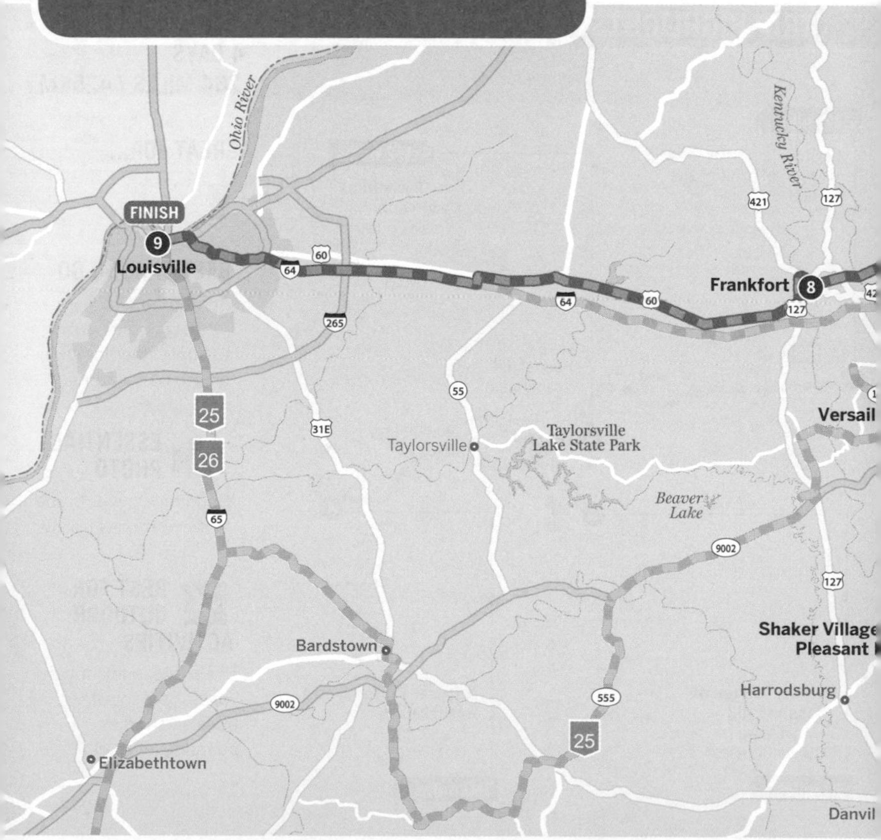

through history, and you can saddle up on a guided trail ride here, too.

To tour a working stable and training facility, visit the **Thoroughbred Center** (www.thethoroughbredcenter .com; 3380 Paris Pike; adult/ child $15/8; ⊗ tours 9am Mon-Sat Apr-Oct, Mon-Fri Nov-Mar), where you can see a day in the life of Derby hopefuls, from morning workouts to cool-downs. At night, put your money on a harness race at the famed **Red Mile** (www .theredmile.com; 1200 Red Mile Rd; ⊗ races held Aug-Oct).

Fans have been cheering from the stands at this red dirt track since 1875. Live races are only held August to October, but simulcasts and off-track betting are offered year-round.

✕ ⊨ p284

The Drive » It's a straight 18 miles from Lexington on US 27, past the suburban corporate bloom, south to the farming town of Nicholasville.

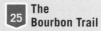

LINK YOUR TRIP

26 Tailgate Tour
Continue your pilgrimage into the soul of US sport, and take in some of America's most mythic speedways, football fields and basketball gyms.

25 The Bourbon Trail
Interspersed between pasturelands and race tracks are Kentucky's fine distilleries, where America's tastiest hooch is crafted and savored.

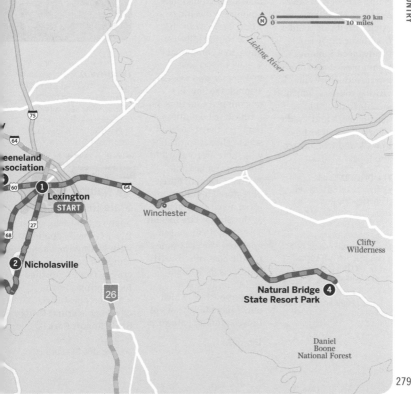

❷ Nicholasville

Strictly speaking, the area surrounding Lexington is what's known as the Inner Bluegrass (or Horse Country), and it has been a center of horse breeding for three centuries. Set on a dead-end road among wooden houses, broken-down barns and stunning pastures stitched with corral fencing, **Sunburst Horsemanship Center** (☏859-224-8480; www.sunbursthorsemanshipschool.com; 1129 Durham Lane; intro lesson $60; 🐎) isn't a stud farm, but rather a horse-riding school that offers clinics to beginners and experienced riders alike, from basic horse safety to advanced jumping techniques. It also offers fun introductory rides to visiting tourists, which include instruction on how to brush and saddle a horse, as well as how to walk and trot, canter and lope.

The Drive » To take KY-1268 to the US 68 west into Harrodsburg is to enjoy the finest scenery in the state. This narrow two-lane road bisects vast pastures, skirts sycamore trees and wraps around hairpin bends that overlook cascading streams. At times the land cleaves and the green Kentucky River snakes along great limestone bluffs known as The Palisades.

TRIP HIGHLIGHT

❸ Shaker Village at Pleasant Hill

As you close in on the **Shaker Village at Pleasant Hill** (www.shakervillageky.org; 3501 Lexington Rd; adult/child $15/5, riverboat rides $10/5; ⏱10am-5pm) the countryside fencing begins to morph from corral to the stone pile flagstone variety, a centuries-old technique that hints at the age of this bucolic settlement, part of an old stagecoach mail route since 1839.

The village itself offers tours but you can take a self-guided tour among the dwellings. In the early 1800s these softly rolling hills were home to a communal society of 500 peace-loving men and women. Though the Shakers worshipped God through uninhibited ecstatic dancing, they practiced strict celibacy (probably why there aren't any left). See their remarkable craftsmanship in dozens of restored buildings and learn about their history at the **Shaker Life Exhibit**. The Shaker Village Inn operates a lovely 3-mile paddle boat ride aboard the *Dixie Belle* (adult/child $10/5) on the Kentucky River, which offers incredible views of those stunning palisades.

🛏 p284

BLAINE HARRINGTON III / ALAMY ©

The Drive » The longest drive of the journey takes you back to Lexington on US 68 to I-64 east. At Winchester veer onto KY-9000 east into the limestone-studded Natural Bridge State Resort Park.

TRIP HIGHLIGHT

❹ Natural Bridge State Resort Park

Eastern Kentucky's Red River Gorge is abundant with jutting limestone bluffs, or palisades, with craggy faces renowned for offering some of America's best rock climbing. **Natural Bridge State Resort Park** (☏606-663-2214; www.parks.ky.gov; 2135 Natural Bridge

Versailles Stud ranch country

Rd; r $70-150, cottages $100-170) is the most accessible of the climbing hot spots in this region, thanks to its abundance of campsites and legendary climbing shop–pizza joint. In fact, your first stop should be Miguel's Pizza (p284), where you'll pick up climbing tips and find out which routes may be closed. In all, the Natural Bridge region offers 20 different climbing routes ranging in difficulty from 5.9 to 5.13b. **Red River Climbing** (www .redriverclimbing.com) is the area's best and most up-to-date online resource for trail and route information. There are also 12 hiking and biking trails in the park, though the majority are rather short. The second-longest option, the **Hoods Branch Trail**, runs for 3.75 miles along the base of the limestone cliffs. At 7.5 miles, the **Sand Gap Trail** is the longest, and runs along an old logging road. It takes four to six hours to complete.

✕ ⊨ p284

The Drive ≫ Double back to Lexington, then head west on Versailles Rd to Keeneland.

⑤ Keeneland Association

Second only to Churchill Downs in terms of race competition, **Keeneland Association** (☎859-254-3412; www.keeneland.com; 4201 Versailles Rd; admission $5) hosts two racing seasons. The first, in April, is a prelude to the Kentucky Derby, and there's another season in October, as well as at least two mega horse auctions that attract big-money buyers from around the world. The thick bluegrass turf on the infield and gorgeous stone grandstand steep the place in history. Show up early on race day and you may see the horses work out from 6am to 10am for free. Every Saturday during race season, Keeneland offers a Sunrise Trackside tour that begins with a full breakfast at 7am and includes a two-hour tour of the facility.

The Drive » From Keeneland take US 60/Versailles Rd then KY-1967 through the rolling pastureland and past corrals full of horses.

- - - - - - - - - - - -

TRIP HIGHLIGHT

❻ Versailles

The landscape around the quaint town of Versailles (pronounced Vur-sails, in these here parts) is simply stunning horse country. Think rolling pastures, stone pile and corral fencing, and gorgeous stallions and steeds basking in pre-eminent stud-ranch country. One zip through the area may be enough to make you jealous of said horses put out to stud, if not their stable mates (and there are plenty of them). Among the thoroughbred ranches you'll find here, **WinStar Farm** (☎859-873-1717; www.winstarfarm .com; 2605 Paynes Mill Rd; ⏰tours 1pm Mon, Wed & Fri) is arguably the most accomplished. Family-owned since the 1700s, this 1864-acre ranch has born, broken and trained numerous champions. Free 30-minute tours of the Stallion Complex are available and require a reservation at least one day in advance. And if you took a beating at Keeneland or Red Mile, drown your sorrows with a taste of Woodford Reserve (p292). Its magnificent distillery can be found among these pastures and streams, and is worth seeing.

The Drive » The countryside stays verdant and luscious as you roll west on the two lane KY-1681 to US 62 west to Midway.

- - - - - - - - - - - -

❼ Midway

Diminutive Midway is the state's first railroad town and home to Kentucky's only all-female college, Midway College. It's darling and historical, with railroad tracks running down the middle of a restored Main St (just one long block), freckled mostly with antique galleries. Age-old wood, brick and stone homes dot the undulating streets on both sides of a town that makes a worthy diversion, and with its surprisingly tempting and cheerful kitchens, it is a terrific place for lunch or dinner.

🍴 p284

The Drive » Take the US 62 east to Leestown Rd, hang a right on KY-1685 and a left on US 460, all of which are thin, two-lane strips through rolling countryside that lead to Frankfort.

DECADENT AND DEPRAVED

Muhammad Ali may be Louisville's favorite son, and for good reason, but Hunter S Thompson – while certainly an acquired taste – is no slouch. After bouncing around newspapers in the '60s, the Good Doctor discovered his way-out voice with an essay for the obscure literary journal *Scanlan's Monthly* in June, 1970, entitled 'The Kentucky Derby is Decadent & Depraved.' Widely considered his first gonzo journalism piece, the possibly insane, certainly drunken (or worse) writer became central to the tale. The essay follows his misadventures in and around his native Louisville during Derby weekend, and in the throes of what he later confessed to be the darkest days of his life. In fact, he thought his career was over, though it would soon launch. British illustrator (and would-be long-time collaborator) Ralph Steadman was along for a ride that included the hijacking of press passes, the spraying of mace, the hoodwinking of rubes and the discovery of a darkness lurking deep inside. It's hilarious, of course, and a must-read.

❽ Frankfort

About an hour east of Louisville is Kentucky's tiny capital, Frankfort. The **Thomas D Clark Center for Kentucky History** (Kentucky Historical Society; www.history.ky.gov; 100 W Broadway St; adult/child $4/2; ⊙10am-4pm Wed, to 8pm Thu, to 5pm Fri & Sat) is a museum with over 3000 artifacts on display, tracing the state's story from prehistoric settlements to the emergence of Muhammad Ali. Architecture buffs will want to tour the **Old State Capitol** (www.history.ky.gov; 300 W Broadway; adult/child $4/2; ⊙tours 3pm Wed & Fri, 3pm & 4:30pm Thu, 10:30am, noon, 1:30pm & 3pm Sat), which looks positively quaint, though it was the seat of power from 1830 to 1910. Learn more about how America's many wars affected Kentucky at the **Kentucky Military History Museum** (www.history.ky.gov; 125 E Main St; adult/child $4/2; ⊙10am-4pm Wed, to 8pm Thu, to 5pm Fri & Sat), housed in the former State Arsenal, built in 1850. And you can visit Daniel Boone's grave in the **Frankfort Cemetery** (E Main St).

The Drive » Take the slow road, US 60, through the Arcadian countryside and the town of Shelbyville where you'll pick up KY-1848 for your last gasp of agrarian vistas. Head south on I-264 to the I-64 west into Louisville.

GRASS IS GENERALLY GREENER

Kentucky's Bluegrass Region covers the north-central part of the state, including the cities of Lexington, Frankfort and Louisville, and is home to half the state's population. Yet, despite the name, the grass is not actually blue. *Poa pratensis*, or Kentucky Bluegrass, gets its name from the bluish-purple buds it sprouts in early summer, which, from a distance, can give the fields a slightly sapphire cast.

TRIP HIGHLIGHT

❾ Louisville

Louisville is Kentucky's most engaging and progressive town. The number of incredible kitchens multiplies every year, especially in the engaging NuLu area, where there are numerous galleries and boutiques to explore. Check them out on the **First Friday Trolley Hop** (www.ldmd.org/First-Friday-Trolley-Hop.html; Main & Market St; ⊙5-11pm, 1st Fri of the month). Downtown parallels the Ohio River, and is a wonderful stroll for fans of sports and culture alike. The **Muhammad Ali Center** (www.alicenter.org; 144 N 6th St; adult/senior & students/child $9/8/5; ⊙9:30am-5pm Tue-Sat, noon-5pm Sun) is a revelation; 'Confidence' is an incisive exhibit about how Ali's swaggering bravado signified a true self-love.

Louisville is also, of course, the crown jewel of horse racing. The Run for the Roses, as the **Kentucky Derby** is known, is the longest-running sporting event in America, and has been held at **Churchill Downs** (www.churchilldowns.com; 700 Central Ave) on the first Saturday in May for the past 138 years. Though most seats are reserved years in advance, if you're around on Derby Day you can pay $50 to get into the overflowing Paddock area. Nobody gets turned away! Though don't expect to see much of the race. You will see plenty of big hats, seersucker suits and perhaps the wildest party in America. Churchill Downs is worth a visit at any time of year, whether you're interested in its history – on display at the **Kentucky Derby Museum** (www.derbymuseum.org; Gate 1, Central Ave; adult/child $14/6; ⊙8am-5pm Mon-Sat, 11am-5pm Sun) – or you wish to glimpse training rides, warm-up races and simulcasts, available from April to November.

✕ ⊨ p284

Eating & Sleeping

Lexington ❶

✕ Table Three Ten   New American $$$

(☎859-309-3901; www.table-three-ten.com;
310 West Short St; dishes $8-32; ⊗4:30-
11pm Mon-Fri, 11am-3pm Sat, 11am-9pm Sun)
Prohibition-era cocktails? Check. Farm-
to-table cuisine? Check. Hipster waitstaff?
Indeed. Every day farmers pull up in old
pick-ups hauling baskets of rabbits, hens, pork
shoulder and veggies – the raw material from
which Lexington's best chefs work. Mains are
listed on the blackboard, and all the dishes are
imaginative and flavorful. To start, they have
a full charcuterie menu, fine cheeses, grilled
Spanish sardines and offer a popular lobster
mac and cheese.

✕ Village Idiot   Gastropub $$

(☎859-252-0099; www.lexingtonvillageidiot.
com; 307 West Short St; dishes $7-17; ⊗5pm-
midnight Sun-Wed, to 1am Thu-Sat) Hip young
foodies descend for dishes comfy and familiar,
but with a twist. Think duck confit and waffles,
or scallop and foie gras Benedict. The baked
brie, wrapped in phyllo dough and drizzled in
fig vinegar, is transcendent. It has a decent
bourbon selection, too.

⌂ Gratz Park Inn   Hotel $$

(☎800-752-4166; www.gratzparkinn.com; 120
W 2nd St; r from $179; P❈✺) On a quiet
downtown street, this 41-room hotel feels like a
genteel hunt club, with mahogany furnishings
and old-world oil paintings in heavy frames, and
a baby grand in the lobby. It's the only boutique
choice downtown.

Shaker Village
at Pleasant Hill ❸

⌂ Shaker Village Inn   Inn $$

(☎859-734-5611; www.shakervillageky.org;
3501 Lexington Rd; r from $100; P✺) Set in
the village's old trustee office, with its elaborate
double-helix stairwell, rooms are large, lovely
and full of light, with high ceilings, wood
furnishings and two rockers to read/snooze in.

Natural Bridge
State Resort Park ❹

✕ Miguel's Pizza   Pizza $$

(☎606-663-1975; www.miguelspizza.com;
1890 Natural Bridge Rd, Slade; mains $10-15;
⊗7am-9:45pm Mar-Nov) The legendary Red
River Gorge pizza joint/climbing shop/climbers
hang. Come for decent pies and expert tips on
area trails and climbing routes. It's closed from
December through February.

⌂ Hemlock Lodge   Lodge $

(☎606-663-2214, 800-255-7275; www.parks
.ky.gov; Hemlock Lodge Rd, Slade; r $70-150,
cottages $100-170) The choice sleep in the
Red River Gorge area. Here are 35 simple yet
comfortable rooms in a mountain lodge with
private balconies overlooking the pool and
surrounding beauty. Cottages are nestled in the
forest and have full kitchens. Rooms offer daily
maid service. Not so for cottages.

Midway ❼

✕ Holly Hill Inn   New Southern $$$

(☎859-846-4732; www.hollyhillinn.com; 426
N Winter St; 3-course brunch & lunch/dinner
menu $18/35; ⊗5:30-10pm Thu-Sat, 11am-2pm
Sun year-round, plus 11am-2pm Fri & Sat spring
& summer) This winsome 1845 Greek Revival
estate, nestled beneath the oaks, houses
one of the best restaurants in Kentucky. The
married chef-owners serve a simple but elegant
multicourse brunch or dinner of wholesome
soups, handmade pastas, locally raised meats
and farmstead cheeses.

Louisville ❾

✕ Garage Bar   Gastropub $$

(www.garageonmarket.com; 700 E Market St;
dishes $7-16) The best thing to do on a warm
afternoon in Louisville is to make your way to
this uber-hip converted NuLu service station
(accented by two kissing camaros) and order
a round of basil gimlets and the ham platter: a

isting of four regionally cured hams, served th fresh bread and preserves. Then move on the menu that ranges from the best brick- en pizza in town to pork meatballs and turkey ngs, and rolled oysters that are divine.

⟨ Hillbilly Tea   Appalachian $$

⟩502-587-7350; 120 S First St; dishes $10-17; ⟩10am-9pm Tue-Sat, to 4pm Sun) An excellent- lue little diner off Main St, it specializes in palachian food with a modern twist, which eans you may find smoked catfish served over nashed potatoes, cornish hen over brussels d parsnips, and its grilled moonshine pork n looks fantastic. There's a muscular tea enu too, with over 20 varieties, but you'll be given if you order the craftsman hooch and a er chaser.

🛏 21c Museum Hotel   Hotel $$$

⟩502-217-6300; www.21chotel.com; 0 W Main St; r from $269; P ✳ 🛜) This ntemporary art museum–hotel would be edgy ywhere; in laid-back Louisville, it's practically

in a different dimension. Video screens project your distorted image along with falling language on the wall as you wait for the elevator. Chandeliers made from scissors dangle weirdly in the hallways. Sexually suggestive sculptures in the lobby make even normally unflappable guidebook authors blush. Urban-loftlike rooms have iPod docks and mint julep kits in the mini- fridge. The hotel restaurant, Proof on Main, is one of the city's hippest New Southern bistros. Parking is $18.

🛏 Brown Hotel   Hotel $$$

See Trip 25 (p294).

The Bourbon Trail

25

They say there's a bourbon for everyone: fiery, stern or with honey droplets of heart-opening heat. Visit the distilleries and taverns of Bluegrass Country, and discover yours.

TRIP HIGHLIGHTS

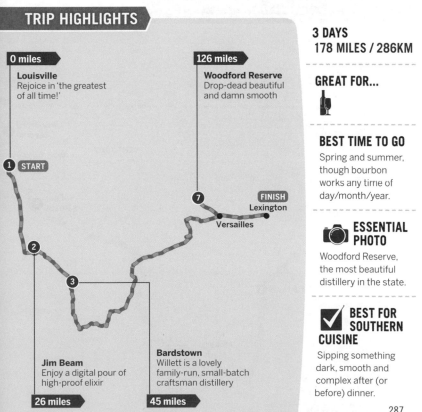

0 miles

Louisville
Rejoice in 'the greatest of all time!'

1 START

2

3

Jim Beam
Enjoy a digital pour of high-proof elixir

26 miles

126 miles

Woodford Reserve
Drop-dead beautiful and damn smooth

7

FINISH
Lexington

Versailles

Bardstown
Willett is a lovely family-run, small-batch craftsman distillery

45 miles

3 DAYS
178 MILES / 286KM

GREAT FOR...

BEST TIME TO GO
Spring and summer, though bourbon works any time of day/month/year.

ESSENTIAL PHOTO
Woodford Reserve, the most beautiful distillery in the state.

✓ BEST FOR SOUTHERN CUISINE
Sipping something dark, smooth and complex after (or before) dinner.

25 The Bourbon Trail

A golden inch of bourbon, silky and mellow with notes of wood and vanilla, is Southern living in a glass. Bourbon was first distilled by a Lexington preacher in 1789, and over 80% of the world's supply is still produced in the state. While all bourbons are whiskey, not all whiskeys are bourbon. Bourbon must be made with at least 51% corn, and aged for at least two years.

TRIP HIGHLIGHT

❶ Louisville

Best known as the home of the Kentucky Derby (p283), Louisville (or Louahvul, as the locals say) is an up-and-coming, progressive city (Kentucky's largest) with good eating kitchens, period architecture, fine museums, leafy streets and some fabulous bars where you may want to sip a little bourbon. After giving downtown museums, like the fabulous Muhammad

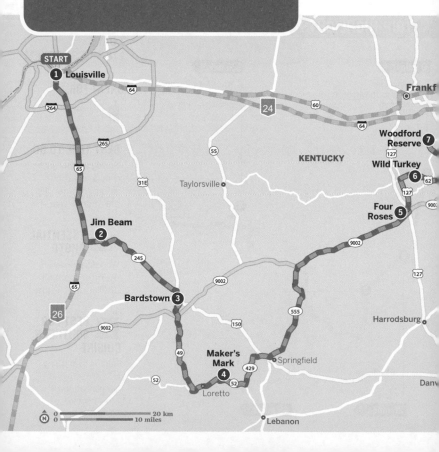

Ali Center (p283) and **Frazier International History Museum** (www.fraziermuseum.org; 829 W Main St; adult/student/child $10.50/7.50/6; ⊙9am-5pm Mon-Sat, noon-5pm Sun), a look, head to **NuLu**, Louisville's nearby arts district. You can taste the good stuff at, well, **Taste** (📞502-409-4646; www.tastefinewinesandbourbons.com; 634 E Market Street; tastings $4-8; ⊙11am-8pm Tue-Wed, noon-late Thu & Fri, 10:30am-late Sat), a high-end wine and bourbon shop on Market St. They

pour craftsman stuff that's hard to find, and you can taste it before you buy it, for $5 a hit. If you'd like a deeper pour and a longer linger, head back downtown to 21c Museum Hotel (p285), where you can peruse edgy modern art and head into upscale Proof (p294) to sample superb cocktails and sip from a fine bourbon list, which may include special editions of Van Winkle.

 p294

The Drive ›› From Louisville head south on I-65 for 24 miles, head left on KY-245S and make another left on Happy Hollow Rd.

TRIP HIGHLIGHT

❷ Jim Beam

The world's largest and best-known bourbon distiller is **Jim Beam** (www.jimbeam.com; 149 Happy Hollow Rd; tours per person $8; ⊙9am-5:30pm Mon-Sat, noon-4:30pm Sun). And though their

namesake hooch won't wow whiskey snobs, you'll soon learn that the Beam family has a history of small batch bourbons. Jim Beam ages all its bourbon for at least four years, twice the legal minimum. Longer aging produces a deeper, smoother character. Absorb the whole operation on the 80-minute tour, or do a self-guided walk along the grounds then head to its fabulous, digitized, automated tasting room. You'll get a half-shot of two bourbons. Beam makes Knob Creek (good), Knob Creek Single Barrel (better), Basil Hayden's (velvety) and the fabulous Booker's (high-proof enlightenment), which is best described as damn smooth with rocket boosters.

The Drive ›› Double back to KY-245 and head south for 15 miles, and head right on Hwy 31E into Bardstown.

◎ LINK YOUR TRIP

24 Kentucky Bluegrass & Horse Country

Bourbon and horses go together like mint juleps and the Kentucky Derby. Take some time to visit legendary race tracks and watch the horses fly. So to speak.

26 Tailgate Tour

Now that you have your bottle of bourbon, follow the nearest sports fan to the basketball arena, horse track or football stadium, and do sip before the action begins.

TRIP HIGHLIGHT

❸ Bardstown

There are seven major distilleries within a 50-mile radius of Bardstown, while the town itself, with its weathered red-brick Georgian churches and fairytale stone cottages, belongs to a different era. For an overview of bourbon history, head to the **Oscar Getz Museum of Whiskey History** (www.whiskeymuseum.com; 114 N 5th St; donations appreciated; ⏰10am-4pm Tue-Sat, noon-4pm Sun), housed in a former Civil War hospital.

Heaven Hill (www.bourbonheritagecenter.com; 1311 Gilkey Run Rd; tours $3-5), one of Kentucky's largest distilleries, is best known for its Evan Williams label. But its higher-end (and higher-proof) offering, Elijah Craig, is what gets whiskey converts salivating. Heaven Hill caters to visitors with its Bourbon Heritage Center displays on bourbon history, an educational film and a tasting bar inside a huge barrel. Elsewhere on campus, 7th-generation master distiller Craig Beam holds the keys to 16% of the world's bourbon supply, and you can certainly smell it in the air.

Willet (📞502-348-0899; www.kentuckybourbonwhiskey.com; Loretto Rd; tours $7; ⏰tours 10am, 11:30am, 1pm, 3pm & 4pm Mon-Fri, 10am, 11:30am, 1pm, 2pm & 3pm Sat; 12:30pm, 1:45pm and 3pm Sun), launched in 1936 and still family-owned, acted as a subcontractor for larger labels for decades, bottling its family recipe for another brand's pay check. Then, in January 2012, the grandson of the label's founder and the new 31-year-old master distiller quit law school and began bottling Willett under the family name once more. You'll enjoy the hour-long tour through the 120-acre property, which includes a prolonged look into the newly refurbished chalet-like distillery, where big stainless-steel corn-mash cookers, and seven 10,000-gallon stainless steel fermenters, are open-topped – their aroma dizzying and tempting.

🍴 🛏 p294

The Drive » The ride from Bardstown south on KY-49 offers the most beautiful countryside at this end of the bourbon trail. Narrow roads wind through classic wooded rolling horse country braided with corral fencing. Follow it south for 8 miles, then head east on KY-52 for nearly five more.

❹ Maker's Mark

South of the Bardstown distilleries, **Maker's Mark** (www.makersmark.com; 3350 Burks Spring Rd; tours $7; ⏰10am-4:30pm Mon-Sat, 1-4:30pm Sun) has

---

WHISKEY TEA

Whiskey tea is a staple of church picnics and family reunions in the Bluegrass State. Ask one of the distilleries if you may buy a freshly dumped oak aging barrel. Take it home and fill it with 10 to 15 gallons of hot tea, then allow it to sit in the sun. At least a quart of whiskey will leach out of the wood, giving the tea flavor and kick.

Maker's Mark Classic Kentucky bourbon

been operating at the same site, near the town of Loretto, since 1805. This makes perfect sense, since the distillery sits on a 10-acre limestone-filtered, spring-fed lake, providing the pure water used in the distilling process. In fact, Kentucky's natural limestone filtration – you will see karsts jutting here and there in the countryside – is precisely why distillers can craft such a fine product here. Touring Maker's Mark is like visiting a small, historical theme park, but in the best way. You'll see the old grist mill, the 1840s master distiller's house and the old-fashioned wooden firehouse with an antique fire truck. Watch oatmeal-esque sour mash ferment in huge cypress vats, see whiskey being double-distilled in copper pots and peek at bourbon barrels aging in old wooden warehouses. At the gift shop you can even stamp your own bottle with the iconic red-wax seal.

The Drive » From Maker's Mark, head northeast on KY-429 to KY-152 to KY-555, and finally KY-9002 towards the town of Lawrenceburg. It's about an hour's drive, and what a pleasant drive it is, with dogwoods sprouting in the springtime and outrageous fall color when the weather turns cold.

- - - - - - - - - -

❺ Four Roses

In Lawrenceburg, **Four Roses** (✆502-839-2655; www.fourrosesbourbon.com; 1224 Bonds Mills Rd; ⊗9am-4pm Mon-Sat, noon-4pm Sun, closed summer) sits on the banks of the Salt River. Check out the unique architecture – red-roofed Spanish Mission–style buildings like these are rarely seen in this neck of the woods. For years, Four Roses was only sold overseas and some labels, like its Platinum, are still only available in Japan. But the company made a triumphant US comeback in 2002, when for the first time since the 1960s you could actually have a Four Roses Manhattan in Manhattan. Take a walking tour of the distillery and have some free sips afterwards in the tasting room. Note that the distillery shuts down in summer, but the gift shop and visitors center remain open. You can also call to arrange a free private tour of the aging warehouse, about an hour away in Cox's Creek.

The Drive » No need to leave Lawrenceburg for your next tipple. Just follow US 127 north for 9 miles.

- - - - - - - - - - - - -

⑥ Wild Turkey

The **Wild Turkey** (www
.wildturkey.com; Hwy 62
E; ◷9am-3pm Mon-Sat,
noon-3pm Sun) distillery
sits on Wild Turkey Hill overlooking the Kentucky River. More industrial and less self-consciously old-fashioned than some of the distilleries, Wild Turkey offers a frills-free tour of the facilities. If you're lucky, you'll get to meet master distiller Jimmy Russell, who's worked here since 1954. Wild Turkey is made slightly differently from most bourbons, aged in a heavily charred barrel for extra-deep amber color, with very little water added at the end of the process.

The Drive » Backtrack on US 127 then get ready for more deep beauty, because Versailles – a thoroughbred epicenter – is laced with streams and swathed in Kentucky bluegrass, which you'll glimpse, point and shoot as you roll east on US 62, which intersects with the stunning KY-1659 in historical Versailles. Head north on KY-1659 to Woodford Reserve.

TRIP HIGHLIGHT

⑦ Woodford Reserve

Set just outside the town of Versailles (pronounced locally as 'vur-sails' despite the spelling and the area's Louisiana Purchase history), **Woodford Reserve** (www .woodfordreserve.com; 7855 McCracken Pike; tour per person $7; ◷10am-5pm) is one of the most beautiful distilleries in the state. You are smack in the middle of thoroughbred stud country, on a 700-acre ranch originally settled in 1812. That's when the owners, who were cattle ranchers, started distilling for themselves and made their first 10 barrels. Two decades later there were nearly 2000 distilleries operating in the Kentucky hills, with a still for every 200 citizens. The Woodford Reserve label was launched much more recently, in 1996. It's known for its 72% corn mash concentration, and triple copper pot distilling method, which it claims removes three times as many sulphates as single distilled products. Critics might counter that it hurts its flavor. We enjoy it. And its new Double Oaked label, which hit shelves in 2011, is aged an extra six to 12 months for a

THE KENTUCKY BOURBON FESTIVAL

This annual Bardstown shindig draws whiskey aficionados from all over the world. The weeklong **festival** (www.kybourbonfestival.com; Bardstown), held each September, includes taste tests from local distilleries, bourbon barrel relay races, liquor-infused cooking demos, and bourbon and cigar dinners. Kids will dig the historical train rides and night-time ghost tours of old Bardstown. And everyone can get into a competitive round of Kentucky's state game – cornhole (a sort of beanbag toss).

IT GETS BETTER WITH AGE

The years that go by matter. Time adds accent and detail. We get older, sure, and with it our character deepens, becomes more complex and interesting. The same is true of bourbon. In fact, you can't actually even call it 'bourbon' until the whiskey has aged. Before then it's called 'green whiskey.' Most widely available bourbons are aged no longer than eight years, but some ultra-premium labels are aged 14, 16 or even 21 years. With each turn of the calendar, the bourbon gets just a little bit darker and often a hell of a lot smoother.

Kentucky, as it happens, has the perfect climate for aging bourbon. Hot summers cause the whiskey to expand into the wood of the barrel, where it sucks up toasty, caramelized flavors, which are released when the liquid contracts during the cold winters. The barrels sit, stacked several stories high, in wood and metal 'rackhouses' that dot the central Kentucky landscape like massive barns. You'll see them at all the distilleries; unsurprisingly, these barn-like facilities are highly flammable, and several distilleries, including Jim Beam and Heaven Hill, have had apocalyptic fires in the past several years.

smooth and smoky finish that's pretty special.

The Drive >> Go slow and take the Old Frankfort Pike – a national scenic byway – from Versailles to Lexington. Head south on KY-1659 to US 60 east to the US 62 to the Old Frankfort Pike.

- - - - - - - - - - - - -

❽ Lexington

Lexington is home to million-dollar houses and multimillion-dollar horses. Once the wealthiest and most cultured city west of the Allegheny Mountains, it was tagged 'the Athens of the West', and is home to the University of Kentucky. The small downtown has some pretty Victorians and intriguing restaurants. It's also home to an up-and-coming bourbon label, **Barrel House Distilling Company** (www .barrelhousedistillery.com; 1200 Manchester St; ⊙noon-5pm Thu & Fri, 11am-3pm Sat & Sun), a micro-distiller set in the barrel house of the now defunct Pepper Distillery. It bottles moonshine, vodka and a product called 'oak rum' and is currently maturing barrels of bourbon. Rumor has it that the first bottle of the smooth stuff may be ready in 2014. Before leaving town, stop by the quirky **Headley-Whitney Museum** (www .headley-whitney.org; 4435 Old Frankfort Pike; adult/ student $10/7; ⊙10am-5pm Wed-Fri, noon-5pm Sat & Sun), a jewelry designer with a remarkable collection of stones, trinkets, doll houses and sea shells. History buffs will want to visit the childhood home of **Mary Todd-Lincoln** (www.mtlhouse.org; 578 W Main St; adult/child $10/5; ⊙10am-4pm Mon-Sat). You know, Abe's wife. And if it's basketball season, catch a KU game at Rupp Arena (p304).

✗ ⊨ p295

Eating & Sleeping

Louisville ❶

✗ Eiderdown Gastropub $$

(☎502-290-2390; www.eiderdowngernantown
.com; 983 Goss Ave; dishes $4-17; ☺4-10pm
Tue-Thu, 11:30am-11pm Fri & Sat, noon-10pm
Sun) When this Kentucky born, 30-something,
French-trained chef fled the corporate confines
of a local Outback kitchen, he envisioned this
exposed-brick, dark-wood destination pub
suffused with the aroma of duck-fat popcorn,
cabbage, bacon, and spaetzle – a melange
of root vegetables and sausage dripping
with sage butter. It's in the still gritty, mostly
residential corner of Louisville known as
Germantown.

✗ Proof New Southern

(☎502-217-6360; www.proofonmain.com; 702
W Main St; mains $17-36; ☺7-10am, 11am-2pm
& 5:30-10pm Mon-Thu, to 11pm Fri, 7am-
3pm, 5:30-11pm Sat, to 10pm Sun) Arguably
Louisville's best restaurant, and certainly its
most lauded, the cocktails here are special, the
bourbon (they're known to pour from special
barrels of Woodford Reserve and Van Winkle)
and wine list is long and satisfying, and mains
range from a bone-in pork chop to a succulent
bison burger to a high-minded take on chicken
and dumplings. The art is loud and inspired,
the servers hip and deadly serious, and the bar
crowd well dressed and festive.

⌸ Brown Hotel Hotel $$$

(☎502-583-1234; www.brownhotel.com; 335
West Broadway; r from $250; ⓟ ✻ ⓦ) Opera
stars, queens and prime ministers have trod
the marble floors of this storied downtown
hotel, now restored to all its 1920s gilded
glamor with 293 comfy rooms and a swank bar.
Parking is $18.

Bardstown ❸

✗ Old Talbott Tavern American $$

(☎502-348-3494; www.talbotts.com; 107 W
Stephen Foster Ave; mains $8-20; ☺11am-8pm
Sun-Thu, to 10pm Fri & Sat, bar to 1am Thu-Sun)
Daniel Boone and Abe Lincoln passed through
this old limestone tavern, now a restaurant,
inn and bar. With worn wooden floors, stone
walls and beamed ceilings, it does basic dishes
like a chicken caesar wrap, and a BLT with
fried green tomato on top, as well as a catfish
sandwich and a slow-roasted pot roast. The
food is fair, the history intriguing. It has good-
value rooms and suites upstairs, too.

✗ Chapeze House Inn $$$

(☎502-349-0127; www.chapezehouse.com; 107
E Stephen Foster Ave; bourbon tasting dinners
$30-99, cottages $99-169; ☺by arrangement)
Michael Masters (known only as 'the Colonel')
will lead you through a tasting from his
collection of more than 100 premium and
vintage bourbons. Afterwards, wife Margaret
Sue, president of the Kentucky Bourbon
Cooking School, will serve a homemade feast in
the candlelit dining room of their lavish Federal-
style mansion. The Masters are so well known
for their expansive Southern hospitality (the
Colonel's drawl is frequently heard on the Food
Network and Fine Living) they've earned the
title 'the Host and Hostess of Kentucky.'

⌸ Jailer's Inn Inn

(☎502-308-5551; www.jailersinn.com; 111 W
Stephen Foster Ave; r $125) Sleep in a former cell
in the Old Nelson County Jail, now outfitted with
floral wallpaper and antique furniture. Not to
mention impenetrable stone walls.

Lexington ⑧

✗ A la Lucie   Bistro $$$

(📞859-252-5277; www.alalucie.com; 159 N
Limestone St; mains $19-30; ⏱11am-2pm
Tue-Fri, 5-10pm Mon-Thu, to 11pm Fri & Sat)
An intimate and whimsically decorated bistro
serving the classics: a lamb shank here, steak
frites there. Don't overlook the white wine and
herb braised Kentucky rabbit. The local choice
on date night.

✗ Table Three Ten   New American $$$

See Trip 🔢 (p284).

🛏 Gratz Park Inn   Hotel $$

See Trip 🔢 (p284).

Talladega Superspeedway
America's fastest NASCAR circuit

Classic Trip

Tailgate Tour

26

Visit the holy temples of Southern sport, where fanatics converge to visualize, embrace and celebrate victory...before the game even begins.

TRIP HIGHLIGHTS

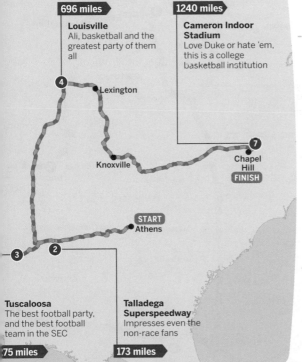

696 miles
Louisville
Ali, basketball and the greatest party of them all

1240 miles
Cameron Indoor Stadium
Love Duke or hate 'em, this is a college basketball institution

Lexington

Knoxville

Chapel Hill
FINISH

START
Athens

Tuscaloosa
The best football party, and the best football team in the SEC

75 miles

Talladega Superspeedway
Impresses even the non-race fans

173 miles

6 DAYS
1250 MILES /
1250KM

GREAT FOR

BEST TIME TO GO
February when basketball heats up, and September when football kicks off.

 ESSENTIAL PHOTO
Talladega Motor Speedway, one of the iconic sports venues.

 BEST FOR HISTORY
Feeling the gravity (or self-importance) of US sports history.

26 Tailgate Tour

In the American south, football is king, car racing is a constitutional right and basketball is a religion. The most legendary venues have become pilgrimage sights for devoted fans who, before the lights shine, the whistle blows and the flag falls, gather in college quads, nearby sports bars and parking areas to make questionable dietary choices and rejoice in the teams they love. Join them, won't you?

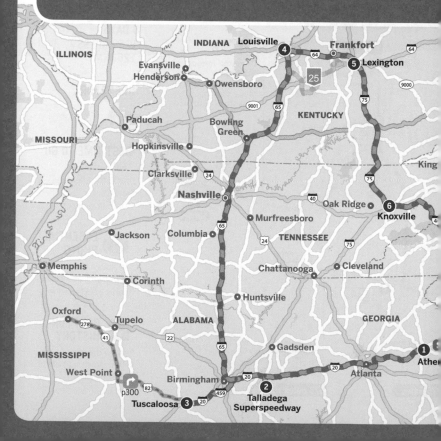

1 Athens

Beery, artsy, laid-back and roughly 70 miles east of Atlanta, Athens is a prototypical American college town. The **University of Georgia** (www.uga.edu; 210 S Jackson St) drives the culture of Athens and ensures an ever-replenishing supply of young bar-hoppers, concert-goers and sports fans. And the University of Georgia – part of the fabled Southeastern Conference (SEC), college football's most competitive league – has a devoted following. The games take place on fall Saturdays at **Sanford Stadium** (☏706-542-9036; www.georgiadogs.com; 100 Sanford Dr) in the middle of the lovely, leafy campus that rambles over rolling hills east of a pleasant downtown. If you can't get a ticket, make your way to **Cutter's** (www.facebook.com/cutterspub; 120 E Clayton St; ⊙2:30pm-2am Mon-Fri, from noon Sat), a popular sports bar with gargantuan flat screens. Before the game it's buzzing, and if victory is grasped, the interior becomes a sloshed dance hall of depravity – in a good way. The hipster vortex of **Normal Bar** (www.facebook.com/pages/Normal-Bar; 1365 Prince Ave; ⊙4pm-2am Mon-Thu, from 3pm Fri & Sat) is a much more sophisticated place to watch the game. Any game.

✕ 🛏 p306

The Drive » There's nothing especially pretty about the 173-mile high-speed run from Athens into Alabama on I-20, but then again, this next stop is all about speed.

TRIP HIGHLIGHT

2 Talladega Superspeedway

Nestled in the East Alabama hills, the **Talladega Superspeedway** (☏877-462-3342; ww.talladegasuperspeedway.com; 3366 Speedway Blvd;

LINK YOUR TRIP

25 Bourbon Trail

As long as you're in Kentucky, why not stay and sip awhile? Visit America's best distilleries and drive away with some good hooch for your next pre- or post-game party.

8 North Carolina's Outer Banks

From Tobacco Rd in the triangle, head to the wild windswept beaches of North Carolina's Outer Banks.

tickets $45-200) rises like Ricky Bobby's mock one dream. It's the fastest in the NASCAR circuit thanks to a 2.6-mile oval and high bank turns (30 degrees and over five stories high). The grandstand is a mile long and seats 130,000. You can visit the track on a guided 30-minute bus tour that leaves from the **International Motor Sports Hall of Fame** (www.motorsportshalloffame .com; 3366 Speedway Blvd, Talladega; museum adult/ child $12/5, track tour adult/ child $8/5, combo tickets adult/child $16/8; ☺9am-4pm). The best time to visit, however, is when the cars are running in May and October. True tailgaters will opt for the motorhome camping area called the **Infield**. It's an RV camp in the middle of the track with views of the race. In fact, that's where the drivers live during race week. Of course, they fly in on private planes and live in rock-star tour buses. The most indulgent deal for the rest of us may be the seats overlooking pit row. The ticket price ($190) includes a buffet and unlimited beer and wine. Think of it as a high-end tailgate picnic.

The Drive » One hundred and three miles away, via I-20 and I-459, is yet another leafy college campus, and Alabama's top sports mecca.

DETOUR: OXFORD

Start: ❸ Tuscaloosa

It's a pretty drive down a series of two- and four-lane highways through the countryside from Tuscaloosa to Oxford, Mississippi, and while Ole Miss football has rarely struck fear into the heart of its opponents like the Crimson Tide, even with two-time Superbowl MVP Eli Manning lined up behind center, it can be fun to party with loveable losers. One of the school's great traditions happens on game-day mornings when **The Grove** – a woodland in the heart of the University of Mississippi (p220) campus – is packed with students and fans who merge with the marching band and stomp to the stadium en masse to cheer for the Rebels! Tiny by SEC standards, the **Vaught-Hemmingway Stadium** seats about 62,000.

TRIP HIGHLIGHT

❸ Tuscaloosa

'Roll Tide!' is the call you'll hear, well, pretty much everywhere in Tuscaloosa, but especially on Saturday afternoons in the fall when students and alumni gather in the **University of Alabama** (www.ua.edu) quad, four hours before the game even starts, for a pre-game party like none other. White tents, wired with satellite TV, fill the expansive lawn. Barbecue is smoked and devoured, cornhole (drunken beanbag toss) is played, 'Roll Tide' is shouted and shrieked. At game time all migrate to **Bryant-Denny Stadium** (☎205-348-3600; www .rolltide.com; 920 Paul W Bryant Dr), a 102,000-capacity football stadium that looks out onto the rolling hills and is always packed with rabid fans. And with good reason: the Alabama Crimson Tide has won 19 national championships, including the last two, and three of the last four. Get a full dose of Crimson Tide football history at the Paul W Bryant Museum (p159). Downtown Tuscaloosa unfurls along University Ave, with a student hood a half-mile closer to campus. That's where you'll find **Houndstooth** (☎205-752-8444; www.facebook.com/ pages/Houndstooth-Sports

THE ALSO-RANS

Although the destinations in this trip may be the crown jewels of Southern sport, we'd be remiss without pointing out a few additional options for getting your tailgate (and face paint) on.

University of Florida (www.gatorzone.com) Set in Jacksonville, this perennial football and basketball powerhouse is no stranger to the spotlight. Recent stars Al Horford and Joaquim Noah (basketball) and Tim Tebow (football) prove their pedigree.

Louisiana State University (www.lsusports.net) Set in Baton Rouge, and arguably third in line behind University of Alabama and University of Florida in terms of football supremecy in the SEC, it's also the alma mater of Shaquille O'Neal.

University of South Carolina (www.gamecocksonline.com) Steve Spurrier, the former University of Florida coach, keeps the Columbia-based Gamecocks in contention on the gridiron.

Durham Bulls (www.milb.com/index.jsp?sid=t234) The AAA affiliate of the Tampa Bay Rays, a fictional take on this Durham, North Carolina–based team and stadium, was featured in the iconic Kevin Costner, Susan Sarandon and Tim Robbins baseball flick *Bull Durham*.

Spring Training The Sunshine State has long hosted Major League Baseball teams during spring training in February and March, when there are games nearly every day. The **New York Yankees** (www.steinbrennerfield.com) and **Philadelphia Phillies** (http://philadelphia.phillies.mlb.com/spring_training/ballpark.jsp?c_id=phi) are two of the big league clubs with training complexes in the Tampa–St Petersburg area.

-Bar/118838634902120; 1300 University Blvd; ⏰4pm-2am, to 3am Fri), a quintessential sports bar, generally mobbed before and after the game.

✕ 🛏 p306

The Drive >> From Tuscaloosa find the I-65 north and hammer the gas for 421 miles all the way to Louisville.

- - - - - - - - - - - - - - - -

TRIP HIGHLIGHT

❹ Louisville

Boxing, basketball, baseball and horse racing, Louisville, Kentucky, may be one of the South's most progressive and intellectual towns, but they do love their sport. How could they not, with a favorite son like Muhammad Ali? You can learn all about the iconic Louisville-born heavyweight at the wonderful Muhammad Ali Center (p283). Baseball fans should wander down to that 10-story-tall baseball bat and the **Louisville Slugger Museum** (www.sluggermuseum.org; 800 W Main St; adult/seniors/child $11/10/6; ⏰9am-5pm Mon-Sat, 11am-5pm Sun; ♿). Also downtown

is the charming and antiquated **Louisville Slugger Field** (www.batsbaseball.com; 401 E Main St; tickets $11-22). The outpouring of love directed at the University of Louisville Cardinals men's basketball team, however, is pure and all encompassing. The defending national champion at research time, it plays its home games in a pro-grade downtown arena, the **KFC Yum! Center** (☎502-690-9000; www.gocards.com; 1 Arena Plaza). But when it comes to the

FLICKRVISION / GETTY IMAGES

LOCAL VOICE
JORDAN WHITLEY, NATIONAL SPORTS BROADCASTER

To be born in the South is to be born of tradition. It runs thick, relentless and stubborn in our veins. Mine is a dark crimson. No, not blood – my football team! At the University of Alabama, every Saturday we don our 'Sundie Best' and stand houndstooth hat to seersucker slacks while we exalt, grieve and consume the almighty game. Football, basketball or, God forbid, NASCAR...you want to know the South? Get to the damn game.

Top: The University of Alabama's football team takes to the field
Left: Louisville Slugger Museum
Right: Basketball game between Duke and North Carolina

tailgate party, no venue, event and or sport can match that of the Kentucky Derby (p283) at Churchill Downs (p283). A **festival** (www .kdf.org) kicks the party off two weeks ahead of time, and on race day everyone with $50 is welcome in the gates where the mint juleps are a-flowing.

✕ ⊨ p306

The Drive » It's less than a 90-minute drive from here on I-64 to yet another basketball hot bed in the state of Kentucky.

- - - - - - - - - - -

❺ Lexington

Lexington may be the heart of throughbred country, but the people of Kentucky consider basketball their first and deepest love, and in Lexington it's all about the **University of Kentucky** (www.uky .edu). The Wildcats have the all-time best record in the history of men's college basketball and are second only to UCLA in national titles. They are a juggernaut, famous for their title teams – the most recent of which was crowned champion in 2012. And their Goliath-like fall in 1966 (when their Pat Riley–led all-white starting five lost the title game to Texas Western's all-black squad) is the stuff of legend. UK plays its home games in the

center of town at **Rupp Arena** (www.rupparena.com; 430 W Vine St), and when it runs, hotels sell out, downtown bars and restaurants are full and the party spills into the streets. If you do love the horses, don't miss nearby Keeneland Association (p281), perhaps the best track in America not named Churchill Downs. The pre-Derby races are especially high class.

✕ 🛏 p306

The Drive » From a men's basketball mecca it's less than three hours down I-75 south to the epicenter of the women's game.

THE OTHER GREAT COACH

Names like Dean Smith, Roy Williams and Mike Krzyzewski are sacred in North Carolina, but there's another championship baskteball coach that you may not have heard of. Jim Valvano coached at North Carolina State for 10 years. He burst onto the national scene when the brash New Yorker won a title in just his third year as NC State's coach. In the aftermath of the miracle alley-oop that defeated the heavily favored University of Houston team, led by Hakeen Olajuwan, he was seen sprinting up and down the court, in disbelief, looking for someone to hug. He is also known for an inspirational speech he gave on national TV just eight weeks before he died of cancer in 1993, at just 47 years of age. During that speech he announced the founding of his V Foundation for Cancer Research, a nonprofit that has raised and donated millions toward the search for a cure.

➏ Knoxville

Knoxville is home to the University of Tennessee, the alma mater of Peyton Manning and long-time residency of the greatest women's basketball coach ever. Pat Summitt has won more games than any coach in the history of NCAA basketball (that includes the boys). She coached for 40 seasons, and her Lady Volunteers won eight national titles, before she retired in 2012 after being diagnosed with Alzheimer's. The best place to get an appreciation for Summitt and her basketball teams is at the **Women's Basketball Hall of Fame** (www.wbhof.com; 700 Hall of Fame Dr; adult/child $8/6; ⏰10am-5pm Mon-Sat summer, 11am-5pm Tue-Sat winter), easily identified by the the the Baden Ball – a 30ft-high 10-ton basketball that sits atop the building. Exhibits date all the way back to a time when women played in full-length dresses. Naturally, Pat Summitt headlined the first class inducted in 1999, along with Cheryl Miller – one of the greatest to ever play the woman's game. Peyton Manning first made his name at **Neyland Stadium** (☎865-974-0953; www.utsports.com; 1600 Stadium Dr), on the otherwise forgettable University of Tennesee campus.

✕ 🛏 p306

The Drive » It's a 336-mile drive east on I-40 to the ultimate rivalry in American college basketball.

TRIP HIGHLIGHT

➐ Durham

In North Carolina, 11 miles separate two college basketball powerhouses. **Duke University** (www.duke.edu) in Durham is home to the great Mike Krzyzewski's Blue Devils. Duke fans worship inside **Cameron Indoor Stadium** (☎box office 919-681-2583; www.goduke.com; 115 Whitford Dr), which first opened for business in 1940. As of the 2011–12 season, the

LEGENDS OF TOBACCO RD

These days the Raleigh-Durham area is referred to as the Research Triangle, or simply the Triangle, thanks to the abundance of top-shelf universities and researchers, but to sports fans it will always be Tobacco Rd. The moniker originally referred to the state's cash crop, but when it comes to basketball riches North Carolina stands alone. Legendary coaches? How about Dean Smith (UNC) and Mike Krzyzewski (Duke), two of the winningest ever. The greatest player of all time, some guy named Michael Jordan, was born and raised in North Carolina and played at UNC. Two of the NCAA Men's Basketball Tournament's iconic moments involved these teams. Jordan sank a last-second game winner to win the 1982 title over Georgetown, and Grant Hill made a spectacular three-quarter court pass to Christian Laettner who sank a turn-around shot to pull out a miracle victory that propelled Duke to the Final Four, and its second straight title in 1992.

men's home record was 751 wins, 150 losses, for a winning percentage of more than 80%. If there's not a scheduled event, you can step inside the stadium during normal business hours and occasionally sit in on team practice. Off the court, check out the old photographs and the **Duke Hall of Fame**. So how to score tickets? Your options are limited. You can sell your first born, get accepted to Duke and camp out with students, or follow @duke_tickets on Twitter. You can also call the ticket office in early October to find out when tickets will go on sale. Your best bet is either a nonconference game or a game played over Christmas break.

🚌 p307

The Drive › Drive 11 miles south down US 501, otherwise known as Tobacco Rd.

---

❽ Chapel Hill

Chapel Hill, known as Blue Heaven to basketball fans, is actually the (much) cuter and more progressive town whose culture revolves around the nearly 30,000 students at **North Carolina University**. Less historical than Cameron Indoor, the Tar Heels play at the **Smith Center** (www.goheels.com; Old NC Highway 10), named for its legendary coach, Dean Smith, who retired with 879 career wins and two national titles, which at research time was exactly 58 victories and two titles fewer than Krzyzewski – arguably the second-best coach ever, behind John Wooden. Of course, Tar Heels fans would counter that their current coach, Roy Williams – certainly no slouch – has won two titles himself. So they're even. Only, they don't quite see it that way. Probably because the politest way to describe college basketball fans in North Carolina would be...fanatical. With an occasional foray into rabid.

🍴 p307

Classic Trip

Eating & Sleeping

Athens ❶

🍴 Farm 255 — American $$

(www.farm255.com; 255 W Washington St; mains $12-21; ⏱5:30-10pm Tue-Thu, to 10:30pm Fri & Sat, 11am-2pm & 5:30-9:30pm Sun) This stylish, light-filled bistro gets much of its meat and vegetables from its own 5-acre, organic/biodynamic Blue Moon Farms outside Athens. The operative word here is *fresh*.

🍴 Ike & Jane — Cafe $

(www.ikeandjane.com; 1307 Prince Ave; mains $3.50-7; ⏱6:30am-5pm Mon-Fri) If your idea of a balanced breakfast is doughnuts and coffee, you are a police officer, an 85-year-old man or you should find this sunny little shingle in Normal Town, where the doughnuts involve creative ingredients like red velvet, caramel glaze, peanut butter, banana and bacon. The coffee is gourmet, and it does quiche, bagels, gourmet soups, salads and sandwiches, too.

🛏 Hotel Indigo — Boutique Hotel $$

(📞706-546-0430; www.indigoathens.com; 500 College Ave; r weekend/weekday from $159/139; 🅿❄@🛜🏊) Athens' first – and desperately needed – boutique hotel is part of the Indigo chain, and is a LEED Gold–certified sustainable standout (the first of InterContinental's 4500 hotels worldwide). Green elements throughout (regenerative elevators, priority parking for hybrid vehicles, 30% of the building constructed from recycled content) mean it's environmentally sound, and the 130-room eco-chic hotel is steeped in local color (Jittery Joe's coffee instead of Starbucks, reclaimed barn-wood-framed posters of R.E.M. and the like).

Tuscaloosa ❸

🍴 Nick's Original Filet House — Steaks $

(📞205-758-9316; 4018 Culver Rd; mains $7-15; ⏱5-9pm Mon-Thu, to 10pm Fri & Sat, closed Sun) Also known as Nick's In The Sticks, this is a rickety backroad joint if ever there was one, and it's a Tuscaloosa classic. Nestled in the trees about 5 miles out of town, with a flock of signed dollar bills stapled to the ceiling, it does tender filet mignon on the cheap (as well as ribeye) and it fries all parts of the chicken (think: livers and gizzards). Oh, and about that Nicodemus. Um, it's a drink. Beware the Nicodemus.

🛏 Hotel Capstone — Hotel $$

(📞205-752-3200; www.hotelcapstone.com; 320 Paul Bryant Rd; r from $145) A decent three-star room within walking distance of the quad and stadium. Digs are spacious with flat screens, wide desks and cottage cheese ceiling regret. But it's on campus and has room service and a lobby bar. Reserve ahead on game day.

Louisville ❹

🍴 Garage Bar — Gastropub $$

See Trip 🚗(p284).

🛏 21c Museum Hotel — Hotel $$$

See Trip 🚗(p285).

Lexington ❺

🍴 Village Idiot — Gastropub $$

See Trip 🚗(p295).

🛏 Gratz Park Inn — Hotel $$

See Trip 🚗(p284).

Knoxville ❻

🍴 Tupelo Honey Cafe — New Southern $$

(www.tupelohoneycafe.com; 1 Market Sq; mains $9-19; ⏱9am-10pm Mon-Thu, to 11pm Fri, 8am-11pm Sat to 9pm Sun) New South flavors are the order of the day at this bustling, eclectic dining room set in the light-flooded ground floor of a historical building on Market Sq. Think chorizo-crusted sea scallops, pulled pork with jalapeño BBQ sauce, and shrimp and goat cheese grits. It does a handful of vegetarian dishes, too.

🛏 Oliver Hotel   Boutique Hotel $$

(📞865-521-0050; www.theoliverhotel.com; 407 Union Ave; r from $145) Knoxville's only boutique hotel has 28 lovingly appointed rooms with marble sink tops and rainshower heads in the baths, plush linens, iHomes and more. Service is outstanding and the vibe is modern and upmarket. Good value.

Durham ❼

🛏 Duke Tower   Hotel $

(📞866-385-3869, 919-687-4444; www.duketower.com; 807 W Trinity Ave; ste $88-98; 🅿❄🛜🖥) For less than most local hotel rooms you can enjoy a condo with hardwood floors, full kitchen and a Tempur-Pedic mattress. Premium suites have flat-screen TVs. Located in Durham's historical downtown tobacco-mill district.

Chapel Hill ❽

🍴 Neal's Deli   Breakfast, Deli $

(www.nealsdeli.com; 100 E Main St, Carrboro; breakfast $3-6, lunch $5-9; ⏱7:30am-7pmTue-Fri, 8am-4pm Sat & Sun) Before starting your day, chow down on a delicious buttermilk breakfast biscuit at this tiny deli in downtown Carrboro. The egg, cheese and bacon is some kind of good. For lunch, Neal's serves sandwiches and subs, from chicken salad to pastrami to a three-cheese pimiento with a splash of bourbon.

Stax Museum of American Soul Music *Stories of soul legends*

Memphis to Nashville

27

When two of America's legendary musical towns are within three hours of one another, they must be linked. Your journey will include a shot of history (and whiskey) along the way.

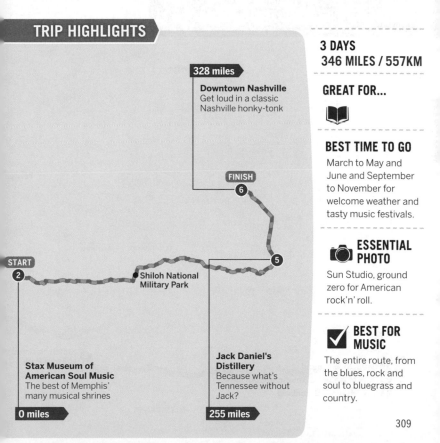

TRIP HIGHLIGHTS

328 miles

Downtown Nashville
Get loud in a classic Nashville honky-tonk

FINISH
6

START
2

● Shiloh National Military Park

5

Stax Museum of American Soul Music
The best of Memphis' many musical shrines

0 miles

Jack Daniel's Distillery
Because what's Tennessee without Jack?

255 miles

3 DAYS
346 MILES / 557KM

GREAT FOR...

BEST TIME TO GO
March to May and June and September to November for welcome weather and tasty music festivals.

ESSENTIAL PHOTO
Sun Studio, ground zero for American rock 'n' roll.

BEST FOR MUSIC
The entire route, from the blues, rock and soul to bluegrass and country.

Memphis is a warm summer night on the riverside. Nashville is a springtime picnic in the sun. Memphis is a smoky blues club, offering grit with a smile, a twisted history and sweet memories. Nashville is a glamour girl – a fine Southern town with cowboy crass, platinum-blonde diamond beauty and beer-soaked stages. Nashville is bluegrass. Memphis is blues. There's a tug of war between Memphis and Nashville devotees. But why choose sides when you can enjoy their differences?

❶ Beale Street & Around

By the early 1900s Beale St was the hub of African American social and civic activity, becoming an early center for what was to be known as blues music. In the '50s and '60s, local recording companies cut tracks for blues, soul, R&B and rockabilly artists such as Al Green, Johnny Cash and Elvis, cementing Memphis' place in the American music firmament. Sprinkled on

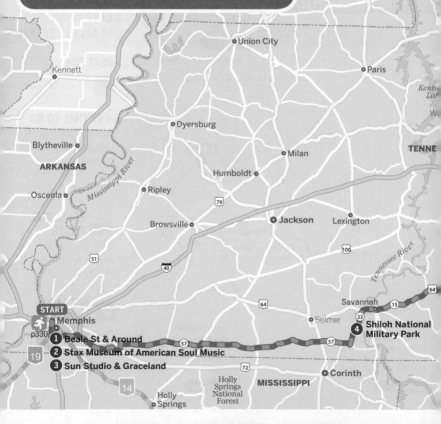

Memphis' most famous block are BB King's (p228), the original nightclub from the Mississippi kid who came to Memphis and became a star; the **New Daisy Theater** (☎901-525-8971, events hotline 901-525-8979; www.newdaisy.com; 330 Beale St; ⊙varies), which regularly hosts indie rock acts; and **A Schwab's** (☎901-523-9782; www .a-schwab.com; 163 Beale St; ⊙noon-7pm Mon-Wed, to 9pm Thu, to 10pm Fri & Sat), with three floors of quirk – don't miss the cool antique gallery upstairs.

Gibson Beale Street Showcase (www.gibson .com; 145 Lt George W Lee Ave; admission $10, no children under 5; ⊙tours 11am-4pm Mon-Sat, noon-4pm Sun) offers a fascinating 45-minute tour where you can see master craftspeople transform solid blocks of wood into legendary Gibson guitars. Journey back into the roots of the American popular music at Memphis Rock 'n' Soul Museum (p274). Its audio tour has over 100 songs, and explains how gospel, country and blues mingled in the Mississippi Delta to create modern sound. The blues are palpable once again when you visit the National Civil Rights Museum (p330), which chronicles the ongoing struggles for African American freedom and equality in the US. Visit Beale St on our walking tour (p330).

The Drive >> Make your way over to 3rd St then head south to E McLemore Ave, where the ragged edge of Memphis begins to show.

- - - - - - - - - - - - -

TRIP HIGHLIGHT

② Stax Museum of American Soul Music

There are few (or no) funkier places on earth than the birthplace of soul music. The **Stax**

LINK YOUR TRIP

19 The Blues Highway

As long as we're getting musical, why not follow the blues trail south from Memphis to the Mississippi Delta, where American popular music all began?

14 Civil Rights Tour

Martin Luther King Jr met his end in Memphis, but you can follow him back to the beginning on this inspirational and historical roadtrip.

27 MEMPHIS TO NASHVILLE

0 ——— 50 km
0 ——— 25 miles

6 Downtown Nashville
7 South of Downtown and The West End
8 Grand Ole Opry

Nashville ⊙
🚶 FINISH
p328

Dickson
40

Murfreesboro
65
24
10

Centerville

Columbia
Mt. Pleasant

Shelbyville

43
15

Jack Daniel's **5**
Distillery
Lynchburg
10
55

enceburg
Pulaski
64
15
Fayetteville

Lexington

ALABAMA
65
10

311

(☎901-942-SOUL; www.staxmuseum.com; 926 E McLemore Ave; adult/child $12/9; ⊙10am-5pm Tue-Sat, 1-5pm Sun Mar-Oct, closed Mon Nov-Mar) experience begins with a moving 20-minute introductory film and the exhibits build on that. This is the label that used an integrated house band to back legends like Sam Cooke, Booker T Jones, and the amazing Otis Redding. Ike Turner is given reverence as the visionary he was. His guitar and Tina's dress are on display (his domestic violence history conspicuously absent). Named for brother-sister founders Jim Stewart and Estelle Axton, there was always was a record shop in front of the studio (now it's a gift shop that sells CDs). It was originally a country label, but neighborhood demographics changed and African American musicians began drifting in. The unique combination of gospel, country and blues formed what became soul music. You can walk through the guts of the recording studio, and enjoy splashy displays for Albert King, the Staple Singers and the great Isaac Hayes, the headliner of the 1972 Wattstax festival, the label's high-water mark. Eventually the label went under, but it is now on a campus of the Soulsville

Foundation that includes the Stax Music Academy, a public charter school.

The Drive » Head back across town on the I-240N, take the Union Ave exit and head west.

---

❸ Sun Studio & Graceland

Sun Studio (p271) is where the rockabilly dynasty of Jerry Lee Lewis, Johnny Cash, Roy Orbison and, of course, the king himself (who started here in 1953), was born. Today packed 40-minute guided tours through the tiny studio offer a chance to hear original tapes of historic recording sessions. Guides spin yarns while you pose for photos in the old recording studio on the 'X' where Elvis once stood. Afterwards, hop on the free shuttle to Graceland (p274). Though born in Mississippi, Elvis Presley was a true son of Memphis: raised in the Lauderdale Courts public housing projects, and inspired by the blues in the Beale St clubs, in the spring of 1957 the already-famous 22-year-old spent $100,000 on a Colonial-style mansion, named Graceland by its previous owners. Priscilla Presley (who divorced Elvis in 1973) opened Graceland to tours in 1982, and now millions come here to pay homage to the king and gawk at the infamous decor.

The Drive » Take the I-240 east to the Bill Morris Pkwy, which will take you out of town. Take the TN-57 east from there for about 52 miles, paralleling the Mississippi border. Head north on TN-22 to the Shiloh National Military Park.

---

❹ Shiloh National Military Park

Located just north of the Mississippi border near the town of Crump, TN, **Shiloh National Military Park** (www.nps.gov/shil; 1055 Pittsburg Landing Rd; ⊙park dawn-dusk, visitor center 8am-5pm) reveals the drama behind one of the early major battles

Memphis Sun Studio

of the Civil War. Ulysses S Grant, then a major general, led the Army of Tennessee. After a vicious Confederate assault on the first day that took Grant by surprise, his creative maneuver on the second day held Pittsburgh Landing, and turned the Confederates back. A relative unknown at the beginning of the war, Grant went on to lead the Union to victory and eventually became the 18th president of the United States. The vast park can only be seen by car. Sights along the route include the Shiloh National Cemetery, the final resting place of 4000 soldiers, an overlook of the Cumberland River where Union reinforcement troops arrived by ship, and various markers and monuments. The visitor center gives out maps, shows a video about the battle, and sells an audio driving tour.

The Drive >> Continue down the Tennessee backroads, and make your way north on TN-22 to TN-15 east. The road jogs so be conscious of signage. After about 45 miles, turn left on TN-50 east which leads into TN-55 east toward Lynchburg.

TRIP HIGHLIGHT

⑤ Jack Daniel's Distillery

Set in tiny Moore County (the smallest in all of Tennessee) is the state's most famous product, **Jack Daniel's Tennessee Whiskey** (www.jackdaniels .com; 182 Lynchburg Hwy, Lynchburg). And strange gets stranger when you consider that it's also a dry county and has been since the soulless scourge of prohibition. Yes, 90 years later dry counties still exist in the South. But, being the South, contradiction is en vogue and you can and will sip a thimble (or more) of the good stuff after the Tasting Tour, which includes an hour-and-a-quarter ramble through the inner workings of the distillery. These enhanced tours are the only type that include a tipple other than lemonade, and they are only available a few times a day, Monday through Saturday, and cost $10. It's best to book ahead. Free tours without a tasting are offered daily on the hour and are available on a first come, first served basis. The distillery itself sells no memorabilia, so if you want some Old No 7 trinkets, visit the **Lynchburg Hardware & General Store** (160 Craig St; ⊙9am-6pm Mon-Fri, from 10am Sat, from 1pm Sun) in town – which is actually owned by the distillery.

The Drive » It's an easy hour-and-a-half drive, mostly off the major interstate, to Nashville. Take TN-55 east to TN-82 north to TN-10 south until you merge with I-24 north for the final 32 miles.

- - - - - - - - - - - - -

TRIP HIGHLIGHT

❻ Downtown Nashville

For country-music fans and wannabe songwriters all over the world, a trip to Nashville is the ultimate pilgrimage. Think of any song involving a pick-up truck, a bottle of booze, a no-good woman or a late, lamented hound dog, and the chances are it came from Nashville. Downtown is where you'll find the lion's share of the honky-tonks, as well as the excellent Country Music Hall of Fame (p328), where Elvis' gold Cadillac and Johnny Cash's guitar are enshrined like religious relics. Visit it on our walking tour (p328). Over on Broadway – the heart and soul of the downtown strip – be sure to duck into **Hatch Show Print** (www.hatchshowprint.com; 316 Broadway; ⊙9am-5pm Mon-Fri, from 10am Sat). For 130 years this classic Nashville printer has been block printing publicity posters. It gets orders from all over the world, and you can buy reprints of original Louis Armstrong, Hank Williams and Bill Monroe shows past. For music in the present make your way to **Robert's Western World** (www.robertswesternworld.com; 416 Broadway; ⊙11am-2am). Name another dive where you can buy boots, have a burger, a beer or something stronger and listen to a rockabilly band for free all day every day. **Tootsie's Orchid Lounge** (☎615-726-7937; www.tootsies.net; 422 Broadway; admission free; ⊙10am-late) is equally appealing: a torn-up linoleum-floor dive bar drenched with boot-stomping, hillbilly, beer-soaked grace.

The Drive » Nashville sprawls a bit, so you will want to drive between downtown and areas south and west. The gridlike streets make it relatively easy to get around.

- - - - - - - - - - - - -

❼ South of Downtown and The West End

Nashville sprawls a bit, and within the shadow of the downtown skyline are a number of can't-miss clubs and sights for music lovers. Our favorite club in town is the

MEMPHIS IN MAY

You've heard of Coachella, you've heard of New Orleans Jazz Fest and you may have heard of Bonnaroo, but Memphis' **Beale Street Music Festival** (www.memphisinmay.org; Tom Lee Park; 3-day pass $85; ⊙1st weekend in May) gets very little attention, though it offers one of the country's best line-ups of old-school blues masters, up-and-coming rockers and gloriously past-their-prime pop and hip-hop artists. It runs over three days and attracts 100,000 people to Tom Lee Park each May. No, the Beale Street Festival is not actually on Beale St.

Station Inn (p329). Sit at one of the small cocktail tables, all squeezed together on the worn wood floor, in this beer-only dive. There is no haunt more momentarily famous than **Bluebird Cafe** (☎615-383-1461; www.bluebirdcafe.com; 4104 Hillsboro Rd; cover free-$15; ⊙shows 6:30pm & 9:30pm). Set in a strip mall in suburban South Nashville, some of the best original singer-songwriters in country music have graced this tiny stage (Steve Earle, Emmylou Harris and the Cowboy Junkies included), which is how it became the central location in the popular television series, *Nashville*. Also in a strip mall, yet still a legit cultural force, is renowned author Anne Patchett's **Parnassus Books** (www.parnassusbooks .net; 3900 Hillsboro Pike; ⊙10am-8pm Mon-Sat, noon-5pm Sun), arguably one of America's most famous indie booksellers. The bright space hosts special events, readings and signings, promotes local authors and even sells e-books. Little nuggets of independence like this may just save our literary souls. The most famous sight on this end of town is **Music Row** (Music Square West & Music Square East), a stretch of 16th and 17th Avenues, home to the

THIRD MAN

Jack White's move to Nashville and away from his downbeat, Detroit White Stripes roots has been well publicized. You can and should visit his excellent new operation, **Third Man Records** (www.thirdmanrecords .com; 623 7th Ave S; ⊙10am-6pm Mon-Sat, 1-4pm Sun), in a still-industrial slice of downtown Nashville two blocks from active train tracks. There's a tiny record shop selling only Third Man recordings on vinyl and CD, as well as White Stripes and Raconteurs (his current band) albums. The T-shirts, stickers and headphones are cool, too. They do live shows in the studio's Blue Room once a month, which are typically open to the public but are only announced a few days in advance, so keep your ear to the asphalt. Often these shows (Jerry Lee Lewis' recent performance comes to mind) become available on limited-edition vinyl sold in the store. The shows are $10.

production companies, agents, managers and promoters who run Nashville's country-music industry. There's not much to see, but you can pay to cut your own record at some of the smaller studios.

The Drive ≫ Take the I-40 east to the TN-155 north and watch for the signs. You really can't miss it.

- - - - - - - - - - - -

❽ Grand Ole Opry

Starting as a radio hour in 1925, country music's signature star-making broadcast operated out of the legendary **Ryman Auditorium** (☎info 615-889-3060, tickets 615-458-8700; www.ryman.com; 116 5th Ave) from 1943 to 1974 before moving out here to the suburbs. After a brief run

as a doomed theme park, these days Opryland is a splashy, labyrinthine resort and shopping mall (complete with IMAX theater), but the signature sight remains the **Grand Ole Opry House** (☎615-871-6779; www. opry.com; 2802 Opryland Dr; tours adult/child $18.50/13.50; ⊙museum 10:30am-6pm Mar-Dec), a modern brick building that seats 4400 on Friday and Saturday from March to November. Guided backstage tours are offered daily by reservation – book online up to two weeks ahead. Across the plaza, a small, free museum tells the story of the Opry with wax characters, colorful costumes and dioramas.

Eating & Sleeping

Memphis

✕ Alcenia's
Southern $

(www.alcenias.com; 317 N Main St; mains $6-9; ⊙11am-5pm Tue-Fri, 9am-3pm Sat) The only thing sweeter than Alcenia's famous 'ghetto juice' (a diabetes-inducing fruit drink) is owner Betty-Joyce 'BJ' Chester-Tamayo – don't be surprised to receive a kiss on the top of the head as soon as you sit down. The lunch menu at this funky little gold- and purple-painted cafe rotates daily – look for killer fried chicken and catfish, melt-in-your-mouth spiced cabbage and an exquisite eggy custard pie.

✕ Dyer's
Fast Food $

(www.dyersonbeale.com; 205 Beale St; burgers $4-7; ⊙11am-midnight Sun-Thu, to late Fri & Sat) Purportedly one of America's best burgers – anointed so by both *Esquire* and *Playboy* – the meat is smacked flat with a spatula at least 4in wide then submerged in bubbling grease, continuously filtered like it is life-giving elixir when, well, it's probably the opposite. But no matter. They've been doing it this way since 1912, and it makes a late-night snack of the gods.

✕ Charlie Vergos' Rendezvous
Barbecue $$

See Trip 🚌 (p236).

🛏 Madison Hotel
Boutique $$$

See Trip 🚌 (p236).

🛏 Pilgrim House Hostel
Hostel $

(☏901-273-8341; www.pilgrimhouse.org; 1000 S Cooper St; dm $20, r $30-50; P ❄ @ 🛜) Yes, it's in a church. No, no one will try to convert you but the chatty young live-in staff may well invite you for a beer down the street, in Midtown's trendy Germantown neighborhood. An international crowd plays cards and chats (no alcohol) in a sunny, open common area resembling an IKEA catalog. Dorms and private rooms are clean and spare. All guests must do a brief daily chore, like taking out the trash.

🛏 Talbot Heirs
Guesthouse $$

(☏901-527-9772, 800-955-3956; www.talbothouse.com; 99 S 2nd St; ste from $130; ❄ 🛜) Inconspicuously located on the 2nd floor of a busy downtown street, this cheerful guesthouse is one of Memphis' best-kept secrets. Spacious suites are more like hip studio apartments than hotel rooms, with Oriental rugs and funky local artwork, and kitchens stocked with snacks. The innkeepers know all the best local restaurants and bars – just ask. Parking costs $10.

Lynchburg

✕ Miss Mary Bobo's Boarding House
Southern $

(☏931-759-7394; www.facebook.com/pages/Miss-Mary-Bobos-Boarding-House/145161592212541?rf=117849681617952; 295 Main St; per person $22; ⊙11am & 1pm Mon-Sat) With just two seatings a day, by reservation only, they've been serving massive and delicious Southern meals family-style at this classic boarding house since 1908. The menu rotates, but includes at least two meats (fried chicken and meat loaf are staples), six veggies, biscuits and corn bread, along with dessert, sweet tea and coffee.

Nashville

✕ City House
New Southern $$$

See Trip 🚌 (p206).

✕ Marché Artisan Foods
Bistro $$

(www.marcheartisanfoods.com; 1000 Main St; mains $9-16; ⊙8am-9pm Tue-Sat, to 4pm Sun) In rapidly gentrifying Five Points, this lovely and bright glass box of a farm-to-table cafe offers a corned beef Ruben on marble rye, a popular lamb burger and a delicious warm broccoli salad with brown rice at lunch. It hosts special beer and wine dinners, too.

✕ Provence
Bakery & Cafe

(www.provencebreads.com; 1705 21st Ave S; mains $7-11; ⊘7am-8pm Mon-Fri, to 8pm Sat, to 6pm Sun) A popular spot in the Hillsboro District, lovers of breads will want to stop here for a loaf or a ready-made turkey, chicken salad or tuna sandwich. It also does frittatas, salads, tasty pastries and a French toast made with a peach compote. Order your flavor and grab a table in the bright dining area that's popular at lunch.

🛏 Hotel Indigo
Boutique $$$

(☎615-891-6000; www.ihg.com; 301 Union St; r from $299) Part of a smallish international chain, the Indigo has a fun, pop-art look, with a lime-green and electric-blue color scheme, a chrome staircase and a huge photo mural above the lobby bar. The king rooms are spacious and hip with brand-new wood floors, high ceilings, flat screens and leather head boards.

Electric guitars mounted on the lobby walls and occasional live music remind you you're in Nashville. The location is excellent, in the heart of the busy West End area near Vanderbilt University. Adjacent to the lobby is Goten, a sushi bar and Japanese steakhouse with a bit of an international-businessman vibe – lots of meat, lots of cocktails.

🛏 Nashville Downtown Hostel
Hostel $

(☎615-497-1208; www.nashvillehostel.com; 177 1st Ave North; dm/r $28/85) Opened in 2012, well located and up-to-the-minute in style and function, the common space in the basement with its rather regal exposed stone walls and beamed rafters is your all-night all-hours mingle den. Dorm rooms are upstairs on the 4th floor, and have lovely wood floors, exposed timber columns, silver beamed ceilings and four brand-new bunks to a room. All come with shared baths. Parking is $12.

Mississippi River
power, ecologic

Big Muddy **28**

It gave us Huck Finn and the blues. Plantations depended on it for commerce, slaves used it to escape and the Civil War streaked it with blood. The Mississippi River is America.

TRIP HIGHLIGHTS

0 miles

Memphis
One of America's great cities, it's full of music, history and soul

99 miles

Clarksdale
Delve into the Mississippi Delta's blues tradition

Helena

4

1

Vicksburg

6

313 miles

Natchez
Antebellum panache, Huck Finn soul

Baton Rouge

8

Venice

518 miles

New Orleans
The river's most glorious city

---

5 DAYS
526 MILES / 847KM

GREAT FOR...

BEST TIME TO GO
September to November and March to May, when the sun is warm yet forgiving.

ESSENTIAL PHOTO
Mud Island River Park, the Mississippi's most visited spot.

BEST FOR HISTORY
The entire route, for the story of America, its people and their song.

319

28 Big Muddy

It bubbles up in Minnesota where the river is still narrow enough to swim across, but in the South it is a commercial artery that ferries fuel, goods and people from the Gulf of Mexico to the Midwest, and back again, as it has for centuries. It twists for 2320 miles, and at nearly every bend there's a story.

TRIP HIGHLIGHT

1 Memphis

Memphis is one of the river's most soulful cities, and the Memphis Rock 'n' Soul Museum (p274) delves into the social and cultural history that produced the blues in the Mississippi Delta. That sound eventually morphed into rock'n'roll when Elvis sang 'Hound Dog', an old blues tune, in Sun Studio (p271), which you can visit as part of our walking tour (p330). But long before Elvis and Otis, this section of the river was used to shepherd slaves to freedom. Learn the details at the **Slave Haven Underground Railroad Museum** (☏901-527-3427; www.slavehavenundergroundrailroadmuseum.org; 826 N 2nd St; adult/child $10/8; ☺10am-1pm Mon-Sat). It's set in a modest clapboard house laced with tunnels fed by trapdoors.

The **Mississippi River Museum** (www.mississippirivermuseum.com; 350 East 3rd Street; adult/child $15/10; ☺10am-5pm Apr-Oct) is the place to learn more about the cultural and natural history of the Big Muddy. Check out the scale model of the lower Mississippi which includes a 40,000-gallon Gulf of Mexico aquarium teeming with sharks and rays. It's part of **Mud Island River Park** (☏901-576-7241; www.mudisland.com; 125 N Front St; ☺10am-5pm Tue-Sun, later in summer). Linked to Memphis by a monorail, you can rent kayaks, canoes and bikes and explore.

✖ 🍴 p326

The Drive ☵ Pick up the Blues Highway, US 61, in Memphis and drive through the city's rough edge into the wide open spaces of the Mississippi Delta, where the blues were born.

2 Tunica

The gateway to Delta Blues country is the juke joint mock-up that is the Tunica Visitors Center (p228), where interactive digital guides offer background checks on famed blues musicians and can't-miss destinations on the Blues Trail itself. You will learn, for instance, that Robert Johnson, the original blues star, was born in Tunica, Mississippi, yet this small riverside town has morphed into a maze of casinos, which aren't worth your time. Best to check out the Visitors Center and keep moving.

The Drive ☵ Blitz through the flat, green, big sky delta on US 61, before heading west on US 49, across the river and into Arkansas.

180 miles to Missouri

Jonesboro

Jackson

ARKANSAS

TENNESSEE

Bald Knob

1 Memphis

Holly Springs National Forest

Tunica **2**

Sardis Lake

Helena **3** Lula

ine Bluff

Clarksdale 4

Tupelo

Arkansas River

Grenade Reservoir

18

Greenville Leland

Tombigbee National Forest

MISSISSIPPI

Delta National Forest

Meridian

Vicksburg 5

Jackson

Bienville National Forest

Natchez **6**

Brookhaven

Laurel

Homochitto National Forest

Hattiesburg

LOUISIANA

Baton Rouge

Lake Pontchartrain

Biloxi

afayette

New Orleans

Donaldsonville

7

The River Road

8

Gulf Islands National Seashore

p262

Raceland

9 Venice

0   100 km
0   50 miles

---

3 Helena

A depressed mill town still hoping for a second wind, it was once home to the late Sonny Boy Williamson, a regular on *King Biscuit Time*, America's first blues radio show. BB King listened religiously as a child, and it was Sonny who introduced King to his first audience on that radio show. The show, which begins weekdays at 12:15pm, is still running, and broadcasts out of the Delta Cultural Center (p230), which is also a terrific blues museum. You're welcome to watch the broadcast live, and you may even get on the air. Down the street is Bubba's Blues Corner (p230), the type of record store – owned

---

LINK YOUR TRIP

20 Cajun Country

Head west from New Orleans, and delve into the blackwater bayous and spiced cultural gumbo that is Louisiana's Cajun Country.

18 Historical Mississippi

Detour from the river in Mississippi to absorb the heartbreaking and soul-stirring history of the river's namesake state.

by an old-school blues vinyl savant – that is a dying breed. If you time it right, you can join the three-day King Biscuit Blues Festival (p230) in October, the one-day only Live on The Levee (p230) concert, held each June, or the two-day Arkansas Delta Rockabilly Festival (p230) in May.

The Drive ⟫ Double back across the river on US 49, skirt Moon Lake and head south in a straight shot for 16 miles on US 61.

- - - - - - - - - -

TRIP HIGHLIGHT

❹ Clarksdale

Clarksdale is the hub of Delta Blues Country. This is where you'll find **the Crossroads** (p221), where legend has it that Robert Johnson made his famous deal with the devil and became America's first guitar hero. And it's here where live music and blues history are most accessible. The

Delta Blues Museum (p231), downtown, has the best collection of blues memorabilia in the delta, including Muddy Waters' reconstructed Mississippi cabin. It will soon go, along with his instruments, records and costumes, into the 'Muddy Wing.' Creative, multimedia exhibits also honor BB King, John Lee Hooker, Big Mama Thornton and WC Handy, whose original 1912 compositions popularized the 12-bar blues. There's live music in Clarksdale at least four nights a week (typically Wednesday to Saturday). **Cat Head Delta Blues & Folk Art** (www.cathead.biz; 252 Delta Ave; ⊙10am-5pm Mon-Sat) is the best place to inquire about local shows, but if you land here on a weekend, head to directly to Red's (p231), a ragged downtown juke joint run with in-your-face charm by its

JOHN COLETTI / GETTY IMAGES ©

namesake. Sometimes he has moonshine behind the bar.

✕ ⟫ p326

The Drive ⟫ US 61 parallels the Mississippi all the way to the Louisiana border, but Helena will be your last glimpse of it until you reach Vicksburg, 144 miles south.

- - - - - - - - - -

❺ Vicksburg

Most famous for a pivotal battle that turned the Civil War into the Union's favor, this charming, if struggling, town offers sublime Mississippi River vistas from its bluffs. And it was control of

---

OIL!

Think land traffic is hazardous? On July 24, 2008, a cargo barge collided with an oil tanker on the Mississippi in New Orleans, causing a 500,000-gallon oil slick. Within minutes 100 miles of the river were closed to boat traffic, costing the Port of New Orleans up to $250,000 per day. Downriver waterfowl were covered in the thick, black sludge, and there were concerns about contamination of urban tap water supplies and the estuaries along the Gulf Coast. Thankfully the clean-up was swift, but the spill served as a reminder that this great and powerful river is not indestructible.

New Orleans Streetcar

that river that drove General Ulysses S Grant to besiege the city for 47 days, until its surrender on July 4, 1863. Inland at Vicksburg National Military Park (p224), you can drive, or pedal, along the 16-mile Battlefield Dr that winds past 1330 monuments and markers, including statues, battle trenches, a restored Union gunboat and a National Cemetery. It makes for a fascinating afternoon. The **Lower Mississippi River Museum** (📞601-638-9900; www.lmrm.org; 910 Washington St; 🕙9am-5pm Tue-Sat year-round, 1-5pm

Sun Apr-Oct), downtown, delves into such topics as the famed 1927 flood, and a background of the Army Corps of Engineers who have managed the river – for better and worse – since the 18th century. Kids will dig its aquarium and rambling around the dry-docked research vessel, the M/V *Mississippi IV*. Art buffs shouldn't miss the wonderful **Attic Gallery** (📞601-638-9221; www.atticgallery.net; 1101 Washington St; 🕙10am-5pm Mon-Sat). There are some fabulous finds here.

🍴 p326

The Drive » From Vicksburg, US 61 once again drifts inland, rolling over mogul-like foothills before bending back to the riverside in Natchez.

- - - - - - - - - - - - -

TRIP HIGHLIGHT

6 Natchez

Historical antebellum mansions will greet you in Natchez, Mississippi. In the 1840s there were more millionaires per capita here than anywhere in the world. When Union soldiers marched through with orders to torch the place during the Civil War, there weren't any men in town. Legend has it the women greeted the soldiers at their doors, and Southern hospitality saved the city. Those mansions are open to visitors during the twice annual 'Pilgrimage seasons' held in the spring and fall. The Visitor and Welcome Center (p224) is your best pilgrimage resource. You may visit the Auburn Mansion (p205) year-round.

When Mark Twain passed through, during his riverboat captain days, he crashed in a room above the local saloon. Under the Hill Saloon (p205) remains the best bar in town, with terrific free live music on weekends. The name works, because the saloon is built into a hillside and overlooks a captivating bend of the Mississippi.

📖 p326

The Drive >> Cross the Louisiana state line and US 61 bleeds into the I-110 south, which merges with I-10 in Baton Rouge. Take US 44 south to LA-70 west to LA-18 toward Donaldsonville, just off of Louisiana's River Road (actually a series of highways that skirt both sides of the Mississippi).

- - - - - - - - - - - - -

❼ The River Road

Elaborate plantation homes dot the east and west banks of the Mississippi River between New Orleans and Baton Rouge. Indigo then cotton and sugarcane brought great wealth to these plantations, many of which are open to the public.

Laura Plantation (www.lauraplantation.com; 2247 Hwy 18; adult/child $20/6; ⊘10am-4pm), in Vacherie on the west bank, offers the most dynamic and informative tour. It teases out the distinctions between Creole, Anglo and African American antebellum life via meticulous research and the written records of the Creole women who ran the place for generations.

Next, step into the **River Road African American Museum** (www.africanamericanmuseum.org; 406 Charles St; admission $5; ⊘10am-5pm Wed-Sat, 1-5pm Sun) and learn the region's seldom-told African American history. You'll learn the truth about slave ships, the vicious toils of slavery, slave revolts, the Underground Railroad, reconstruction and Jim Crow from antiques, artifacts, photographs and video interviews. When slaves escaped the Donaldsonville plantations, they ran or floated south to New Orleans, where they could blend in with free African Americans, rather than north, where they would have to cross Mississippi, Tennessee and Missouri to find freedom.

The Drive >> From Donaldsonville take the I-10 east, skirt Lake Pontchartrain and follow it all the way into the Crescent City.

- - - - - - - - - - - - -

TRIP HIGHLIGHT

❽ New Orleans

No city is better associated with the Mississippi River than New Orleans – for better and worse. New Orleans

---

PHATWATER CHALLENGE

If you're into aquatic self-propulsion (ie you really dig kayaking) then you'll enjoy the Phatwater Challenge, a marathon kayak race (the future Olympic sport you've never heard of) that runs downriver from the Port of Grand Gulf 42 miles to Natchez, MS. For one full day barge traffic is halted as paddlers own the Mississippi. Join the party and you can stop for breaks on beaches and sand bars, and you may even see a 12ft gator or two. The race wraps with a bluegrass jam at the historical Under the Hill Saloon.

is best experienced on foot, so be sure to enjoy our walking tour (p262). This city, packed with life, passion, music and angst, has been formed, nourished and flooded by the river for centuries. **Jackson Sq** (☎504-568-6968; www .jackson-square.com; Decatur & St Peter Sts) is a clear choice for just soaking up the local street scene. Don't miss the **French Market** (N Peters St from St Ann St to Barracks St): New Orleanians have been trading goods for over 200 years from this spot on the Mississippi riverbanks. The river is nearby, up the levee, and you get nice views over the sweet, brown, polluted, sloshing water from there.

When the moon rises over the Mississippi, it's time to seek night music. For live music that's on the river, you can't really go wrong with the **Rivershack Tavern** (☎504-834-4938; 3449 River Rd; ⊗11am-midnight Mon-Thu, to 3am Fri & Sat). Alternatively, head to **Chickie Wah Wah** (☎504-304-4714; www.chickiewahwah.com; 2828 Canal St; ⊗shows around 8pm). Not on the river – but it's close enough (as is all of Frenchman St) – it's a

DETOUR: MISSOURI

Start: ❶ Memphis

Whether you're more interested in the great **Mark Twain** (www.marktwainmuseum.org; 415 N Main St; adult/child $11/6; ⊗9am-5pm), who grew up on the river as Samuel Longhorne Clemens (1835–1910) in Hannibal, or you're partial to St Louis, Lewis and Clark, and the **Gateway Arch** (☎877-982-1410; www .gatewayarch.com; 707 N 1st St, Jefferson National Expansion Memorial; observatory adult/child $10/5; ⊗8:30am-9pm Jun-Aug, 9:30am-5pm Sep-May), Missouri has as much Mississippi River gravitas as any other state on its shores. And don't leave St Louis until you grab a Bud at **Anheuser-Busch Brewery** (www.budweisertours.com; cnr 12th & Lynch Sts; admission free; ⊗9am-4pm Mon-Sat, 11:30am-4pm Sun, to 5pm Jun-Aug, from 10am Sep-May). The tour through this cereal-smelling Victorian-era complex shares trade secrets. For instance, at one time the brewery used Mississippi River water to make beer, and stored barrels in artificial caves dug into the cool riverbanks. Don't worry, you'll be rewarded with two frosty ones.

dependable jazz venue. Local legends like the Sweet Olive String Band and Meschiya Lake make their way across that small stage regularly.

✗ 🛏 p326

The Drive » From New Orleans take the 428E through Algiers and head south on LA-23, a continuation of the Great River Rd that follows the river's west bank until it ends 70 miles south of New Orleans amid the stilted vacation homes, oil infrastructure and sport fishing marinas of Venice.

- - - - - - - - - - - -

❾ Venice

This is the mouth of the Mississippi and you'll see the river spread into rivulets that flood a vast estuary protected by the Fish and Wildlife Service as the **Delta National Wildlife Refuge** (www .fws.gov/delta). There are redfish and speckled trout in the wetlands, and tarpon, snapper and grouper in the Gulf. Charter a boat for a day, or you may wish to cast off a defunct offshore oil platform.

Eating and Sleeping

Memphis ❶

✗ Alchemy — Southern Tapas $$
(☎901-726-4444; www.alchemymemphis.com; 940 S Cooper St; tapas $10-13, mains $23-28; ⏱4pm-1am Mon-Sat, until 10pm Sun) A flash spot in the Cooper-Young district, it serves tasty Southern tapas like diver scallops with truffled cauliflower purée, roasted asparagus with Benton's bacon, and cornmeal-dusted and flash-fried calamari. The kitchen stays open until 1am.

✗ Cozy Corner — Barbecue $$
See Trip 23 (p275).

✗ Sweet Grass — Southern $$$
(☎901-278-0278; www.sweetgrassmemphis .com; 937 S Cooper St; mains $21-27; ⏱5:30pm-late Tue-Sun, 11am-2pm Sun) Contemporary lowcountry cuisine (the seafood-heavy cooking of the South Carolina and Georgia coasts) wins raves at this sleek new Midtown bistro. Shrimp and grits, a classic fisherman's breakfast, is a crowd-pleaser. However, the vibe can be a bit stuffy.

⛏ Sleep Inn at Court Square — Hotel $$
(☎901-522-9700; www.sleepinn.com; 400 N Front St; r from $114; ❄ 🛜) Our pick of the cheaper downtown digs, this stubby stucco box, part of a jumble of corporate sleeps, has pleasant, airy rooms with flat screen TVs. Parking is $12.

Clarksdale ❹

✗ Abe's — BBQ $
See Trip 19 (p236).

⛏ Shack Up Inn — Inn $
(☎662-624-8329; www.shackupinn.com; Hwy 49; d $75-165; P ❄ 🛜) At the cheeky Hopson Plantation, this self-titled 'bed and beer', 2 miles south on the west side of Hwy 49, evokes the blues like no other. Guests stay in refurbished sharecropper cabins or the creatively renovated cotton gin. The cabins have covered porches

and are filled with old furniture and musical instruments. The old commissary, the Juke Joint Chapel (equipped with pews), is an atmospheric venue inside the cotton gin for live-music performances. The whole place reeks of downhome dirty blues and Deep South character – possibly the coolest place you'll ever stay.

Vicksburg ❺

✗ Rusty's Riverfront Grill — Southern $$
(www.rustysriverfront.com; 901 Washington St; mains $17-29; ⏱11am-2pm, 5-9:30pm Tue-Fri, 11am-9:30pm Sat) Set at the north end of downtown, this downhome grill is known for its terrific ribeye, but it has a nice selection of Southern-style seafood fare too, including crab cakes and blackened redfish, and a nice New Orleans–style gumbo.

Natchez ❻

⛏ Mark Twain Guesthouse — Guesthouse $
See Trip 16 (p217).

New Orleans ❽

✗ Elizabeth's — Cajun, Creole $$$
(www.elizabeths-restaurant.com; 601 Gallier St; mains $16-26; ⏱8am-2:30pm & 6-10pm Tue-Sat, 8am-2:30pm Sun) Elizabeth's is deceptively divey, way too dark and probably too laid-back. The food is overly simplistic at times; startlingly out-of-the-box at others. But it tastes as good as the best haute New Orleans chefs can offer. Be sure to order some praline bacon, no matter the time of day: fried up in brown sugar and, as far as we can tell, God's own cooking oil.

✗ Gautreau's — Modern American $$$
(☎504 899-7397; 1728 Soniat St; mains $22-35; ⏱6-10pm Mon-Sat) Chef Sue Zemanick has seemingly won every award a rising star can garner in American culinary circles. Gautreau's, her HQ, is unsigned and tucked away in a

residential neighborhood. Savvy diners enjoy fresh, modern American fare – gnocchi with truffled parmesan cheese and grouper in salsa verde, for example – within a local culinary treasure.

🛏 Columns   Historical Hotel $$

(☎504-899-9308; www.thecolumns.com; 3811 St Charles Ave; r incl breakfast weekend/weekday from $170/134; ❄🔊) A steal in low season, still a good deal in high, this stately 1883 Italianate mansion in the Garden District is both elegant and relaxed, boasting extraordinary original features: a stained-glass-topped staircase, elaborate marble fireplaces, richly carved woodwork throughout etc. To top it off, there's a lovely 2nd-floor porch overlooking oak-draped St Charles Ave and a damn inviting bar.

STRETCH YOUR LEGS
NASHVILLE

Start/Finish: Country Music Hall of Fame & Museum

Distance: 2.7 miles

Duration: Three hours

Nashville will spin you around and leave your ears ringing with the sound of steel guitar. But it has a brainy side too, with great museums, and grand old government buildings not far from those addictive honky-tonks.

Take this walk on Trips

`16` `27`

Country Music Hall of Fame & Museum

Head directly to downtown's **Country Music Hall of Fame & Museum** (www .countrymusichalloffame.com; 222 5th Ave S; adult/child $22/14, audio tour additional $2, Studio B Tour 1hr tour adult/child $13/11; ◉9am-5pm). Here you can gawk at Patsy Cline's cocktail gown, Johnny Cash's guitar, Elvis' gold Cadillac and Conway Twitty's yearbook picture (back when he was Harold Jenkins). Exhibits trace country's roots from the original banjo-pickin' hillbillies of the early 20th century through to today's tattooed and pierced stars, while listening booths give you access to the vast archives of sound.

The Walk » Head north for one block on 5th Ave and make a right on Broadway.

The District

Lower Broadway between 2nd and 4th Aves is famous for its neon-lit honky-tonks, the crowds of tourists in painfully new cowboy boots, and the kid on the corner singing his heart out on a battered guitar. For rockabilly tunes, we love Robert's Western World (p314). Tootsie's Orchid Lounge (p314) is a classic beer-drenched joint, too. Both have free live music from 11am. And don't miss Hatch Show Print (p314), a long-running block print company with a tremendous archive.

The Walk » Continue down Broadway until it dead ends at 1st Ave and the Cumberland River. Head upriver to Church St and make a left. Between Church and Union St you'll find Printer's Alley.

Printer's Alley

Cobblestone-paved Printer's Alley, now lined with bars and restaurants, used to be home to the city's thriving printing industry. Beginning in the early 1800s, horse carts carried paper and ink to the alley's mostly religious publishing houses. The printing of Christian hymnals gave way to secular music

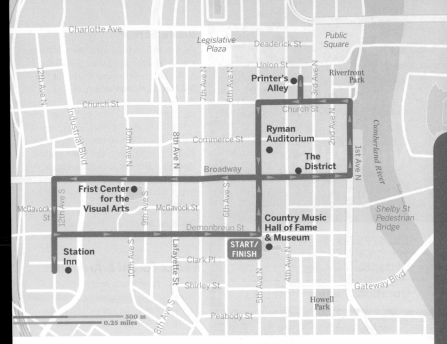

publishing, which helped attract the large record labels in the 1940s and '50s.

The Walk » Take Church to 5th Ave. Make a left and walk two long blocks to Nashville's most historical venue.

Ryman Auditorium

Ryman Auditorium (www.ryman.com; 116 5th Ave N; self-guided tour adult/child $13/6.50, backstage tour $17/10.50; ☉9am-4pm) is a soaring Gothic Revival building commissioned in the late 1800s by crusty old riverboat captain Thomas Ryman, after his soul was saved by a popular Christian evangelist. These days, the 2000-seat Ryman hosts distinctly secular acts such as alt-rock giants The National.

The Walk » Take 5th Ave to Broadway, make a right and walk for several blocks.

Frist Center for the Visual Arts

This massive **art museum** (www.frist center.org; 919 Broadway; adult/senior/child $10/7/free; ☉10am-5:30pm Mon-Wed & Sat, to 9pm Thu & Fri, 1-5pm Sun) is on par with those you'll find in the world's great cities. It has a collection that spans indigenous American pottery to Picasso to mind-melting modernist sculpture; contemporary works are installed on the 1st-floor gallery.

The Walk » Continue on Broadway to 12th Ave and make a left. In four blocks you'll find our favorite place in town for night music.

Station Inn

Station Inn (☎615-255-3307; www.stationinn .com; 402 12th Ave S; ☉open mic 7pm, live bands 9pm), an unassuming stone building, and beer-only dive, is the best place in town for serious bluegrass. The room is lit only by stage lights, neon signs and the lightning fingers of bluegrass savants. We are talking stand-up bass, banjo, mandolin, fiddle and a modicum of honey-throated yodelling.

The Walk » Walk two blocks to Demonbreun St, which leads you back to the Hall of Fame.

STRETCH YOUR LEGS
MEMPHIS

Start/Finish: Beale Street

Distance: 2.5 miles

Duration: Three to four hours

Memphis is alive with blues, soul and rock 'n' roll, pulsating out of bars, concert halls and...museums? A gritty city of warm smiles, smoky barbecue and deep history, its best sights are huddled close and demand a stroll.

Take this walk on Trips

Beale Street

This is where the blues bloomed from a wild Mississippi Delta seed into American popular music. From the **WC Handy House Museum** (☎901-522-1556; www.wchandymemphis.org; 352 Beale St; adult/child $6/4; ⊙11am-4pm Tue-Sat winter, 10am-5pm Tue-Sat summer), a homage to the Father of the Blues, to the original BB King's (p228) to the **Elvis statue**, Memphis royalty is honored here. And this pedestrian street remains a giant street carnival, with free live music nightly.

The Walk » Walk a block over from the pedestrian rave to the FedEx Forum campus on 3rd St.

FedEx Forum & Around

The FedEx Forum, home of the Memphis Grizzlies, hosts two special attractions on its sprawling plaza. The Gibson Beale Street Showcase (p311) offers a 45-minute tour of the factory where the iconic guitars are crafted. Around the corner, the Smithsonian-affiliated Memphis Rock 'n' Soul Museum (p274) shows Memphis' many influences and how this cross-cultural stew revolutionized American music.

The Walk » Continue down 3rd St, turn right on Vance Ave and head left onto Mulberry St until you see the preserved Lorraine Motel.

National Civil Rights Museum

Housed across the street from the 1950s-era Lorraine Motel, where the Reverend Dr Martin Luther King Jr was fatally shot on April 4, 1968, is the gut-wrenching **National Civil Rights Museum** (www.civilrightsmuseum. org; 450 Mulberry St; adult/student & senior/child $10/9/8; ⊙9am-5pm Mon & Wed-Sat, 1-5pm Sun Sep-May, to 6pm Jun-Aug). Extensive exhibits include a detailed timeline, and incredible human cost of the movement for African American freedom and equality.

The Walk » Continue on Mulberry to Patterson Ave. Hang a right, then another onto South Main St.

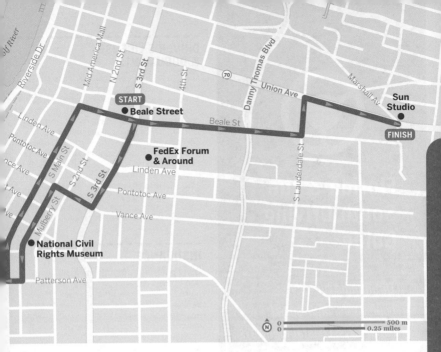

South Main Street

Head to this up-and-coming arts district and make like Elvis – pop into Arcade (p236) for breakfast. Crowds still descend for sublime sweet-potato pancakes. We absolutely love **Hoot & Louise** (www.facebook.com/hootandlouise; 109 GE Patterson Ave; ☺10:30am-6:30pm Mon-Sat, noon-5pm Sun), a new vintage-inspired boutique two doors down from Arcade. If it's late, find **Earnestine & Hazel's** (531 S Main St), a spooky brothel-turned–dive bar, named after its late madams.

The Walk » If you have it in you, head back to Beale, and walk to Union Ave, via Lauderdale St, for more Elvis lore.

Sun Studio

Sun Studio (p271) is where founder Sam Phillips took a chance on a series of scrawny nobodies barely out of their teens. (Ever heard of Elvis, Johnny Cash or Roy Orbison?) Tours are led by enthusiastic guides, many of them country singers themselves. Descriptions of the studio's history are interspersed with loudspeaker clips, such as Elvis' first recording. Pose with the old-school mic in the recording studio then hop the free shuttle back to Beale St.

Florida & the South Driving Guide

Thrumming big-city boulevards, high-speed causeways, coastal highways and winding backcountry roads connect every corner of Florida and the deep South.

Driving Fast Facts

➡ **Right or left?**
Drive on the right

➡ **Legal driving age?** 16

➡ **Top speed limit?** 75 mph
(on interstate)

➡ **Best bumper sticker?**
Remember Who You Wanted
To Be

DRIVER'S LICENSE & DOCUMENTS

Foreign visitors can legally drive in the USA for up to 12 months with their home driver's license. However, getting an International Driving Permit (IDP) is recommended; this will have more credibility with US traffic police, especially if your home license doesn't have a photo or is in a foreign language. Your automobile association at home can issue an IDP, valid for one year, for a small fee. You must carry your home license together with the IDP. To drive a motorcycle, you need either a valid US state motorcycle license or an IDP specially endorsed for motorcycles.

INSURANCE

Don't put the key into the ignition if you don't have insurance, which is legally required, or you'll risk financial ruin if there's an accident. If you already have auto insurance (even overseas), or if you buy travel insurance, make sure that the policy has adequate liability coverage for a rental car; it probably does, but check.

Rental-car companies will provide liability insurance, but most charge extra. Always ask. Rental companies almost never include collision-damage insurance for the vehicle. Instead, they offer an optional Collision Damage Waiver (CDW) or Loss Damage Waiver (LDW), usually with an initial deductible of $100 to $500. For an extra premium, you can usually get this deductible covered as well. However, most credit cards now offer collision-damage coverage for rental cars if you rent for 15 days or less and charge the total rental to your card. This is a good way to avoid paying extra fees to the rental company, but note that if there's an accident, you sometimes must pay the rental car company first and then seek reimbursement from the credit-card company. Check your credit-card policy. Paying extra for some or all of this insurance increases the cost of a rental car by as much as $15 to $30 a day.

RENTING A CAR

Car rental is a very competitive business. Most rental companies require that you have a major credit card, that you be at least 25 years old and that you have a valid

Road Trip Websites

AUTOMOBILE ASSOCIATIONS

American Automobile Association (www.aaa.com) Offers roadside assistance 24 hours per day.

Better World Club (www.betterworldclub.com) Offers the same services, and donates 1% of its profits to environmental nonprofit organizations.

ROAD RULES
Department of Motor Vehicles (www.dmv.org)

CONDITIONS & TRAFFIC
Federal Highway Administration (www.fhwa.dot.gov)

MAPS
Google Maps (www.maps.google.com)

Rand McNally (www.randmcnally.com)

driver's license (your home license will do). Some national companies may rent to drivers between the ages of 21 and 24 for an additional charge. Those under 21 are usually not permitted to rent at all. **Car Rental Express** (www.carrentalexpress. com) rates and compares independent car rental agencies in US cities; it's particularly useful for searching out cheaper long-term rentals.

National car-rental companies:

Alamo (www.alamo.com)

Avis (www.avis.com)

Budget (www.budget.com)

Dollar (www.dollar.com)

Enterprise (www.enterprise.com)

Hertz (www.hertz.com)

National (www.nationalcar.com)

Rent-a-Wreck (www.rentawreck.com)

Thrifty (www.thrifty.com)

Rental cars are readily available at all airport locations and many downtown city locations. With advance reservations for a small car, the daily rate with unlimited mileage is about $35 to $55, while typical weekly rates are $200 to $400, plus myriad taxes and fees. If you rent from a non-airport location, you save the exorbitant airport fees, but may pay a fee for a drop off out of state.

An alternative in Miami and Atlanta is **Zipcar** (www.zipcar.com), a car-sharing service that charges hourly/daily rental fees with free gas, insurance and limited mileage included; pre-payment is required.

BORDER CROSSINGS

Rental cars from Canada and Mexico are eligible to cross the border and operate in the US. Leased cars are also eligible, though you must have a letter of permission from the leasing company. If you own your car, you will more than likely be allowed to cross the border without filling out a customs bond, but the border officer does reserve the right to ask for the bond to be completed.

MAPS

Rand McNally (www.randmcnally.com) is a long-time publisher of high-quality road maps. But they won't show you any more than **Google** or **Map Quest**. **National Geographic Road Atlas** (www.nationalgeographic.com) is the best ink-and-paper map going, with special attention paid to national parks and forests.

ROADS & CONDITIONS

The vast majority of all roads you'll encounter will be free, and paved. Though gravel roads, otherwise known as fire roads, do exist, as does the rare tollway, which requires a fee of 50¢ or more. Interstates are eight lane (at least), high-speed freeways. Highways can be two to six lanes in width and are the most common long-distance strip of asphalt in America. In the

Road Distances (Miles)

	Asheville, NC	Atlanta, GA	Charleston, SC	Chattanooga, TN	Clarksdale, MS	Durham-Chapel Hill, NC	Fort Lauderdale, FL	Jackson, MS	Laffayette, LA	Lexington, KY	Little Rock, AR	Louisville, KY	Memphis, TN	Miami, FL	Nashville, TN	New Orleans, LA	Orlando, FL	Oxford, MS	Savannah, GA
Atlanta, GA	210																		
Charleston, SC	270	320																	
Chattanooga, TN	225	120	435																
Clarksdale, MS	580	390	710	380															
Durham-Chapel Hill, NC	220	380	310	445	775														
Fort Lauderdale, FL	770	640	560	755	1000	810													
Jackson, MS	590	380	700	385	155	760	890												
Laffayette, LA	790	580	540	600	365	960	950	230											
Lexington, KY	285	380	855	280	495	470	1020	625	855										
Little Rock, AR	640	515	835	475	150	860	1130	265	355	555									
Louisville, KY	360	420	615	305	460	530	1065	590	815	80	520								
Memphis, TN	505	385	700	340	80	725	965	210	440	425	135	385							
Miami, FL	790	660	585	780	1025	830	30	910	975	1045	1150	1080	1015						
Nashville, TN	295	250	550	135	285	510	890	415	645	210	350	175	210	910					
New Orleans, LA	680	470	740	490	335	850	840	185	135	745	425	710	395	865	535				
Orlando, FL	585	440	380	555	800	625	215	690	750	820	925	860	765	235	690	640			
Oxford, MS	530	330	650	295	65	710	915	160	390	445	215	410	80	940	235	345	735		
Savannah, GA	310	250	110	365	640	350	465	580	750	585	765	670	630	485	495	640	280	580	
Tampa, FL	640	455	435	575	790	680	265	705	770	835	940	880	810	280	705	660	85	745	335

cities, traffic can back up between 7am and 9am and between 4pm and 7pm for rush hour. In the country, traffic is virtually nonexistent.

ROAD RULES

If you're new to US roads, here are some basics:

➡ The maximum speed limit on interstates is 75mph, but that drops to 65mph and 55mph in urban areas. Pay attention to the posted signs. City street speed limits vary between 15mph and 45mph.

➡ Police officers are generally strict with speed-limit enforcement, and speeding tickets are expensive. If caught going over the speed limit by 10mph, the fine is upwards of $150.

➡ All passengers in a car must wear seat belts or you may be cited and fined. All children under three must be in a child safety seat.

➡ As in the rest of the US, drive on the right-hand side of the road. On highways, pass in the left-hand lane (but pushy drivers often pass wherever space allows).

➡ Right turns on a red light are permitted after a full stop, unless signs dictate otherwise. At four-way stop signs, the car that reaches the intersection first has right of way. In a tie, the car on the right has right of way.

PARKING

In the countryside parking is generally free. In cities you will have to pay at a parking meter (the cheapest), in a designated lot or structure, or you can look for free neigh-

Driving Problem-Buster

➡ **What should I do if my car breaks down?** Call the service number of your car-hire company and they will call out a tow truck. If you're bringing your own car, it's a good idea to join AAA (American Automobile Association), a 24-hour roadside assistance service which can be called out to breakdowns at any time. You can join, on call, at the time of your breakdown.

➡ **What if I have an accident?** For minor accidents you can simply exchange insurance information with the other party and then call your insurance (and/or rental-car company) immediately to report it. If you distrust the other party, call the police, who will fill out an objective report.

➡ **What should I do if I get stopped by the police?** Show your license, passport (if necessary) and proof of insurance (mandatory). And whatever you do, act natural.

➡ **What if I can't find anywhere to stay?** This is likely only a problem in big cities during a major event or festival. If you head out of town (not too far) on the interstate, you are likely to find a cheap corporate motel that will have a room.

borhood street parking. There is usually a time limit, and occasionally permit-only parking, so read the signs, or you may get an expensive ticket.

FUEL

Gas stations are extremely common, except in national parks and high in the mountains, though you will never be more than 50 miles (at the very most) from a gas station. The vast majority sell unleaded, unleaded plus and premium gas, as well as diesel. Unleaded is cheapest and will be fine for your rental car.

SAFETY

Country roads generally lack road lights, and unless you are used to dark highways it can be intimidating. Generally, these are also the highways where cows or deer may try to cross the road. Be very careful. Cows kill. Seriously.

Cities such as Atlanta, Memphis, Miami and New Orleans certainly have their rougher areas, though driving through any neighborhood in daylight is rarely a problem. Be sure to keep all valuables out of sight and doors locked while parked to avoid theft.

RADIO

➡ 90.7 FM, WWOZ, New Orleans' best jazz station, and one of the best in the country. Featured in the HBO series *Treme*.

➡ 960 AM, WABG, broadcasting blues from the Mississippi Delta

➡ 89.9 FM, WEVL, Memphis' only listener-supported, independent radio station, broadcasting blues, rock, world, and bluegrass music.

➡ 100.1 FM, WRLT, Lightening 100, Nashville's independent radio station brings a number of local and well-known artists into the studio.

➡ 107.9 FM, Atlanta's premier hip-hop station deluxe.

BEHIND THE SCENES

SEND US YOUR FEEDBACK

We love to hear from travellers – your comments help make our books better. We read every word, and we guarantee that your feedback goes straight to the authors. Visit **lonelyplanet. com/contact** to submit your updates and suggestions.

Note: We may edit, reproduce and incorporate your comments in Lonely Planet products such as guidebooks, websites and digital products, so let us know if you don't want your comments reproduced or your name acknowledged. For a copy of our privacy policy visit lonelyplanet.com/privacy.

OUR READERS

Many thanks to the travelers who used the last edition and wrote to us with helpful hints, useful advice and interesting anecdotes: Dave Connelly, Mark Sauerhoff.

AUTHOR THANKS

ADAM SKOLNICK

Thanks to Stephanie Greene, Dana McMahan, Carla Carlton, Phoebe Lipkis, Kristin Schofield and Louisville Basketball in Louisville; Jennifer Bohler and Shanna Henderson in Nashville; Nealy Dozier, Walter Thompson, Chloe Friedman, Lydia Hardy, and Chi Bui in Atlanta; and Keith, Peggy and Melissa in Natchez. My love and appreciation goes out to best Savannah buds Alicia Magee, Anna Cypris Jaubert and (by proxy) Joe Bush. Thanks also to my co-authors, Jennye Garibaldi, Clifton Wilkinson and the whole Lonely Planet team for your guidance,

collaboration and assistance. It's a joy and privilege to work with and know you all!

AMY BALFOUR

Thank you Jennye Garibaldi for entrusting me with this great assignment! Big thanks to my friends and experts in the Carolinas: Mike Stokes, Jay Bender, Dan Oden, Lacy Davidson, Deborah Wright, Paige Abbitt Schoenauer, Barbara Blue, David Kimball, Noell and Jack Kimball, and Jennifer Pharr Davis of Blue Ridge Hiking Co.

ADAM KARLIN

Thank you to the Lonely Planet crew: Adam Skolnick and the rest of the South team, the fabulous editorial team of Suki Gear, Bruce Evans, Alison Lyall and dear departed Jennye Garibaldi; mom and dad for raising me right; and Rachel Houge, who I married right after I turned this book in.

MARIELLA KRAUSE

Thanks to Jay Cooke for sending me to Florida the first time, which meant there'd be a next time and a time after that. Thanks also to Tim Bauer for making sure I ate during write-up and for holding down the fort at home. And thanks to all the amazing artists of Wynwood for providing a day of art-filled inspiration.

PUBLISHER THANKS

Climate map data adapted from Peel MC, Finlayson BL & McMahon TA (2007) 'Updated World Map of the Köppen-Geiger Climate Classification,' *Hydrology and Earth System Sciences,* 11, 1633–44. Cover photographs: Front (clockwise from top): Oak Alley Plantation, Louisiana, Massimo Ripani/4Corners; Flamingo mailbox, Sanibel Island, Florida, Ocean/Corbis; Ford Thunderbird, Sun Studio, Memphis, Andrew Woodley/Alamy. Back: Magnolia Plantation Gardens, South Carolina, Pat Canova/Alamy.

THIS BOOK

This 2nd edition of Lonely Planet's *Florida & the South's Best Trips* guidebook was researched and written by Adam Skolnick, Amy Balfour, Adam Karlin and Mariella Krause.

This guidebook was commissioned in Lonely Planet's Oakland office, and produced by the following:

Commissioning Editors Jennye Garibaldi, Suki Gear, Clifton Wilkinson
Coordinating Editors Andrea Dobbin, Pete Cruttenden
Regional Senior Cartographers Alison Lyall
Coordinating Cartographer Julie Dodkins
Coordinating Layout Designer Mazzy Prinsep
Managing Editor Bruce Evans
Senior Editors Catherine Naghten, Karyn Noble

Managing Layout Designer Jane Hart
Assisting Editor Carly Hall
Assisting Cartographers Fatima Basic, Mick Garrett
Cover Research Naomi Parker
Internal Image Research Kylie McLaughlin
Thanks to Anita Banh, Ryan Evans, Larissa Frost, Genesys India, Jouve India, Trent Paton, Gerard Walker

INDEX

Adam Karlin Born in Washington DC and raised in rural Maryland, Adam has written close to 40 guidebooks for Lonely Planet, from the Andaman Islands to the Zimbabwe border, but the place he decided to settle is New Orleans, one of his favorite cities in the world. For this book he wandered the bayous of Louisiana and the backstreets of his adopted hometown, and loved every minute of it.

My Favorite Trip 20 Cajun Country for unique landscapes and cultural encounters, from crawfish boils to fiddle dancing.

Mariella Krause As someone who was born in Oklahoma, lived in Texas and writes about Florida, Mariella considers herself an expert on states with a panhandle. Seven years ago, she had an epic Florida adventure while researching her first-ever Lonely Planet guidebook, and this marks the third time she's cruised up and down the entire length of the state in search of the best key lime pie, alligator encounters and tacky tourist attractions.

My Favorite Trip 5 Overseas Highway to Key West because you get to drive out into the middle of the ocean.

OUR WRITERS

OUR STORY

A beat-up old car, a few dollars in the pocket and a sense of adventure. In 197 that's all Tony and Mauree Wheeler needed for the trip of a lifetime – across Europe and Asia overland to Australia. It took severa months, and at the end – broke but inspired – they sat at their kitchen table writing and stapling together their first travel guide, *Across Asia on the Che* Within a week they'd sold 1500 copies. Lonely Planet was born.

Today, Lonely Planet has offices in Melbourne, London and Oakland, with more than 600 staff and writers. We share Tony belief that 'a great guidebook should do three things: inform, educate and amuse'.

Adam Skolnick Adam writes about travel, culture, health and politics for Lonely Planet, *Outside*, *Men's Health* and *Travel & Leisure*. He has co-authored 20 Lonely Planet guidebooks to destinations in Europe, the USA, Central America and Asia, and will from here on blame the state of Kentucky for his growing bourbon dependency. You can read more of his work at www.adamskolnick.com, or find him on Twitter and Instagram (@adamskolnick).

My Favorite Trip `19` **The Blues Highway** takes you from one of America's secretly great cities, Memphis, to the fertile ground where American popular music was born.

Amy Balfour Like her Scots-Irish ancestors, Amy has rambled – and sipped 'snake-bite medicine' – a over the South. A Southerner, she's been visiting th Outer Banks since she was a child and never tires of running down Jockey's Ridge. Amy has authored or co-authored more than 15 books for Lonely Planet, including *Los Angeles Encounter*, *Arizona*, *Hawaii* an *Southwest USA*. She has also written for *Backpacke Every Day with Rachael Ray*, *Redbook*, *Southern Livin* and *Women's Health*.

My Favorite Trip `7` **The Great Smokies** for the safari-like drive through Cades Cove, where deer, turkeys and a bear or two romped just beyond the windows.

← MORE WRITERS

Published by Lonely Planet Publications Pty Ltd
ABN 36 005 607 983
2nd edition – Feb 2014
ISBN 978 1 74179 813 5
© Lonely Planet 2014 Photographs © as indicated 2014
10 9 8 7 6 5 4 3 2 1
Printed in China

MIX
Paper from responsible sources
FSC™ C021741

Paper in this book is certified against the Forest Stewardship Council™ standards. FSC™ promotes environmentally responsi socially beneficial and economically viable management of the world's forests.